A MENNONITE FAMILY IN TSARIST RUSSIA AND THE SOVIET UNION, 1789–1923

David Rempel

A Mennonite Family in Tsarist Russia and the Soviet Union, 1789–1923

David G. Rempel
with
Cornelia Rempel Carlson

UNIVERSITY OF TORONTO PRESS
Toronto Buffalo London

Toronto Buffalo London
Printed in the U.S.A.

Reprinted in paperback 2011, 2012

ISBN 978-0-8020-3639-1 (cloth)
ISBN 978-1-4426-1318-8 (paper)

Printed on acid-free paper

TSARIST AND SOVIET MENNONITE STUDIES

A publication series sponsored by the Research Program in Tsarist and Mennonite Studies, a program within the Centre for Russian and East European Studies, University of Toronto. The series includes research guides, source collections, and studies.

General Editor, Harvey L. Dyck; Associate Editor, John R. Staples

---

National Library of Canada Cataloguing in Publication

Rempel, David G
A Mennonite family in Tsarist Russia and the Soviet Union. 1789-1923 / David G. Rempel with Cornelia Rempel Carlson.

Includes bibliographical references and index.
ISBN 978-0-8020-3639-1 (bound). – ISBN 978-1-4426-1318-8 (pbk.)

1. Rempel family. 2. Mennonites – Ukraine – History. 3. Ukraine – History – 20th century. I. Carlson, Cornelia Rempel II. Title

BX8119.U45R44 2002 929'.2'088287 C2002-902473-0

University of Toronto Press acknowledges the financial assistance to its publishing program of the Canada Council for the Arts and the Ontario Arts Council.

Canada Council for the Arts Conseil des Arts du Canada
ONTARIO ARTS COUNCIL CONSEIL DES ARTS DE L'ONTARIO

University of Toronto Press acknowledges the financial support for its publishing activities of the Government of Canada through the Canada Book Fund.

To the memory of Laura Rempel and my brother John G. Rempel, whose love and knowledge of Mennonite and Russian history and literature were an inspiration and valuable source of information to me throughout my public life.

– D.G.R.

Contents

List of Maps and Genealogical Figures

Maps

Figures

Background of This Book

CORNELIA REMPEL CARLSON

For years two portraits, tacked above my desk amidst the detritus of contemporary life, have directed my mind back nearly a century in time. The larger of these, taken in the early 1900s, features six women whose faces proclaim their kinship. They are my grandmother, her four sisters, and their mother. They posed formally, clustered in a corner around an appropriately skirted table, in front of the photographer's canvas backdrop depicting an incongruous amalgam of Russian birch and decaying Roman landscape. I search these women's faces from time to time, hoping they will reveal something of their Mennonite experience, something I might grasp as my heritage. Their dignity, self-assurance, and quiet pride are obvious, yet their modest, averted gazes veil their aspirations, the histories of their triumphs and tribulations, and their core beliefs. No more enlightened, I turn to the second, smaller photo, which is a candid shot of an elderly man, his white head topped by a worn purple velvet embroidered Russian cap, his animated expression suggesting he is engaged in a vivid interchange with the photographer. The elderly man is my father, David Rempel, author of this book and source of my understanding of what it means to be a Mennonite.

David Rempel was born in 1899 in Nieder Khortitsa, a Mennonite village on the Dnieper River, in what is now Ukraine. The boyhood he recalled in family conversations, and in this memoir, was typical of a middle-class Mennonite child's life in a turn-of-the century village – endless summer hours of play in the river, chafing at chores, delight in school, envelopment in a stable, close-knit family. The outbreak of war in 1914 halted this idyllic life. Soon after, it was obliterated altogether by six horrific years of revolution, civil war, bandit depredations, a typhus epidemic, and famine. Thus, in 1923 my father, two of his brothers, and one sister, joined a mass Mennonite emigration to Canada, where they could live, worship, and study freely. After working on a distant relative's farm in Saskatchewan to repay the cost of his passage to the New World, my father set off for college, where he pursued his passion for history, ultimately earning a doctorate in Russian history from Stanford University. In 1934, while at Stanford, my father accepted a teaching position at the College of San Mateo (in California), and except for a hiatus as an army historian during the Second World War, he remained at the college until he retired in 1964. During these years, and especially during a 1962 sabbatical in Moscow and Leningrad, my father began acquiring what would become a major collection of books and archival material on the Mennonite experience in Russia.

After his retirement in 1964, my father published several important articles on the establishment of, and early conflicts within, the Khortitsa Settlement. He wrote a number of unpublished manuscripts as well, among them this family portrait, whose original title, *Branches across the Wall*, alluded both to the ancient Khortitsa oak and to the various family branches that lived in Russia, many of which remained in the diaspora behind what were then Soviet 'walls.' Initially, my father wrote a sketchy 225-page version. Then, as relatives and Mennonite scholars grew interested in the project, he saw the need for a more complete study that fleshed out the individual family members, placed them within the cultural and political context of their time, and showed thereby how they reflected the totality of the Mennonite experience in southern Russia during the nineteenth and early twentieth centuries.

David Rempel began the present version of this memoir in the early 1970s and had completed all but the final two anticipated chapters when he died in 1992. I had read portions of the manuscript as it progressed, but always as fragments. Regrettably, I did not read the entire work until the manuscript passed to my sister Sonia and me after my father's death. Then, in an attempt to learn more of my background, and if possible to publish the book, I discovered it had grown from its modest first rendition to nearly a thousand pages, still clearly a first draft, typed (and frequently typed over), with handwritten marginal notes that were barely discernible.

What I thought would be a simple matter of typing the manuscript into my computer evolved into the more ambitious effort of editing and – most often – rewriting the material. This book is the result. The reader who compares it with the original manuscript will, I hope, find that it is easier to read than it would otherwise have been. I have attempted to retain all essential material, but by trimming repetitions and as much passive language as possible, I have pruned it to about half its original length. I have added material as well, drawing parts of Chapter 1 ('Two Russian Mennonite Families') from material in two of my father's published articles.[1] Small bits of Chapters 17 ('The Outbreak of War') and 19 ('Revolution and Reform') I based on several of my father's unpublished manuscripts. Limited portions of Chapter 12 ('Life at Home') and Chapter 15 ('Class Conflicts within the Khortitsa Settlement') I drew from his unpublished letters. I considered using the same sources to write the final two chapters that my father had envisioned (and would have entitled 'The End of the Civil War and the Famine' and 'European and American Relief Efforts and Emigration to Canada'). I am unable to say why he did not write these, as he had completed the remainder of the book some time before his death, and worked extensively on other projects during the intervening years. I suspect, however, that the famine, which followed the terrors of war and disease, and then his parents' deaths, represented a final loss of innocence and, perhaps, a crisis of faith that he chose not to confront in writing. Notably, my father's earlier 'complete' manuscript also ended without a discussion of these two painful events. In the end, I knew that I could not recreate those tragic occurrences, and I therefore left these chapters blank. In their stead, I have tacked a brief coda onto the final chapter. That chapter, entitled 'More Desperate Years,' gives, I hope, some sense of the horror of the time, as well as enumerating the tragic fates of those members of the extended family who remained in the Soviet Union. The Epilogue I drew from material my father had placed elsewhere in his manuscript.

Transliterations of text in Russian and Ukrainian follow the Library of Congress system with some modifications. Low German (*Plautdietsch*) orthography is based on the dictionary compiled by Jack Thiessen, *Mennonitisch-Plattdeutsches Wörterbuch/Mennonite Low German Dictionary* (Steinbach, 1999).

I reiterate my father's thanks to the people he acknowledged in his preface, and add the gratitude I know he felt towards several scholars with whom he corresponded after he had written that section. His letters and conversations with Dr James Urry of Victoria University (Wellington, New Zealand) were a high point of his intellectual life. Discussions with Dr Leonard Friesen of Wilfrid Laurier University (Waterloo, Ontario), who helped with references, excited him about the potential of fresh generations of Mennonite historians. I suspect that there are many others who deserve recognition, as do several distant relatives and former Khortitsa Settlement neighbours who helped my father verify information after he wrote the preface. I regret that I cannot adequately credit their contributions.

I would personally like to thank my sister Sonia for patiently supervising all other matters related to our father's massive collected materials, and my husband Mel for encouraging me to work on this project. Alexander and Elena Prusin and Anya Galkina corrected what seemed to me indecipherable Russian quotes, as did Larysa Iarovenko, whose added knowledge of Ukrainian facilitated many translations. No simple thank you can express my appreciation to Dr Jack Thiessen, who offered encouragement and a selfless expenditure of time to review Low and High German text. His wry commentary expanded my view of Mennonite character. I am likewise immensely grateful to William Schroeder for the speed, skill, and enthusiasm he applied in rendering the maps, to Dr John Staples for his expertise in indexing this work and his readiness to answer numerous questions, and to Dr Peter Letkemann who provided data on Nieder Khortitsa for the years following 1923. My thanks to Dr Hildi Tiessen of Conrad Grebel College and Susan Burke of the Joseph Schneider Haus Museum for permission to include Henry Pauls's painting of Khortitsa on the cover of this work; likewise to Robert McNair for his photography. Above all, I wish to thank the Pauls family for their enthusiastic support of the painting's inclusion in this work. Like my father, I am indebted to Richard Rempel (David's nephew), Professor Emeritus of McMaster University (Hamilton, Ontario), who unfailingly encouraged my father in his efforts, read his manuscript innumerable times, and then spent many hours of his all too precious time reading and commenting on this version.

To Dr Ronald Schoeffel, editor at the University of Toronto Press – my thanks for your patience, insight, and encouragement. My thanks also to Harold Otto for scrupulous copy-editing.

No one deserves more credit than Dr Harvey Dyck, Professor Emeritus of the University of Toronto, and general editor of the series in which this book appears. Upon reading my first draft of this memoir, Professor Dyck immediately saw its potential as a larger book, one reflecting more than a single family's experience. From that time onward he has shepherded the volume through numerous rewrites, devoting countless hours to each version. In every case, drawing on his breadth of knowledge of Russian Mennonite experience, Professor Dyck offered cogent insight and supportive suggestions. I gratefully acknowledge both his encouragement and assistance.

While Soviet walls fell just before my father's death, in 1992, and the noble Khortitsa oak died just after, many descendants of the family branches trapped in the former Soviet Union remain in that once-walled region. I thank all those who can disseminate this book to these distant family members, and to other Mennonites still in the diaspora. This was my father's fervent wish.

Preface

DAVID G. REMPEL

This is the story of an extended Mennonite family in southern Russia, spanning the time from their arrival there in the late eighteenth century to the early 1920s, when many of their descendants sought out a new home in Canada. It portrays that family – my own – within the larger framework of the Mennonite experience in pre-Soviet Russia, showing how events outside of the Mennonite world touched its members' lives and influenced their behaviour and activities. To this end, I draw on recollections (mine and those of many family members and friends) and on decades of research in primary and secondary documents covering Imperial Russia, as well as Russian Mennonite, matters. Above all, I have attempted to write this history free of the narrow parochialism, anti–Russo-Ukrainian biases, and self-justifying mythologies that afflict too many Mennonite-generated studies.

I began this study at the behest of relatives and friends, most of whom I grew up with in southern Russia (now southern Ukraine). Soon after, the children of these family members and friends voiced even greater interest in learning about their roots and Russian Mennonite culture. These 'children' were born either on the eve of the First World War, during that war, or in the first two decades of the Bolshevik regime. As parents, having experienced the extreme hardships of war, revolution, anarchy, disease, and famine, most of us had little time or inclination to talk about our Mennonite heritage. Or, if we were willing to open up, the conversations of many of us dwelled on bemoaning the loss of the prosperous and contented years that we all allegedly enjoyed under Tsarist rule.

Then, in 1970, this project acquired greater urgency when I discovered that the latest generations of Mennonites scattered across the

USSR had perhaps even less knowledge of their Mennonite heritage than did our children in Canada and the United States. I first became aware of this from an unexpected source – a New Year's greeting from a long-lost nephew, Jacob Pankratz, in Siberia. He was the second son of my older sister Neta and her husband, the senior Jacob Pankratz. Born in 1910 in Nieder Khortitsa, my nephew had moved with his family to Arkadak, one of the Khortitsa daughter colonies. I had last seen his parents in 1920, when they had returned to Nieder Khortitsa to visit their parents, only to find that both sets had perished months earlier during the typhus epidemic of 1919–20. My last communication with Neta and Jacob had been in late 1934 or early 1935, shortly before they were exiled to Siberia.

This New Year's greeting was as unexpected as it was welcome. My nephew's brief note stated that should I respond, he would write in detail about his family's fate over the past half-century. Evidently he had obtained my address from a cousin living in Novosibirsk, who had received it from her sister living in Winnipeg. Nephew Jacob now wished to hear about what had become of his relatives who had either emigrated to Canada in the 1920s or been forcibly resettled in German-occupied territory in 1943. He assumed that the latter cohort may have ultimately emigrated to Canada as well.

Promising to duplicate any material I might provide and distribute it to his two brothers and three sisters scattered across European and Asiatic Russia, Jacob begged me for any information that I might be able to provide about his ancestors, from their original migration from the west of Europe to the Dnieper region of Russia. His comment, 'We [his sisters and brothers] are about the last in our family who have some acquaintance with our Mennonite background,' suggested that life in the diaspora and marriage outside the Mennonite faith had virtually obliterated knowledge of their families' Mennonite heritage. The non-Mennonite names of his nieces and nephews and sons- and daughters-in-law indicated this break with the past. Among their first names were Oleg, Svetlana, Evgenii, Vania, Iura, Genia, Ira, Ivan, Natasha, Irina, and Elena, while family names included Shuia, Peregudov, and Kulenko. Perhaps it was not surprising, then, that only two elderly relatives were farmers – the classic Mennonite occupation. Jacob's other relatives included doctors, professors (of philology and of German literature), engineers, an architect, a dental technician, an economist, and a high school English teacher.

Drawing on the material that my brother Johann had compiled from church records, and my own research, I was able to give my nephew an extensive picture of our ancestry. Our correspondence furnished much of the nucleus of this story.

My interest in Mennonite history began already while I was in elementary school. Over the years, my mother had amassed a library that included virtually all German texts on the topic of the Russian Mennonites. From Mother, Johann and I learned about the Mennonite brotherhood's history and its current experience, but it was her mother, my Grandmother Pauls, who could tell us about our ancestors and the early life of the colony. Grandmother Pauls was a true Hildebrand and, as such, very proud of the prominent roles that her father (Jacob Hildebrand), grandfather (Peter Hildebrand), and great grandfather (Jacob Höppner) had played in establishing the Khortitsa Settlement. Perhaps through the sense of social responsibility characteristic of this line of the family, they had all attempted to preserve materials that they deemed to be of historical significance. In addition to Grandmother's influence, I suspect that the unsettling events that led to the family's exodus in 1923 solidified my love for the Mennonite legacy and deepened my understanding of its meaning and the message it had to offer both those within and without the Mennonite church.

Beyond the milieu of the family home and my personal experience in Russia, I had the privilege of studying under several outstanding teachers in high school and at the Teachers' Training Seminary in the Mennonite village of Khortitsa (in present-day Ukraine). Among them were Peter Penner and the brothers Heinrich and Peter Epp. Years later, in the United States, I studied with the well-known Mennonite historian Dr C.H. Smith at Bluffton College. This directed my choice of dissertation topic at Stanford University: 'The Mennonite Colonies in New Russia. A Study of Their Settlement and Economic Development from 1789 to 1914.'

The selection of material to include in this study has sometimes proven difficult. Regrettably, I have had to exclude information on lateral family members about whom I lack a complete or coherent view. Furthermore, it has been impossible to accede to the many requests to include material on my brother Johann's influential ministerial services in Canada during the period 1925 to 1955, in part because his children were persuasive in insisting that they wished a more extensive treatment of their father's life and experience.

Relatives and old friends in Canada have been of inestimable value in refreshing my recollections of significant episodes and people. Three relatives were of special help – my brother Johann, my sister Mariechen (Mrs Henry Klassen), and my mother's youngest sister Tante Sus. Johann's appeals to his former teaching and ministerial colleagues in Russia yielded an especially rich harvest of information. Three cousins – Mrs Justina Janzen Sawatzky, Mrs Maria Janzen Koslowsky (later Mrs Peter Peters), and Henry Pauls – assisted in untangling the extended Hildebrand-Pauls family relationships. These three, along with Tante Sus, were most helpful in supplying photographs. Cousin Henry Pauls deserves special notice for placing many of his paintings of Insel Khortitsa at my disposal. On some aspects of life in Nieder Khortitsa I have drawn from the recollections of two former neighbours, the Reverend Kornelius Warkentin and Mrs Marie Siemens. Recollections of several other former Nieder Khortitsa residents, as well as the diary of Johann Funk (who was both secretary to the mayor of Nieder Khortitsa prior to the First World War and chairman of the village's soviet during 1918–20), have also proven valuable.

On more general phases of the Khortitsa Settlement's experiences in prewar Russia, I am especially indebted to: Franz Petrovich Thiessen and Katjuscha Dyck Thiessen, his wife, and to Nikolai Iakovlevich Klassen, son of the long-time executive secretary of the Khortitsa volost administration. Visits with them were delightful experiences that also yielded a wealth of historical material, among it Franz's notes on his wartime service in Moscow, and the voluminous diary of Abram Dyck, Katjuscha's father, for the years 1899 to 1919. Abram Dyck was a well-known Mennonite, a partner in the Niebuhr flour-milling concern, well travelled, and acquainted with many prominent business and political figures. Through an extended correspondence with Nikolai Klassen I gained a rich treasure of notes, sketches, letters, maps, and commentaries on various aspects of Mennonite life and history, as well as enlightened views on Russian history and literature.

To all these people, and others too numerous to list here, I wish to express my sincerest appreciation for their various forms of assistance. To several of them, unfortunately, these expressions of thanks come posthumously, although many of them had an opportunity to either discuss with me or read substantial portions of this story some years ago.

Finally, there are several close relatives who deserve special recognition. The first of these are my niece Laura Rempel Wiens and her husband Henry, of Dundurn, Saskatchewan, who have not only taken great personal interest in this project, but also extended substantial financial support. My niece Hilda Rempel Klassen and husband Jake, of Edmonton, Alberta, rendered great service in connection with the preparation of the negatives and prints of many of the photographs included here. Above all, I am greatly indebted to my nephew Richard Rempel, Professor of History, McMaster University, for valuable assistance in editing large portions of this family account.

I, of course, bear complete responsibility for emphasizing the worldly and historical aspects – while minimizing religious convictions and experiences – of the lives of family members in Russia. My object has always been to portray the secular side of the life of an average middle-class Russian Mennonite family, an area in which I have some competence. I leave the religious side to persons better qualified for that task. It is my hope that this biographical story will be of interest and significance to the readership for whom it is intended.

Introduction

HARVEY L. DYCK

David G. Rempel's posthumously published memoir/history of Mennonite life in southern Ukraine is a significant work grounded in close observation and distinguished scholarship. Set in the picturesque village and settlement of his birth on the banks of the Dnieper River near the Zaporizhzhian cataracts, where he spent the first quarter-century of his life, it spans the history of David Rempel's extended family and community, from the first Mennonite immigration to tsarist Russia in the late eighteenth century until his emigration to Canada in the early 1920s. The work concentrates on the late tsarist and early Soviet period, which was a watershed in the experience of the Mennonite community. Marked by troubled change and then revolutionary tumult, the period saw the breaking out of Mennonites from their sheltered communities into the larger world, a central theme of this book. Written by the acknowledged doyen of tsarist and Soviet Mennonite studies, Rempel's work combines the sweep of an epic with the intimacy of a finely drawn family portrait.

David Rempel brings to this story the seasoned historian's mastery of time and place, buttressed by a decades-long inquiry into published Russian-, Ukrainian-, German-, and English-language sources and Soviet and Western archival documents. Above all, the study draws on the author's vivid recollections of people and events, and a lifetime of table-talk and correspondence with a host of eyewitnesses. The result is an engrossing and shaded portrait of David Rempel's extended family, village, and multivillage settlement community. By faithfully evoking the heartbeat and rhythms of family, community, and regional life, this story also opens to view the tsarist empire and southern Ukraine as a complex multiethnic, multireligious, and multicultural creation. Presented, with qualifications, as a microcosm of the larger Mennonite world, the memoir offers a unique window on one of tsarist and Soviet Russia's smallest, but, at the time, best known and most dynamic ethnoreligious and ethnocultural minorities.

David Rempel lived into his nineties and his active scholarly career stretched over six decades. Born in 1899, in the southern Ukrainian Mennonite village of Nizhniaia Khortitsa (Nieder Khortitsa, in German), he was a boy in the economically buoyant and volatile decade before the First World War. This period of community life he views with a fond but critical eye. As a young man, Rempel experienced the full horrors of the Russian Civil War in southern Ukraine – an anarchic time of traumatic episodes in which Rempel's grandmother, parents, a brother, and a tenth of the people of his village and settlement community perished.

In 1923 David Rempel migrated to Canada. Ten years later he graduated from Stanford University with a doctorate in history and the glimmerings of what became his life's work. Rempel's dissertation, entitled 'The Mennonite Colonies in New Russia: A Study of Their Settlement and Economic Development from 1789 to 1914,' constituted the backbone of much of his later work. There followed three decades of teaching and administration at the College of San Mateo in California, interrupted by voluntary, non-combatant service in the Second World War as a military historian with the U.S. Army Air Force.

The wartime interval, with its break from the commonplace, was pivotal to David Rempel's development as a scholar. Attached as a historian to the Supreme Headquarters of the Allied Expeditionary Force (SHAEF), it was Rempel's duty to listen in on all telephone conversations between Supreme Commander of the Allied Expeditionary Force General Dwight D. Eisenhower, and Field Marshal Lord Alanbrooke, Chief of the Imperial General Staff.[1] This unusual task left Rempel with a finely tuned sense of the contingent in historical events and of the strengths and human limitations of great leaders. David Rempel also contributed key chapters to an official U.S. history on air power in the Allied drive into Germany.[2]

Second World War experiences in Washington, Paris, and Versailles, and research and analysis of large, tangled events like the Battle of the Bulge and the Crossing of the Rhine, expanded David Rempel's world enormously. Moreover, while schooling himself in the finer points of military doctrine and strategic and tactical thinking, his wartime service honed his research, story-telling, and analytical skills. Measuring himself against his accomplished wartime colleagues may also have given him the confidence to tackle the huge canvas of this book crammed with the people, events, and volcanic forces out of his storied past. In any case, throughout his career and wartime service, Rempel snatched fleeting moments from heavy teaching or wartime schedules, bouts of family illness, and family and related duties, to pursue his lifelong passion – the story of his beloved tsarist Russian and Soviet Mennonite world. His most significant scholarly contributions, however, date from his later, less-crowded, almost thirty-year formal retirement, which ended with his death in 1992.

The Mennonite world around which David Rempel's productive scholarly career revolved had its origins in the reign of Catherine the Great (1764–1796).[3] In the late eighteenth century the Russian Empress, as part of a strategic vision of southward imperial expansion and power, invited Mennonite agrarian and artisan families from the West Prussian Vistula estuary, along with others, to pioneer cattle-raising, the trades, and plowland agriculture on the grassy steppeland frontier of New Russia (today, southern Ukraine). There, in 1789, Mennonites founded their first settlement, known as the Khortitsa Mennonite Settlement, or the 'Old Colony.' This was David Rempel's ancestral family home. More than a decade later, in 1804, a further group of Vistula lowland Mennonite immigrants established a second, larger settlement, the Molochna Mennonite Settlement, some hundred miles to the southeast. As spelled out in negotiations by the crown and imperial administration, the role of these state-sponsored settlements was to help populate New Russia's raw frontier and to be 'models' of enterprise and deportment to other foreign colonists in tsarist Russia.

The Mennonite immigrants who spoke Low German were Christian pacifists of Dutch and German background who traced their origins as Anabaptists to the Reformation. Vistula-area Mennonite immigrants were well known as able tradesmen and agriculturalists, and they had made their fame by helping to drain the Vistula Lowlands using dyking techniques developed in their Netherlandic home. The name 'Mennonite' comes from one of their early leaders, the Frisian Dutchman Menno Simons (1496–1561).

The establishment of the Mennonite settlements was followed by two generations of hard pioneering. From the mid-nineteenth century onward, however, the expansion of settlement emerged as a major preoccupation in Mennonite community life. This drive was triggered by high rates of natural population increase, expanding international grain markets, landlessness, community disputes over pastures, and rising affluence. Pushing out from their original 'mother' settlements, Mennonites established landed estates and multivillage, compact 'daughter' settlements throughout Southern Ukraine. Similarly, they moved into the Crimean Peninsula, and the Northern Caucusus, Volgan, Trans-Volgan and Western Siberian regions to found multivillage settlements. Members of David Rempel's family joined this spread eastward and southeastward across the Russian Empire. During this time both mother and daughter settlements adapted to a fitfully modernizing external world, while experiencing economic growth and often wrenching inner conflict and change themselves. In David Rempel's classic formulation, common administrative and social networks, institutions, culture, and a way of life, coupled with considerable administrative autonomy and religious independence, fused Mennonites into a coherent, distinctive, and somewhat separate world across tsarist Russia. It was a 'state within a state,' he wrote, a veritable 'Mennonite Commonwealth.'[4]

By 1914, Mennonites resided in some 350 village communities, grouped mainly in a few dozen larger multivillage settlements, and on scores of khutor-farmsteads and estates. Mennonites had, moreover, evolved from a simple agricultural people into a complex, somewhat religiously diverse, layered, and modernizing society enmeshed in many areas of Russian national life. With colour and nuance, David Rempel brings to life the confessional, socioeconomic, village, regional, generational, and even ideological differences in his own family and, by extension, in his broader community. The result is a vibrant three-dimensional picture of the variety that characterized what too-often is regarded as a homogeneous, undifferentiated Mennonite community.[5] One can only regret that David Rempel largely refrains from discussing the Mennonite religious experience, as reflected in popular culture and in the worship and outlook of traditional and non-traditional Mennonite confessional groups. Yet he does make clear the differences between the life of Mennonites and that of their Slavic neighbours. Mennonites had avoided the relatively weak 'melting-pot' effect of tsarist imperial culture. Later, however, in the vacuum and chaos of revolution and civil war, Mennonite distinctiveness in language, religion, village layouts, architecture, and, above all, in standards of living, had tragic implications. At that time, Mennonite communities, along with German colonist settlements and Jewish shtetls, became easily identifiable and especially vulnerable targets of untrammelled Ukrainian peasant banditry and extreme revolutionary violence.[6]

At the top of tsarist Mennonite society was a thin layer of wealthy industrialists, milling entrepreneurs, and owners of estates. They were the acknowledged socioeconomic elite, and they strongly influenced community policies, helped establish and fund charitable institutions, smoothed over problems, and mediated political and economic relations with the larger imperial world. The middle strata of Mennonite society were mixed and variegated. They comprised a proto-intelligentsia of teachers and officials, who shared broader horizons and were often involved in church and public affairs, a large group of church officials (including elected lay elders, ministers, and deacons) with their varied roles and standings, a differentiated group of village landholders (the majority), with merchants, tradesmen, and artisans providing the yeast in the mix. At the bottom of this social system were the landless (a minority). These people worked rented land, or they were employed in the trades as day labourers. This group, which included boyhood friends and branches of his family, piqued David Rempel's special interest and compassion.

As part of an ethnoreligious minority, many Mennonites remained inward-looking. As a group, however, Mennonites came to play a vital role in the social, agrarian, industrial, and religious developments in the areas where they lived. Today, they are again remembered by scholars in Ukraine and Russia as a varied, dynamic, and respected group that stood in the vanguard of economic and social modernization in late tsarist times.[7]

The year 1917 marked a violent discontinuity, a sharp and permanent rupture, in both the surrounding world and in Mennonite life. During the Russian Civil War and the decades of Soviet rule that followed, the fate of Mennonites as members of a German-speaking, relatively prosperous, still largely religious community closely linked to émigré fellow Mennonites in the West, was tragic. In the 1920s, while seeking to adapt to their strangely unfamiliar Soviet world, Mennonites were ultimately frustrated in their efforts to advance their common economic interests, independent identity, and religious principles. About a fifth to a quarter of Soviet Mennonites – including David Rempel, two brothers, and a sister – managed to emigrate or flee to Canada, Paraguay, and Brazil.[8]

In the 1930s and 1940s, the Mennonite majority still in the USSR suffered victorious Stalinism with its attendant terror. The results were humiliation, discrimination, arrests, imprisonment, overwork, starvation, deportations to labour camps or places of wartime exile, and a large and disproportionate number of executions.[9] Mennonite communities were ruined or vanished totally. By the end of the Second World War virtually no Mennonites remained in Ukraine. Overall in Soviet times, around a third of all Mennonites perished, including many of David Rempel's acquaintances, friends, and relatives. Yet while the Soviet inferno cast dark shadows across his work, Rempel insisted that the revolution, civil war, and Soviet rule be explored objectively. He did so as a meticulous professional himself, writing about larger regional and imperial contexts, major roots of change, and generational and socioeconomic fault-lines within Mennonite society. Rempel was especially keen on uncovering and understanding the deeper wellsprings of the violence he had experienced firsthand during the long civil war occupation of his community by Ukrainian peasant insurgents and terrorists.

From the start of his academic career, David Rempel, along with other Mennonite scholars,[10] became passionately engaged in every aspect of helping to recover, record, and explain all sides of the Mennonite story. He concerned himself equally with its ups and downs, and he was as curious about its cameos as its vistas. This became a lifelong task. As a historian, Rempel wrote about the Mennonite story himself, of course, but he recognized that more was required if tsarist and Soviet Mennonite studies were to jell as a scholarly field. It was necessary to record the experiences of his afflicted generation, track down and preserve sources, nurse along specialized archives and libraries, support popular and specialized publishing outlets, enlist and train a younger generation of scholars, and raise funds to support all of these activities.

In pursuit of this larger challenge, David Rempel helped fellow émigrés to draft, edit, and publish memoirs and studies.[11] To place his own, sometimes unconventional views before his émigré peers, Rempel wrote letters to the editor and numerous popular articles, many with a secular, left-liberal viewpoint and polemical edge. These addressed essential facets of the Mennonite story including its neuralgic points. Rempel's journalistic writings appeared episodically, often in the Mennonite émigré weekly *Der Bote*.[12] There they prompted rejoinders and more recollections. Through a mammoth correspondence with researchers and librarians in Canada, the United States, Germany, and the Soviet Union, Rempel further hunted down, purchased, or copied rare studies and sources and shared them with other scholars.[13] In the Khrushchevian early 1960s, Rempel was among the earliest group of Western researchers to be admitted to Soviet archives in Moscow and Leningrad. From these he emerged exultant with a 10,000-page microfilm collection of precious Mennonite-related tsarist state documents, a path-breaking first in Mennonite studies.[14] In the late-1980s Perestroika lowered Soviet barriers to archival research, and this filled Rempel with new hope. Thrilled when a 140,000-page cache of long-missing, 'in-group' documents on tsarist Mennonite history turned up in the Odessa Regional State Archive in 1990, Rempel quickly offered words of encouragement to scholars and financial help for microfilming and the preparation of a companion research guide. The find, he rejoiced, was 'incredible in its historical significance.'[15]

In other areas, David Rempel generously donated specialized books and periodicals and reels of microfilmed newspapers and documents to several Canadian and U.S. archives, libraries, and research centres. Especially noteworthy was his vigorous interplay with colleagues in the field and his warm and friendly mentoring of budding specialists – a younger generation of new blood in Mennonite studies. 'He was consistently encouraging and supportive,' recalls Leonard Friesen, a Canadian historian of Russia and Ukraine who worked closely with Rempel in the early years of Friesen's career. 'He had a razor-sharp memory, and he recalled events from the start of the twentieth century as if they had happened yesterday. Rempel cared passionately about Mennonites and about the larger Slavic world in which they lived. And he loved the landscape of southern Ukraine, especially the walks home from Rosental to Nieder Khortitsa.'[16] New Zealand–based anthropologist and historian James Urry, a specialist on Mennonites, conducted a mutually fruitful twenty-year correspondence with David Rempel and became his good friend. Urry writes, 'He humoured me, chided me for youthful impetuousness, forgave my impertinence, and gently guided me towards a richer and fuller understanding of Russian history and Mennonite life.'[17]

Every facet of the Mennonite story excited David Rempel's interest, but not equally. What he found most riveting was what he knew best, the eventful story of his own eighteen-village Khortitsa Mother Colony. It is in the foreground of his dissertation, of his most important articles and, as noted, of this book. Sometimes he even indulged in a bit of Old Colony flag-waving, a whimsical echo of tsarist Mennonite intersettlement rivalries. At the end of the nineteenth and in the early twentieth centuries, the Old Colony had a population of around 10,000 to 12,000 Mennonites. Most of its villages lay nestled in a 220-square-mile hilly region, intersected by prairie streams and sharp defiles, along the high west bank of the Dnieper River at its great bend. Several villages were in earshot of the dull roar of the Zaporizhzhe rapids.

The Old Colony was part of a mixed commercial grain-growing and evolving industrial area. At its doorstep were rail lines and the mighty Dnieper River linking the Old Colony with Black Sea and European grain and flour markets in the south and southwest. Nearby were rich coal and iron ore deposits, a cornucopia of strategic raw materials for late tsarism's on-again off-again industrial revolution, and the foundation of southern Ukraine's burgeoning iron and steel industry. Prominent Old Colony villages such as Einlage, Khortitsa, Osterwick, and Schönwiese had booming farm-implement factories and mammoth, tall-smokestacked, steam-driven flour mills. Regionally, these heralded the dawn of the modern world. The Mennonite Old Colony, together with other Mennonite settlements, played an animating and dynamic role in southern Ukraine's late nineteenth- and early twentieth-century commercial and industrial breakthroughs.

As a boy and youth before the First World War, David Rempel, like others of that transitional age, did not travel widely. He had no opportunity to set foot in the region's Molochna or other Mennonite settlements, and he had scant personal knowledge of Mennonite landed estates (including several belonging to relatives), or regional urban centres, except nearby Alexandrovsk. As if to compensate for a dearth of broader travel, he developed an extraordinary familiarity with his own settlement and village world. Rempel's natural curiosity and powers of observation, awakened by his lively home life, schooling, and family visits, were fed in summertime by daily, half-toilsome, half-exhilarating grain-buying trips as coachman with his merchant father to almost half of the Old Colony villages. Within the larger Old Colony world, Rempel knew three locales best – the village of Khortitsa, the Island of Khortitsa (also with a village), and his home village of Nieder Khortitsa. They were the hubs around which Rempel's early life turned, and they form the setting for much of this book.

The village of Khortitsa, with its churches, schools, pedagogical program, settlement administration, hospital, factories, mills, bookstores, commercial outlets, railway station, and much more, was the unchallenged centre of the Old Colony and of its daughter settlements. It was equally a religious, cultural, and institutional focus for the entire tsarist Mennonite world. For David Rempel, Khortitsa was home to prominent branches of his mother's family, including that of his maternal grandmother's clan, and the object of frequent family visits. Rempel lived in Khortitsa while attending high school and the teachers' seminary.

Close by, across the narrow western arm of the Dnieper River, reachable from the village of Khortitsa by ferry, lay the enormous Island of Khortitsa, the largest on the Dnieper River.[18] With a recorded past that long predated the arrival of Mennonites, the island had been the fabled stronghold of the raiding and freedom-fighting Zaporizhzhian Cossacks of the Black Sea steppe frontier in the sixteenth, seventieth, and early eighteenth centuries.[19] Taras Shevchenko, the great nineteenth-century Ukrainian writer and most influential founder of Ukrainian nationalism, paid the island a memorable visit in 1843. Subsequently, Shevchenko authored several poems stereotyping Mennonites as 'Germans' on the island, indifferent to Cossack honour[20] – an ominous stereotype in light of the civil war atrocities to come. Shevchenko portrayed the Cossack inheritance as a call of freedom for all ethnic Ukrainians. Ironically, Khortitsa Island Cossack traditions of a decidedly social revolutionary and anarchic strain may well – along with social circumstances and the political vacuum in the region at the time – have helped shape the bloody outlook of the Makhnovites, bands of armed Ukrainian peasants, who raped, pillaged, and killed Old Colony and other Mennonites during a reign of terror in Southern Ukraine during the civil war.

David Rempel experienced the island in his own way. Throughout his childhood and youth, Mennonite ploughmen on the island still turned up rusting bits of Cossack sabres, rifles, cannon, and shot – relics of the island's military past. More memorable for Rempel, however, was the pre-First World War island with its bucolic mood. He remembered its mix of hardwood forests, plowed fields, gardens, orchards, sandy beaches, rocky bluffs, marshy lagoons, a small village, a graveyard, and a family history dating to the first Mennonite settlement. These evoked Khortitsa Island for him less as a launch-site of epic Cossack raids, or a spawning ground of Ukrainian national myths, than as a Mennonite refuge of unsurpassing beauty and repose. It was where a distinguished branch of Rempel's pacifist family had first settled in the late eighteenth century, and where his cherished grandmother and a great-uncle had taken long and memorable walks. After a short rowboat crossing from Nieder Khortitsa, the island awaited the young Rempel, his siblings, and companions, with perhaps a school picnic, a swim in the Dnieper, or boyhood escapades into the lagoons or woods. Visits with family and friends often ended with a stop at the historic grave of a celebrated ancestor, the early Mennonite leader Jacob Höppner.

Down the river, within an easy row of the southern tip of the Island of Khortitsa, was David Rempel's home village of Nieder Khortitsa.[21] Its Mennonite population in 1914 was around 1,000. Nieder Khortitsa is unquestionably the centre-stage for Rempel's unfolding story. Its natural and historic features made it one of the most beautiful Mennonite villages anywhere in the Russian Empire. Shaded by large cottonwoods and weeping willows, its sandy beach meandered among gigantic rocks, boat landings, and the secluded estuary of the Nizhniaia Khortitsa Stream. Inland, on the hilly steppe, bisected by a stream bed and among burial mound landmarks of ancient steppe warrior-princes, lay communal pastures, watering ponds, and village plowlands. The latter were broken into fields, and these into family strips. Nieder Khortitsa's windmills, house-barn-garden-orchard plots, streets, streetscapes, schoolhouse, cemetery, and painted picket fences were all Mennonite Netherlandic-style to the last detail. The addition of a handful of grain storage sheds, small flour mills, and shops gave Nieder Khortitsa a built-up form resembling that of most other Mennonite villages.

For all its conventional Old Colony layout, appearance, and way of life, Nieder Khortitsa, as portrayed by David Rempel, was also a uniquely troubled place, arguably one of the most class-ridden and proletarianized of the tsarist Mennonite villages. Perched at the extreme southeastern edge of the Old Colony, next door to the Ukrainian village of Razumovka, Nieder Khortitsa looked outward onto the river and its many unusual activities and occupations. Social anxieties were cutting and deep. The landless class was exceptionally large, accounting for approximately a third of all the families. Some of the landless men and boys were employed in such unusual occupations for Mennonites as bargemen and teamsters. Here they rubbed shoulders with lower-class elements of tsarist society and could get by in Yiddish, Ukrainian, and Russian.

Part of the Nieder Khortitsa landless class lived huddled together in substandard housing near the river. They emerge from the pages of David Rempel's memoir-history as a kind of hereditary semiproletariat, often bitterly alienated from the – landed – top society of the village. Culturally, the village had a rustic feel. This image of David Rempel's home is confirmed by Khortitsa district (*raion*) Communist Party reports for the mid-1920s. They portray Nieder Khortitsa as the only Old Colony village where Communist Party workers stood any chance of fomenting the class struggle. This, according to Bolshevik lights at the time, was a necessary precondition for the regime to sink roots among the poor and to sovietize local society.[22]

In 1991, during the last year of his life, David Rempel witnessed the sudden and unexpected collapse of the Soviet Union. Already during the late 1980s' ebb tide of Perestroika, Rempel had expectantly weighed up the scholarly promises of the coming age. While Soviet barriers to archival research crumbled and the dawn of intellectual freedoms in Russia and Ukraine arrived, Mennonite participant-observers from the USSR flooded into Germany with their life-stories. Among the latter were a number of David Rempel's surviving relatives.

In the years immediately following David Rempel's death, a small group of young Russian and Ukrainian archivists and scholars, including specialists in minority studies, emerged to study the Mennonite story, long officially muffled and suppressed. Intrigued with their early findings, they plunged into the Mennonite-related documentary record in nearby regional archives. There they were soon joined by a handful of equally keen Western colleagues. Together these two groups sparked a renaissance in tsarist and Soviet Mennonite studies.

A landmark event in this rebirth was Khortitsa '99, a collaborative international scholarly conference of Ukrainian, Russian, and Western scholars, archivists, and museologists. In the spring of 1999 it convened in the southern Ukrainian industrial city of Zaporizhzhe for a wide-ranging examination of the Mennonite experience in its historical context. The conference venue encompassed several one-time Old Colony Mennonite villages, including two of David Rempel's favourite haunts, the village of Khortitsa and the Island of Khortitsa, the latter now a regional nature preserve and city park featuring a Cossack museum.

The emotional climax of the conference was the unveiling of a historical marker in the cemetery of David Rempel's home village of Nieder Khortitsa – this was done in the presence of Ukrainian villagers, conference participants, scholars, and a Ukrainian Orthodox village priest. Coinciding with the centenary of his birth, Khortitsa '99 paid tribute to David Rempel's legacy of pioneering leadership and scholarly accomplishments. Program notes made clear David Rempel's important place in the field of tsarist and Soviet Mennonite studies. That same day, David Rempel's daughter Sonia placed flowers at the foot of a new historical marker in the Nieder Khortitsa village cemetery, this one in honour of the Mennonites buried there, including a long line of Rempel family members. Occupying an honoured place beside the new marker was a restored cast-iron memorial to one of them, rescued from the banks of the Dnieper, where it had been dumped by vandals. During a moonlit dinner at an outdoor Cossack restaurant on the Island of Khortitsa, on a bluff overlooking the gorgelike ancient arm of the river, conference participants talked glowingly about David Rempel's love of the island and his mastery of its past. The accolades were based on a reading of the manuscript for this book.

A MENNONITE FAMILY IN TSARIST RUSSIA AND THE SOVIET UNION, 1789–1923

CHAPTER ONE

Two Russian Mennonite Families

I was born on 30 November 1899 in southern Russia (now Ukraine), in Nieder Khortitsa, a village in the Mennonite settlement of Khortitsa, often called the Old Colony. This enclave of eighteen villages, flanking the Dnieper River, was founded in the late eighteenth century by Mennonites escaping economic and political repression in their home region in and around Danzig. Over the following years the immigrants created a stable and highly prosperous agrarian culture, isolated to a significant degree from the Russian world surrounding them. However, as the nineteenth century ended, this Mennonite community underwent a series of transformations, similar in character (although muted in force) to the revolutionary changes occurring in the Russian Empire itself – rapid industrialization, a shift from an agrarian to a mixed economy, and the absorption of Western European intellectual and cultural influences. Concomitantly, social unrest was growing in both Mennonite and Russian quarters over the inequality between rich and poor and the entrenched power of the clerical and political authorities. As a result, the social fabric of both communities was to undergo far-reaching change.

My parents' marriage in 1891 exemplified many aspects of the transformation in the Mennonite sphere, in that it challenged this group's traditional social, economic, religious, and professional barriers. My father belonged to the Flemish branch of the Mennonite church, which virtually banned marriages to unconverted members of the Frisian branch. Although Father owned a farm in a distant daughter colony, he leased it to someone else, and instead became a grain merchant and shopkeeper. At that time, farming was the sine qua non of wealth and stability, while the commercial path my father chose was of marginally middle-class status and generated an uncertain income.

Father's birth and residence in Nieder Khortitsa further undermined his status, since much of the settlement viewed our village as the cultural backwater of uncouth, 'Russified' Mennonites. An exceptionally high percentage of the village's residents owned no land – probably one-third by the late nineteenth century – and much of this group formed a Mennonite proletariat. Alcoholism was common among this downtrodden group, my father's own father included. A remark another village's school principal made to a teacher moving to Nieder Khortitsa summarized the view of the 'better sorts of villagers' towards Nieder Khortitsa: 'What? To Nieder Khortitsa? Only two respectable families live there!' (*Was? Nach Nieder Chortitza? Da gibt es ja nur zwei anständige Familien!*).

In contrast, my mother was born in Rosental, a village that prided itself on its cultural attainments. She was the descendant of two of the settlement's most notable founding families and of a long line of prosperous farmers whose children married up into the Mennonite 'aristocracy.' Her father was a preacher as well as a successful farmer. The same was true of both her grandfathers and at least one great grandfather, as well. Certainly, none of her family were alcoholics. Furthermore, Mother was a member of the Frisian branch of the Mennonite church. She had earlier rejected the marriage proposal of the scion of an extremely wealthy family. To choose my father instead meant marrying 'down' rather than 'up.' Mother's parents reluctantly sanctioned the marriage, but only after my father agreed to change his church affiliation.

Mother's independence of action seemed an apostasy to her family's most conservative relatives and neighbours. It was, however, merely a harbinger of the course her younger siblings – and much of the settlement's youth – took ten years later. Her sisters Lena and Sus commented on that time, 'There was a kind of revolt taking place in our house. And it was your mother, David, who first resisted our parents.' Mother's heart and mind were right – my parents' marriage proved the happiest in both extended families, even if they had come from different ends of the Russian Mennonite spectrum.

This book portrays my parents, their diverse ancestries, their children, and life as it unfolded through a period of radical change within Mennonite society and the far broader Russian world. Stories of my father's rough-and-tumble ancestors fill Section One. Those of my mother's more genteel people appear in Section Two. The final three sections describe life as I experienced it through the turbulent first two decades of the twentieth century. For the benefit of readers unfamiliar with Mennonite history, I first provide a sketch of the central events of the founding of the settlement of Khortitsa as they relate to this story.[1]

The Founding of Khortitsa

Two hundred and twenty-eight Mennonite families left their homes in Danzig and its environs in 1789 and journeyed towards Southern Russia. Their plan was to settle near Berislav where they hoped to establish prosperous farms and enjoy freedom of religion. At least four of these families were among my mother's ancestral clans: the family of Jacob Höppner, Peter Hildebrand, Franz Pauls, and Filipp Kovenhoven.

Three years earlier, Catherine the Great, recognizing the need to populate her newly seized southern territories with industrious families, had sent a recruiting agent to Danzig to entice Mennonites to settle in this virgin land, then called New Russia. Catherine was keenly aware of the Mennonites' aptitudes in farming, dairying, business, and crafts, and likewise cognizant of their dissatisfaction with the discriminatory measures increasingly imposed on them by the Danzig and Prussian authorities. Among the most nettling were a series of special taxes, restrictions on establishing various businesses, and a prohibition on purchasing land except from another Mennonite. In other words, Mennonites in Danzig could never increase their landholdings or provide land for their offspring except at the expense of other Mennonites. To be sure, these measures did not affect their religious beliefs directly. However, Mennonites could obtain relief only if they compromised their positions. For example, a Mennonite could gain exemption from special taxes if he rendered military service. Or he could buy land if he gave up his membership in the church. For many Mennonites the only ways out were to compromise their religious beliefs or to emigrate. Thus, they were ripe for Catherine's invitation.

Catherine's agent Georg Trappe came armed with her 1785 manifesto that detailed the rights and privileges she was guaranteeing all foreign colonists (listed in Appendix I). Although the promised rights appealed to the Mennonites, they were too sober a people to accept the offer at face value, and instead they chose delegates both to evaluate the land and negotiate detailed terms of settlement with Viceroy Potemkin and higher authorities in St Petersburg. Trappe assured the two Mennonite delegates that his government would fund their trip and reward them generously if their efforts produced at least 200 emigrant families. With these promises, Johann Bartsch and my mother's great, great, great grandfather, Jacob Höppner, left Danzig for Russia in November 1786.

Bartsch and Höppner scoured numerous sites on the eastern bank of the Dnieper River and a large part of Crimea before selecting the choice Berislav tract, which was not far from Kherson. The site replicated Danzig's lowland topography and climate and was thus ideally suited for transplanting their current farming endeavours – growing crops and raising livestock. Furthermore, the location on the Dnieper would furnish good fisheries and a source of transportation to supplement the nearby road, which was the main route to Crimea. Proximity to Kherson and other ports and towns, built or projected, added value in providing convenient markets.

With the site selected, Bartsch and Höppner returned to the fortress-city of Kremenchug to submit their detailed list of conditions, including the requested land (sixty-five dessiatins, or about 175 acres per family). Fortuitously, both Potemkin and Catherine the Great were there, and the Tsarina enjoined them to travel with her retinue back to St Petersburg where their petition would be signed. Appendix II lists the petition's most important provisions, but essentially it granted Mennonites various subventions, tax deferments, freedom to practise their religion, and a permanent exemption from military service. The document clearly reflected the Mennonites' understanding of the value they would add to their adopted country.

As soon as Bartsch and Höppner returned to Danzig, they related their findings before an assembly of Mennonites. Initially, they described the site, terms of settlement, and their meeting with Catherine the Great. Then Trappe produced two other documents for the excited audience, detailing a series of special privileges the government granted to Höppner and Bartsch – extra land, free travel, as well as other allowances, plus the rights to operate flour mills, breweries, stores, and bakeries (see Appendix III). The two documents were identical, written in German, dated on the day of the meeting (19 January 1788), and signed by Trappe and the Russian minister in Danzig (Sokolovskii). No one questioned these generous extra privileges at the time, although bitter discord arose from them later.

As emigration fever swelled among Danzig's Mennonites, worried civil authorities attempted to curb the exodus, falsely charging that the Russian government would settle the Mennonites on Potemkin's land, and not grant them state-owned lands. When propaganda failed to dampen the potential emigrants' enthusiasm, the authorities actively thwarted any attempt to leave. Although officials in Danzig seriously impeded the exodus of even those of modest means, the Prussian government went further, prohibiting the departure of any would-be emigrant who possessed a home or other property. This forced wealthier Mennonites to secretly sell property, and flee at night to outlying fishing villages to board a vessel for Riga. Because many of the wealthiest Danzig Mennonites were unable or unwilling to sacrifice their property, a majority of the original settlers in Khortitsa were families with modest resources. Their lack of capital was bound to make their early years in a new homeland difficult, even if conditions had been more favourable.

The 228 families who left Danzig (less than a quarter of those wishing to leave) reached Riga by late 1788 and early 1789.[2] Those who owned wagons travelled overland, while the Russian government transported the remainder by boats and wagons. Reaching Riga, each family received the first 100-ruble payment, as promised. They rested there briefly, then continued to Dubrovna, a small town on the Upper Dnieper and one of Potemkin's numerous estates.

The authorities treated the immigrants well on arrival at Dubrovna, but difficulties arose immediately. First, ancient dissension between the Flemish and Frisian factions of the Mennonite church broke out. Next, the authorities were tardy in paying the second 100-ruble stipend and the daily living allowances. The settlers most bitter disappointment came a few months later when they learned that the government would not give them the land promised. Instead, they would receive parcels of one of Potemkin's estates. This new site, called Khortitsa homestead (*Khortitskoe urochishche*), was north of Berislav, lying just below the Dnieper's southernmost rapids, where two small steppe streams (the Upper and Middle Khortitsa) joined the river.[3] No one knows why the authorities switched the sites, but I would suspect it was primarily Potemkin's doing. Deeply in debt to the government, he must have realized that the presence of these industrious settlers would greatly enhance the value of his property.

The families left Dubrovna in July and reached Khortitsa a few weeks later. Those who came by barge debarked at a site that was to become the *Tsarskaia pristan* wharf, alleged to be the spot where Catherine's flotilla had briefly stopped while visiting Potemkin's temporary 'palace.' Oral tradition indicates that the settlers camped briefly near a rock formation called Pig's Head (*Schwienskopp*), where the Upper Khortitsa steppe stream empties into the Old Dnieper River. Those who arrived in Khortitsa by their own conveyance or government wagon camped farther inland, near the century-old oak *(hundertjährige Eiche)* in the Khortitsa Valley.

The tract, comprising about 23,000 dessiatins (about 62,000 acres), represented some of the most picturesque scenery in southern Russia, with abundant forests of oak, elm, and wild pear (locally known as *grushi*). The beauty of the site, however, did not quell the settlers' apprehension concerning its topography. In contrast to the strategic location of the Berislav tract, and to its lush, ponded lowland which was ideal for dairying and cultivating grain, Potemkin's land appeared to be a barren series of high steppe plateaus, bifurcated by steeply banked, broad valleys, with water available only in or near the Upper (*Vysshaia*) Khortitsa Stream, its tributary Kantsirskaia Creek, and the Middle (*Sredniaia*) Khortitsa Stream.

The arriving settlers were blind to the land's real potential, and their optimism turned to anger, which exploded as more problems mounted. Initially, these were the universal difficulties any immigrant faced when settling virgin land – discomforts of living in haphazard shelter, adapting to new soil, and the depredations of locusts and gophers, drought, and similar natural disasters. However, government inaction vexed them more. Instead of being paid in five months, as promised, the loans and subsistence allowances trickled in over an eight-year period. The lumber arrived over seven years, much of it of inferior quality or damaged in transit over the Zaporog rapids. Corrupt government authorities demanded 5 per cent payoffs to deliver goods or payments. The surveyor that they had been promised did not come. Finally, when their household goods arrived, the settlers discovered substantial theft and damage. In fact, the government failed the colonists on a majority of the petition's promises. The colonists, perhaps because they could not vent their frustration on the government, turned their wrath on blameless Höppner and Bartsch. Yet despite this inauspicious beginning, the Mennonites rapidly established a stable community structure and prosperous farms, and subsequent waves of emigrants were eager to come to settle in Khortitsa.

Father's ancestors, the Gerhard Rempels, journeyed with a second wave of emigrants straggling out of Danzig over a four-year period that began in 1793. Several factors may explain the protracted exodus, most having to do with political events in and between both the Danzig area and Russia itself. Perhaps this group also had more difficulty in obtaining exit permits because most of the 118 families requesting them were prosperous farmers.

Socioeconomic Factors

In the late eighteenth century, many of Danzig's Mennonites were prosperous and influential in various business circles, notably banking, shipping, brewing, and distilling. However, the majority of them were poorer, and most of Khortitsa's settlers came from the less-affluent group. These colonists were simple folk, accustomed to toil and hardship and adept at various trades and crafts. They were truck farmers, pedlars, innkeepers, carpenters, blacksmiths, millers, tanners, tailors, brewers, cartwrights, and fishermen. They must have been a tough, resourceful group, who had been able to earn a living despite their exclusion from trade guilds and the harassment endured while plying their trades. Although their modest financial resources may have been a hindrance, their manifold skills proved invaluable in developing a diversified economy in Russia.

Most of the wealthier emigrants seem to have been yeoman farmers, as records indicate that they brought large numbers of livestock with them from Danzig. Deputy Höppner's requests for provisions along the trek for a minimum of 400 horses and considerable herds of cattle bolster that assumption, as do the settlement's 1797 census records, which indicate large numbers of sheep, horses, pigs, and cattle just a few years after colonization. That these well-to-do farmers evaded exit regulations may reflect bribery, or artful deceptions, but in a few cases the authorities may have simply wanted to be rid of the economically competitive, religiously nonconformist group.

Decades after the emigration, a variety of myths arose about the economic status of Khortitsa's original settlers. Many who became wealthy in their new homeland ascribed their prosperity not just to personal industriousness and the benevolence of Providence, but also to higher-class origins, claiming that their forebears had made the 1788–9 journey from Danzig to southern Russia in their own covered wagons, rather than by government transport. In a contrary version, the emigrants were so poor they had 'pushed a wheelbarrow [*Schubkarren*], loaded with their few belongings, all the way to Khortitsa.' Records showing that the Russian government upheld its promise of transportation make this but a fable.

Another, more insidious, myth about our ancestors' original social status arose during the middle of the nineteenth century, when increasing numbers of Mennonites joined the poor, landless class. At this time, many of those who held land and wealth asserted that the cottagers, day labourers, and the few shiftless ne'er-do-wells in most villages stemmed from the vast numbers of improvident original emigrants. Although there might be a grain of truth in this idea, it is mostly false. Until the Reform Era of the 1860s and 1870s, most of the disaffected, landless people were the children and grandchildren of farmers whose original allotment was indivisible, by government edict. Considering the large size of typical Mennonite families, it is easy to see how rapidly a landless class developed, irrespective of ancestral status.

Ethnic and Religious Background

Although the Mennonites who established the Khortitsa Settlement came most recently from Danzig and its environs, relatively few of their ancestors were natives of this Prussian region. Some, presumably, came originally from various principalities of what was once the Holy Roman Empire. The vast majority, however, had moved to Danzig from the Low Countries – Flanders, Holland, and Frisia – to escape religious persecution during the sixteenth century. Certainly, when I was a child, those who reminisced about the past were exceedingly proud of their Dutch ancestors who, in the Vistula region, had reclaimed vast stretches of land from the sea, much as they had done in their previous homelands.[4]

Individual branches of Mennonitism developing in Flanders and Frisia divided on issues of doctrine, ritual, dress, discipline, and attitudes towards 'the world.' The distinctions remained in Danzig and among immigrants to southern Russia, although, ironically, by the nineteenth century the congregations in their ancient homeland had essentially merged.

Much of the difference between the so-called Flemish and Frisian churches in Russia, and its resultant friction, may be related to the settlers' obduracy and propensity to split hairs over meaningless matters. The primary differences involved the Frisians' use of a shorter catechism and slight differences in the mode of baptism. In the Frisian church the deacon dipped water into the bishop's or elder's cupped hands, who in turn poured a small amount over the head of the youth to be baptized. In the Flemish church the elder poured a little water out of a pitcher onto the youth. Yet both recited virtually identical words during the ceremony. Despite a common dogma and only trivial differences in ceremony, these immigrant groups endeavoured to live apart from each other and banned intermarriage. Perhaps this ancient apartheid related to early occupational and economic differences – the Frisians were usually prosperous farmers and the Flemish more often crafts- and tradesmen. Or perhaps remnants of ethnic differences lurked in the recesses of both groups' collective memories. Whatever the cause, the division remained acute until the twentieth century.

The Khortitsa Settlement

The original nucleus of the Khortitsa Settlement (*Ansiedlung*), established in 1789–90, included eight villages, called 'colonies' (*Kolonien*).[5] These were Khortitsa, Rosental, Einlage, Neuendorf, Insel Khortitsa, Neuenburg, Schönhorst, and Kronsweide (except for usage of the Russian 'Khortitsa' throughout the text of this book, the village names are rendered in High German; Appendix IV lists them in Russian and Low German, as well).[6] Most of the original families settled in these villages, while a few moved elsewhere shortly after their arrival. Two families moved to St Petersburg, although they reputedly moved back to the settlement later. Several moved to Ekaterinoslav permanently.

The first group of 228 families included members of both the Flemish and the Frisian churches, living together, it appears, inharmoniously. When the time came to choose homesites, the Frisians banded together to found the villages of Kronsweide and Insel Khortitsa. These two villages did not offer enough homesites, however, which left a few Friesens to settle among the Flemish groups, primarily in Einlage and Rosental. Since Khortitsa was the 'capital' of the settlement, and most of its members belonged to the Flemish church, the term 'Khortitsa church' gradually replaced 'Flemish church.' Similarly, the concentration of Frisian church members in Kronsweide led to a gradual replacement of the term 'Frisian church' with 'Kronsweide church.'

Members of both churches also participated in the second migration (1793–6).[7] The Flemish members evidently settled in the established villages first, then moved to other newly created villages. As in the first migratory group, the Frisian minority adamantly refused to settle among their Flemish co-religionists. The Russian government, acceding to their demands, gave them two tracts of land to establish the villages of Schönwiese and Kronsgarten.[8]

Over the next twenty-seven years the immigrants and their descendants founded six more villages: Burwalde, Nieder Khortitsa, Schöneberg, Rosengart, Blumengart, and Neuhorst. These eighteen villages comprised the Khortitsa Settlement until the eve of the Second World War. They appear on Map 1 (page 12), except for Kronsgarten, which was to the north of the area designated on this map.

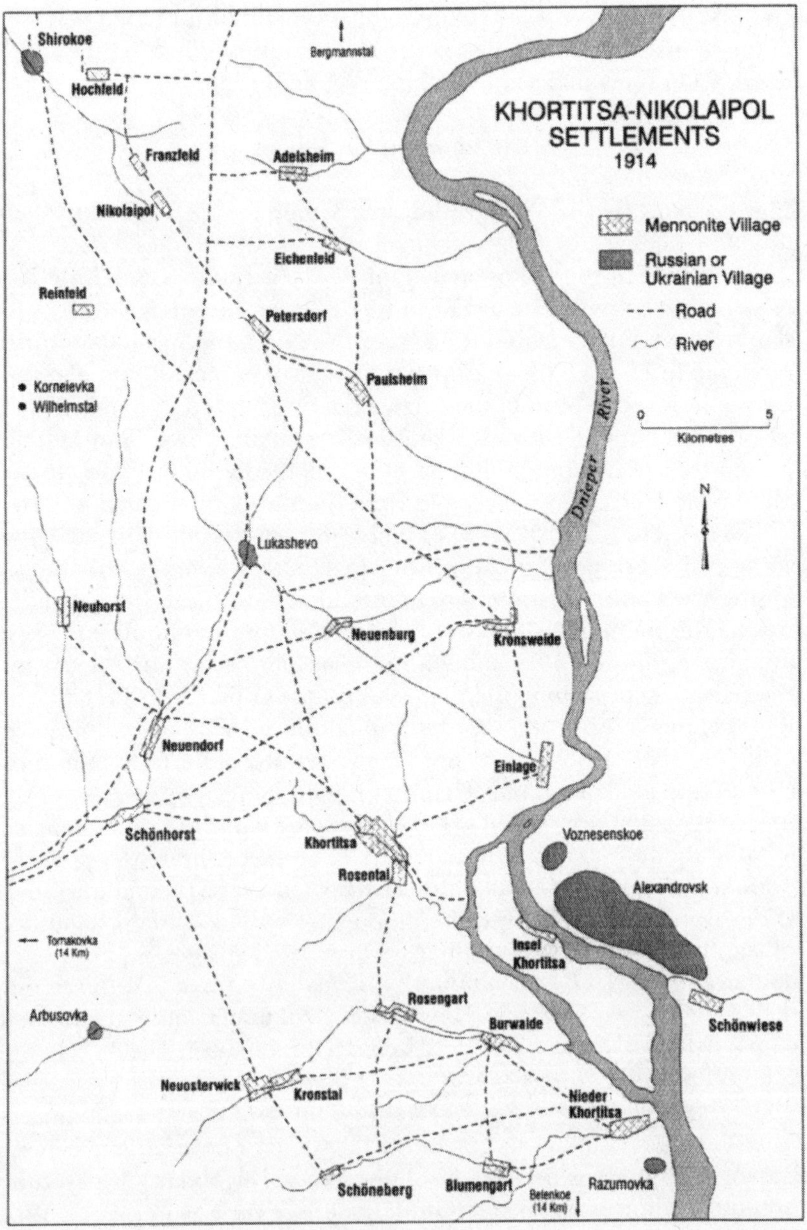

KHORTITSA-NIKOLAIPOL SETTLEMENTS 1914
Mennonite Village
Russian or Ukrainian Village
Road
River
0
5
Kilometres
N
Dnieper River
Bergmannstal
Shirokoe
Hochfeld
Franzfeld
Adelsheim
Nikolaipol
Eichenfeld
Reinfeld
Petersdorf
Paulsheim
Korneievka
Wilhelmstal
Lukashevo
Neuhorst
Neuenburg
Kronsweide
Neuendorf
Einlage
Schönhorst
Khortitsa
Rosental
Voznesenskoe
Alexandrovsk
Tomakovka (14 Km)
Insel Khortitsa
Rosengart
Schönwiese
Arbusovka
Burwalde
Neuosterwick
Kronstal
Nieder Khortitsa
Schöneberg
Blumengart
Betenkoe (14 Km)
Razumovka

Map 1

PART ONE

Father's Ancestral Family: The Rempels

CHAPTER TWO

Cherkessy with Broken-Tipped Knives: The Rempel Clan

In Nieder Khortitsa the Rempel name, or *Rampel*, as it was pronounced in Plautdietsch or Low German, which was the Mennonite mother tongue, was as common as Petersen in a Danish village or Jones and Smith in an American town. It was so common, and the choices of given names so small (Jaet or Jearad, Hendritj, Peta, Jasch, Jaun, Jehaun or Hauns, Welm, and Doaft were typical) that nicknames became identifying tags.[1] If, for example, a wife dominated family affairs, the husband was known as Susanna's Rampel (*Sauntje Rampel*) or Greta's Rampel (*Jretje Rampel*). Nicknames based on profession, trade, residence, or height and/or girth were even more common. Thus, my father's nickname, Shopkeeper Rempel (*Lauftje Rampel – lauftje* being a Mennonite corruption of the Russian word *lavka*, or shop), distinguished him from numerous other *Jeat Rampels* in the community. We called the preacher, Preacher Rampel (*Predja Rampel*), the auctioneer Out-caller Rampel (*Utroopa Rampel*), and the photographer *Aufnehma Rampel*. Other Rempels included Corner Rampel (*Atj Rampel*), Dnieper-end Rampel (*Nippaenja Rampel*), Khutor or Estate Rampel (*Küta Rampel*), tall (*Groota*), short or little (*Tjleena*), and even *Ungasch Rampel*, named because either he or his wife had been raised by a family named Unger.[2]

Although their nicknames indicated a diverse group, all Rempels shared several character traits: they held strong personal views and convictions, were self-assertive, chafed at demands to conform – traits which despite a clannish nature often led to intrafamily contention. Another trait our extended family shared was the pleasures of the table. And since there were no taboos against moderate drinking at special social occasions, some enjoyed an occasional drink of beer or 'strong water' (vodka or schnapps) from a bottle labelled 'Father's medicine' (*Voada siene Meditzin*), kept in the parents' bedroom corner cabinet.

Because of the prevalence of the Rempel name in Nieder Khortitsa (which was settled by immigrants of the second migratory group), and its relative scarcity in other villages, it was often assumed that none had arrived in New Russia until the end of the second migration in 1796. This was, indeed, true for my branch of the family, but not for all Rempels, since there were at least four Rempels (named Heinrich, Wilhelm, Isbrand, and Benjamin) from Danzig, East Prussia, and perhaps even Lithuania, who immigrated with the first group. And the Khortitsa Settlement sheets for October 1797 indicate that most of the Rempels in the eight original villages lived in Schönhorst and Einlage.[3] The identity of all these Rempels and their places of residence are difficult to establish precisely, because in the early years many settlers moved from one village to another. These same sheets indicate that most were prosperous farmers, owning horses, cattle, and sheep.

Traditional family accounts hold that the Nieder Khortitsa Rempels had been skilled tradesmen in Danzig, claiming no high-born lineage nor particular achievements. True, some Nieder Khortitsa Rempel descendants eventually became prosperous farmers, or were successful in business, industry, or commerce. But more simply fared well plying the same trades and crafts as their ancestors had in the 'old country.'

To the best of my recollection, none of the local Rempels were particularly concerned about their ancestry, or that the clan consisted of anything but plain, unsophisticated, and hard-working people, even though a few later descendants fancied themselves a bit superior to other branches of the family. Certainly, none of the men would have objected to being referred to by Nieder Khortitsa's nickname, *Cherkessy* with broken-tipped knives (*Cherkessy met aufjebroakne Massasch* or *Cherkessy met aufjebroakne Tjniefs*).[4]

This moniker lay in the legend that the villagers of Nieder Khortitsa had an ancestral memory of their Danzig days, when – excluded from the Free City's guilds – they had of necessity plied their trades and defended person and property pugnaciously. A likelier explanation is that Nieder Khortitsa lay on the settlement's frontier, across the river and slightly south of a one-time fort (and later city of Alexandrovsk), and near the broad *plavni* – thick wooded lowlands flanking the Dnieper and inhabited by numerous lawless elements in the early decades of the settlement. Consequently, Nieder Khortitsa's men were accustomed to defending themselves. Mennonites, as pacifists, did not own firearms, except for hunting. Therefore, they fought with their pocketknives. But these were also tools used around the house, barn, or stable, and the blade points were inevitably broken off. Thus, the Low German nickname.[5] Perhaps the real implication is that a Nieder Khortitsa male's bark was worse than his bite.

Whatever the reason, nicknames fostered good-natured intervillage banter. My father not only endured, but relished, farmers' jesting '*Cherkessy* Rempel, where is your broken-tipped knife?' (*Cherkaussy Rampel, woa es dien aufjebroaknet Massa?*). He protested that, although being a *Cherkauss*, his knife did not have a broken tip, and he could prove it. With considerable flourish he groped in his jacket or vest pocket, produced the knife, and opened the blade. Invariably its tip was broken, and as expected, Father then teased his challenger on his home village's nickname.

CHAPTER THREE

The First Three Generations of Rempels

Great, Great, Great Grandfather Gerhard sired two branches of the Rempel family that reunited a century later with the marriage of his great, great grandchildren, Gerhard and Maria Rempel (Figures 1 and 2*). This couple was my father and his first wife.

According to family legend, this first Gerhard lived with Anna, his wife, and their son in a Mennonite community in or near the Free City of Danzig or perhaps in a village in the adjacent Vistula Delta. In the early to mid-1790s they began an overland trek via Riga towards a new home in southern Russia as part of the second migratory group. No one knows precisely when the family reached the Khortitsa Settlement, although I imagine it was sometime in 1796. According to family tradition they settled, at least briefly, in Schönwiese before moving to Nieder Khortitsa when it was founded in 1803. Khortitsa church records attesting to their residence in Schönwiese in 1797 are the only documentary evidence of the family's existence in Russia.[1] Even the official Russian records of immigrants for the years 1793 to 1796 fail to list this family. However, a notation follows a list of the 118 family names: 'this leaves six families unaccounted for.' Thus, the Gerhard Rempel family began their sojourn in Russia as 'unaccounted' souls. Their absence from other records suggests they either moved from one village to another and were thus absent when censuses were taken,[2] that the father died prior to Nieder Khortitsa's 1814 census, or that the couple was too old to establish a farm and lived instead with their son who married in 1799.

* All figures refer to the genealogical figures in Appendix VI, which begins on page 272.

The Second Generation: Great, Great Grandfather Rempel and His Wives

The life of Great, Great Grandfather Gerhard (the next generation of Rempels in Russia) stands out from the remaining hard-working *Cherkessy*-farmer Rempels in only one way: he holds the family record as to number of marriages, or as the church's register states, how many times he got *kopuliert* (Figure 2). His first marriage in 1801 to Johann Janzen's widow, Anganetha (née Hübert), took place shortly after young Gerhard arrived in Russia with his parents. Anganetha's death two years later ended that marriage, but its brevity did not deter Gerhard. Shortly thereafter, he married Eva Janzen, who bore him four sons and then died less than a year after the fourth child's birth. Again, Gerhard sought a new wife to care for his young sons, this time marrying an older widow, Anna Peters (née Rempel). Her maiden name suggests the couple was at least distantly related. In any event, Anna cared for the motherless boys, and ultimately married off two of her granddaughters to Gerhard's sons. Her relation to these girls thus became simultaneously grandmother and stepmother-in-law. By the time Anna died in 1837, Gerhard's children were grown, yet in less than a year he married his fourth wife, the family maid, Helena Dyck.

The marriage between the sixty-five-year-old groom and the eighteen-year-old bride was clearly one of convenience and provided generous fodder for family tales.[3] The aged groom acquired a housekeeper to tend to his needs, while the bride received the inalienable right to the comforts and conveniences of a well-furnished house and a generously stocked larder. According to family lore, immediately after the wedding ceremony Old Jeat (Great, Great Grandfather Gerhard) took his young bride to the summer room (*Sommastow* or *Sommerstube*). It had been Helena's room when she had been the maid.[4] Allegedly, Old Jeat told his new wife, 'Helena, this is your room. Here no one will disturb you' (*Lentje, hia es diene Stow. Hia saul di tjeena schteare*). The family rehashed the story so often that each member had a slightly different rendition of the old man's statement, but the meaning was always the same. Old Jeat continued to use the corner room (*Atjstow*), which in most Mennonite farmhouses was the parents' bedroom. Certainly, the young wife could have no illusions about her position, despite her legal status. Tradition reports nothing about any financial settlement made by Old Jeat for Helena, nor whether she resented her relegation to the position of glorified maid. At her age she could bide her time.

The event that thrust Helena to the forefront of family gossip occurred right after Old Jeat died. Within two days of the funeral, she married her old beau, Jacob Löwen. The two had been engaged while still teenagers, and for reasons unknown, Helena had broken the engagement and married Old Jeat instead. As tit-for-tat Jacob married an elderly widow. Since his old bride died sometime before Old Jeat, the latter's death freed the young couple to resume their romance. They celebrated their union with a bounteous repast of freshly baked breads and pastries – 'but nothing stronger than coffee,' the story went. When the celebrants had eaten all the goodies, Helena excused herself, went to the pantry, and returned with a huge platter of *Tweebaktjes* (favourite Mennonite pastries) left over from the funeral a few day's earlier. Reputedly, her comment to the merrymakers was, 'Now let's enjoy what was baked for another event a few days ago.'

Although the family tongues wagged eternally over Helena, everyone regarded her fondly. Evidently Old Jeat's sons and their wives visited Helena and Jacob often, addressing them as *Murratje* and *Vurratje.* Their use of the endearing forms of mother and father speaks to the bonds of their relationships, since the Löwens were more than a decade younger than their stepchildren. Even when the Löwens moved to Neuendorf, about twenty miles from Nieder Khortitsa, they retained close ties. And, according to tradition, they were mightily annoyed to hear the Neuendorf neighbours sniff at their stepmother as 'that barefoot grandmother.'

The Third Generation: Great Grandfather Johann

Great Grandfather Johann (see Figures 1, 2, and 3) was known for two striking traits: his physical strength and his obstinacy. His physical prowess was legendary – until the very last of his seventy-nine years he could scythe as much grain as any hired man. Evidently he exercised this strength more colourfully at home when an obnoxious man named Wiens married Great, Great Grandfather's brother's widow. Wiens felt that his in-laws failed to appreciate him, and once when visiting the family, he crept behind an unsuspecting relative and slapped him 'upside the head' or on the neck, using the excuse that the victim was asleep and needed to wake up. This odious behaviour so annoyed Great Grandfather Johann that one day he picked Wiens up by his coat collar and set him down so hard on the family's nearby treasure box that its lid splintered. This put an end to Wiens's visits. Any other piece of furniture in the living room or great room (*Grootestow*) might have been damaged without causing a family schism. But this chest held the family's heirlooms and daughters' dowries. Every Mennonite farmer owned such a large and treasured chest, made of cedar, oak, or walnut, and embellished with brass buttons, handles, and fancy hinges and keyholes. Splintering the top meant an irreparable family split.

Johann's other characteristic – his obstinacy – may have been no more marked than that of the average nineteenth-century Mennonite settlement farmer. But his reputation reached storied proportions because as the mayor (*Schulz*) of Nieder Khortitsa, he faced-down none other than the great Johann Cornies, the authoritarian chairman of the Agricultural Union of both Khortitsa and Molochnaia (another Mennonite settlement), who wielded such absolute power in the 1830s and 1840s that many colonists called him 'the Mennonite Tsar.' Great Grandfather's contest with Cornies revolved around two basic issues. The first pertained to teaching methods and was basically a contest between progressive villagers and those with traditional views. The second concerned land use. Here the contention was whether to relocate part of the village of Nieder Khortitsa.

The skirmish over education occurred when Cornies demanded that the elementary school in Nieder Khortitsa adopt some 'improved' teaching materials. These consisted of various pictures, wall displays, and the like. All of the other villages in the Khortitsa Settlement approved their use, apparently with little opposition – except in Nieder Khortitsa, where the quality of elementary education was allegedly extremely poor. Here the opposition proclaimed vocally that the materials were not only bad, but contrary to Mennonite doctrine. This was a standard canard that the political or religious conservatives used against any reform they did not like. Mayor Johann, his assistants (*Beisitzer*), and the church and other lay leadership led the opposition. The community followed solidly behind. Fortunately, the autocrat died in 1848 in the midst of the fray.

The land issue was more complex and involved a large number of farmers, as well as a few cottagers, living on the south side of one of the village's main streets – an area often flooded during the Dnieper's spring thaw. Compensating for minor flood damage, the inundated lowlands briefly became excellent fishing grounds and, when the water receded, lush grassy areas for grazing and/or haying.

Cornies viewed the situation differently. As he saw it, the chief damage to the farmers was not to their buildings, but to their orchards and tree plantations. As director of the Agricultural Union, Cornies commanded every farmer and cottager to plant certain numbers and kinds of trees at the rear of each landholding. These trees were not merely Cornies's pride and joy; they were his obsession. To enforce his directives he had on occasion inflicted corporal punishment, even on those who lackadaisically weeded the area. No wonder many called him the 'tree devil.'

Cornies's solution to Nieder Khortitsa's problem was this – if occasional flooding damaged the farms' obligatory trees, move the farms. To accomplish this he directed the Khortitsa district officials to work out a relocation plan with the leaders of Nieder Khortitsa. The area selected by Cornies was close to much of the existing location and immediately adjacent to the community's general tree plantation. It was higher than the land in question, but still close to the *plavni,* the low Dnieper banks which were heavily wooded with poplar and willow. The result would put much of the village on the *Hügeln* (huggels, i.e., hills). This local elevated landmark was a sandy pasture land beyond the conceivable reach of flood waters.

Cornies issued his directive in 1847. Nieder Khortitsa's officials, headed by Mayor Rempel, and supported by the community, refused to cooperate. Fortunately, Cornies died the following year, before he could mete out his usual punishment for such recalcitrance. Although such forms of punishment seem out of keeping with Mennonite tradition, there is ample evidence of Cornies's brutish methods. Furthermore, the Odessa-based Guardianship Committee (the governmental agency of the Ministry of State Domains overseeing colonist affairs until its abolition in 1871) must have approved of Cornies's directives, if not necessarily his methods. When the regional inspector for the committee, and the Khortitsa district mayor (*Oberschulz,* something akin to the district – or settlement – governor) complained, the Committee removed Mayor Rempel and one of his assistants from office.[5]

But Nieder Khortitsa remained unaltered. Had Cornies won the battle, Nieder Khortitsa would have become an Old World equivalent of our suburban tract developments. Rows of neat, orderly houses would have lined the one main, overly wide street. Each house would have been of identical size, style, and material, and each spaced equidistant from the others. Every vegetable garden, orchard, and tree plantation would have been located in the same place on each property. That had been Cornies's way in other villages – neatness, orderliness, attractive symmetry, but overwhelming, stultifying sameness. There was a saying in the Khortitsa Settlement that thanks to Cornies, if authorities in any of

Molochnaia's villages ordered every householder to open his front and rear door at a given hour, one could have seen through every house from one end of the village to the other.

Instead of this fate, Nieder Khortitsa remained one of the settlement's most beautiful villages until the Russian Revolution and ensuing tragedy devastated the region. It boasted an attractively asymmetrical layout, with a large, slightly uneven quadrangle in the centre. Some of its largest farmsteads lay here, and they, in turn, abutted a large communally-owned and heavily wooded area which included many varieties of fruit trees. Near it meandered the Nizhniaia Khortitsa stream from which the village got its name. Its broad lowlands encircled more than half of the best farms. All this – in combination with the beauty of the sandy Dnieper beaches and the view across the narrow Old Dnieper to the densely wooded southern tip of Khortitsa Island – gave our village a picturesque appearance. While one might deprecate obstinate Mayor Rempel for thwarting Cornies, the village's descendants owe this obdurate man and his community supporters a debt of appreciation.

The Third Generation: Great Grandfather Peter Rempel

Johann was my great grandfather. His younger brother Peter was likewise a great grandfather of my oldest sister and brothers. This convoluted relationship (depicted in Figure 1) developed when my father married his second cousin. Father was Johann's grandson. His first wife was Peter's granddaughter. I know nothing about Peter. His wife, Maria, however, was the subject of family banter even almost a century after her death. Theoretically, she was the daughter of Johann Peters and Helena Enns. But family gossip attributed her quick temper and red hair to an alternative, illicit source – a putative liaison between Helena and a French officer serving in the Russian army.

Seeds of Trouble: The Fourth Generation

Although Johann and Peter's father Gerhard set the record for the greatest number of marriages (*kopuliert*), these two excelled in 'begetting.' Johann sired thirteen children over a twenty-three-year period (Figure 3). Peter stopped after eighteen years with a mere eleven (Figure 4). Although they began their families only thirty years after their grandparents' arrival in Khortitsa, the strain of this fertility on individual lives and on the social structure of the village is evident already by this early date. Since a family could not divide its farmstead, many of the children of the larger families had a hard time acquiring land, and thus of making a living.[6] Although Peter's descendants generally fared well (Chapter 4), Johann's children struggled. At least four of them had to move to daughter settlements. One, Anna, finally resettled in Manitoba, Canada, with her husband and ten children after leasing a series of parcels in various daughter settlements. Another, Peter, eked out a modest, landless existence in Nieder Khortitsa, working as a *Nippaenja* boatman ferrying passengers and freight to Alexandrovsk. He became an alcoholic, a condition not unheard of in this rather desperate class. His brother, my Grandfather Gerhard, acquired the same illness. His rocky life is described in Chapter 5.

CHAPTER FOUR

A 'Better' Class of Rempels: The Maternal Lineage

Although most of the Nieder Khortitsa Rempels had few aspirations beyond operating a successful farm, one branch of the family fancied itself as classy and certainly superior to the hoi polloi of their relations. Members of this branch of the Rempel clan (Figure 5) were Father's distant cousins. As mentioned, one of these cousins – Maria – was destined to become Father's first wife. Maria's parents were Gerhard and Anganetha Rempel, who had built one of the most attractive farmsteads in the village. Yet despite the hint of superiority, we all maintained close ties. Even after Maria died, and Father had remarried, all of us children of this second marriage, considered Father's first wife's brothers and sisters to be our own aunts and uncles.

Apart from Maria and one of her sisters, the tonier Rempel family siblings tried to make their fortunes outside of farming and beyond Nieder Khortitsa itself. Most returned to our village only briefly when they were flush with success or for longer stays when their financial balloons burst. Photographs show them as my memory recollects – self-assured, nonchalant, as though sitting for the photographer were part of the day's routine. The brothers' handsome features, tall stature, and imposing bearing, so different from most of the village's Rempel males, are obvious here, too. What the camera does not catch is their joie de vivre, their propensity for venturesome enterprises, and talent for showy, although sometimes short-lived, success. All of them could both put on the dog and fall with aplomb.

Johann, the eldest child, was typical. An auctioneer with an uncertain income, success eluded him throughout his life, yet this failed to dampen his high spirits. When he visited our village, we assumed that he would claim that pickpockets on the train had stolen his wallet, or that he had mislaid his last ten-ruble note in one of the homes he had visited. So we would lend him the fare back home to his village of New York (named by the Duchess Ignatieva on whose estate the Ignatievo colony was founded). His brother Gerhard, who lived in the same village, established a flour mill on minimal capital, assuming grain prices would remain high. Unfortunately, numerous other Mennonite men shared his get-rich-quick dream at the same time, creating a 'Mennonite mill fever.' For a time, Gerhard prospered, but as grain prices dropped, he – as many others – went bankrupt.

Peter, the handsomest brother, married Agatha Heinrichs, daughter of wealthy landowning Mennonites. His future father-in-law, Peter Heinrichs, considered the young man a scoundrel, so the couple eloped to elude the parental ban.[1] Still Agatha brought a handsome dowry to the union, and of all our relatives, no family displayed a more ostentatious lifestyle. Yet their fortunes seemed to waddle as wildly as a small boat on a storm-tossed sea. They moved frequently, sometimes visiting their poor relations in Nieder Khortitsa in a handsome phaeton, drawn by a beautifully matched team of horses and driven by a liveried coachman. Later, when they lived in Rostov-on-the-Don, Uncle Peter usually came by train, appearing outwardly to be a prosperous merchant or industrial entrepreneur, yet unable to pay the taxi driver who brought him from the station.

Maria and her three sisters – with their pleasant round faces and ski-jump noses – resembled their Wieler ancestors. Yet they inherited the same brains and joie de vivre as their handsomer brothers. For example, Aunt Anna married Peter Dyck, a young teacher from Rosental, who like his brothers-in-law, succumbed to 'mill fever,' with even more dire effect. Peter Dyck was an intellectual and, perhaps spurred by his failed enterprises, acquired a vivid interest in post-1905 revolutionary events, especially the strikes and peasant jacqueries, the growth of political parties, and the political repression that followed. His Nieder Khortitsa relatives (perhaps primed by Anna's exclamations of 'Oh Peter and his poor!') regarded Peter as red-tinged (*rot angehaucht*). He was definitely critical of the Mennonite lay and clerical establishments. And while he may not have formally been a Menshevik, he was certainly sympathetic to their program.

The classier Rempels's insouciant spirits evidently developed in childhood, much to the bedevilment of the stepfather they acquired after their father died in 1880. At the time the children were eight to twenty-four years old, and most still lived at home. The poor stepfather, Johann

Siemens, who was commonly known as Old John (*Oole Jaun* or *Oole Jehaun*), had a strained relationship with his stepsons, and as an added burden, his lively stepdaughters thwarted his attempts to rein them in. Throughout the next decade, the boys' friends and the girls' suitors gathered daily along the Friesen family's fence, across the street. Or if they were itching to arouse Oole's anger, they lined up at the Rempel-Siemens's fence itself and began whistling and shouting. Oole soon appeared on the porch to announce: 'Well boys, I'll let you know when I need you' (*Na, Junges, etj well jünt saje lohte wann etj jie bruke well*). No sooner said than the young men defied him, climbed over the barrier, and waited for their friends on the garden benches.[2]

Long after the older generation died out, my own peers remained faintly awed by this branch of the family. Two cousins were my chums at high school in Khortitsa, and they certainly knew the ways of the world, while we Nieder Khortitsa Rempels were real country bumpkins. And although many of my classmates at the Boys High School had their eyes on my beautiful cousin Sonia (Uncle Gerhard's daughter), some felt she held her nose higher than a Mennonite should.

Family accounts ascribed the panache of the classier Rempel branch to the putative illicit French affair of many generations back. I, however, suspect that the family's determined independence reflected a streak of the maternal Wielers. Both of Anganetha's brothers, Johann and Gerhard Wieler, played significant roles in the religious upheavals that shook the Russian Mennonite community during the 1860s and 1870s.

Initially, the uncles threw themselves into the Mennonite Brethren church (the splinter group influenced by the German evangelist Eduard Wüst) which dissented from the established church's doctrine and ritual. In 1860, the Russian government recognized the Mennonite Brethren as a separate church (called the *Mennoniten Brüder Gemeinde*) with all the rights and privileges of the parent church (now called the *Kirchliche Gemeinde*). But Gerhard Wieler's fractious behaviour extended beyond his severance with the established church. Soon after becoming a Brethren leader, he proclaimed himself an apostle with the rights and obligation to baptize, ban, or excommunicate whomever he wished, thereby splintering this separatist group as well.

Somewhat later the uncles became involved in the fledgling Russian Baptist church, a movement that caused even greater consternation among the established Mennonite church than the Brethren had. With characteristic zealousness, Gerhard proselytized among members of the

Orthodox church, an activity strictly prohibited by Russian law. Ultimately, the government jailed him for his efforts.

Johann, the more stable brother, played a more constructive role in both dissident churches. From 1882 to 1884, he presided over various joint conferences between dissident groups, including the Mennonite Brethren, dissident German Lutherans, Russian Baptists, Shtundists, Molokans, Dukhobors, and others. The Russian government, threatened by these movements, banished him in 1884. He first found sanctuary in Germany, until Russia pressured that country to oust him, as well. He fled next to a haven of Russian Baptist émigrés in Rumania. There, while constructing a Baptist church, he was seriously injured and died shortly thereafter.

A few Mennonites may have secretly and uncharitably deemed the means of Johann's demise poetic justice, for the schism between the Brethren and established churches engendered such bitter feeling that often family members severed virtually all contact with other members if they were of the opposite branch of the faith. For a member of the old church to 'convert' (the Brethren's favourite expression for joining its membership) to the new was regarded as a betrayal of true Mennonite faith. These tensions grew even more frequent and intense after the October Revolution, when in addition to the Brethren, the Kirchliche Gemeinde endured a second schism in the formation of Alliance congregations.[3]

I distinctly recall the estrangement these schisms produced within families. During the winter of 1922–3 I taught elementary school in Schöneberg. My salary consisted of a heated room in the teacherage, millions of worthless rubles, and three meals during each teaching day (Monday to Saturday). I boarded with a wonderful, once-prosperous, elderly couple, the Bückerts. My father had often bought grain from them, and they had known each other well. Two of the couple's married children lived with them, and both had recently converted to the Brethren. Except for routine discussions relating to farm business, the two generations barely communicated at table. Right after each meal, the young couples would retire to their own quarters. Old man (*Oomtje*) Bückert lamented, 'How does it look? Here we are all Mennonites, but on Sunday morning Mother and I go to church service in the school, but they go to the other end to a house they call church' (*Wo sit daut doch. Hia sent wie aula Mennisten oba aum Sindach morjen, dann gohne Mutta en etj too Tjoatj enne Schoal, en de gohne noam aundren Enj noh een Hus, daut se Tjoatj nanne?*).[4]

CHAPTER FIVE

Tribulations: My Paternal Grandparents

Grandfather Gerhard Rempel died a few weeks before my second birthday; thus I have no personal recollections of him, nor can I recall any relatives ever mentioning his name. Even stranger is the fact that my grandmother, although married to him for forty-six years, never mentioned him to me, even though I saw her almost every day until she died when I was fourteen. In fact, I never thought about this man until decades later, when I began this family history. Then, unavoidably, I found the family's unspoken pact of silence puzzling.

At this late time, I asked my brother Johann, who was ten when grandfather died, what he could remember of this mysterious man. Johann's response was: 'I dimly recall one thing. He seemed to be easygoing, perhaps lazy as some people said. But I clearly remember the time of his death. Our schoolteacher, Mr Reimer, was teaching us surveying. We were measuring the width of a street at the corner of David Epp's farmstead directly across from grandfather's shop when someone shouted from the window, "Hans, come quickly. Your grandfather has just died"' (*Hauns, komm schwind. Dien Groatvoda ess jrohts jeschtorwe*). Later, when I asked my sister Mary how our father had felt about his own father, she shot back a laconic, 'He loathed him.'

I regret never asking my parents about Grandfather Rempel. Perhaps in later years there might have been a more charitable memory of him. I do recall one hint of this. During my teenage years, Mother marshalled us boys to go to the cemetery to weed and spruce up the ten or eleven mounds in the family plot. She invariably gave primacy and her personal attention to four of these. The first was a tiny site where her firstborn child was buried. Then she tended the only two family sites with grave markers, those of our father's first wife and of this wife's father.[1] And finally she cared for the adjacent site – the grave of our infamous grandfather. This routine took place several times a year between April and October. As far as Mother was concerned, it was an act of love and respect. I must add that for us young draftees, this Saturday afternoon occurrence was rarely an exercise in kind devotion, for it took away from our frolics in the Dnieper.

Gerhard Rempel was a small farmer and shopkeeper. His landholding may have been a quarter farm (*veadel Wirtschauft*) of sixteen and one-quarter dessiatins (roughly forty-four acres). I presume he inherited it as a part of his father's full farm because the Russian government finally permitted subdivision of these sixty-five-dessiatin farms into half and quarter farms in the mid-1860s, at the height of the rancorous disputes between the farm owners and the landless cottagers. This was a decade after Grandfather's 1855 marriage and two decades prior to his father's death in 1885. Initially, at least, Grandfather must have been successful at both his enterprises because he built a very nice, large, brick home with the general store at one end, along with a separate brick stable and a barn. I remember the place well from my teenage years, for after Grandfather died the family sold it, including the business, to an Old Believer named Golubkov, father of two of my companions, Efim and Maker.

These two boys spoke Low German as well as anyone born to the language and were to all intents and purposes an integral part of all Nieder Khortitsa's youth activities, except in attending the Mennonite church. Such integration into the Mennonite community might seem strange in view of the Russian government's absolute prohibition against different religious groups living together. From the outset, the government settled each group of new colonists in separate communities – Mennonite, Lutheran, Roman Catholic, or any other – to avoid religious strife. No one outside the specific faith could settle in these villages, although seasonal labourers and factory workers could live there temporarily. In such cases the government required factory owners to provide separate housing, schools, and even, in one case, an Orthodox church. Nor could the colonists proselytize among one another or within any established Russian Christian church, especially the Orthodox. Moslems, however, were fair game, as were the Old Believers, who the Russian church and state viewed as lost souls anyway. Thus, many of the villages had Old Believers, at least one of whom was typically a shopkeeper. In fact, old man Golubkov had operated a smaller general store before he purchased Grandfather's enterprise. We viewed Golubkov, as we did other Old Believers, as the most honest and successful of the ethnic Russian businesspeople. However, Golubkov reputedly drank himself to death, which was unusual, since Old Believers were strictly abstemious.

Another measure of Gerhard Rempel's success is the comfortable cottage with adjoining farm buildings that he built for his daughter Elizabeth in 1891, when she married. This home was located in a section of Nieder Khortitsa known as *kutok,* a cul-de-sac of small landholdings whose tenants combined small-scale farming with jobs in crafts, trades, or drayage.

Despite Grandfather's evident success, he had one serious failing. He was an alcoholic. This profoundly affected my father, and particularly my grandmother, who was left destitute by Grandfather's death. When new owners tore the old stable down in 1925, they unearthed numerous empty vodka and schnapps bottles that Grandfather had hidden under the floor planks and behind the wallboards. I assume that his alcoholism was a major, or perhaps the singular, reason why no one in our household ever mentioned his name. Yet as I reflect on my boyhood experiences, it appears to me that there must have been another side to this man considerate, affectionate, humorous, and tolerant of other people's foibles. Two examples support this: the type of home he built for my grandmother and his relations with one of his grandchildren.

To understand how revolutionary this house was, and how thoughtfully it met Grandmother's needs, it is necessary to appreciate how it differed from the usual Mennonite farm home. Typically, Mennonite houses were built according to a set pattern, with the rooms arranged in the same way they had been in sixteenth- and seventeenth-century Flanders and Frisia, eighteenth-century Poland, and now nineteenth-century Russia. Only the wealthier farmers made minor changes to this plan. One could say with no fear of contradiction, 'If you had seen one, you had seen them all.' In this interior arrangement almost every room used for living, sleeping, eating, and general work was large, naturally well-lit, and ventilated. But that was not true of the kitchen, the area in which the farmer's wife spent the majority of her time. The cooking and baking area were invariably in a narrow niche with no outside light except to the vestibule (*Väaschtow*), where most of the meals were served between April and October. The ventilation, limited to a duct channelled into the main chimney, was as bad. Most housewives endured this arrangement, except those who had a small building in the backyard, called the summer kitchen, with its own drawback. Located in the vegetable garden, the aroma of food failed to mask the odours of the nearby chicken coop and pigsty. Still, there were utilitarian reasons for this arrangement – eggs were within easy reach, and the pigs proved a convenient garbage disposal.

Grandfather's house, however, was different. He made the kitchen one of the largest, brightest rooms in the house, with its window protected from the afternoon sun. To the best of my knowledge, the only other men who broke with the practice of relegating their wives to the Mennonite household's 'black hole,' even up to 1917, were my father – who built two such homes – and four farmers, whose homes had burned down. Such an innovation was apparently regarded so much as a matter of course within our family that rarely did anyone give Grandfather credit for his considerate action.

Grandfather's relations with my cousin Elizabeth (*Listje*) reflect his gentleness, as well. She recalled his store as a happy meeting place for the neighbourhood's retired farmers. Furthermore, he bought her an accordion and encouraged her to play, despite Grandmother's distaste for 'the thing,' the accordian being an instrument that she regarded as suitable for the hired help, such as Ukrainians from the Poltava or Chernigov areas, but not for good Mennonites. Grandmother disliked any frivolous items, and banished from her household anything encouraging vanity, such as mirrors and photographs.

Elizabeth played the accordion well and took it on boating parties during the spring weekends when the Dnieper flooded the lowlands behind the village. If a Sunday event, it meant someone had to sneak into Grandmother's room while she napped, to fetch the accordion because the old woman kept it there to insure no one broke her prohibition of Sunday entertainment. Since my brother Johann was the youngest, the teenagers usually enticed him to snatch the instrument. He rarely succeeded, for she seemed to anticipate the plan. To the grandchildren, then, Grandmother was the spoiler.

They could not have understood the tragedies of her marriage. Grandmother (Elizabeth, née Funk), had grown up in a middle-class farming family in Burwalde, brought a dowry to her marriage, and surely expected to live in similar comfort with Grandfather. Instead, with his drinking, she took on much of his work, overseeing the farm, the store's operations, and frequently performing her husband's communal work (*schoawoatj*), in addition to her own duties as wife and mother. For example, during the 1860s, when the Dnieper's spring flood waters threatened to inundate Rosental and Khortitsa, every household in the settlement's villages was ordered to furnish one able-bodied person to help erect a dam across a broad valley where the Khortitsa and Kantsirskaia steppe streams emptied into the Dnieper. It was Grandmother, then in her mid-thirties and mother of several children, who took her husband's place during the emergency. Beyond this, Grandmother endured two other great sorrows – her eldest son's death and her estrangement from two of her remaining three children (Figure 6).

Johann, the eldest child, married Katharina Pätkau in 1879. Their four children were born in rapid succession. While the youngest was still an infant, Johann died. This was a profound blow to Grandmother, not just because she lost her first and cherished son, but she had counted on his taking over the family farm, relieving her of exhausting tasks. To compound the loss, the widowed daughter-in-law dumped her four children on the Rempel grandparents when she married a widower, Wilhelm Pankratz, the father of eight children, and moved to a distant Fürstenland village. Although my father and his first wife soon assumed charge of the youngest two, both mere infants, Grandmother cared for the two eldest for more than a decade.

That my grandparents' former daughter-in-law joined the Mennonite Brethren church may have compounded their alienation from her. This religious movement probably contributed to a distancing of Grandmother's two youngest children, David and Elizabeth, from the family, as well. Both joined the Brethren after moving to Orenburg, a Khortitsa daughter colony situated east of the Volga River and founded between 1894 and 1897.[2] Elizabeth and her husband, Johann Harms, must have moved to this new settlement shortly after Grandfather built their house for them in Nieder Khortitsa in 1891, and presumably at roughly the same time as her brother David, and his new wife, Elizabeth Wiens moved to the new territory.

Non-religious reasons may also have contributed to Uncle David and Aunt Elizabeth's detachment. They may have shared my father's disgust for their father Gerhard and his drunkenness. Or it may have simply been too difficult to travel to and from Orenburg, especially since settlers to that region experienced particularly difficult early years. Most, coming from poor families, were undercapitalized, and further pauperized by a succession of droughts. In addition, two institutional linkages between mother settlement and daughter colonies dissolved about that time – the establishment of a new high school in the Orenburg settlement village of Pretoria and of a government forestry camp in western Siberia. This meant young men in the daughter colonies no longer came west to Khortitsa for education or alternative service. To the best of my knowledge, David returned home only once to visit Grandmother, and I cannot recall that Elizabeth ever did. Certainly, neither came to her funeral in 1913.

Yet Grandmother's life was not entirely one of sorrow. Even before Grandfather's death, my father (her second-eldest son) helped out, and following that time, he supported her entirely, housing her in a rented cottage on a property abutting our vegetable garden. Living so close, I remember Grandmother well, often working in our garden, her long skirt and petticoats tied high around her waist. An independent woman until her last days, she usually prepared her own breakfast and evening meals, but Mother sent her main midday meal over, recruiting one of us to take it there. None of us minded, since Grandmother was not a talkative woman and seldom detained us with questions or with her own reminiscences.

Later I regretted my lack of interest. For in the few instances that she did reveal snatches of her past, she offered compelling pictures of long-gone times. Most of all, I remember vignettes of her experiences during the Wagon Time (*Podvody Tiet*) during the Crimean War. Perhaps the story began in reference to bread. Then she recalled the district administration's directive to prepare vast amounts of dried fruit and toasted slices of bread which were the Russian soldier's staple ration (*sukhari*). At times her husband had to transport these from Khortitsa, Alexandrovsk, or even Ekaterinoslav, south to the Tavrida guberniia. Occasionally, they transported soldiers or military goods, as well. Sometimes the drivers, who might be as young as teenagers, took these as far as the Crimean Peninsula, returning home weeks later, their wagons now loaded with sick and wounded soldiers. The Russian authorities preferred the Mennonite ladder wagons (*Leiterwagen*) to the typical Russian peasant carts, because the carts could carry only two wounded soldiers or a small quantity of material, while the wagons (which Russians called German Wagons), drawn by four horses and equipped with ladder extensions, could carry much more material or up to eight wounded soldiers. The teamsters then left the patients in towns with established hospitals, or in improvised Mennonite and German colonist village facilities, where they were tended by Sisters of Mercy (*Barmherzige Schwestern*) recruited from among the village women, or even in private homes. The space was freely offered, or as often, commandeered. To the credit of the Mennonite and German colonists, these teamsters carried thousands of wounded hundreds of versts (about two-thirds of a mile) from the front to their home villages to be nursed back to health. I should note, however, that contrary to Mennonite belief, these trips were not always voluntary, but frequently made on orders from the government, which reimbursed them for horses and wagons, based on the trip's length. Per diem payments for the teamsters appear to have been the responsibility of the settlement or village. Records indicate that the government conscripted as many as 400 teams and wagons from the Khortitsa settlement for one particular journey.[3]

Throughout life, Grandmother was a composed, deeply religious, woman, and I often recall her reading aloud from her small collection of books, the Bible especially, possibly a few other religious books, and D.H. Epp's *Die Chortizer Mennoniten, Gesangbuch zum gottesdienstlichen und häuslichen Gebrauch der Mennoniten-Gemeinden Russlands* (The Khortitsa Mennonite Hymn Book for Service and Home Use of the Mennonite Churches in Russia) and *Palmblätter* (Palm Leaves). Certainly, her books supported her through a life of misfortune to which she seemed resigned. Only on one occasion can I recall her sigh: 'Boy, life has been hard at times' (*Jung, daut Lewe es maunchmoal schwoa jewese*). But it was decades before I wondered whether she meant this in a material or psychological respect.

CHAPTER SIX

Father and His First Wife

My father rarely spoke of his childhood or teenage experiences, and I always surmised that he preferred to veil the memories of those times, and especially of his alcoholic father. The only occasions on which he discussed his early life occurred when I accompanied him to buy grain. After reviewing his notes on the amount and expected harvest date of wheat he had contracted that day, Father would stuff his notebook and stubby pencil into his breast pocket. Then, but only occasionally, he would talk of his past, perhaps opening up because my exasperation with these tedious treks reminded him of his own childhood frustration with the drudgery of farm work.

Most often Father mentioned his inadequate six-year education, which while average in most settlement villages, was distinctly mediocre in Nieder Khortitsa at the time he attended school. He had passionately wanted to go on to the Khortitsa Boys High School, but his parents had neither the money nor the inclination to provide for his dream. Without this formal training his command of High German was poor, although he could read a modicum of it. This deficit did not affect his business, however, since he spoke fluent Plautdietsch with the Mennonites, and excellent Russian, Ukrainian, or Yiddish with his other customers.

Yet his sense of educational deprivation was acute, and it abetted his conviction that his children most certainly had to have a higher education. This view was most uncommon among Mennonite farmers, not only in Nieder Khortitsa, but throughout the Khortitsa Settlement. The wealthiest farmers, in particular, found Father's emphasis on higher education foolish, but my father pursued his conviction with determination, even if it meant denying himself and his family comforts and temptations of a more passing nature.

Apart from his regret over missed educational opportunities, and his dislike of farm and household chores, Father indicated that his childhood had not been especially hard. Yet life in his parents' home obviously displeased him in a general way. Once, in a rare revealing comment, he mentioned that at an early age he had vowed to strike out on his own as soon as possible, to get married, and to start his own business.

Often I would secretly wonder, as we meandered back over the monotonous dusty roads towards our house, whether as a child he had ever threatened, or even contemplated, running away from home. Much later I realized how difficult it would have been for a Mennonite youngster in the 1870s to shake off the shackles of the parental household and depart for places unknown. The most important barrier to this adventure would have been the fact that a Mennonite, of any age, could not legally leave, or live outside a Mennonite settlement, without official permission of village and volost (district) authorities. I also realized that as a schoolboy, Father had not read – as I had – Mark Twain's tales and Maine Reed's adventure stories of the American Indians.

Father's realization of his teenage objectives of marriage and career depended less on his venturesome spirit than on several factors beyond his control. First, his marriage required the consent of both his and his prospective bride's parents. Equally important, the Mennonite Brotherhood required the potential groom to take a government-administered physical examination to determine his fitness for military service. Under the provisions of the Compulsory Uniform Military Service Act, which took effect in 1880, every man had to take the examination before he was twenty-one. Mennonites found fit had then to give four years of service to the government. In peacetime, they spent these years in a forestry or tree-nursery camp. In wartime, some men were assigned to these same camps, but more often they spent their time in hospital or related medical service. It would seem that in the early years of this act, the provision regarding the timing of the examination, and the Mennonite's prohibition on marriage prior to taking it, were loosely enforced. In Father's case, the exam revealed a chronic heart murmur which disqualified him from service. Thus, he could marry at a slightly earlier age than most of the village's men.

Curiously, Father never discussed the one aspect of his childhood which had indelibly marked his life – his father's alcoholism. Nevertheless, we children knew instinctively how he felt about alcohol from his actions around the home, and that just as he abstained from all hard liquor, he expected us to follow suit. However, he did not preach or exhort anyone to follow his lead, believing other people's behaviour was their own business. Furthermore, he followed Mennonite custom in serving vodka to everyone who came for the annual neighbourhood hog-slaughtering, both during early morning hours when men assembled to sharpen knives or boil cauldrons of water for the scalding troughs and after the butchering was complete, when most men drank one, or many, small glasses of vodka. Although Father willingly provided the bottle, he himself always found some ruse to escape the proceedings.

Within my memory, Father did not smoke either, although virtually every other man in Nieder Khortitsa did. Perhaps he had once smoked but later quit because the Pauls family (his second set of in-laws) frowned on the practice. None of the Paulses' sons smoked, and my aunt claimed that no Rosental maiden would ever marry a man who did. This reflected her own or her family's opinion, because it did not comport with my observation. More likely Father had simply never liked to smoke, since my brother Johann, while still of school age, observing Father's awkward attempts to smoke at a social occasion, wanted to tell him, 'Dad, I can do that better than you.'

My father's disgust with hard liquor did not extend to lighter brews. Although he did not care for wine, which was rarely available in Mennonite homes anyway, he did not object to young people drinking a glass or two at weddings and similar ceremonies. Beer was a different matter. On hot summer days Father enjoyed a glass of beer at home. Or if he drove to Alexandrovsk, he often stopped on the way home at Janzen's Brewery in Schönwiese for a refreshing bottle. And when he wished a great treat after an active business day, he asked Mother to cook beer soup for him. I do not recall how it tasted, but Father obviously considered it a rare delicacy.

Although Grandfather's drinking created stress throughout Father's childhood, it moulded his in the opposite direction – in ways he impressed on us – towards self-reliance, respect for the rights of others, independence of thought, and having the courage of our convictions. All these would sustain us later during the horrific final years of our life in Russia.

Father's First Marriage

In the circumscribed Mennonite world of nineteenth-century Russia, where marriages outside the faith were virtually prohibited by the church and state, and even marriages between Frisian and Flemish congregants were frowned upon, it was not unusual for second cousins to marry one another. And so it was in 1883 when my father, Gerhard Rempel, married his first wife (and distant cousin), Maria Rempel. Both were nineteen.

Maria reputedly resembled her eldest child Neta, with her round face, mischievous eyes, and slightly plump build.[1] Known for her vivaciousness, she also had evident good taste and artistic talent. Several of her items remained off-limits to the children, in the glass-doored china cabinet (*Glausschaup*).[2] I particularly recall her china and a folder of her school artwork.

The only specific story I recall of Father's first wife relates to the home they built shortly after their marriage. Maria came from a prosperous farming family, and she wanted a new, large home. Thus, they moved the existing dwelling off the lot and built an attractive, fire-resistant home on the original site, which was strategically located for Father's business, in the centre of a number of very prosperous farms, and straight across from the two Niebuhr-Wiebe flour mills. I suspect that both the couple's parents helped defray the costs of this solid building, or perhaps Maria's inheritance was sufficient to fund the construction. Whatever the source of money, Father engaged bricklayers and construction began. Maria wanted the house a particular size, and so she periodically appeared on-site to measure foundation walls and interior rooms, using her apron as a ruler. A crisis arose after the bricklayers laid the foundation and then asked her for the measurements before they erected the walls. These measurements revealed the foundation to be ten inches short. The brief recriminations led nowhere, as the future mistress of the house blamed the workmen for not being able to count, and they in turn blamed her for wearing aprons of different widths at different times. But it was too late to extend the dwelling, and so the family sacrificed proposed staircases to the attic and cellar and substituted trapdoors in the kitchen ceiling and dining-room floor.

Maria's death from smallpox in 1891, just as she reached her twenty-seventh birthday, cut Father's first marriage to less than eight years and left him with three small children: Neta who was six, three-year-old Gerhard, and a toddler, Johann (Figure 7). By the time I was old enough to know that Father had been married once before, none of these children had any clear recollections of their mother.

Beyond the tragedy of Maria's early death, in a sense her passing marked what was transpiring in the family as a whole – the end of one hundred years of preoccupation of the two branches of the Nieder

Khortitsa Rempels with themselves, their interests, follies, and fecundity. The descendants of the first Rempels in Russia (the couple's great, great, grandparents, Gerhard and Anna Rempel) were now widely dispersed. There were some in each of the Khortitsa Settlement's eighteen villages (Map 1, page 12). Others could be found in the daughter settlements of Ignatievo, Orenburg, Arkadak, Nepliuevo, Fürstenland, and in Paulsheim, Neu Schönwiese, the so-called *Judenplan,* and in numerous other places in New Russia, Little Russia, and the Don Cossack Territory (Maps 2 and 3, pages 41 and 42), while those who had once settled in Bergtal now lived in Canada. Some achieved striking success. Others failed entirely. Over the century most lived by farming, but in more recent times many had turned to commerce and manufacturing, Father among them. My father's next marriage took him further from the insular Rempel family fold and from the parochial Nieder Khortitsa outlook, since Maria Pauls, his second wife, came from the prominent Höppner, Hildebrand, and Pauls families of Rosental and Insel Khortitsa.

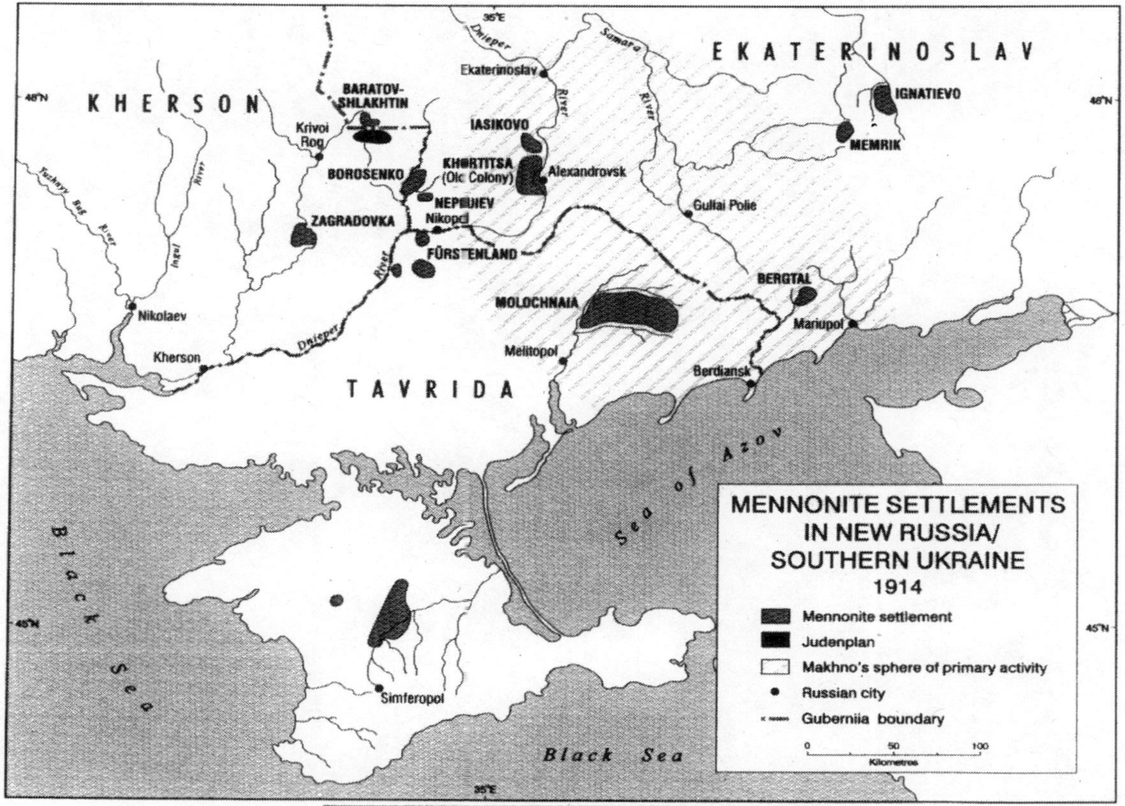
MENNONITE SETTLEMENTS IN NEW RUSSIA/ SOUTHERN UKRAINE 1914
Mennonite settlement
Judenplan
Makhno's sphere of primary activity
Russian city
Guberniia boundary
0
50
100
Kilometres
EKATERINOSLAV
KHERSON
TAVRIDA
BARATOV-SHLAKHTIN
Krivoi Rog
BOROSENKO
ZAGRADOVKA
KHORTITSA (Old Colony)
NEPLIUEV
Nikopol
FÜRSTENLAND
IASIKOVO
Alexandrovsk
Ekaterinoslav
Dnieper
River
Samara
Gulai Polie
IGNATIEVO
MEMRIK
BERGTAL
Mariupol
Berdiansk
MOLOCHNAIA
Melitopol
Nikolaev
Kherson
Yuzhnyy Bug River
Ingul River
Simferopol
Sea of Azov
Black Sea
Black Sea
35°E
48°N
45°N

Map 2

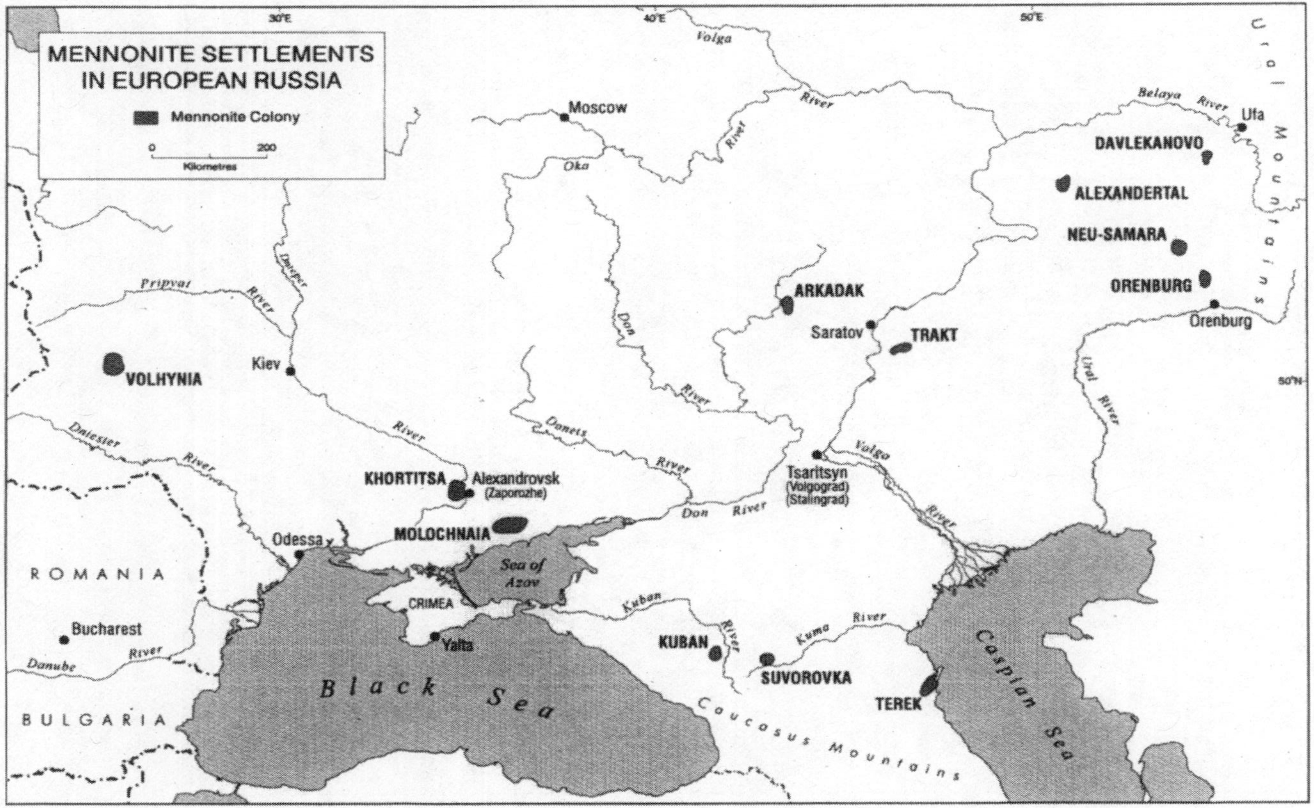
MENNONITE SETTLEMENTS IN EUROPEAN RUSSIA
Mennonite Colony
0
200
Kilometres
30°E
40°E
50°E
50°N
Volga
River
Moscow
Oka
Belaya
River
Ufa
Ural Mountains
DAVLEKANOVO
ALEXANDERTAL
NEU-SAMARA
ORENBURG
Orenburg
Ural
River
ARKADAK
Saratov
TRAKT
Dnieper
Pripyat
River
Don
River
Kiev
VOLHYNIA
Donets
River
Dniester
River
KHORTITSA
Alexandrovsk
(Zaporozhe)
Tsaritsyn
(Volgograd)
(Stalingrad)
Volga
River
Don
River
MOLOCHNAIA
Odessa
Sea of
Azov
ROMANIA
CRIMEA
Kuban
River
Kuma
River
Bucharest
Yalta
KUBAN
SUVOROVKA
Danube
River
TEREK
Caspian Sea
Black Sea
BULGARIA
Caucasus Mountains

Map 3

PART TWO

Mother's Ancestral Families: The Höppners, Hildebrands, Kovenhovens, and Paulses

CHAPTER SEVEN

Unjust Charges: The Fate of Jacob Höppner

With a magnanimous spirit fostered by decades of success, the Khortitsa colonists celebrated the settlement's centennial in 1889 by erecting marble monuments over the graves of the two men who were instrumental in its founding: Johann Bartsch and Jacob Höppner.[1] The gesture must have seemed ironic and particularly poignant to the Bartsch and Höppner descendants, for the colonists' gratitude contrasted sharply with the early settlers' cruel and unjust treatment of these two dynamic men: the church shunned both, and the community forced Höppner's imprisonment. The reasons the Mennonite settlers initially chose Bartsch and Höppner to negotiate for them, then later nearly destroyed both, are of more than academic interest to me, because Jacob Höppner was my great, great, great grandfather (see Figures 1 and 8).

Prior to founding the settlement of Khortitsa, Jacob operated an inn, general store, and tenant truck farm in Bohnsack, a village just east of Danzig. His compatriots' willingness to place their futures in his hands suggests that these businesses flourished and that he was a trustworthy man. Certainly, the future colonists must have felt that he had a worldly point of view and persuasive personality, one dynamic enough to negotiate with representatives of the Tsarina. This former attribute was obvious by the time he settled in Russia. From then on Jacob Höppner travelled back and forth to Danzig several times, corresponded frequently with Mennonites remaining there, and simultaneously hobnobbed with the local Russian landed gentry, often exercising his passion for the hunt on the Miklashevskii, Lukashevich, Ivanenko, and Markusov estates.

These contacts, however, especially with the Russian gentry, exacerbated the bitterness the colonists vented on Höppner and Bartsch, whom they perceived as the sole source of their disappointed expectations – the change of site, the government's failure to make payments and supply timber on time, the graft of local officials, and even the first years' poor harvests. Then, too, Höppner's friendship with the gentry reminded the disgruntled colonists of the special privileges originally granted to the deputies (see Appendix III), despite the fact that the government treated Höppner and Bartsch with equal disregard, giving them only one of the promised benefits, the loan of 800 rubles, which both repaid in any case.

Beyond these petty jealousies, I believe that the colonists' fury towards Höppner and Bartsch was mainly caused by their selecting choice building sites near, or at the entrance to, Potemkin's two large tree plantations. Höppner built his home on Khortitsa Island, on Potemkin's cherry orchard, and Bartsch, after a brief stay on that island, erected his home at the entrance to the settlement's orchard (*Koloniesgoade*) in Rosental. Höppner abandoned his homestead a year later following a harrowing incident. Returning home one night, he encountered brigands, who threatened to kill the entire family and might have done so if Potemkin's elderly watchman had not scared the bandits off. To escape further potential attacks, Höppner moved his family to the island village. Yet the colonists continued to resent Höppner's previous possession of the site, perhaps suspecting that Potemkin and other influential people awarded it to Höppner, along with other requested favours. For example, in a letter (now in the Leningrad Historical Library), Höppner asked Viceroy Potemkin for some windows from an abandoned palace in Kremenchug. We do not know whether he intended them for personal use or for the settlement as a whole, nor do we know Potemkin's response, but in that bitter climate, anything hinting at favouritism must have fueled the colonists' smouldering resentment.

Finally, Höppner's success in breeding livestock probably nourished the colonists' envy. Census figures for 1797 show that just eight years after arriving at Khortitsa Höppner owned eighteen horses, fifty-five horned cattle, 205 sheep, and ten pigs. The same data reveals that only a few other farmers, in Kronsweide, Schönhorst, and Kronsgarten, owned similar numbers of livestock. Just three years later, a Russian inventory shows that Höppner's stock had increased to twenty-four horses, seventy-one head of cattle, 399 sheep, and thirteen pigs.

The hostility towards Höppner and Bartsch escalated through the 1790s, until finally a vocal group of church and lay leaders levelled legal charges against the two. Bartsch apologized for his 'misdeeds,' just to gain peace of mind, but the more obstinate Höppner refused to plead guilty to the unfounded charges.[2] Two centuries later the indictment is obscure and supporting evidence non-existent. The official document that the Mennonites submitted to the Russian authorities is vague, and official Russian records similarly offer neither a list of charges nor details of the trial itself. Unfortunately, Höppner's son-in-law, Peter Hildebrand, who witnessed the events, failed to present a clear picture of the affair in his retrospective history of the settlement's founding years.

With Bartsch recanting, the community turned its full fury on Jacob Höppner and one of his brothers, Peter. As best I can discern, the brothers were charged with misusing public funds and misappropriating 287 public timbers to construct their homes. Finally, the colonists claimed Jacob Höppner's most reprehensible acts included 'his wilful, selfish character, which at a recent barn-raising affair had led him to use physical force against a fellow-Mennonite' and that his brother Peter had invariably supported him in all his 'arbitrary acts.'

To the best of my knowledge, there are no documents substantiating any of this. Unfortunately, Samuel Contenius, assigned by the Russian government to review the unruly early affairs of both the Mennonite and Lutheran colonies, unquestioningly accepted the colonists' version of the conflict and stated in a written report that the charges against the Höppners were 'already proven.' He, too, gave no substantiating evidence.

The missing timbers exemplify the dubious nature of the charges. We know that the merchant who sold the timbers, Chernikin, failed to deliver a considerable number, and that Baron von Brackel (the colony's director) misappropriated others. Beyond these losses, many logs floated down the Dnieper and smashed on the rapids, while peasants from the Ukrainian village of Voznesenskoe across the river, stole many more. Even the later director of the colonies, Ivan Brigontsev, reported that as late as 1801 no one could establish who had acquired the timbers, and that the Höppners' guilt lay in not taking sufficient precautions in guarding them.

Despite the spurious nature of the charges, the Flemish church banished the Höppner brothers. Briefly imprisoned, the two were pardoned by a general amnesty issued by Alexander I to commemorate his coronation in 1801. The pardon included only those with debts less than 1,000 rubles, but while Jacob's 'debt' was about 1,845 rubles, he had satisfied most of this by auctioning portions of his property in 1800. In this case, Höppner's friendship with the local Russian gentry helped, since that group bought most of the property, and gave a portion back to the family. The auction realized 1,758 rubles, which left a debt of eighty-seven rubles. The authorities then scheduled additional sales. These must not have occurred, as Contenius reported to the Senate that on the basis of the Imperial Amnesty Decree the two Höppners were freed and that their remaining debts were uncollectable. This is puzzling, since the decree specifically cancelled the debts of those pardoned. Even stranger is the fact that Peter Höppner's debt of 535 rubles was not cancelled, forcing him to sell his home in Khortitsa to Peter Siemens and his windmill to a Greek Orthodox priest.[3]

Release from debt and prison did not end the brothers' troubles, because the Khortitsa Settlement authorities refused to let them return to their villages or rejoin their church. Again one of the local gentry, Privy Counsellor Miklashevskii, rescued Jacob, housing him on his large estate at Belenkoe. Later the Höppner family moved to Alexandrovsk, joined the Schönwiese Frisian church, and eventually resettled with their son on the old family farm on Khortitsa Island. Although he again prospered, the trauma of his imprisonment and vituperative treatment at the hands of his co-religionists remained vivid, and shortly before his death in 1826, Jacob Höppner demanded that he be buried on the family farm, not with other Mennonites. Seventy-three years later, grateful colonists erected a memorial to him in the small family plot.

The grave sat on a high bluff, with an unsurpassed vista of the Dnieper, with its east and broader arm gracefully curving slightly to the southwest to meet the narrower west arm some seven versts away, at Nieder Khortitsa. Alexandrovsk was visible to the southeast, along with portions of Schönwiese, the remainder of that village hidden behind the broad and heavily wooded lowlands (*plavni*) that flooded during the spring thaw. Looking straight south along the island itself one saw *Bütendick*, and to the right of it, the remnants of Potemkin's cherry orchard where the Höppner family had made its first home in 1789.[4]

A lush carpet of brush and trees marking a number of valleys (*balki*), sloping steeply to the Dnieper, lay to the right of the island's ploughlands. In Höppner's days the *balki* had been favourite spots to hunt wolves, foxes, and deer, and by the time I was a boy, although the wildlife was gone, my friends and I often passed the remains of Höppner's wolf-shed where the hunters had lain in wait.[5]

Along with its beauty, the island's history and folklore were equally magnetic. We called one valley General's Valley (*Generaulsläajcht*) where, according to tradition, a Russian general had fallen and been buried during the Russo-Turkish War of 1739–40. Traces of Zaporozhian Cossack trenches and redoubts dating to this same war also dotted the island. These were but a few reminders of the real events and folklore of the land – military adventures against the nomadic Pechenegs and Khazars, the exploits of Prince Oleg and other heroes of the Kievan period, Cossack deeds, and taunts of the Turkish sultans.

One can only hope that Höppner's walks up the deep and winding dale just in back of his farmstead, and through the serene, thickly wooded path to the high point of his homestead (*Hüskoagel*), solaced the bitter memories of his abuse at the hands of his brethren. At the least, life with his wife, Sara, and his family provided this. We will meet the couple's daughter, Helena, equally central to our story, in the next chapter.

CHAPTER EIGHT

Mennonite Service and Supernatural Tales: The Hildebrands

The marriage of Jacob and Sara Höppner's daughter Helena to Peter Hildebrand seems an unlikely alliance. She was seventeen, he more than twice her age. She was the daughter of the famous Mennonite deputy Höppner, he a recent convert to the faith. But he had one advantage in courting Helena: he was her father's long-term friend and employee. Born and raised a Lutheran in Ladekop, a village near Danzig with a large Mennonite population, Peter had had extensive contacts with Mennonites, and began working for Jacob Höppner some time prior to 1786. The men's closeness and mutual respect must have been great, because in 1788, when the Höppner family departed for Russia, Hildebrand cast his lot with the émigrés. Then when they reached their destination, Hildebrand accompanied Höppner on numerous important missions.[1] Helena and Peter's relationship probably developed over these years, blossoming just as she approached a marriageable age in 1793.

Whatever the background of this marriage, the couple apparently settled immediately into the normal course of Mennonite farming and procreation. Over the next twenty-three years they produced nine children (Figure 9), while simultaneously building a successful farm on the virginal soil of Khortitsa Island. Census figures of the Khortitsa farmers (14 October 1797) reveal that Peter and Helena's farm flourished from the outset and possessed as much livestock as those of most of the other prosperous farmers, although somewhat less than that of Jacob and Peter Höppner.

Although Peter came late to the Mennonite religion, he embraced it wholeheartedly, and by 1810 was elected minister of the Kronsweide (Frisian) church.[2] Peter's piety and sense of mission must have been strong, at least according to an 1819 report of two visiting Quakers, William Allen and Steven Grelett. They paint a picture of Hildebrand family contentment in the bucolic setting of 'the island of Cortetz, situated in the Dnieper':

> I went with the governor in one cart, and my companion with the assessor of the colony in another; the river having overflowed and covered a great deal of the country. We had to pass through much water ... there are great masses of granite rock, at thirty feet high ... which with trees ... make a beautiful landscape. The island is nine versts long and five broad, and contains one village of the Mennonists' colonies; we drove across one end of it, and came to the road by the main body of the river; on our landing, the pious pastor came to meet us in a little cart; we were both struck with the sweetness and simplicity which appeared in his countenance. After the first salutation, he set off full speed to give notice to his wife of our coming; as we approached the avenue leading to the house, we found the path strewed with lilac blossems, the rooms were also ornamented with flowers; everything bore the marks of neetness and comfort. The mistress of the house is apparently a very clever woman; and has taught her children arithmetic, etc. herself. They have five or six children, some of them nearly grown up; we were much delighted in meeting with this truly Christian family, with whom we had some religious communication; the pastor went with us as guide to Schönwiese, the next village; we had to go across the Dnieper in two little boats ...[3]

Peter served the Frisian church almost until he died, at the age of ninety-six. His greatest service to the Mennonites as a whole, however, was his collection of letters, memoranda, and sheets of statistical and genealogical data that made up the nucleus of his booklet, *Erste Auswanderung der Mennoniten aus dem Danziger Gebiet nach Süd-Russland.* As the materials cover the period 1786 to 1836, I suspect that shortly after his arrival in Russia he recognized the historic moment of the Mennonite exodus and the need to preserve documents relating to it. Initially, the collected papers were intended exclusively for the family, or at least were not to be published until everyone connected with the settlement's early conflicts had died. Peter's grandchildren finally published the booklet in Halbstadt in 1888, to commemorate the founding of the Khortitsa Settlement.

I recall Grandmother cherished a copy of the initial printing. Original copies are now rare, but the volume has been republished several times.[4] It remains one of the few sources of information on life in the settlement's first decades. Unfortunately, the book lacks historical scholarship and suffers from Peter's political naiveté and his studious avoidance of the real causes of the conflicts that nearly tore the settlement asunder. Apart from these failings, the materials became the foundation of one of the most remarkable collections of documents on the settlement, covering the first half-century of its existence. Peter's son and grandson expanded the collection, which is commonly called the *Hildebrand Nachlass* or Hildebrand Papers. Tragically, most of this was lost in 1919 during our area's occupation by Makhno and his bandit cohorts, when few people, and no trained historians, had viewed the material.

Despite Peter's esteemed place in Russian Mennonite history, I do not recall my grandmother (who was his granddaughter) ever mentioning the man, even though she must have known him during her early childhood. In contrast, she often spoke of her great grandfather Jacob Höppner. Her tie to the elder man, who had died long before her birth, may relate to his loftier place in Mennonite lore (especially following the 1889 centenary celebrations of the settlement's founding) and to her son Bernhard's purchase of the ancestral Höppner farm in 1907. But I suspect another factor explains my grandmother's reticence towards Peter Hildebrand's memory – the scandalous taint surrounding his wife's strange disappearance and death. My grandmother never spoke of the events in my presence, and only after she herself died in 1920 did her daughters (my Tante Sus and Tante Lena) relate the story of Helena's tragic drowning, with its attendant supernatural myths, befitting Gogol's tales. My aunts' injunction that 'this is for your ears only' measured their desire to keep this mysterious matter hidden from all but family members.[5]

The facts are simple. During the night of 18–19 June 1833, Helena slipped out of the Hildebrand's house, clad only in her white nightgown and black nightcap. When her disappearance was discovered the next morning, searchers found her footprints in the Dnieper's shallow waters, leading south, past the big rock formation on the shore of the neighbouring Bernard Dyck farm, where the prints disappeared. Shortly after noon, her cousin Jacob Höppner was fishing near the mouth of Middle Khortitsa (*Sredniaia Khortitsa*), when a group of Russians shouted at him over the water that they had earlier seen a drowned Jew lying in the shallow waters near the *Bütendick*. Höppner disregarded the remark, until he went to the Hildebrand home later that afternoon and found that Helena had disappeared. A search party hurried to the site and discovered Helena's body. It was still clothed as on the night before, her black cap misleading the fishermen to believe the corpse was that of a Jew.

No one knows the true cause of Helena's death, but the most likely explanation is that Helena walked out of the house in her sleep, briefly along the water's edge, and then slipped and fell into a deep eddy, where she drowned. However, those who related the tragedy rarely accepted this reasoning. Two aunts intimated that Helena had fallen in love, while still in her teens, with one of the Russian gentry who visited her father while the family lived in asylum on the Miklashevskii estate near Belenkoe and that perhaps Helena had renewed this interest. Others suggested that the twenty-one-year age difference between Helena and Peter had become an issue for the couple and she had committed suicide.

Whatever the cause, a litany of superstitious fables soon surrounded her death resembling such Gogolian tales as *May Night, or the Drowned Female* or *Evenings on a Farm Near Dikanki.* First a neighbour, Mrs Dyck, recalled hearing the family's dog howl, then creep to the back of the house. Getting up, she hurried to the street-side window and caught a glimpse of three white-clad figures approaching, then walking past their house. Petrified, she extinguished the lamp, jumped back into bed over her husband's sleeping body, and hid under the covers.

Another neighbour, Peter Wiens, revealed a spookier tale. Returning at sunset from a day of fishing, he pulled his boat up onto the beach, but left it and his catch there when his wife called him home for supper. After eating, he and his wife went to retrieve boat and catfish and, looking downstream, saw another boat with two men in it, approaching swiftly. Although neither man rowed, the boat glided smoothly across the water's glassy surface. Puzzled, Mr Weins watched the men disembark without beaching the boat, then walk across the street, melt *through* a fence rather than climbing over it, and head towards the Hildebrands' orchard. Concerned that the boat might drift away, Wiens called to the men – first in Plautdietsch, then Ukrainian – to pull their boat onto higher ground, but they ignored his calls. Assuming the boatmen were headed to the Hildebrands' orchards to pick mulberries, and would therefore be back soon, Wiens decided to pull the boat up himself. When he got close, the boat disappeared.

Meanwhile, at the nearby farm of Peter and Helena's son Jakob, a maid saw two ghostlike figures passing the window. She dashed out and ran to the corral to tell her mistress of the apparition. Looking up, Mrs Hildebrand caught a glimpse of two white figures. She called to them, but they seemed to float away, disappearing behind tall weeds.

Jakob was away while these mysterious things took place, but another strange occurrence was in store for him. Having ridden a borrowed horse into the steppe behind the village to round up some of his own horses for the next day's work, Jakob passed the village cemetery. The horse suddenly balked and refused to move. Looking up, Jakob saw two white-clothed figures that he believed to be Mr and Mrs Neufeld, a pair of no-good alcoholic Mennonites, trying to sober up or play pranks. They ignored him, and Jakob finally persuaded the horse to move on.

So ended the hours of the strange appearances (*merkwürdige Erscheinungen*) which neighbours and relatives claimed accompanied the mysterious disappearance of Deputy Höppner's daughter. My Uncle Kornelius Braun, recognizing the resemblance of such stories to the region's Ukrainian folklore, and aware of the extensive contact the islanders had with the nearby peasant village of Voznesenskoe, voiced caustic remarks about the superstitions (*Aberglauben*) prevalent among Insel Khortitsa's villagers.

Perhaps my family's reluctance to discuss the matter related to its occurrence in a preacher's family. Both at the time it happened and many decades later, when I was a child, there was a sense among the most conservative contingents of Mennonites that the event was God's retribution for some imagined act by the bereaved husband. Others may have ascribed Helena's drowning to punishment for her father's 'guilt as already proven,' for did not the Bible say the Lord 'was visiting the inequities of the fathers upon the children unto the third and fourth generation?' Even in those days there were plenty of superstitious or self-righteous busybodies among our people.

Village gossip seldom lacks reasons or excuses to contrive fanciful explanations for unseen acts, or those surrounded by mysterious circumstance. And opportunities for peddling tales surely abounded in the Mennonite settlements, especially on the periphery of an alien world. However, some relatives suggest that family resentment over Peter's immediate remarriage may account for its silence on the issue. Eighty-one years old at the time of his wife's death, Peter again took a younger wife. In this case the bride was Jacob Friesen's widow, Anganetha. She was fifty-three and still in charge of three under-age boys. She was also the mother of Peter's son's wife, Katharina. This younger couple had married ten years earlier. Now, with her own remarriage, Anganetha became simultaneously Katharina's mother and mother-in-law, and likewise Peter, his son's father and father-in-law. Such convoluted relationships were not unusual in the village's tight world.

The Next Generation of Hildebrands

Jacob Hildebrand was Peter and Helena's only son, and heir. In that couple's careful fashion, they had recorded his birth in the family register – six o'clock in the evening of 3 September 1795. As the only son, his youthful responsibilities must have included long hours of work in the multifarious tasks connected with growing grain and raising sheep and other livestock – jobs expected of well-to-do Mennonite farmers' sons. Perhaps, however, he shouldered these at an earlier age than usual, since his father became a minister when Jacob was barely fifteen. This burden may account for his rather late marriage (at age twenty-eight) to Katharina.

Although Jacob was a successful farmer, his greatest distinction lies in his years in the ministry, serving the Frisian churches throughout the Khortitsa Settlement. He was called to service first by the Insel Khortitsa congregation, who elected him church servant (*kirchlicher Diener*), or church teacher (*kirchlicher Lehrer*), in 1825. A year later, they elected him church elder, a position rarely bestowed on such a young man, or one who had served such a short ministry. Elder Franz Görz, of Molochna's Rudnerweide church, came to ordain him.

Jacob carefully recorded his services as teacher and elder from 1825 to 1866, delivering an astonishing 1,278 sermons during regular church services and 161 at funerals, marrying eighty-five couples, baptizing 775 youths, and offering communion to 1,152 souls. Beyond these routines, he corresponded extensively with fellow preachers in the Khortitsa and Molochna settlements, and was active in publishing church hymnals, catechisms, and other church materials, functions extending his reputation beyond the Mennonite community, to which visits by Count Coremba and John Melville attest. Apparently he gave up his duties in the last year of his life, 1867, except to supervise the election of new ministers and to administer communion in Kronsweide.

My Grandmother Hildebrand and Her Siblings

In typical Mennonite fashion, Jacob and Katharina had ten children, the youngest of whom was my Grandmother Maria. A healthy group, only one died in infancy, and most lived to at least the age of seventy (Figure 10). All the children were extremely conscious of their identity and heritage, first of all as Mennonites, but only slightly less so as the offspring of a historically important family, one they considered a cut above those in the common Mennonite farming class. All except Peter (who remained a bachelor) became (or the daughters married) successful men, one even becoming the district mayor. But the family's involvement with the ministry essentially evaporated. Only one son answered the call, and I believe no one in subsequent generations did.

Although my grandmother Maria was twelve years younger than her brother Kornelius, the two were almost inseparable in the last two decades of their lives. Kornelius was an inveterate tinkerer and either invented or adapted numerous pieces of farm equipment. He began his career as a clockmaker's apprentice (as had several other Mennonites who later became successful industrialists producing agricultural machinery, motors, and wagons), then set up two factories, one in Khortitsa, the other in Schönwiese. Since Russia did not belong to the International Patent Union, Russian entrepreneurs, including Mennonites and other colonists, freely copied and/or adapted European, and especially English and American, machinery. According to Grandmother, whenever Kornelius heard someone had purchased a new (and imported) piece of equipment, he hurried to examine it. Invariably, he returned home with his suit covered in grease, mud, and dust, for his habit was to crawl over, under, and into pieces of machinery to find out how they were made and worked. Clearly, Kornelius's aptitude was for invention not business acumen, and eventually near-bankruptcy forced him to turn the factories over to two of his sons and a son-in-law.

Kornelius possessed a fine sense of humour, an observing eye, and a narrator's gift for story-telling, whether of his childhood experience – especially his frolics along the Dnieper, and pranks he had played on mates – or later recollections of relatives, friends, and his tinkering enterprise. His contributions to the Hildebrand Papers do not possess the historical value of his grandfather's, nor of his father's factual portrayal of the demands made on a Mennonite minister's time, finances, and other resources. However, for sheer human interest, Kornelius's stories surpass those of his immediate ancestors.[6] Perhaps Kornelius gave freer rein to his vivid imagination because he never received a call to the ministry nor faced the difficulties of reconciling conflicting interests, and he wrote in an easy, flowing style, uninhibited by knowledge of grammar or punctuation.

I recall an object he made which depicted the Mennonite migration to Russia and the colony's subsequent development. It was an elaborate, museum-quality assemblage of wood carvings, figurines, and what appeared to my childish eyes as 'things.' Years later, as I researched Mennonite history, I remembered that the first part of Kornelius's depiction portrayed a traditional Mennonite myth, to wit: our ancestors had come to Russia in 1788–9 largely *per pedus apostolorum*, with their miserably poor belongings loaded on wheelbarrows, which they pushed from the Vistula Delta to Khortitsa. In reality, of course, none did.

The Hildebrand homestead, on which the nine children grew up, stood near the Höppner farmstead on Insel Khortitsa (see Map 4, page 80), sharing the same idyllic splendour. Both spots held magnetic attraction for several generations of the extended family. I suspect this idyllic setting in part explains why the Hildebrand offspring were known for their joyous approach to life. Here on the island, as scarcely anywhere else in the settlement, many farmers, utilizing its rocky soil, cultivated grapes. As youngsters, we looked forward to island visits with a special thrill in late summer and early autumn as the grapes ripened, because we rarely ate that fruit at home. In retrospect, I wonder if any Mennonites made wine from these grapes. Perhaps some did. Certainly, in 1825–6 various levels of Mennonite and Russian authorities considered what to do with a Mennonite woman from Insel Khortitsa named Liske, who had sold a half-bucket of illicit spirits to a Voznesenskoe resident named Joseph Bugutskii. Although of seemingly insignificant import, the matter wove its way from local Mennonite authorities to the Russian district law enforcement to the Guardianship Committee, and finally to the Senate in St Petersburg. The issue was that Mennonites could brew and distill spirits, but only for their own consumption. Since the government derived substantial revenue from the excise tax on spirits, any infraction, no matter how small, had to be prosecuted. The matter was finally settled at the lower level of the Guardianship Committee, when the Senate concluded that the expense of bringing the woman to St Petersburg and trying her there would cost more than they could assess in fines. The affair illustrates how early in our Russian experience the insular and supposedly self-ruled Mennonite world became involved in the affairs of the larger world around them.

CHAPTER NINE

Piety and Pain: Mother's Paternal Ancestors

In 1832 Heinrich Pauls and Maria Kovenhoven joined in an ill-fated marriage that lasted until Heinrich's death fifty years later. Both came from Rosental's few Frisian families, and both were grandchildren of Kronsweide's founding families who had arrived with the first migratory group – Franz and Anna Pauls and Filipp and Magdalena Kovenhoven (Figures 1, 11, and 12) – so their difficulties did not lie in incompatible backgrounds. Evidently the couple's problems began even before the wedding. Maria was in love with a Lutheran man, but when her parents adamantly refused to consent to her marrying outside the faith, she reluctantly accepted Heinrich's proposal. More disappointments filled Maria's subsequent life and her behaviour reflected this. At first she was simply moody, but eventually she became insane.

I suspect that Maria would have become mentally unbalanced no matter what her situation, but perhaps it was aggravated by her husband's demanding life. Heinrich was both a prosperous farmer and a minister of the Kronsweide (Frisian) church. This latter position often imposed onerous duties and, because it was unpaid, demanded financial sacrifice. In Heinrich's case the duties were particularly taxing because, rather than serve his home village's congregation, he ministered to several congregations in the outlying villages of Kronsgarten, Priiut, and Wiesenfeld. To reach his congregations he left early each Sunday morning, or even several days in advance. And beyond carrying out Sunday services, his position required numerous other duties, all time-consuming, and none paid.

The Mennonite clergy, until just prior to the First World War, consisted of one elder and several deacons for the settlement's congregations, and one or two ministers in each of its constituent villages. The elder administered communion and baptism ceremonies once a year in the daughter colonies of the Khortitsa Settlement, except in the most remote, which elected their own elders and deacons. In addition to these church servants (*kirchliche Diener*), both branches of the Mennonite church had several functionaries to perform quasi-religious duties which the elder oversaw. For example, until the late nineteenth century, the Khortitsa Settlement had a Church Mother (*Tjoatjemutta*) whose function was to prepare young women for baptism. She ensured that the girls dressed modestly and that they had parted their hair in the centre for catechism instructions and the service itself. Both my grandmothers used to talk of another church institution maintained until the late nineteenth century. Convened by the preacher and deacon each month on specified Thursdays – designated Green Thursday – (*Jreen'donnadach*), the officials admonished parishioners who had committed various proscribed acts since the previous session. My Grandmother Pauls humorously referred to those as 'Thundering Days.'

The entire male congregation elected the clergymen by majority vote, from a slate of candidates previously selected by the members of a screening and nominating committee, who themselves came from the 'best, solid citizenry.' In theory, the entire membership appointed the committee members. But in actual practice the committee was selected by the minister and a small group of leading citizens. As none of the clergy received salaries, the committee often nominated men on the basis of their wealth and ability to simultaneously take care of their farms as well as the religious flock. The members' self-interest also often played a role in their selections. Most of the committee members played dominant roles in the village's temporal affairs, usually as part of the village council meetings (*Schultebott*), and so these 'leading citizens' were just as likely to base their choices on how they expected the nominees to align themselves with the council. Parenthetically, the non-democratic aspects of the nominating process included the fact that the congregation's sisters (*Schwestern*) had absolutely no voice in governing, but were left to decorate the church for festive occasions and to serve food to the brethren (*Brüder*).

Towards the end of the nineteenth century many congregations demanded better-trained ministers, and at this point it became common practice to choose a local teacher as the minister. The farmers accepted the selection of their preachers from the teaching profession, as much because they believed they had already paid the teacher for his services as through a sense that the teachers were learned (*jeleat*) or literate (*jegrommt*).[1] Moreover, they assumed that the teacher could shake a sermon out of his sleeve without much work on a Saturday night to preach them a soul-stirring sermon (*eine herzergreifende Predigt*) on Sunday morning.

Despite these numerous ministerial duties, the Pauls family developed a successful farm and staffed the household with at least one servant girl. Material comforts aside, life in the household was unhappy, the spectre of impending crises always hanging over it. Whether the mistress's increasing malaise was the cause or the effect of this stress one can only guess. However, I imagine that the pious, uptight attitudes that characterized the Frisian Pauls family did not help matters. They were solemn moralists. They viewed life as a deeply serious affair, and regarded simple pleasures and diversions from the meek day-to-day tasks to be dangerous flirtations with the forces of evil. Furthermore, they were quite ready to contend with anyone who failed to share their religious beliefs and zealously propagandized their point of view.

Maria evidently disliked the rigid environment of her husband's heavy ministerial duties and was perpetually moody, the condition intensifying following her mother's death in 1845 and her father's seven years later. Her depression deepened further in the 1870s, when several of her relatives emigrated to Canada and the United States. Earlier still others had moved to the Bergtal villages and subsequently to Canada. Adding to Maria's misery was that some of her children joined the separatist congregations (*Brüder Gemeinde*), a matter which (as already discussed) often caused embittered schisms within a family.

By the time her husband Heinrich died in 1882, Maria had slipped into full-blown insanity of a decidedly paranoid character. This was exemplified by her certainty that the family was poisoning her and her ensuing demand that everyone at table taste some food on her plate before she herself would eat. As she clearly could not remain on the Kovenhoven farmstead in Rosental, even with hired help, the children sold the farm and moved Maria into a cottage on the Rosental farmstead belonging to her son Heinrich and his wife – that is, my grandparents.[2] At first, Maria lived a seminormal life, assisted by a maid. But after a year the family could no longer afford the maid, who tried by the old woman's aberrant behaviour was eager to leave anyway. For example, the disturbed woman demanded the maid sew linen shirts for all of the beggars from the neighbouring peasant villages who would visit Mennonite villages on specified days.

With the maid's departure, Maria allowed only her son and several grandchildren into her room. Usually, this meant my mother and her sister Tina, or the foster son Abram Kröger, who stayed with Maria both day and night. The grandchildren's chatter and playful activities calmed her fears. This arrangement worked for several years, until she started her nightly wanderings, getting out of bed, arranging the room's chairs, and talking to the furniture as though it was a human gathering. Angered by lack of response from the imagined audience, she would become violent and threatened the grandchildren. The final blow came when suddenly one night Maria seized my mother by the throat and tried to choke her. With no private or communal Mennonite institutions for the insane, the family moved the old woman into the main house to keep her under constant surveillance. For a time, her son's pleading temporized her aberrant behaviour but she soon resumed her deranged conduct, which continued to escalate until her death in 1889.

Maria's insanity was clearly as much a stain as a strain on the family. Perhaps they believed it to be retribution for some act of omission or commission, because relatives spoke of her mental illness, long after her death in 1889, in hushed tones, always admonishing me, 'But you must not mention any details of this to anyone since this is only for your information.' Since everyone knew the details, this struck me as irrational. Maria's death must have relieved the family, yet I do not recall my grandmother (the afflicted woman's daughter-in-law), who certainly experienced prolonged tribulation, or my mother, who had helped care for the sick woman for years, ever speaking of their ordeals.[3]

In reality, Maria's personal and family experiences during the last decades of her life, when her mind was tortured with totally irrational fears for her life, were not unique. Although she had tendencies we would now call paranoid, I believe much of her malaise stemmed from the stresses within the family and the community. Over the century between her grandparents' arrival in Khortitsa in 1789 and her own death in 1889, the extended family had experienced all the Russian Mennonites' divisive conflicts: the friction between the Flemish and Frisian branches of the church, the bitter land quarrels between those who had a land allotment and those who did not, the dispersion of families to the daughter colonies, the irreparable split between the *Kirchliche* and *Brüder Gemeinde*, and the large-scale exodus to the New World. Probably similar tragedies, although varying in detail and the forms in which they manifested themselves, occurred in a great number of Mennonite families during the second half of the nineteenth century. I assume that similar problems existed in the German Lutheran and Catholic colonies, as well.[4] Certainly, dissent splintered the other Protestant faiths, leading to the formation of the Brethren, Shtundists, Baptists, and Templars, and an extensive emigration to Canada and the United States.

The Pauls Offspring

Despite Maria's fragile mental state and Heinrich's overburdened life, none of the couple's seven children suffered overtly from the family's stressful environment. All but one married into higher social strata and several achieved successful and/or happy lives (Figure 13). The entry of five of the children into the *Gutsbesitzer* class of prosperous estate owners came about because this elite circle of families needed an infusion of 'fresh blood.' Much of the rise of this wealthy class occurred when enormous tracts of land came on the market throughout European Russia after the serfs were freed. In the Ekaterinoslav county (*uezd*), in which Khortitsa was located, individual Mennonite families, and/or groups of related families, purchased a majority of the land. Many of the Mennonite economic elite established their wealth through this process, in particular the Peterses, Martens, Friesens, Wallmans, Bergmanns, Neustädters, Epps, Zachariases, and Sudermanns. The Heinrichs family was probably the largest landholder, whose huge estate, Korneevka, was really a small village. By the end of the nineteenth century, Mennonites owned virtually all the territory in a thirty- to forty-mile-wide strip west of the Dnieper River from Khortitsa to Ekaterinoslav, about fifty miles northward. That left a handful of peasant villages and remaining gentry-owned estates as islands between the Mennonite villages, hamlets, and estates. The expansion was so extensive that the landed gentry petitioned the Council of Ekaterinoslav to prohibit further Mennonite purchases. Their petitions, lodged between 1887 and 1889, disingenuously alleged that their concern was for the peasants, too poor to compete with Mennonites in buying land. Despite their protestations on Mennonite land acquisitions, many abetted the group's control by selling or leasing their estates to them.

As wealthy classes tend to do, the *Gutsbesitzer* (estate-owning) families practised a high degree of intermarriage. Frequently, first cousins married each other. In consequence, a significant percentage of this group's progeny was mentally or physically handicapped. A perusal of the records of the Niebuhr, Töws, Thiessen, Klassen, Wiebe, Dyck, and Heinrichs families corroborates this. To remedy the situation, many of the Gutsbesitzer sought mates for their offspring among the more prosperous farming, business, manufacturing, and professional families (especially teachers) to expand the gene pool. The children of these groups were regarded as possessing a degree of culture. Or at least they seemed susceptible to acquiring the social graces needed in the real or assumed state of cultured people (*kul'turnye liudi*), the skills that would enable them to fit in with other select families when vacationing in the Crimea or consulting doctors in Kharkov, Simferopol, Yalta, or Moscow, or taking the waters at health resorts (*Kurorte*) in Germany, Austria, or Switzerland.

Although the marriage of my grandfather Heinrich Pauls to a Hildebrand lifted him into an elevated cultural milieu, it did not propel him into the wealthy *Gutsbesitzer* class, and except for his youngest brother Johann, who married into the prominent Heinrichs family, considerable friction existed between Grandfather Pauls and all his *Gutsbesitzer*-joining siblings. My aunts and uncles (Grandfather Pauls's children) loved to regale my family with stories of *Khutoriane* (inhabitants of a *khutor*, the Russian word for an individual, large farmstead, ranch, or estate) visits to their home, especially the Neustädters' idiosyncratic eating and sleeping habits or of the bratty behaviour of several of the *Gutsbesitzer* children. Whether these derisory stories were deserved or not I cannot say, for I knew only a few of their sons as schoolmates between 1913 and 1917.

The only one of Grandfather's siblings who I knew personally was Great Uncle Kornelius Pauls, the only one who did not 'marry up.' Father visited Kornelius and his wife whenever he went to Kronstal to buy grain, with me frequently in tow. Although Kornelius was no longer actively farming, he still lived on the farmstead. All its buildings were arranged in the traditional Mennonite *Winkelhaus* form, surrounded on one side by a large vegetable and flower garden, and an extensive number of fruit trees and berry bushes to the right of the long drive that led from the village street to the house and barn. I have fond memories of Kornelius's wife and the delicious watermelons and pastries – especially *Pirozhkie*, *Schnettje*, and *Tweebaktjes* – served along with thin 'coffee' (*Pripps*) for Father, and milk for me.[5]

Great Uncle Kornelius was an ordained minister in the Kronsweide (Frisian) church. Since Kronstal had few members of this congregation,

Reverend Pauls spent much time preaching to scattered congregations in other villages, just as his father had done before him. I remember him often stopping at our home on Saturdays en route to Schönwiese and Neu Schönwiese. Occasionally he delivered the sermon in Nieder Khortitsa as well, an unusual event for a Frisian minister in a Flemish church. His preaching manner was much like a revivalist's, exhorting all to repent. Some of our parishioners observed that no matter what his biblical text might have suggested, the sermon was always the same.

I vividly recall some of his visits to our home, occasionally accompanied by the Kronsweide Church Elder Johann P. Klassen, who lived in Schönwiese. Each of these visits had a strange, mysterious air about it. The clergymen met with my parents in the living room, with the doors shutting us out. Were these meetings designed to keep them from straying from the Kronsweide (Frisian) church's narrow path? This seemed curious to me since my parents went to the services affiliated with the Khortitsa (Flemish) church where we children had been baptized. Perhaps Kornelius even noticed the Khortitsa catechism that stood in a cabinet in that very same living room.[6] According to my Rosental Pauls relatives, all of Kornelius's children, except one daughter, eventually joined the Mennonite Brethren church. Kornelius himself leaned towards that group and perhaps would have left his own church except that he found it easier to recruit converts from his position in the established church.

That my parent's relationship with Great Uncle Kornelius was warm and friendly perplexed me, because I never saw him in my grandmother's (his sister-in-law's) home in Rosental, nor even heard his name mentioned there. It was not until after my grandmother's death in 1920 that other relatives explained the situation. Visits between Great Uncle Kornelius and our Grandfather Heinrich (his brother) had once been frequent and intimate. But after Grandfather developed stomach cancer, Kornelius bored into his ailing brother with his evangelizing manner and exhorting tone – 'Brother, confess thy sins!' To this Grandfather invariably replied, 'I have nothing to confess. I am at peace with my Lord and my fellow men.' As Grandfather's condition deteriorated and his pain became insufferable, he demanded Kornelius be kept from his room. From that time on, all contacts between Grandmother and her brother-in-law Kornelius Pauls and his family ceased for good. Grandfather's story comes next.

CHAPTER TEN

A Burdened Life: Grandfather Heinrich Pauls

Photographs of Grandfather Pauls show a man of serious mien, one burdened with heavy responsibilities, more involved in life's disappointments than in its pleasures. One is a family picture, of Heinrich, his wife Maria, and their surviving ten children. It was taken around 1889 or 1890. The other is of him, alone, probably taken a few years earlier. In part, his demeanour must reflect the difficulties in caring for his mother during her final demented years. This responsibility, however, was only one painful aspect of the final two decades of my grandfather's life. It combined with his disappointment in his eldest daughter's marriage, the bitter estrangement with his brother Kornelius, his eldest son's dwarfism, and the long and painful struggle with stomach cancer, from which he died the year after I was born.

I know far less of Grandfather Pauls and his life than of many of my ancestors, and I wish that more of the family's conversations had touched on his life and experiences. But perhaps after all his years of suffering, many who survived wished to draw a curtain across past sorrows and problems. Still I – and I suspect most of my generation – wanted to know everything about my Mennonite heritage, the difficult and unhappy experiences, as well as 'the good old times in the old Russian homeland' (*die gute alte Zeit in der alten Heimat Russland*).

Grandfather Pauls seems never to have embraced his step-grandchildren, my three oldest siblings. This contrasts to Grandmother Pauls, who considered them her true descendants. The reasons for Grandfather's distant attitude are unclear, although relatives surmise it related to his daughter's husband. As we shall see in a later chapter, Grandfather Pauls, a devoted Frisian church member, allowed his daughter Maria to marry my father only after the prospective groom agreed to change his church affiliation to that of his future in-laws. But granting approval did not mean Grandfather was happy with the match. He also felt his daughter was marrying beneath her station. The Pauls family were mainstays of the community, successful farmers, and he himself had married into the founding Höppner-Hildebrand family, while most of his siblings had married into the *Gutsbesitzer* class. Thus, my grandfather may have disapproved of his daughter marrying a sort of foreigner (*Ütlenda*) to their class, and a non-farmer who had only recently joined the correct church.

A further cause of Grandfather's distress must surely have been the steady flow of relatives who considered his capacious farmstead their own 'home away from home' on interminable visits. The house and out-buildings were located on Rosental's main street, built in the typical right-angle 'Winkelhof' style (with the stable attached to the house proper) that our forebears had used in Poland and Prussia during the seventeenth and eighteenth centuries, and earlier in Holland and Flanders. The one indelible memory I have of this homestead is of the wagon wheel perched atop the barn on which storks built their nests each spring on their return from Africa. The male storks swooped from the nests to the nearby pond or marshy wetlands along the Dnieper to forage for frogs and water snakes, returning with them to feed the new chicks. Often one of my uncles would band a bird just before the flock migrated again to their African winter home, and of course each subsequent spring the same family of birds would return. Local folklore held (as it does in much of Europe) that the storks and their nests brought good luck and sure protection from fires.

As welcome as the storks' springtime arrival was, the same could not be said for the interminable, year-round visits from people. Every near and distant relative, it seemed, used the Pauls home as an inn and livery stable whenever they came to Rosental to conduct business in the adjoining village of Khortitsa. Mennonites took this practice for granted. Most enjoyed the conviviality and, at least for the women, the relationship tracing (*nohfaedme*) that was a common part of their conversations. The Pauls relatives, however, tended to abuse the privilege. One spring, for example, the family had only one day's respite from visitors during the forty-day period between Easter and Ascension Day.

The frequent trips to adjoining Khortitsa were really a necessity since this village was essentially the settlement's capital, with administrative and judicial offices, those of doctors and a dentist, several mills and factories, and various shops. In Khortitsa was Zhukov's Inn (*Auffahrtshof* or *gostinyi dvor*), with stabling facilities. The Pauls relatives, however, preferred to combine visiting (*Schpetsiere*) with business (*Jeschaft*), and therefore, they relied on Grandfather and Grandmother's hospitality. This meant feeding the self-invited guests, their teams of horses, often their coachman (*Kutscher*), and on rare occasions even a nursemaid (*nianka*), if the relatives' trip related to their child's illness. Invariably, these relatives, such as the Heinrichs, Neustädters, Peterses, and Unraus, were far wealthier than my grandparents, and they could easily have afforded to stay at Zhukov's Inn, which admittedly was hardly distinguished for its accommodations and fare.

All the children who remained at home during those final years of Grandfather's life felt that although the visits were sometimes pleasant, they were more often a barely tolerable imposition for them, and an unbearable burden for their ailing father. Finally, Uncle Jacob Pauls, who managed the farm during the last years of Grandfather's illness, locked the oat bins in the barn, telling any visitor, or his coachman, that he could have straw and roughly ground grain (*Schrot*), but he would have to bring his own oats. The results seem to have been minimal, because when none of the Pauls sons were around, the coachmen would snitch some feed from the bin in the stable. As a final resort, the sons locked the stable door. Similar behaviour occurred at table. One visitor, a veritable glutton when ham (*Schinkenfleisch*) and fried or roasted potatoes (*geröstete Kartoffeln*) were the main fare, was warned to bring his own accustomed portion of *Schinkenfleisch* from home in future. Obliging, he would come to the table, unwrap a huge chunk of smoked ham, grunt with satisfaction as he ate the meat, but never offer to share his tasty dish (*Leckergericht*) with anyone else present.

Grandfather's health deteriorated rapidly in 1898. A visit to a reputed cancer specialist in the Crimea was to no avail, and the cancerous condition of his stomach made it difficult for him to eat or retain food. The family hired a nurse, a Lutheran woman, whose soul Uncle Kornelius constantly attempted to save. His wheedling failed, for the nurse maintained she was happy with her own faith, but Kornelius's proselytizing so unnerved her that she deserted her sorely tried patient and his family.

Relief came to Grandfather on 15 November 1900. In Grandmother's words, 'My husband Heinrich Pauls died with dignity on 15 November 1900, after a lengthy illness, on Wednesday at two in the afternoon, and will be buried here in the cemetery on Sunday on the 19th of November,' (*Mein Mann Heinrich Pauls starb 1900 den 15. Nov., nach langjähriger*

Krankheit, Mittwoch 2 Uhr Nachmittags u. wurde Sonntag den 19. Nov. hier auf dem Friedhofe begraben).

Although a series of Job-like trials plagued Grandfather's latter years, his life was not without pleasure. Certainly my grandmother's zest for life, so characteristic of the Hildebrand clan, infused the household with joy, in part offsetting the grim life posture typical of the Pauls family. And while his eldest daughter's marriage displeased him, he was proud that two other daughters married into the *Gutsbesitzer* class. Then too, my Uncle Bernard Pauls recalled many happy childhood moments, particularly the toys my grandfather made for him, and Sunday drives the father and son took through the surrounding countryside. Bernard also recounted stories that a Russian peasant, Ostap Belonos, told him about Grandfather Pauls.

Ostap and his father worked for three generations of Pauls families each summer season, from the 1870s to the First World War. This practice was common in New Russia (now southern Ukraine), the hired help was especially from the Poltava and Chernigov guberniias. Often these seasonal jobs passed from father to son, and both might become virtual members of the employing family. Over the years some peasants would become proficient enough in farming to be promoted to foreman or supervisor of the construction of new farm buildings or operator of the smithy. Some even saved enough from their earnings to start their own farms or set themselves up in a trade.

In the earliest years of this arrangement, sheep-rearing was an important Mennonite occupation and Ostap's father worked as a shepherd. Ostap himself, although quite young, took care of the ewes and lambs. Much later he reminisced about how the mistress would send him off in the morning with a lunch bag and the enjoinder to take good care of the animals entrusted to him. Ostap and his father were viewed as family members in the Heinrich Pauls household, and the same arrangement pertained when Ostap later worked for their son, Bernhard Pauls. In Bernard's home on Insel Khortitsa, we addressed him as Onkel Ostap. When he ate with the family he would bow his head during grace, cross himself, and join in the Amen with the words, 'Lord be merciful. Amen' (*Gospodi pomilui. Amin*). Then, having become fluent in Plautdietsch, Ostap would join in the conversations on a wide range of topics – including religion, a dangerous subject to discuss if the state and church authorities knew of it.[1]

There must have been a good deal of mutual respect in the relationship because I know that Grandmother and her brother Kornelius visited Ostap in his home. On one such occasion, while enjoying a festive lunch, the conversation drifted into religious topics, including the Mennonite objection to icons. Ostap commented, 'Your German God perhaps hears without Icons, but our priest says: "Ostap, thou must pray before the icon, for we are the Right believers"' (*Jün dietscha Jeist heat velleicht uck ohne Ikone, oba ons Diakoon sajt: Ostap, Dü mottst verre Ikone beden, wiels wie send de Rajchtjleewje*).

According to Ostap, my grandfather was of medium height, slightly corpulent in his later years, although when he was younger he had been trim, fit, and an excellent rider and marksman. One of Ostap's favourite stories attested Grandfather's skills. Two dogs had slipped into the sheep corral one night, mauling and killing most of the stock. Ostap's father noticed as they scooted through the gate when it was opened in the morning. He called Grandfather, who immediately leaped on to his horse, set off in hot pursuit of the predators, and while in mid-gallop, managed to overtake one of the dogs and kill it with a single shot.

Heinrich and Maria's Children

Following Russian Mennonite tradition, Heinrich and Maria (née Hildebrand) Pauls had twelve children (Figure 14). They later expanded the family by one more when they assumed the foster care of a young orphan, Abram Kröger. Most of the male Pauls children viewed life as seriously as their father did, and all except the youngest, Johann, found it difficult to unbend. This Uncle Hauns, as we affectionately called him, had a ready smile, delightful sense of humour, and the time to tell stories – traits some relatives considered laziness. He was an inveterate hunter. One of the greatest treats he could give his nephews was a view of his bedroom, replete with rifles, fishing rods, powder pouches, and his hooked hunting belt used to carry home the quail and other small game he caught.

Heinrich, the oldest son, was a dwarf. He had a normal torso, but stunted arms and legs. Although Heinrich was a bright child, his disability was a blow to the family and especially his father. The Mennonite God, like the Jewish one, was sometimes viewed as a vengeful God, and a mishap like this was interpreted as punishment for sins of omission or commission. Heinrich's incapacities prevented him from assuming control of the family farm, as was customary for the eldest son, so Heinrich took up tailoring. He plied his trade in his room in the family home, a room I, like everyone else, never entered until bidden. Invariably, Heinrich sat on the huge table, measuring tape around his neck, surrounded by bolts of cloth, big scissors, spools of thread, needles, a lump of wax, and his sewing machine. Often, when he was not busy sewing, he would read German books, mostly paperback romances, perhaps a travel story, or occasionally a serious book. I have no idea where he obtained his favourite romances – which he would frequently take down to the orchard to read – since as far as I know he never ventured to the Enns bookstore in Khortitsa. Perhaps Tante Sus got them for him, for she was not a bashful, Puritan maiden. Uncle Heinrich earned a sufficient income to take care of his personal needs, and his room and board at home were free. His only domestic task was to feed the chickens and gather eggs. I have a vivid memory of him feeding the chickens, with whip in hand, to ensure that the domineering roosters not deprive the timid hens of their share.

Except with family members, Heinrich was intensely shy. I do not recall ever seeing him walk outside the perimeter of the yard and orchard, and when visiting relatives, even in town, he always went by carriage. As is the case with many shy people, Heinrich was very observant. When he was in the mood, he would tell interesting stories about the foibles and idiosyncrasies of some of the *Gutsbesitzer* relatives, especially the Neustädters. Largely self-taught, Heinrich was prone to one-sided views, prejudicial, and argumentative on issues on which he felt better informed than the person with whom he conversed. Although he never married, he underwent a transformation after he emigrated to Canada with his brother Bernhard and sister Susanna. In this new homeland, Heinrich became more outgoing; he hauled grain to the railroad elevator, shopped in town, and visited friends and relatives without hesitation.

When Grandfather Pauls could no longer manage the family farm, this role devolved to the second eldest son Jacob. Tallest of the uncles and every inch a Pauls, Jacob was serious of mien, humourless, decisive, purposeful, and demanded action now, not eventually. Although we affectionately called him Onkel Jasch, none of his nieces and nephews would dare challenge his authority when we visited. There is little that I remember about the old farmhouse prior to 1905, except for Grandfather's rocking chair in the living room and Onkel Jasch's instructions for me to keep off it.

Later I was able to observe Onkel Jasch's resolute nature when a neighbour's home and adjacent farm buildings caught fire. Because fire could easily spread into a general conflagration enveloping neighbouring farms, the authorities required each farmer to have certain tools (such as ladders and buckets) ready should a fire break out on his property. To assure compliance, outlines of the tools were drawn on the outside of every farmer's stable door. In this case, when the neighbour's fire broke out, three of the Pauls sons raced to the flames with the prescribed tools. Unhappily, the fire had already consumed the house, and all they could do was attempt to rescue the horses and other livestock. Uncles Jacob and Kornelius rushed into the stable and were bringing out several horses, when they noticed that an itinerant Prussian labourer, who had accompanied them, had panicked. But instead of helping them, the labourer was kneeling and in a loud voice praying for God to assist the other men. Uncle Jacob rushed over, slapped his face, issued the peremptory command, 'Up with thee, thou stupid Prussian. The dear God helps only him who helps himself' (*Opp mett die, dü domma Preuss! De leewe Gott halpd bloos dem, de sitj selwst halpd*).

Jacob must have assumed the role of farm manager (*de Weat* or *Wirt*, or in Russian *khoziain*) when very young. He carefully husbanded the farm's income for a household of numerous members and the seemingly endless train of unexpected visitors. Operating the farm must have been a demanding and trying experience during the last years of Grandfather's illness because Jacob tried to defer to his father's judgments on matters like selecting crops and livestock, replacing outmoded equipment, and which major repairs to make or defer, while in reality his ailing father could not decide even the most imperative matters.

At about the time Grandfather died, Jacob bought half the farmland and some of its movable assets, purchasing the remainder in 1905 when Grandmother moved to her new smaller home in the village. That year he married, at age thirty-three, which was old by Mennonite standards (of twenty-one to twenty-five). Jacob and his bride, Anna Hamm, then transformed the farm into one of the most successful in Rosental. Their establishment exuded an air of industriousness, contentment, and comfort, outfitted with the newest buildings and most modern equipment.

In sharp contrast to the family's rather dour sons, the daughters resembled their Hildebrand forebears, who found life joyous. Maria, the eldest child, was my mother. Her story appears throughout the remainder of the book. As alluded to previously, Grandfather Pauls was unhappy with Maria's choice of husband. This contrasted with his pleasure over the marriages of his next-eldest daughters, Katharina and Anganetha, who married into wealthy *Gutsbesitzer* families. At the time, even more than in their parents' generation, this affluent class shopped for their children's prospective mates as much outside as inside their circle, to avoid the deleterious effects that close interbreeding had wrought in the past.

Aunt Katharina married Jacob Janzen, of the Wilhelmstal (Vasilievka) estate, about forty versts (twenty-five miles) northwest of Khortitsa. Although Wilhelmstal lay near the massive estates of Zachariasfeld, Friesental, Korneevka, and those of the Wallman and Bergman families, Janzen was a *Grossbauer* (a farmer who owned more land than a full farm of sixty-five dessiatins, but less than a true estate). His home was in the typical Kronstal style, although larger, and surrounded by the usual farm buildings – stable, barn, sheds, servants' quarters – and an orchard. It was not, however, large enough to support the allied enterprises of the most substantial estates, which often had their own flour and grist mills, smithies, and other workshops.

Anganetha married higher still, choosing Heinrich Heinrichs, scion of one of the wealthy Heinrichs families. They lived in Eichenfeld, about thirty-five miles from our home, so, in a time when travelling meant going by horse and wagon, we rarely saw them. I recall their visiting us only three times prior to 1917, and then, although Uncle Heinrich visited a local horse trader, he refused to visit a relative, a badly crippled old man who had evidently strayed from the family fold.

While my aunts' *Gutsbesitzer* marriages during the 1890s followed expected custom, the family's rigid traditions, already loosened earlier by my mother's independence, fissured as the twentieth century opened. None of the remaining children would entirely conform to the old ways. Bernard was the first to break two absolute patterns: he initially abjured farming, becoming instead an administrator, and he married outside the Kronsweide (Frisian) church. While these may seem trivial matters to us, at the time they were of great import to that family. Over generations, only a few of the Paulses converted either to the Khortitsa (Flemish) or *Brüder Gemeinde* congregations, and as far as I know, none of the Hildebrands took such steps. Bernard's marriage to Helena Epp, daughter of the Khortitsa church elder Heinrich Epp, however, took place in 1902 after Grandfather died and could no longer object to 'marrying outside the faith.' By this time, too, views on other issues had loosened, and business pursuits were considered viable options to farming.

By the time Bernhard and Helena married, her father had also died, so Bernhard assumed operation of the Epps' run-down ancestral farm in Rosental. I suspect he regretted leaving his intellectually stimulating administrative job, but he continued to manage the Epp farm until 1907. Then he purchased the Jacob Höppner farm on Insel Khortitsa. Owning this historic and beautiful tract of land must have more than reconciled him to his task.

Bernhard's younger brother Kornelius Pauls renounced farming altogether and opened a general store in Rosental. At first it was located on the village's main street, then the family farmstead, and finally, following Grandfather's death and the sale of the farm, in the working-class neighbourhood – where it thrived for about a decade. When Kornelius was called up for alternative service in September, 1914, his wife – a jolly fat woman – took over the business, and for a time it stayed afloat. But, as it became impossible to obtain stock, it began to deteriorate. Following the October Revolution of 1917, the business folded entirely.

My mother's two youngest sisters took independent paths as she herself had done. Susanna refused to marry until she was in her mid-thirties, and Helena married Rosental's elementary school teacher, Kornelius Braun. A brilliant man, Kornelius had a razor-sharp tongue, sarcastic gallows humour, emotive body, and rather high-pitched, musical voice. His talents were obvious during the years in which he directed the acclaimed Rosental men's chorus (*Gesangverein*). A consummate actor, Kornelius could mesmerize audiences when reading aloud from his extensive library of German and Russian literature, especially Fritz Reuter (in original Low German), Gogol's Russian tales, and Shevchenko's Ukrainian writings.

Kornelius taught at the Rosental school for roughly two decades, immediately establishing his reputation as a resourceful and innovative teacher, likewise as a strict disciplinarian. His piercing brown eyes intimidated any show-offs on the school grounds (and, his children claimed, at home). Some of his in-laws branded him a radical or 'red-tinged' (*rot angehaucht*) because he voiced liberal political views probably derived from his extensive reading and his comprehension of the enormous gap between the affluent Mennonite farmers and entrepreneurs from their Ukrainian compatriots. Aside from my father, Kornelius Braun was the only one of my relatives who foresaw the enormous political, economic, and nationalist forces at work in our larger imperial surroundings – along with their potentially horrendous consequences.

The youngest child Susanna Pauls weighed less than three pounds at birth. In those days, before incubators and the paraphernalia of modern medicine, no one expected her to live. Nevertheless, Tante Sus grew up to lead a full life. She outlived three husbands who she married later in life, and died just a few weeks short of her ninety-fifth birthday. Grandmother reigned over the Pauls household, a bit like a grand dame, but it was Tante Sus who actually ran it. Tante Sus decided what to stock in the larder, what to cook and how to serve it, what to buy beyond the kitchen's necessities, how many and which of the many boarding applicants to accept in the home, and the myriad other matters of this household. Tante Sus cleaned the house, and sometimes with help from Heinrich and Johann, planted and harvested the vegetable garden, and then canned and pickled the abundant harvest.

Tante Sus became the village beauty. The young men of Rosental called her Pauls's Little Rose (*Pauls Röschen*). But she refused to marry any of her many suitors. She was the favourite of her siblings and the extended relations within and beyond the Khortitsa Settlement. No one loved her more than her numerous nieces and nephews. So on our visits to Grandmother's home we had no doubt about who would reward us for our good behaviour, or punish miscreants. Likewise, we all looked forward to her visits to our home, since she so obviously communicated her joy in living. However, as a spinster aunt, she could find fault with our behaviour, as when we grumbled at Mother's instructions to wash our hands before meals, or if we had dirty feet when we went to bed, or perhaps came home late from swimming in the Dnieper. At these times, after the initial ardour of her visits had cooled, I remember rare moments when we would whisper to each other, 'I love Tante Sus dearly, but when will she go home?' (*Etj sie Taunte Sus sea goot, oba wann woat de noh Hüs foahre?*). How often she would remind me of this remark decades later when we were both safe in the New World!

CHAPTER ELEVEN

Equanimity: Grandmother Pauls, 1901–1917

My grandmother Pauls's years of widowhood were anything but reclusive or dependent. Normally, the Mennonite settlement's Orphans Department (*Waisenamt*) assigned a Good Man (*guter Mann*) to advise widows with minor children on financial matters. Grandmother refused such help, asserting that she and the older children could successfully manage the farm as they had done throughout the years of her husband's illness.[1] Only in 1905, when she negotiated the purchase and remodelling of a new home, did she relent and allow a *guter Mann* (her neighbour, Franz Enns) to briefly assist.

Moving from the farm to her new house on the hill had a profound effect on my grandmother and those of her children who remained at home. None of the memories of her mother-in-law's insanity or her husband's long and painful illness burdened this new abode. Moreover, it was too small to accommodate the many relatives who had used the old farm as their inn whenever they visited the area, ending this taxing burden. The benefits of the move became immediate and obvious. A neighbour (a Mennonite elder who knew everyone in the village) pointed out he knew no other household so content, unruffled, and harmonious, especially considering its disparate members. During these years they included Grandmother, her sons Heinrich and Johann, daughter Susanna, and a steady flow of students boarding there while attending one of Khortitsa's high schools or taking sewing lessons from the local seamstress.

The new home on the high south bank rising from the Khortitsa-Rosental Valley sat close to a steep, narrow lane off Rosental's main street. This section of the village included about a dozen attractive homes, inhabited mostly by retired, or semiretired people, one of whom was the famous clockmaker Kröger, whose clocks were found in virtually every house in the settlement.

The area had once been a mulberry plantation, one of many decreed by Alexander I and Nicholas I in an attempt to foster the silk industry. These plantations reached their zenith between 1830 and 1848, when Johann Cornies (the so-called Mennonite Tsar or Tree Devil) ruthlessly coerced his co-religionists into planting many orchards and tree plantations. The farmers abandoned the mulberry plantations when southern Russia's silk industry collapsed halfway through the nineteenth century, as France's industry recovered. At this same time, the Crimean War (1853–6) stimulated the need for grain, and these crops rapidly replaced the mulberry groves. The local farmers divided the orchard among themselves with no restrictions on each parcel's use. By good fortune, my grandfather drew his lot close to his own homestead, and he planted an assortment of fruit trees on this new parcel, terracing them up its steep slope. Years later, during the last decade of the nineteenth century, much of the original tract was converted into a residential district.

Grandmother's new house had been built recently by Dietrich Epp[2] who had earlier emigrated to the United States, but disliking the new country, returned to Russia. Finding no other suitable building site in Rosental, he bought the small site on, or adjacent to, my grandfather's parcel of the former plantation, levelled a small section, and built a one-and-a-half-story home which my relatives referred to as being in the 'American style.' I do not know whether Epp finished the interior or built its small stable and carriage house. Evidently an argument with the village officials, and much of its citizenry, forced him to abandon the project before he completed it.

The roots of this quarrel stemmed from Dietrich Epp's Seventh Day Adventist practices and proselytizing. Having zealously adopted this new religion in America, he set about propagating the new faith among his Mennonite neighbours. When Rosental's leaders resisted his attempts, Epp chose a creative form of vengeance. Rosental's population made a great deal of noise throughout the week pursuing the normal activities of farmers and tradespeople. That noise continued through Saturday, which was Epp's day of rest and worship. Epp retaliated in kind, hammering and sawing throughout the Mennonite neighbours' Sunday morning worship. Each Sunday the sound of the nearby Orthodox church's bells filling the countryside signalled Epp to begin construction. His hammering reached an offensive crescendo between ten and twelve o'clock when the churchgoers set off for services, then slackened until the Mennonites left church, when he would resume his abrasive construction.

When Grandmother bought the house, her sons removed the upper half-story, rebuilt it completely, enlarging and adding rooms and an enclosed verandah. The main kitchen was on the ground floor, and heavily shaded by shrubs, so it remained a cool haven in summertime despite the large stove and blazing oven that seemed always full of fragrant pies and *pirozhkie*. The large dining room, complete with a dumb waiter to send food upstairs (where the family ate in winter), was adjacent, with the ample pantry just behind it, typically filled with an hypnotic array of canned fruits and preserves. The living quarters were on the second story, with a dining area adjoining the living room, and several bedrooms, virtually all of which had grand views of the surrounding countryside. Surmounting these was the steeply roofed attic, with its collection of cast-off tins, chests, decrepit furniture, and litter of old papers and letters. What a magnet this was for us grandchildren, who loved to rummage through these 'treasures' or spy out onto the grand vistas from the windows at either end.

Considering Grandmother's limited income, and the spacious house, the family decided to board students from the girls high school in Khortitsa in one of the larger bedrooms. The school enjoyed an outstanding reputation, and many Catholic and Lutheran parents, as well as Mennonite families in distant areas, sent their daughters there.

A steady stream of grandchildren who visited *Grootmau* (or *Oma*) joined these little lambs (*barashki*), as the local boys called them, both groups adding zest to the cheerful household. Of the twenty-eight grandchildren born prior to the First World War, the sixteen who lived close to Grandmother's 'America House,' carried lifelong memories of happy hours spent romping, eating, or listening to Grandmother's stories, in their youngest years, and the serious conversations between the two generations of adults that they were later privileged to join.

The kitchen garden was among the home's prime attractions, full of fruit trees (primarily apple, pear, cherry, plum, and apricot) and of grape, gooseberry, and raspberry vines. Whatever the season, there was always some form of fruit treat to relish – fresh, dried, pickled, or preserved. However, the treats gave Tante Sus a weapon. She would withhold them if we failed to comply with her rules. Beyond the fruit, the orchard's terraced slopes and steep alley just beyond provided physical delights. In summer, we raced through the garden, jumping from level to level, while in winter, the alley – absent traffic – became our favourite sledding course.

From the highest points in the garden as well as from the second floor of the house, the view was superb, with history marking so many sites. For example, Tsar's Landing (*Tsarskaia pristan'*) on the Dnieper – so named because Catherine the Great allegedly disembarked there for Potemkin's estate on her 1787 journey to the Crimea – was the point where many Mennonites landed in 1789. A massive, high rock formation called *Opekopp* (or *Affenkopf*), because of its resemblance to an ape's head, and the equally inelegantly named *Schwienskopp* (*Schweinskopf*) or pig's head landmark rose to the right of the landing. Close by, Rosental's early settlers erected their first primitive dwellings, each on a separate tract of land rather than in close village form.[3] Still further to the right, on clear days you could see the narrow, winding road leading to the Khortitsa Island ferry, and the high, rocky northern end of the island, with its remarkable landmark, the so-called Jew's Rock (*Judesteen* or *Judenstein*). Here the land dropped a hundred feet or more to the water. According to local Russian folklore, the Zaporozhian Cossacks used it to mete out 'justice' to Jewish traders they suspected of cheating. Immediately east of it lay the island's tip, where the Dnieper River divided into two channels – the eastern or New Dnieper and the western, narrower Old Dnieper.

Grandmother, who was a history buff, liked to point out that the Franz Enns farm lying about 150 feet below the steeply terraced section of her Rosental property originally belonged to Johann Bartsch, one of the settlement's two founders. Until it burned to the ground in the late 1890s, the wooden house and barn on the lot had been among the last structures remaining from the time that the village was founded. Grandmother and Tante Sus alleged that the high quality of the lumber accounted for the dwelling's longevity and perhaps substantiated the early settlers' complaints that Höppner and Bartsch appropriated the best materials and sites for themselves. Unquestionably, Bartsch's homesite was one of the loveliest in the entire settlement, located at the entrance to what had been Potemkin's orchard, and near the small steppe stream, called *Kantsirskaia*, that flowed into the Upper Khortitsa Stream which the earlier settlers had called their 'Jordan River.'

Lifting your eyes from the valley floor to the high western bank of the stream, you could see the village cemetery, with its obelisk-shaped monument erected to Bartsch in 1889, and left of that, a few red rooftops of the new farms. Beyond them was the heavily wooded Khortitsa-Rosental

Valley and glimpses of the Dnieper, while many of Rosental's main farmsteads, including the former Pauls farm, and neat cottage of the last Bartsch descendant, lay closer. The Colony Garden (*Koloniesgoade*) – a large park, a few minutes walk from my grandmother's house – was the most interesting sight. It was in a deep, narrow valley, called Kantsirskaia, with many trees probably antedating Potemkin's 1775 appropriation of the vast tract[4] surrounding the garden. What pleasure it used to be to stroll beside the Kantsirskaia creek, which meandered its way across meadows and around clumps of trees, some so dense sunlight barely penetrated their branches. The canopy sheltered innumerable birds, whose endless daily chirping silenced at sunset, only to resume with the nightingales' melodious trills.

With such a spectacular setting, the village's name – Rosental (that is, Rosedale) – seemed perfect. Some claimed that the first settlers, as sober minded and sorely disappointed as they were, chose the village's name. However, according to oral tradition, Bartsch named his house Rosedale, and when the early settlers moved their temporary shelters from Schwienskopp to the orchard area, they adopted Rosedale as the village name.

My grandmother spent the last fifteen years of her life in this pastoral splendour, often roaming through it with her older brother Kornelius, who – having relinquished management of his factories – spent his days tinkering with inventions and adding his memories to the already described Hildebrand Papers. Frequently the two would hike for hours in Rosental's hills and valleys, then head for the Dnieper, and take the ferry to the island where they then walked the four miles to the village of Insel Khortitsa. After visiting with relatives and acquaintances, they would resume their leisurely walk, exploring the island's landmarks (Map 4, page 80). Favourites included Potemkin's one-time cherry orchard where Höppner built his first home and several deep ravines, among them Deer Valley (*Rehläajcht*), General's Valley (*Generaulsläajcht*), and the Pine Woods (*Fichtewoold*). Occasionally they would extend their hikes to the *Bütendick*, the island's southern tip, call a boatman to ferry them across the smaller branch of the Dnieper to Nieder Khortitsa, and visit us, after which we took them home.

My grandmother loved these walks passionately. If Kornelius should come when she was resting in bed and inquire, 'Where's your mother?' (*Woa es diene Mutta?*), and was told, 'Oh Mother's not feeling well today' (*Na, vondoag feehlt Mutta sitj nich sea goat*), Kornelius would respond, 'That's too bad. When the weather's so nice, I wish she'd come

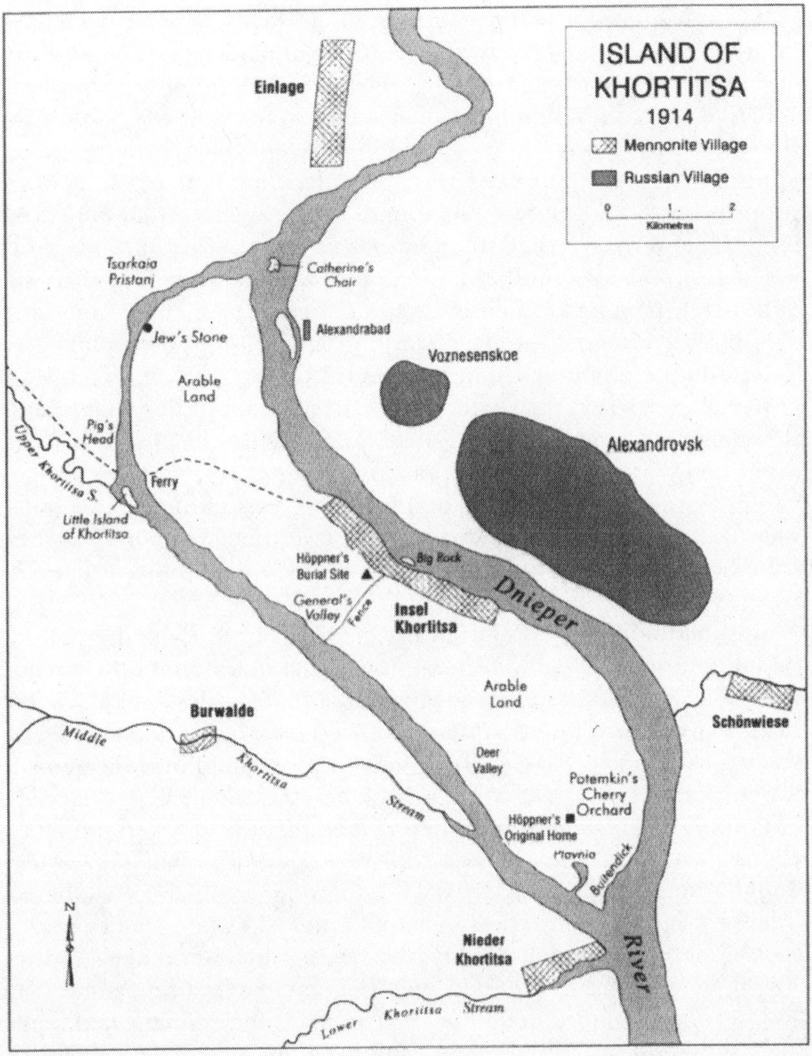

ISLAND OF KHORTITSA 1914
Mennonite Village
Russian Village
0 1 2
Kilometres
Einlage
Tsarkaia Pristanj
Catherine's Chair
Jew's Stone
Alexandrabad
Voznesenskoe
Arable Land
Pig's Head
Upper Khortitsa S.
Ferry
Little Island of Khortitsa
Alexandrovsk
Höppner's Burial Site
Big Rock
General's Valley
Fence
Insel Khortitsa
Dnieper
Arable Land
Burwalde
Middle
Khortitsa
Stream
Schönwiese
Deer Valley
Potemkin's Cherry Orchard
Höppner's Original Home
Plavnia
Buttendick
N
Nieder Khortitsa
River
Lower Khortitsa Stream

Map 4

with me to the island.' (*Daut es oba schohd. Wann daut Wadda so scheen es, dann wull etj daut se met mie noh de Kaump gohne saul*). Somehow Grandmother invariably would hear her brother's voice, divine his intentions, and call, 'Yes, yes. I feel much better already. Wait a bit and I'll be ready' (*Joh, Joh. Etj feel mie aul gauns bäta. Wacht mol en tjlien bestje en etj sie foadig*). And off the two would go. They maintained these hikes until Insel Khortitsa was sold, under duress, to Alexandrovsk in 1917. The civil war broke, and gangs of bandits sweeping the area made all travel dangerous after that. By then, Grandmother was in her early seventies and Great Uncle Kornelius in his mid-eighties.

Both my grandmother and Kornelius shared the legendary Hildebrand memory, and they were veritable storehouses of Mennonite history and lore. I believe my interest in Russian and Mennonite history stems from Grandmother's vivid stories of our ancestors' past, the significant roles they played in the settlement and the historical events she herself witnessed. Beyond her facility in story-telling, the most indelible memory I have of my grandmother, which has stuck with me into my own old age, is of her vitality and her dignified bearing. Serene and unflappable, the activities of the children and teenagers interested and invigorated her as much as did the activities of her peers.

Everyone in the household loved to read, and lively discussions filled the house, especially during afternoon coffee break. I remember discussions mainly from my Khortitsa schooldays of 1913 to 1919, but one when I was about ten, also remains clear. We went to Grandmother's after a doctor's visit in Khortitsa. My brother Johann, Tante Lena, and her husband Kornelius Braun, and their baby were there, too, along with the household occupants, Tante Sus, Uncles Heinrich and Johann, and Grandmother. I was the youngest and sat between the two eldest, Grandmother and Uncle Heinrich.

These two began discussing the Boer War (1899–1902) and the later Boer Trek, emphasizing the alleged wickedness of British imperialism and its atrocities against the Boers and President Kruger in particular. Both had recently read a German book on the topic. Uncle Heinrich characterized Britain as '*Der perfide Albion.*' Uncles Johann and Kornelius Braun, who were close friends, shot condescending responses to Uncle Heinrich's opinions, which in part reflected their disdain for Heinrich's taste for romance novels. But the two were more concerned with other political matters, especially the Stolypin land reforms and other issues before the State Duma. I understood these Russian matters only vaguely from discussions overheard when Jewish grain traders visited our home.

Although my father tended to be anti-British, because his grain-trading business suffered whenever Britain pressured Turkey to threaten to close the Dardenelles Straits, he too felt that other political matters were of greater import to the Mennonites – whether the ever-present Balkan problems would stir up animosities between the Russians and Turks, and whether the land reforms might assist our village's landless families to finally obtain allotments.

I did not understand much of the politics. Eighty years later, however, I still can recall the seating arrangement around the table, and the vigour with which most of us pressed our views. Perhaps I remember the scene so well because such heated political discussions were commonplace in our home, and in Kornelius Braun's and Uncle Bernhard's – but not so likely at my grandmother's house. Second, I was proud that my father held his own, despite his modest education. In retrospect, I am also amused that later that afternoon, Father told a story in the Jewish dialect which he had acquired through his transactions with Jewish grain traders. He could have told this story without embarrassment in almost any home in Nieder Khortitsa, and in Rosental to my uncles, but not in Grandmother's presence! Mother was visibly uneasy over the event and en route home let my father know that such an ethnic story was not the sort told in the Rosental Pauls home. Finally, I remember Grandmother's poise, the deference everyone accorded her and her views, and the sense of repose that pervaded her home. Those were unfailing traits that lasted until the day she died.

PART THREE

Boyhood

CHAPTER TWELVE

Life at Home

My father and mother wed on 26 November 1891, and the new marriage radically changed the Rempel household. In the immediate sense this meant that Father's three small children again enjoyed a mother's love. In the longer view, it affiliated the Rempel clan with the Pauls-Hildebrand family, who had a deeper commitment to real or professed Mennonite beliefs, who were perceived to be of better social and economic standing, and who held broader cultural interests. Finally, the Pauls family's knowledge of our Mennonite past and the reasons for migration to Russia fostered a keen sense of heritage in all the family's children. And, although the family's contacts with Father's first wife's family remained intimate, the household's focus shifted towards the Pauls relations in Rosental and Insel Khortitsa. Together, the dual view of two extended families, belonging to different social strata and different branches of the church, gave us a deep appreciation of the Mennonite experience in Russia.

My parents' marriage differed from ordinary course of matrimony in Nieder Khortitsa. Most often villagers married Mennonites from within their own village or one nearby, and the prospective spouse was almost always of the same religious affiliation. The widower Rempel, however, went farther afield, to Rosental, and he chose a member of the Frisian church, while, as noted, he himself belonged to the Flemish.

How did Father meet Maria Pauls? I never heard this discussed until after both my parents had succumbed to typhus (in 1919–20). Then, reminiscing with my brothers and sister about happier times, my older siblings offered their views. The consensus was that my mother often used to visit her cousin, Mrs Sara Siemens, who lived next door to my father and his first wife. When there, she would certainly have met the couple. They also felt that Mrs Siemens may later have helped to arrange her newly widowed neighbour's second marriage.

Whatever these preliminaries may have been, my brother Johann told how Father went to Rosental to woo Maria. One day in early autumn, Father had asked a local teamster to drive him to Rosental, using the better of his two teams of horses and a neighbour's box wagon that had a spring seat, as well. Just as they were about ready to leave, a friend of the Rempel family, who had evidently made up her mind that she was going to marry the new widower, came by. Perhaps sensing that 'her' Jeat Rampel might have other plans, she implored him to take her along. With some effort, Father dissuaded her, insisting he would be gone all day and that materials he would be purchasing in Burwalde would leave no room for passengers. Father and the teamster did not stop in Burwalde, but drove straight to Rosental instead. When they passed the Pauls homestead, something 'broke' on the wagon. Father went to the Pauls house on the pretext of borrowing a wrench to tighten up a few bolts on the coupling of the wagon shaft. He was handed the wrench and he took but a few minutes to make the 'repairs.' However, he took a long time returning the wrench. Father, evidently seemed at ease, and very happy, on the way home.

Two of my mother's siblings, Lena and Kornelius, who were eight and ten years old when this incident occurred, corroborated the events. They remembered that one day Maria had unceremoniously shoved them out of the house, remarking that the family expected a visitor and that they had better stay out of sight. Then, a stranger arrived and asked for a tool, which Maria procured for him, and afterwards the man spent a long time with Maria and her parents in the *Grootestow.*

From hints several Rosental relatives later dropped, my impression is that Maria's parents consented with some hesitation to their first born daughter's marriage to Gerhard Rempel. Earlier she had rejected a proposal from Jacob Hermannovich Niebuhr, the scion of Schönwiese's wealthy Niebuhrs, who had made their fortune in milling. Instead, Maria was intent on marrying a recently widowed man with three small children, whose profession of small businessman lacked a farmer's assured income. Furthermore, this Rempel belonged to the Flemish church, a disturbing matter to a Frisian church family, especially one whose members were often elected to its ministry. Well, at least he did not belong to the *Brüder Gemeinde,* which would have been a more serious matter.

Father agreed to join the Frisian church, and this evidently assuaged the parents' concern on that issue. But a fourth factor remained: Father was from Nieder Khortitsa, a village which many of the settlers held in low esteem. Its inhabitants had a reputation of being uncouth, too russified (*verrusst*), and its menfolk tough devils ready to fight at the slightest provocation. No wonder the other villages, as noted, had nicknamed the men of Nieder Khortitsa *Cherkessy* with broken-tip knives (*Cherkessy met aufjebroakne Massasch*). Certainly, those from villages claiming to be the standard-bearers and guardians of Mennonite 'culture' (especially Khortitsa, Rosental, and Schönwiese) took the Nieder Khortitsa residents to be uncultured people. These villages delighted in ridiculing our villagers' mode of speech. Our Low German was virtually devoid of any High German words, and the 'cultured' villagers deemed our everyday vocabulary and pronunciation to be that of country bumpkins, much as a New Englander might view a brash Texan. This reputation notwithstanding, and in spite of the Pauls parents reservations, my parents married several weeks later.

Life at Home in the Early Years

Maria Pauls was a handsome woman, with the erect bearing typical of the Pauls family. Although her height of about 5'8" was no greater than Father's, she appeared taller than her husband, who carried his stocky but wiry body with a slight stoop. Both enjoyed vigorous health, and I remember only the rarest instances when either was sick enough to leave their work and retire to bed or even rest on the ubiquitous bench beside the oven (*Owebeintj* or *Ofenbank*).

The household duties that Mother assumed in 1891 left no time for homesickness, especially since the youngest of Father's three children, Johann, was a year-old, delicate infant. Their own first child, born a year after the marriage, died of diphtheria at the age of two (Figure 7). Johann recalled Father coming into the room where he and Gerhard were playing, to tell them in tears, 'He is dead.' The loss of this son, if anything, strengthened Mother's attachment to Johann, or Hauns, as we usually called him.

For at least nine months of the year, Father was out of the house all day on business, leaving my mother to manage the hectic household and family. Eventually there were seven of us: Neta, Gerhard, and Johann from Father's first marriage, and Maria, Heinrich, Jacob, and myself from the second. In addition to the nuclear family, Father's niece and nephew, Grandmother's Elizabeth and Grandmother's Gerhard (*Grootmaus Listje* and *Grootmaus Jeat*) lived with us for prolonged periods. Some of their belongings were stored in our attic, including Listje's accordion, which we were not allowed to touch. As a child, although I was fond of these older cousins, I often wondered why someone called Grandmother's Elizabeth or Grandmother's Gerhard was always at our home and never at Grandmother's.

Several of Father's first wife's relatives, especially her brothers, also frequented our home, and their relationship with our mother was so strong they treated each other like actual sister and brothers. In addition, we often had to accommodate Father's business acquaintances, or on occasion, government officials, because Nieder Khortitsa had neither an inn nor a restaurant.[1] Then besides all of these relatives and business associates, Mother fed the peasant girls who weeded Father's melon fields (*Baschtaun*)[2] and the men hired to guard the seven or eight acres of watermelons and cantaloupes from predatory crows and thieves.

Of course, as my sisters grew, they helped. But Neta left in 1906 when she married, and by the time Maria was sixteen (in 1910) Father had commandeered her to help in his grain trade. Maria often took charge of receiving the teamsters' loads, checking the weight and purity of the shipments, and supervising their sacking and loading onto barges and *berliny* for further shipment to Alexandrovsk or Kherson. However, throughout most of my childhood, an ageless peasant woman from nearby Razumovka, known to us simply as Marika, often helped Mother. During the busiest months of the year, Marika became a de facto family member, assisting in the house, yard, granary, and watermelon patch. Marika had been around for so long and understood Low German so well that as Mother started instructing her in the day's work, she would respond: 'Enough said. I understand everything' (*Jenauch etj vestoh aules*). We also employed Priska, Marika's daughter, and her deaf-mute niece Nastia, both labouring outside with the strength of tough peasants (*muzhiki*).

In keeping with the times, we produced almost all of our own food, harvesting fruit and vegetables, and two cows provided all our dairy products. Most of the meat we ate was home-raised – either poultry (mostly chickens, but ducks and geese, as well) or pork products, such as hams, sausages, ribs, and lard which we cured or rendered at home after the neighbourhood hog-butchering event in late autumn. We ate fresh beef, veal, mutton, or lamb occasionally, but only during the warmer months when a local farmer slaughtered these animals.

Preparing food to fill the larder occupied most of my mother's time from early spring until just before winter set in. At the beginning of the season she would plant our potatoes, beets, onions, cucumbers, beans, cabbages, radishes, carrots, tomatoes, and so forth. In summer she made preserves of the garden's bounty of cherries, apricots, pears, plums, apples, berries, and little wild pears (*Kruschtje*). By late fall all her time went to pickling cucumbers and watermelons, boiling the melon juice down into syrup, and roasting pumpkin seeds.

In our community we fed the pumpkin flesh to the animals, reserving only the seeds for a winter pastime that most young and old alike enjoyed – artfully tossing toasted seeds into our mouths, cracking them, and spitting the shells onto the floor. Our family did not 'chew.' In most of the village's households, however, as winter shadows fused into night, everyone crunched pumpkin seeds – the children while doing their homework, mothers while sewing or knitting, and fathers while poring over their paperwork. Thus, the housewives' final evening task was sweeping up hulls.

No matter what the season, my mother was busiest on the days that she baked, usually at mid-week and on Saturday. As in other Mennonite homes, Mother's staples included small white loaves of bread (*Tweeback*), large tall loaves (*Bultje,* from the Russian *bulki*), and double-decker rolls (*Tweebaktjes*). Although some housewives also made their own rye bread, Father usually bought the darker Russian rye bread, which we liked best, from the bakeries in Alexandrovsk after he had finished his day's business there. As a treat, especially if we expected guests, Father brought home a loaf of French (*Franzeesischet*) or twisted Vienna bread, both of which Mother served with tea rather than coffee. In summer, Mother baked special pastries to serve with fresh fruit, and indeed an authentic summertime midday Mennonite meal (*en ajchtet mennischet Mohl*) was *Schnettje en Arbus* (*Schnettje,* a rolled pastry like a twisted Danish roll, and *arbus* – watermelon). On Saturdays she baked specialties for the week-end, particularly *Tweebaktjes* made with butter instead of lard. In addition, Mother often made *Pirozhki,* typical Russian pastries, which in summer she filled with fresh cherries, plums, or apples, and in winter, with canned fruits. Or she made *Plautz,* a fruit- or preserve-topped sheet cake. For an extra special mid-afternoon 'coffee' break (*Vaspa*), Mother might make a special coffee cake with cottage cheese and streusel (*Glommskuake*).

We did not have a summer kitchen, and so Mother baked everything in our outdoor brick oven (similar to an American brick barbecue pit). The aroma alone of freshly baked breads and pastries was sufficient inducement to keep us boys busy with our Saturday chores, weeding and sweeping in the garden, for Mother always rewarded us with ample samplings of these treats.

This was not daily fare. Nor was our table sumptuous, nor even portions always abundant. Our meals were neither as rich nor as generous as those in a typical well-established Mennonite farm home. Moreover, since we relied on home-grown foods, we husbanded them carefully, eating rather frugal portions of meat, sugar, and dairy products (especially butter and cream). With the relative scarcity of lard at home, my mother often cooked with sunflower seed oil, which Mennonites at the time regarded as fit only for the poorest of their members, or for peasants. Using sunflower seed oil demeaned a proper housewife. But this was before anyone recognized the dangers of saturated fats, so Mother's necessary frugality turned out to be an extra blessing for a family with congenital heart murmurs. I should point out, too, that while we rarely ate lavishly, we never ever missed a meal – until the turmoil of the October Revolution.

Father liked a nice home and tidy surroundings, and within his means built up a fine homestead in which the family lived for the first twenty years of the marriage (see Map 5, page 122). However, in 1912 my father decided to build a new, larger, and more comfortable homestead. To raise the extra capital he sold the Orenburg farm that he had purchased years before and selected an empty site down the street from our original home. Throughout 1912–14 he engaged a contractor and local Ukrainian bricklayers to build the house, granary (*Spitja*), stable, and barn – a common practice. Mennonites put up their own wooden structures (a majority of the farm buildings), but hired Ukrainian labourers for the brick buildings. Our house and out-buildings were, with a few exceptions, the nicest in the village, pleasing Father immensely.

My father's desire for neatness was universal, and he insisted we dress in tidy clothes. Mother made all her own clothes, and until we reached high school age, most of her children's as well, except shoes and caps. I assume Mother helped Neta and Maria sew their dresses, too, although a local seamstress may sometimes have helped. We all inherited hand-me-downs from our older siblings, and Mother spent much of her evening adapting clothes and darning or patching endless bits of wool reinforcement into the heels and toes of socks to make them last longer. As to shoes, the preschool children wore them only on Sundays or for special occasions, while the school-age boys and girls both wore thick-soled wooden sandals (*Schlorren*) during the week and good shoes likewise on Sunday. My mother carefully tended our limited wardrobes, and on Monday mornings, especially in the summer, we boys had to help brush our Sunday clothes before we put them back in the wardrobe.

Money was tight and we boys knew that if we were careless or extra hard on our clothes, we would have to wear them patched. But I had a particular problem during the warmer months when fresh paint or boat tar would be lying always in wait, virtually leaping out at me when I approached the riverbank. Consequently, I wore many a stained shirt or pair of trousers, even on Sundays, as a reminder that the Dnieper beaches held hazards for me.

As we grew older, Father occasionally added a ready-to-wear item or two to our wardrobes. Uncle Heinrich Pauls made some of our clothes, but more often Benjamin Goldman, a Jewish tailor from Alexandrovsk, fashioned them. While anti-Semitism was common throughout southern Russia, and even Mennonites were not free of this disease, within my experience it never reached the virulence seen outside our community, and during pogroms Jewish residents from nearby cities often found asylum in local Mennonite homes. Certainly, there was ample commerce between Mennonite and Jew. In fact, Benjamin the tailor spent so much of his time in Nieder Khortitsa that he knew Plautdietsch and we called him *Bunjamin*. At times he spent days, or even weeks, sewing garments for customers while living in some villager's home. Often that was ours and in compensation he tailored a few items gratis. When Benjamin stayed in our village for weeks he brought his best bolts of cloth along, and as fate had it, a fire occasionally broke out in his Alexandrovsk store under suspicious circumstances. When it had become habitual, I remember Mother telling him that he could use the vestibule (*Veaschtow*) for as long as he needed it, but he should not have a fire at home during that time.

Although Father liked his family neatly dressed, and his house orderly, he had little time to develop an appreciation for beautiful things or those without obvious utilitarian value. An example was his utter disdain for the appearance of his wagons and teams of horses. At best the horses could be called old, worn-out nags (*kliachi*), the sort a poor peasant or peddlar might own. Seemingly, Father only cared that the horse had a neck and shoulders to hold the harness, four legs to move steadily, and a long tail to swish flies. It was not that he begrudged them feed. Rather, his horses were *kliachi* because they had no redeeming features to begin with, which mortified my brother Heinrich and me when we drove with him, because the proudest possession of every

Mennonite farmer, and especially of his sons, was a matched pair of horses used exclusively for pleasure drives plus a substantial number of sturdy horses for farm chores.

As if my father's *kliachi* horses were not bad enough, they pulled an equally nondescript wagon. And, while we twice persuaded Father to buy a nice box wagon from the local blacksmith and wagon-maker, Tall Martens (*Groota Moatess*), he sold each almost immediately to some farmer from whom he bought grain. One of his wagons I remember with special abhorrence – a contraption that we used for an entire year. It was cannibalized from several wagons. The front axle was at least eight inches wider than the rear one. That wagon was a sight, and it would elicit derisive catcalls from the farmers' kids wherever we took it. Father was not in the least bothered by this, but their 'hee-haws' constantly horrified me. The rationale of this conveyance was not obvious until, years later, Father pointed out that in all the time he had traded in grain, often carrying large sums of money with him, he had never been robbed. This was true even in the troubled years of 1905 to 1907, when bandits and revolutionaries infested the *plavni* around Alexandrovsk and the countryside on the other side of the Dnieper.

Finally, in 1912, Father bought a respectable team and wagon, and then only to placate Heinrich, who agreed to help in the store on that condition. Father bought a decent wagon, fine harness, and selected a good-looking pair of dappled colts, which unfortunately did not have a chance to develop into strong mature horses because they were worked too hard for their ages. In early 1916, when the army requisitioned all horses, Father sold the pair to a farmer in Schöneberg, and bought such a nag that neither the military nor even the Makhnovites confiscated it during the troubles in late 1919.

What my father lacked in appreciating the beauty of either beast or nature, my mother possessed in abundance. She loved birds and garden plants and flowers, and she had an uncanny ability to make things grow. On the lot of our new home, Mother supervised the layout of the garden, which provided attractive walkways, flower and vegetable beds, thirty-six fruit trees, and numerous berry vines. For her, gardening was as much relaxation as chore and during the warm seasons the garden was verdant. I must add that we boys did not merely share in the garden's delights, but were frequently conscripted to labour in it. Much to our discomfort, the chores seemed always to be on Saturdays when we had planned to frolic with our friends in the Dnieper.

The typical Mennonite home did not allow for much artistic expression, with the room arrangement and furnishings virtually identical in all but the poorest cottages. Such variation as existed was mainly in the substitution of cane-seated Vienna chairs for the standard solid oak or walnut ones, or the occasional addition of a combination secretary and desk. Hence, the housewife demonstrated her decorative skill only in her choice of curtains, wall-hung samplers, table linens, embroidered bedspreads, and the numerous pillows stacked high on the guest bed in the living room. Alternatively, some housewives displayed a few pieces of fine china in the china cabinet (*Glausschaup*) or, rarely, a fine samovar. Mother's special pride were the few Kuznetsov cups and saucers Father bought for her when he managed to stretch his budget. These pale pink fragile pieces, thin as Bellique china, were inscribed with 'On the day of the angel' (*V den angela*), referring to the name days of the Orthodox saints, celebrated like birthdays. Father also gave her a lovely, foreign-made table clock, about six inches in height, and a beautiful small papier-mâché box of the famed Russian *Palekh* type, with a delicate painting of some Russian folk tale on its cover.

Our parents did little 'neighbouring,' I suspect that this was because they shared a unique spirit of 'oneness,' which created an emotional self-sufficiency for the two. Also, they must have been too engrossed in taking care of the family's physical needs and providing the children with an environment that nurtured their educational development to have time to socialize across the fence, drink weak 'coffee' (*Pripps*), or exchange small talk or gossip. Father was just as happy to spend the weekend with his family, resting, or catching up with his paperwork, since he met so many people in his business dealings during the week. And Mother disliked gossip and hated to waste time discussing the household trifles that interested most of the village women.

I recall that Mother had few good acquaintances her own age in Nieder Khortitsa beyond two of her cousins, Sara Siemens and Franz Pauls, and their families. While some locals may have thought her aloof, believing that Rosentalers felt superior to people in Nieder Khortitsa, this was not true of Mother. Rather, she preferred to spend time with her extended Hildebrand and Pauls families. Weather permitting, we always drove to Rosental on Sundays to visit my grandmother Pauls and several of her siblings, and if we missed several weeks, Mother abandoned her tasks and rode to Rosental with a friend or relative who had business there or in neighbouring Khortitsa.

However, in the later years of my youth, Father and Mother were perhaps reacting to their ostracism by a group of local farmers who were angered over Father's support of the demand that the poorer residents of Nieder Khortitsa had made for land (see Chapter 15). In a few instances, the farmers' children absorbed their parents' injurious attitudes. I recall a nasty jibe I sustained from one youth: 'Your mother married the wrong man. Had she married Jacob Niebuhr from Schönwiese she would be rich now, would not have to work so hard, and could afford better things to wear.'

If she did not engage in the traditional Mennonite practice of gossipy 'neighbouring,' my mother radiated warmth and happiness, and she particularly enjoyed the company of young people, even my eldest siblings' friends. With them, she seemed so young at heart, that long after she died, many people commented that my mother's favourite greeting and farewell to them had been: 'Beautiful is youth, with happy times, beautiful is youth, it comes never more' (*Schön ist die Jugend, bei frohen Zeiten; schön ist die Jugend, sie kommt nicht mehr*). How ebulliently Mother and my 'half-cousins,' Sonia and Greta Rempel (daughters of Father's first wife's brother Gerhard) exchanged this greeting when the girls visited us during the years they attended the Khortitsa Girls High School. And if anything ever went wrong, Mother always calmed the waters, and soothed everyone with her favourite aphorism: 'Poland is not yet lost' (*Noch ist Polen nicht verloren*).

Father too, though no pessimist, drew comfort from Mother's sunny disposition, composure during stressful times, and optimistic spirit. Whenever business matters were really fouled up, or prices had fallen suddenly, he would be in a gloomy mood until Mother showed him that matters were not so dire after all, her counsel never failing to buoy him.

Another trait of Mother's character, along with her joy in youthful company, was her enormous compassion for those who were defenceless, or in poor physical or mental health, and allied to that, her charitable acts for the poorest members of the village, especially the teamsters' and boatmen's families. They, in turn, held her in high esteem, although she herself considered these to be acts of elementary decency between people, irrespective of their social position. Perhaps Mother's childhood years spent with her deranged grandmother accentuated her natural disposition.

The bonds between Father and Mother and their children manifested themselves in many ways. As example, no one used the terms 'stepmother,' 'stepchildren,' or 'half-brother' and 'half-sister.' Although this may not have been unusual in a community where a parent's death was soon followed by the survivor's remarriage, it was brought to my eight-year-old attention in a way that disturbed me profoundly. It was late one Sunday afternoon in the summer of 1907. My sister Neta and her husband, Jacob Pankratz, visited for the weekend, and I was to return with them to Schönwiese for a week's stay. Jacob's brother arrived with a lovely carriage and team of horses, handsomely decked out, to take us to the Alexandrovsk–Schönwiese boat. I had rarely ridden with such dashing horses and was elated as I took my place next to the driver. Shouting to a neighbour's daughter, about five years older than I, 'These are my sister Neta's husband's family's beautiful horses.' This brought the nasty retort: 'Neta isn't your sister. She is only your half-sister.' The term 'half-sister' puzzled me greatly, and my perturbation grew over the next hours until I was in tears. Neta noticed this at suppertime and asked, Was I homesick already? Finally, I managed to blurt out through my tears that someone said she was only my half-sister. Neta compassionately explained what a half-sister was and that I was not to worry because my mother was truly a mother to all the children.

The question of half-brothers and half-sisters had never come up prior to this rude introduction, and no sense of inequality ever existed within the family. And later, after the revolution and civil war, when part of the family emigrated and we divided the family's home and few remaining possessions, no one gave any thought to what might belong to which set of 'halves.'

Family Reading

Both Mother and Father had only a sixth-grade education. Mother's was of somewhat higher quality since she had attended the superior Rosental school. Nevertheless, she loved to tell stories about some of her teachers who were no better prepared to teach than were her own brothers who were freshmen in high school. One story concerned a lazy teacher who taught multiplication tables by rote. Warned to drill his students on these numbers in both German and Russian in case the government education inspector visited unannounced, this teacher had developed a system of hand signals. If he held up his right hand with two fingers outstretched, it meant the pupils should chorus in German their 'twos': '*Einmal zwei ist zwei, zweimal zwei ist vier,*' and so on. The same signal with the left hand unleashed a Russian chorus: '*Odin raz dva – dva, dvazhdy dva – chetyre.*'

One day the classroom door burst open and the belligerent wife of a well-known farmer advanced menacingly towards the teacher, demanding to know why he had whipped her son Jasch the day before. The teacher replied, 'Your Jasch used very bad words' (*Jün Jasch haft sea schlajchte Weada jebruckt*). The woman's response: 'What kind of words did he use?' (*Waut ferre Weade haft de jebruckt?*) was met with: 'That I will not tell you' (*Daut woar etj jünt nich saje*). Now angrier still the mother advanced on him, threatening to strike him, saying, 'Little teacher, you will tell me!' (*Lehratje, daut woascht dü mie saje!*) To ward off her blow he raised his right hand with all five fingers outstretched, and at once the class started to recite, '*Einmal fünf ist fünf, zweimal fünf ist zehn,*' and so on. Advancing, the mother again threatened the teacher, who now saw his rescue. He raised his left arm with four fingers extended, and the children then chimed, '*Odin raz chetyre-chetyre.*' The game went on for some minutes until the irate mother left in a huff.

Despite their modest schooling, both my parents had a strong commitment to their children's education and to providing them with abundant reading material. This was distinctly different from most Mennonite farmers at the end of the nineteenth and beginning of the twentieth centuries. Most were sceptical of intellectual matters and their homes had few books. My mother's love of books lay both in the pleasure of reading and in their intrinsic value to stimulate her children's interest. For Father, the presence of books was more a matter of a means to an end, for his consuming ambition was that his children receive the best education they could get.

Most of our children's books were in German. I remember especially an illustrated version of Grimm's fairy tales, and a few stories by Hans Christian Andersen, James Fenimore Cooper, and Maine Reed. Those in Russian included some charming, and occasionally lurid, folk tales, one a story of an old witch, *Baba Yaga.* Many decades later, my sister reminded me that once, when visiting Mrs Reimer, the ancient, homely widow of a boatman, I had anxiously asked Mother if the old lady was Baba Yaga.

The older children read books on the heroic exploits of Prince Igor and his victorious battles against the ancient steppe peoples, the Pechenegs and Khazars, and certainly as high school students we were roused by songs of Kievan Prince Oleg's exploits against the plundering Khazars along the lower reaches of the Dnieper. Only *La Marseillaise,* which became popular during the early days of the 1917 Revolution, thrilled us as much.

Mother was a passionate reader, and all her free time in the evening until Father came home she spent with books. She knew little Russian, but had an excellent grasp of spoken Ukrainian as well as spoken and written High German. The latter, of course, facilitated her strong interest in Mennonite history. There were a considerable number of publications in this field in the decades prior to the First World War. As I recall, Mother had copies of every book and pamphlet written by David H. Epp, such as *Die Chortitzer Mennoniten* (1889), Johann Cornies (1909), *Die Memriker Ansiedlung* (1910), and several booklets on religious topics. She had the huge tome by P.M. Friesen, *Geschichte der Alt-Evangelischen Mennoniten Brüderschaft in Russland* (1911), and of course, a copy of her ancestor Peter Hildebrand's booklet, *Die Erste Auswanderung aus dem Danziger Gebiet nach Süd-Russland* (1888). Other books in German that I recall included *Quo Vadis, Die Waffen Nieder*, some plays by Hauptmann and Sudermann, short stories by J.H. Janzen,[3] and collections of poetry by Schiller, Göthe, Heine, Chamisso, and others. There were also several books by Lutheran or Catholic colonist writers, such as P. Keller and Jakob Stach.

Several periodicals held a prominent place at home, including two annual publications, *Mennonitisches Jahrbuch* (1904–14), edited by Heinrich Dirks, then by David H. Epp, and *Christlicher Familien-Kalender* (1897–1914, 1918–1919), edited and published by A. Kröker. My parents also subscribed to *Der Botschafter* (1905–14), edited by David H. Epp, which was more or less a weekly organ of the established Mennonite church (*Kirchliche Gemeinde*). We did not, of course, buy the rival Mennonite Brethren church newspaper, *Friedensstimme* (1903–14).

Religion in Our Home

Our home was, I believe, representative of the typical Mennonite family belonging to the *Kirchliche Gemeinde.* In my childhood days, roughly two-thirds of the Russian Mennonites belonged to this branch, which was in a sense the established church (the remainder belonged to the *Brüder Gemeinde,* or Brethren). The majority of the membership of the *Kirchliche Gemeinde* was religiously conservative, although not fundamentalist in the American sense, nor at all evangelistically inclined.

Mother and Father resembled other *Kirchliche Gemeinde* members in that they themselves refused to proselytize. Nevertheless, they always listened to colporteurs who brought religious tracts to our home or solicited for Russian sectarian churches. Actually there was little verbalizing of religion at home, and I believe that this was because our parents believed that actions speak louder than words. To them, faith was not a sentiment, but an attempt to actively love one's fellow men, even in the midst of the often harsh realities in both our immediate Mennonite world, and in the broader world round about us. But being human and mortal, our family, as I suspect was true for all the other village families, occasionally faltered and failed to live up to its proclaimed ideals of seeking to follow a straight and narrow, righteous path.

As children, most of our religious training occurred in the elementary schools. Almost all of these schools offered a minimum of one hour of religious instruction five to six days each week. No Mennonite could escape this requirement because of compulsory attendance in the brotherhood's schools. Largely because of this, few Mennonite churches maintained Sunday school classes for either the young or the old, although as the century progressed some of both the Brethren and Kirchliche congregations began doing so.

Mother and we children invariably attended Sunday services, although Father rarely came along. Instead, he held his own devotions, locking everyone out of the living room (*Grootestow*) where he read aloud to himself. Usually he selected lengthy passages from the *Palmblätter*, a collection of religious writings.

After services, the family spent the remainder of Sunday either visiting relatives, especially Grandmother Pauls in Rosental, or with Father attempting to collect business debts. When necessary, Father would drive to Marievka or some other peasant village, usually accompanied by one of us boys, in this mostly vain pursuit. Somehow the debtor was never at home during the week. Even on Sundays, I recall Father would make me stop the team of horses a block or two from the individual's house, while he walked the rest of the way in hopes of catching the man before a family member or neighbour could warn of our arrival. This rarely worked, at least to the extent of collecting the sum owed him. Despite the numerous debts, Father ever only took one case to the Belenkoe volost court. The debtor was a Marievka peasant who, from the appearance of his homestead, could well afford to pay his debt. Regrettably, although the court ruled in Father's favour, he never collected the whole sum due. I should note that if the debtor had been another Mennonite or a Ukrainian or Great Russian sectarian or dissident, such as a Baptist or Old Believer, the matter would have been settled long before it would have gone to court.

Discipline

If one of us misbehaved in some significant way, Father gave us a withering look. He never resorted to the switch. Yet I sometimes would have preferred the latter rather than endure the former measure of his displeasure. Since he was away so much of the time, however, Mother was the major disciplinarian. She rarely encountered problems, for by merely talking to us, without ever raising her voice, she was remarkably persuasive in making us toe the line. Although the razor strop, switch, hairbrush, or sandal were all within easy reach, I do not recall that Mother ever used them. My sister Mariechen has avowed that the only spanking she ever received was at the hands of our elder sister Neta. We intuitively knew that if we had not done our schoolwork, we could not go out to play. If our teacher had a harsh word about our behaviour in school, we could expect a verbal reprimand at home. Or if we failed to do our chores, we could not join our gang at the Dnieper. But perhaps Neta's most effective measure was to threaten to take our storybooks away, or not permit us to check books out of the school library. From my earliest memory, books were a treasured joy, and one I was unwilling to forgo. They have always remained so.

Christmas

In our village, Christmas ignited the same anticipation children feel everywhere, although of course we were not awash with presents as children are here in the United States or Canada. Festivities would begin a week before the school holiday, when our teacher would hand each student a folder, decorated with German script. He had ordered these from a stationer in Riga weeks earlier, and they were for our 'Christmas wishes' to others. For the next several days we would diligently practise our penmanship, and when the teacher judged it presentable, he would give us sheets of white paper to write out our greetings for our parents, siblings, aunts and uncles, and grandparents, and also to express wishes for our own Christmas present.

The excitement would reach a crescendo at the Christmas Eve party, held in the largest classroom which had been festooned with garlands. A tree, decorated with candles, stood either in the front or centre of the room, while several of the parents would be stationed adjacent to the tree with water buckets should a candle set the tree ablaze. A pile of nicely decorated packages always lay beneath the tree, the gifts themselves theoretically from the teacher, although they had actually been purchased from the community fund or donated by a community-spirited citizen.

The gifts were simple by modern standards but we relished them – candy, cookies, nuts, perhaps a pencil for the children of poor parents, and in the best years, an orange. Before they were distributed, we would put on a program of songs, plays, and poems. Then the teacher would hand us our Christmas folders, but we showed our parents the covers only, because reading our greetings to them was part of the next morning's ritual. The only thing that would dampen our spirits that night was the fact that the teacher handed out grades at the same time.

At about ten o'clock we would adjourn, and walk home through the crisp night, brilliantly starry if it was not snowing hard, while listening to the occasional sound of sleigh bells off in the distance. Once home we would enjoy a light dinner, then trundle off to bed. We did not sleep long. How often on Christmas did I shout, 'Can we get up now?' at four in the morning? And always our parents' response was, 'No, the Christmas Man hasn't come yet.' Finally, we would all storm out of bed and into the living room (*Grootestow*) to find our presents on the table, the gifts usually being books and small toys such as porcelain horses or dolls. After opening our presents, we would read our Christmas wishes to Father and Mother, and they in return would give each of us a few coins. When the commotion ceased, Mother would make breakfast, a little fancier than usual with eggs, *pirozhkie*, *Tweebaktje*, and jam, while our parents would drink real coffee made from moccha beans.

By ten o'clock we had set out for church service at the school. As usual, the men would sit to the left of the pulpit, the women on the right. Fortunately, the services were short since we were eager to get back home to dinner, which was served as soon as the plates hit the table. Of course, we said grace, then attacked the food, which usually featured a roast goose or duck, mashed potatoes, fruit compote (*Plumemooss*), vegetables, and dessert. For once, we had little appetite for dessert, having stuffed ourselves earlier with our Christmas candy and cookies. Still we were hungry soon enough to enjoy a light *Vaspa* at four, and a more substantial supper later, although as we grew older we became impatient to join our friends and share our day's adventures.

In Mennonite homes, Christmas was celebrated for three days, with the latter two devoted primarily to visiting relatives. Our family would spend the first of these visiting kin in Nieder Khortitsa. We would read them our Christmas wishes, perhaps receive a treat, then rush off to join our chums in snowball fights or skating on the frozen ponds, and in the winters when it was possible, on the Dnieper itself. The main meal that day was usually a cold repast of baked ham and *Plumemoos*, and occasionally, I remember, there would be a rare treat of rice pudding for dessert.

On the third and final day of the Christmas holiday we would journey to Rosental to visit with Grandmother Pauls and all the aunts and uncles. It was our favourite day. If the snow was deep we could travel by sleigh, and even our nondescript horses seemed to delight in the sounds of their collar bells tinkling. At the end of our twelve-mile journey to my grandmother's house we always felt that the celebrations had a special aura and that the food was extra tasty. Finally, would come the drive home. We would be bundled up in fur blankets, with Mother urging us to sleep and our excited anticipation quenched for another year.

New Year's

New Year's Eve and Day were similarly convivial events. As teenagers, we would band together to pull a few innocent pranks. For the young adults, it was a time for New Year's Eve (*Silvesterabend*) parties, with, for some, the regrettable aftermath many of us experience today.

Looking back, however, the most interesting experience was the time-honoured practice that tied the Mennonites to the broader Ukrainian community. Long before sunrise on New Year's Day, a large number of peasants from the nearby Ukrainian village of Razumovka descended on our village, each man with a bag of grain over his shoulders. First, the older men would knock and demand entrance to the parents' bedroom, then they would burst in and shower the couple with grain, chanting, 'We sow and sow, and bless you, and congratulate you on this New Year' (*Seiem, seiem, provivaiem, s novym godom pozdravliaem*). In return, the parents would give the peasants a bit of our Christmas fare, or some coins. Later, the peasant boys would stroll by in groups, carrying a decorated cross, singing, and likewise tossing grain into the entrance hall. They, too, would be rewarded with sweets and coins. Although it must have annoyed housewives to sweep the grain and sponge up the muddy snow from their floors, no one but the most callous Mennonite would have refused the visitors entrance, for the practice was a firm, nearly sacred custom among our neighbouring Ukrainian peasants.

CHAPTER THIRTEEN

Father's Occupations

For several decades Father maintained two businesses – buying and selling grain and running a general store. The grain trade was more lucrative than the store, but it was a seasonal business, occurring mostly between 1 June and 1 October (*Pokrov*)[1] or the middle of that month. During this time Father purchased wheat and barley from neighbouring Mennonite and peasant farmers, and resold it across the river in Alexandrovsk and Schönwiese. This essentially combined city was southern Russia's most important inland port, as well as home to numerous banks and facilities for storing and milling grain. My father sold most of the grain to local mills such as the huge Niebuhr company, the remainder either to the Jewish traders who controlled much of the city's local and export trade or to agents of companies in Constantinople.[2]

Although Father's business was local in scope, it was subject to any upheaval in the broad European grain markets, since at least prior to the First World War, Russia transported most of its grain to Western Europe. The quantity traded fluctuated enormously depending on the harvest, competition from the United States, Canada, and Argentina, and to an extraordinary degree Russia's relations with Turkey[3] – which were affected by Britain's relations with Turkey. When these relations were amicable, the Bosphorus and Dardanelles were open, and Russia's grain trade flourished. It dropped off precipitously whenever Russia and Turkey had a set-to over the Balkans and/or Middle Eastern areas or if England or other countries engaged in 'Balkan bargaining.' At such times the straits connecting the Black Sea with the Mediterranean were either closed or under threat of closure. That Russia's rail network was inadequate to carry most of this grain to alternative Baltic ports meant that exports dropped off radically.

With Father's limited resources, he operated on a narrow margin, which forced him to make daily, or even twice-daily, trips to Alexandrovsk-Schönwiese to collect receipts for the grain his teamsters had delivered the previous day or to collect an advance on the next day's shipment. To get there, Father walked a mile from home to the Dnieper, unless one of his teamsters was on hand with a wagon. From the riverbank, a local boatman ferried him the three miles or so upstream to the city docks, and then he walked the further mile and a half to the Alexandrovsk city centre. If the previous day's grain had gone to the Schönwiese mills, my father walked an additional half-mile. The return trip mirrored the same route. Only when business was very brisk, or when he needed to replenish the stock of the general store, would Father ride with the teamsters to Alexandrovsk. And once there he almost never indulged himself by hiring a cab.

On the most hectic days Father would return from this ten-mile round trip in mid-afternoon. After a hasty snack, and sometimes a brief nap, he would go to Burwalde or Blumengart – each four miles from home – walking if he felt his only pair of horses needed rest. Sometimes he would leave as late as four o'clock, hat invariably pushed to the back of his head, walking-stick held in the curve of his arm, head tilted slightly forward, deeply immersed in his thoughts of the day's business. Although he loved to walk, my Father would occasionally hitch a ride with a farmer returning to his fields to pick up more grain. But if he walked both ways, he would not return home until ten o'clock. Fortunately, Father found it easy to put the day's problems aside, relax, and fall asleep. The next morning he would set off at the same pace. This schedule would be maintained for weeks on end.

Beginning the morning tasks, Father would assign his teamsters to pick up grain in specified villages. There were about twenty-five to thirty such teamsters in our village, most of whom hauled grain from the farmers of the nearest seven villages, who preferred to sell to Father. The teamsters would make two trips per day if their destination was nearby Burwalde or Blumengart. Those who went to the more distant Osterwick, Kronstal, Rosengart, or Schöneberg would make only one trip, and perhaps top the day off with several short local hauls. The grain itself was sacked and weighed at the farm and brought either to the family granary (called a *Spitja* in Low German, a *Speicher* in High German, or an *ambar* in Russian) for temporary storage, or it was carted directly to the Dnieper. Here it was either loaded on flat-bottomed barges (*duby*), for shipment to Alexandrovsk, or huge, river-plying covered barges (*berliny*), for shipment to the Black Sea ports of Kherson and Odessa. As soon as Father had assigned the teamsters' jobs, he would leave for Alexandrovsk and our surrounding Mennonite farms and peasant villages.

The Ukrainian peasant villages with which my father had dealings had been recently established under the Stolypin land reforms. In contrast to traditional Russian or Ukrainian peasant settlements of up to 500 households, these consisted of only fifteen to twenty farms. Every one of these farms was more productive than the old ones had been, and certainly able to produce surplus grain beyond that needed to feed the farm family. The higher yields resulted from at least two conditions: the land lay in a single consolidated plot as opposed to the traditional inefficient separated strips, and the farmers had received favourable servicing from the State Land Bank.

Many of these new proprietors had in past years been seasonal labourers for neighbouring Mennonite farmers, which was obvious as soon as you entered the new village. Both homes and farm structures resembled the Mennonite pattern, although they were of smaller scale. Their farming methods, crops, equipment, and crop rotation were also fashioned on Mennonite practices. And because they had worked for Mennonites in the past, their credit was generally better with the local store owners and farmers than that of the run-of-the-mill peasant. Unfortunately, much later this stamped these successful peasants as kulaks, and they suffered the same fate as one-time Mennonite farmers and teachers – exile to the forced labour camps, with the ensuing horrors.

On rare occasions Father also would visit the poorer, traditional Ukrainian peasant villages of Razumovka and Marievka to buy grain. He visited Belenkoe even less often, since this large village had its own grain-trading centre. Generally, the peasants hauled their own grain to my father to save the cost of hired teamsters, because money was more scarce to them than time, while the converse was true for most Mennonites. When the peasants brought their grain to Nieder Khortitsa they would usually approach Father, whom they all knew intimately; although if prices were rising, a neighbouring grain merchant or the two mills located across the street from our house would also bid on the grain. The neighbour was not a serious competitor, but the mills were. Although called the Wiebe Mills, marriage and other tie-ins made them an integral part of the Niebuhr Milling Company. With its huge capital backing, it was a formidable competitor.

For several years, if my father was not home when grain arrived, he would empower my older siblings to buy the grain at a predetermined price. Gerhard assumed this role until about 1906 or 1907, when Johann briefly took over. But by about 1909 or 1910, my sister Mariechen had assumed many of Father's business responsibilities. At only fifteen she was an efficient assistant and particularly astute in sizing up whether the grade and weight of wheat were up to the seller's claims or whether the farmer had adulterated it with sand. Mariechen's appraisals dismayed many a peasant, because adulterating grain was an all-too-common practice, except among the Ukrainian and Russian sectarians (especially Baptists) who were known for their honesty. She also caught the occasional deceitful Mennonite farmer.

Frequently, Jewish traders would come to the house to buy grain, particularly when it was to be shipped to Kherson or Odessa. Then the discussions, bargaining, and haggling became decidedly animated, generally in Yiddish, and accompanied by furious gesticulations, shoulder-shrugging, and body contortions characteristic of the marketplace.

The busiest part of the day began after dusk, when Father and Mariechen would tally the day's shipments. The calculations included the amount of grain hauled from a particular village by each teamster and the amount unloaded at our granary or onto the barges. In the latter case, they would note how much the teamsters themselves had loaded and how much had been loaded by the special bagmen (*burlaki*). Even though the grain was weighed carefully when it was sacked at the farm or our granary, representatives of the purchaser had a right to check it when it reached the barge. Occasionally, a discrepancy was discovered – the result of unavoidable spillage, a teamster's pilfering, or the purchaser's deceit. When the evening's tallies differed, a violent argument often ensued between the teamsters and the purchaser's agent. One particular autumn, when we dealt with an agent named Makar, there were many such occasions. Despite numerous checks when the grain was loaded at a farm or our granary, and despite using different teamsters, Makar always claimed that the shipment was short. After days of fruitless but furious argument between Makar and the teamsters, the teamsters took drastic measures. It was late autumn and the *Baschtaun* had been cleared of watermelons. A huge pile of tiny melons that we fed to the hogs and cattle during the early winter months sat in the yard. When Makar came to submit his report, he passed between a shed and house. That night the teamsters hid, armed with baseball-sized melons, and as Makar emerged from between the buildings, his avenues of advance and retreat cut off, the teamsters plastered him mercilessly with a hailstorm of melons. The encounter ended after Makar promised there would be no more discrepancies. True to his new word, the accounts squared that evening – and for the remainder of the season. Makar did not return the following year.

Father's business provided an unintentional social service for the neighbouring farms and villages, as his continual rounds forced him into a secondary role as reporter, conveying local, national, and even international news. At the time, telephone communication was non-existent and all mail went to a central distribution centre in Khortitsa. Postal service to a given village was haphazard, depending on whether the mayor, his representative, or some other citizen happening through Khortitsa, picked it up. During the slower winter and spring seasons, families would make frequent trips to neighbouring villages, and so have contact with relatives and friends. During the busy summer and autumn harvest, however, many relied on Father's circuit to convey messages and greetings. If the farmer initiated the message, it usually concerned farming – grain crops, harvest dates, condition of livestock, how new farm machinery was performing, and so forth. Messages from the farmer's wife were more likely to be of a social nature. They usually ran something like: 'Well, Mr Rempel, when you get to Burwalde, do not forget to greet my sister. You know, the Mrs Penner who lives on the side street leading towards Rosengart. Tell her that our Greta is again feeling much better' (*Na, Oomtje Rampel, wann du noh Berwool tjemst, dann vejat nich miene Sesta too jreese. Du weedst, de Mummtje Pannasche de aum Uutwaj noh Rosegoad wohnt? Saj äah, daut onse Trintje mol wada väl bäta es*). And always there were questions – who had died, whose house had been robbed and what had been stolen, or about the health of parents, grandparents, or so and so, or queries concerning livestock epidemics or other common interests of these rural folk.

Having driven Father on innumerable such trips, I knew the names of every farmer in at least seven villages, and in time, even which farmer or wife had relatives of what degree in a different village, and at which farm Father's visit was prone to be a prolonged affair. Even though I was only seven to thirteen when I made these trips there was no way to avoid knowing all the aches and pains of every farmer's Katharina, Susanna, Justina, Greta, and Peter, Jacob, Cornelius, Johann, or Julius (*Trintje, Sauntje, Justintje, Jretje,* and *Peta, Jasch, Tjnais, Jehaun,* or *Jils*), since I heard them so frequently. My assignment was usually to remind Father when we arrived at 'farmer A in village N' that he had a note (*Zaddel*) in his pocket or an oral message to deliver there.

So my father's business dealings along with his role as reporter, political commentator, and messenger often extended the time he had announced our trip would take when we left home. To a boy or young teenager who felt the trip already an unduly large infringement on the interesting undertakings he had planned with his friends, any further delay nettled more. By the end of the afternoon my misery deepened and the roads seemed dustier or muddier and the gnats and flies thicker. Added to the tedium of these drives was that if I took a book along, a farmer's kid was certain to see me reading. The derisive shouts of, 'Look at that lazy kid lying low for hours on the wagon and reading,' were bad enough. Worse yet were the nasty comments on Father's ill-matched pair of horses and his ragged wagon. Fortunately, there was the consoling fact that my father, although friendly and a good listener, was not particularly gregarious, nor did he enjoy gossip or small talk. He was first and foremost a businessman who could listen patiently when necessary, but also could gently but firmly terminate a conversation that threatened to be a drawn-out social affair.

There were pleasant interludes to offset my discomfort. Practically every farmer – and especially the ones in Schöneberg and Kronstal – grew a wide variety of fruit, and Father would usually leave the farmhouse with his hands loaded with produce. If we arrived mid-afternoon, when all work had stopped, and if time permitted, we joined their coffee break (*Vaspa*). More appropriately it was a *Pripps* break, considering the thin drink, made of a whisper of coffee mixed with roasted barley or some other grain. It tasted weak and its nondescript grey colour resembled rinse water (*stremp-foaw Wota*). Actually, during watermelon season only the elderly parents or grandparents deigned to drink *Pripps* at *Vaspa*, while everyone else ate watermelon. Either way, the housewife's freshly baked breads and pastries (typically *Tweebaktje, Schnettje, Plautz, Pirozhkie*, or a slice of *Bultje*) were central to the feast.

Thus, Father's grain business consumed much of his time and demanded tasks of several of the children. Competitive and sometimes risky, it was nevertheless, on the whole, a profitable venture. Combined with his general store, the family's income and living standard were comfortable, allowing the children educational opportunities that later assumed a paramount role in their lives.

The General Store

For several decades my father ran an additional enterprise, the general store that adjoined our house (see Map 5, page 122). In my earliest recollections it was a thriving business, despite local competition from similar stores. Two were owned by other Mennonites and an Old Believer owned another. This reflected the usual ownership in most small Mennonite villages, although Jews also owned stores in the larger villages, which had more diverse populations.

The store's shelves bulged with bolts of cloth, spools of thread, kitchen utensils, garden supplies, small tools and nails, tobacco and cigarettes, and a dazzling array of groceries – flour, sugar, syrup, coffee, tea, spices, sunflower seeds and oil, raisins and other dried fruit, salt, rice, all sorts of candies, and occasionally Russian rye bread. My father supplied a further popular item, kerosene, stored in barrels set outside, next to the pigsty. In the weeks before Christmas the stock would acquire special lustre with the appearance of a large selection of toys and gift items, and special candies and cookies, like the spiced *prianiki* and gaily decorated *gruzniki,* associated with this festive season.

However, to many people the store served more as local gathering spot than commercial enterprise. This social function grew from an absence of communal meeting places. The only public structure in most of the villages of the Khortitsa Settlement was the school, used as such from Monday through Saturday and for church services on Sunday, since only Khortitsa and four other villages had actual church buildings. Similarly, Nieder Khortitsa had no taverns or inns. I believe only Khortitsa, which was both the administrative centre and home to various milling and manufacturing concerns that employed large numbers of non-Mennonite Prussian and Great Russian labourers, had a place selling liquor (*Schentj*), although perhaps Einlage, with its flour mills and industrial enterprises may have supported one as well. In the absence of such communal gathering spots, Father's shop became something like an English pub, except that the only 'alcoholic' beverage sold was the lightly fermented *kvass.* Actually, those who drank beer did so at home, rather than in public, and if you wanted vodka or schnapps, you had to buy it in the largest neighbouring town or a nearby peasant village.

The Mennonite world was strictly a man's world. Only men congregated at Father's store, while the women remained at home, occupied with their manifold duties or visiting friends and relatives. Like other shopkeepers, my father set benches just outside the door and under a large shade tree to accommodate the men. Every weekday during the warmer months, the village's elderly men (*Oomtjes*), who were mostly retired farmers, gathered there in the late afternoon to discuss the day's events, praise or bemoan the weather and state of the crops, and especially to rehash village gossip. In the cooler weather, the benches were brought inside and set in line against the counters; the *Oomtjes* would follow and there they would spend the day, and often the early evening, retreating home just long enough for meals. As men of the soil, they spoke with the coarse earthy humour of paddock talk (*Peadhock reden*).[4] Accompanying the verbal barrage was the ceaseless crack of roasted sunflower seeds and the haze from chain-smoked cigarettes, which were hand-rolled, often using tobacco that was little better than the peasant's vile *makhorka*.

Towards evening, the complexion of the gathering would change, as the *Oomtjes* drifted home and the village's young men took their place. Depending on which group of friends were present, their conversations might be serious matters of the day or simply light banter, but either way their youthful exuberance meant the talk became louder, the laughter more raucous, and the *kvass* consumption heartier. All this was accompanied by the incessant crack of sunflower seeds and wagers of who could eat more halva (*khalva*), drink more *kvass*, or break the tallest stack of *prianiki* or *gruzniki* with one stroke. They, too, chain-smoked, and although they could buy a wide variety of excellent packaged cigarettes, these young sons of farmers viewed them as pretentious and 'citified.' Gradually the air in the shop would become thick with cigarette smoke and from time to time so oxygen-deprived that it extinguished the kerosene lamps. Then everyone briefly poured outside, leaving the shop's doors wide open to air the place. Outside, too, and adding to the evening's masculine bent, the village's teenage boys would perch on nearby fencetops, involving themselves in the universal and time-honoured pursuits of teenage boys – smoking, telling tall tales, plotting to carry out some mischief, bragging about their favourite horses or other beloved possessions, cracking sunflower seeds or otherwise behaving obnoxiously with food, and of course, girl-watching. Thus, during both the day and evening hours men encircled the entrance to my father's store. Women shoppers, both old and young, were often discomfited when passing through a gauntlet of staring eyes and tasteless comments.

Operating a village general store took a lot of stamina, as well as the ability to ignore the presence of goodly numbers of loafers, instead of customers, and the hubbub and nonsense of their conversations. Still, I think Father enjoyed the business, at least in his younger years. He had grown up in a family with a similar store, and had started his own as soon as he left his parental home. Moreover, for several years my mother and elder siblings could tend the shop during the days when Father's grain trading took him away. Or in the evenings, when my father was tired and frankly bored with the neighbourhood small-talk, my mother or siblings could answer the tinkling of the bell that hung over the entry or stay in the store until closing time.

Gradually things changed as my elder siblings grew up. Neta married in 1906 and moved to Schönwiese, where her husband worked at the Niebuhr milling concern. Gerhard became a bookkeeper in Alexandrovsk, and Johann and Mariechen were away at school from about 1903 to 1910. Heinrich, who had displayed the greatest aptitude for Father's business, began showing symptoms of a serious heart condition. He was tall and appeared robust, yet the slightest physical exertion caused him severe chest pains. Sometimes he even bled from his mouth. It became clear that Heinrich might never have the strength to take over the business. By this time, too, I suspect that Father's interest was shifting more towards the grain trade. The economic reforms of 1906 had stimulated the economy enough that trading grain appeared to be a viable, permanent occupation.

Thus it was that, along with her numerous household tasks, the shop gradually became Mother's burden, and she disliked many aspects of it. She did not mind waiting on customers during the day. But she became increasingly unhappy with the all-pervasive tobacco stench and smoke, the evening's clublike atmosphere, the incessant gossip, and *Peadhock* language. Mother's distaste for the men may have been intensified by her somewhat Puritanical attitude about wasting time or talent. Or perhaps she was concerned that the men's language and stories might corrupt us younger boys when we occasionally waited on customers or were directed to stick around to prevent the 'customers' pilfering the marzipan and cookies piled in the tall jars along the counter. Growing up, as we were, in a farming community, where we heard so much from our elders and observed the barnyard livestock day in and day out, Mother was hardly capable of shielding us from knowing plenty about the 'facts of life.' Perhaps the children did have some erroneous notions about sex and human mating practices; nevertheless, they did not need to be told much about the 'birds and bees.' When I was seven or eight, for example, Father, having to remove a sickly cow from the common pasturage, had me take it out grazing along the road to

Burwalde. One day the bone-setter, 'Doctor Hildebrand,' drove by. Halting his team he inquired, 'You are Rempel's David, aren't you? Whats wrong with your cow?' (*Dü best doch Rampels Doft? Na Jung, waut ess daut doa mett jüne Kooh?*). To which I replied, 'Mr Hildebrand, she has been abused by the bull. That I heard from Father and the cowherd. He says that the bull abuses her terribly every day' (*Oomtje Hilbraunt! De haft de Boll äwa'tjwält. Daut hab etj von Voda enn de Hoad jeheat. De Hoad sajt, daut de Boll de Kooh jieden Dach schratjlijch tjwäle deit*).

The business provided a comfortable income for many years. Still, Mother must have been relieved when political events caused its unforeseen collapse in 1909. The origins of its demise and how these same events affected Father's grain trade are discussed in Chapter 15.

CHAPTER FOURTEEN

Apprehension Following the 1905 Revolution: Premonition of Chaos to Come

Bloody revolts broke out in 1905 following Russia's defeat in the Russo-Japanese War. These were outbursts of the rage that had been seething among the peasants and the working class. After they were quieted, many Mennonites, and certainly much of Russia's middle and upper class, remained concerned about the government's long-term stability. Still, I suspect that few people could imagine how explosively that rage would erupt in another twelve years. Anyone with open eyes should have seen that the repressive measures the government used to restore order – for example, deploying Cossack troops against striking workers and rampaging peasants – would leave a volcano of bitter hatred against the established political and economic order, just waiting to erupt.

My father may have had an inkling of the times to come. His political views were conservative, but the plight of the underclasses concerned him keenly. Of course he, like everyone else, knew the dangers of speaking openly about the need for political change or the revolutionary sentiment throughout the land. Therefore, he was circumspect about what he said, and to whom he spoke. Nonetheless, Father occasionally came home from Alexandrovsk with a flyer expressing distinctly socialist views. I assume he received these from business acquaintances, since no one dared distribute them in public. Certainly, his daily contacts with Jewish businessmen and dock workers in that important industrial city made him aware of the influence the Bolsheviks, Mensheviks, and Social Revolutionaries exerted on the city's workers. No one doubted that many had joined these parties.

As the months progressed, however, the government must have felt increasingly secure. It had established a semblance of order, not solely with repression, but also by issuing the October Manifesto of 1905 which created the state Duma, and by granting a series of ostensibly inalienable rights. These rights included freedom of conscience, property, assembly, organization, and a slightly liberalized electoral process. However, these promised rights represented a fragile form of constitutionalism. For example, the government prematurely dissolved the First and Second Dumas. Both had been theoretically elected for five-year periods, but the government could not tolerate their liberal tenor. The tsarist government obtained its compliant Third Duma by curtailing suffrage, so that the parliamentary representatives were now elected not by direct vote, but through a series of electoral curia that were heavily weighted in favour of the propertied classes.

Actually, the restoration of peace came about in large part through the autocratic leadership of the premier, Petr Stolypin. One of Stolypin's primary actions to inhibit future rebellion was to set up a system of land redistribution. Under this plan the government allotted all state-owned land in the *udel'noe vedomstvo*[1] to qualified peasants. The amount of land granted was based on the number of 'souls' (males sixteen to sixty years old) in the family, possession of a minimal amount of equipment, credit, livestock, and personal characteristics indicating likely success. Between 1906 and 1909, many small Ukrainian peasant villages were formed under this program, mostly arranged on the Mennonite model. They were a startling success.

These measures did not entirely quell the popular unrest. Over the next decade, many Mennonites felt the wrath of the peasants. Typically this involved the looting or torching of buildings. Fire reports often bore the notation: 'Incendiary origin suspected' (*Man vermutet Brandstiftung*). Revolutionary slang termed this 'raising the red rooster.' One of my most vivid childhood memories is of a conflagration which, fanned by winds, consumed the village school along with at least six or seven farm buildings. The next day, standing in Peter Rempel's farmyard, I beheld the school's smouldering ruins across the street, smelled the stench of burned livestock in the nearby barn, and watched farmers shoot other burned horses to put them out of their misery. Arson was the cause.

Worse fates befell some of the richer Mennonite estate owners. Those kidnapped for ransom were lucky. Others were murdered, including the head of the Niebuhr family in Khortitsa and several of my late Grandfather Pauls's relatives. These included his brother-in-law, Abram Neustädter. Then, in 1912, peasants killed his niece and grandniece on the estate of Reinfeld, along with the child's nursemaid.

Alarmed by these acts, some Mennonites contemplated emigration, possibly to Argentina. A few families, including four from Nieder Khortitsa, emigrated to Canada. The Redekopp family were the first to leave in 1912, soon followed by the Peter Pätkau, Jacob Peters, and Dietrich Neufeld families. The latter three, after a year spent enduring Saskatchewan's brutal climate and barren aspect, returned to our village.

The vast majority of Mennonites remained, and their reaction to the unrest was mixed. A few actually joined the Bolsheviks and Mensheviks. No one was willing to speak of their heresy except to make surreptitious comments that they were ne'er-do-wells or mentally unbalanced.[2] My brother Johann met the most notorious of these revolutionaries, Kornelius Thiessen, in about 1910 when he roomed at Thiessen's mother's home in Neuendorf.[3] Years earlier, Johann's friend, Johann Hildebrand, had told him of Thiessen's exploits, some of which also involved one of our distant relatives, Peter Rempel.[4] At the time, Johann shared the common assumption that such people were dangerous plotters bent on changing the existing political and social order. Presumably, he agreed with the well-known Mennonite preacher and versifier, Bernhard Harder, whose portrait of a subversive person was: 'There slinks with frowning countenance, that furtive democrat' (*Da schleicht mit finsterem Angesicht, der dunkle Demokrat*). In other words, whoever was a democrat was a revolutionary.

The only radical I knew personally was Kornelius Hübert, an odd fellow who lisped. Perhaps this impediment, joined with his swarthy complexion and thin face, accentuated his furtive appearance, which reminded one of a stereotypical anti-tsarist plotter. Kornelius lived with his equally odd father and younger brother Peter in a small brick cottage at the western end of Nieder Khortitsa. They lived in half the building and plied a variety of trades – as blacksmiths, tinkers, and repairmen – in the other half. My friends and I sold the trio scraps of iron, rags, and bones in exchange for a few kopeks. The musty place, filled with trays of bolts and nails, and piles of junk and mechanical gadgetry, reminded me of a mysterious alchemist's shop. But the most curious aspect of the family was its sense of gentility. All three men wore suits, or at least suit trousers, despite their manual labours, and spoke with a literary vocabulary.

On one occasion, I caught a glimpse of a booklet there that had influenced Russian youths during the second half of the nineteenth century.[5] Entitled *What Is to Be Done?* and written by Nikolai G. Chernyshevskii, I recognized it only because my brother Johann also had a copy. Chernyshevskii was one of the most famous revolutionary writers of the nineteenth century, a populist philosopher, literary writer, and critic who spent years in prison and forced exile in Siberia. Actually, I have no idea whether Kornelius Hübert joined any of the radical parties. Remarks I heard from local people who knew him suggested that he was simply a harmless critic of the existing order, spinning impractical dreams of changing the status quo in the Mennonite establishment.

A far less radical, and somewhat larger, group of Mennonites held liberal views. Many were sympathetic to the political changes advocated by the Constitutional Democrats, the strongest bourgeois party. Although this group (also called the *Kadet*[6] party) recommended remunerated expropriation of land, which frightened landowners, its promotion of a constitutional monarchy modelled on the British system appealed to Mennonite intellectuals and professionals. Few of the settlement's students joined this party, but many agreed with its views. This was particularly true for those few who attended either the grammar (*gimnaziia*) and commerce schools in Alexandrovsk, Ekaterinoslav, or Kharkov, the engineering schools in Riga or Kiev, or the teachers' training institutes in St Petersburg, Ekaterinoslav, or Moscow. These institutions were often hotbeds of dissatisfaction with the political and economic status quo. Some Mennonite youths attending them were swept up in the sentiment, but most had a more practical sense of achievable goals than did their Russian colleagues. I was much younger, but I remember many students singing lusty renditions of the *Marseillaise,* bawdy songs about the Russian Orthodox church, and especially anti-tsarist, revolutionary songs. Among these – after Russia's defeat in 1905 – was a popular revision of the lyrics to 'Sing, Swallow, Sing,' which went, 'Sing, Nikolai, sing; Port Arthur is no longer thine; Korea-Manchuria Thou wilt not see; Sing, Nikolai, sing.' Parenthetically, I should note that years later, in the diaspora in Canada, these same Mennonites vehemently disavowed their youthful liberal taint.

Actually, a Russian higher education, coupled with living in a metropolitan setting, often had quite opposite effects on different young men, even those belonging to the same family. This was the case for two sons of the prominent Khortitsa village Epp family, Dietrich and Heinrich. Their forebears had played prominent roles in the colony since its settlement, beginning with *Oohm Doft,* who was instrumental in securing the Mennonite Charter of Privileges in 1800. The boys' father was Elder Heinrich Epp.

Heinrich, the Elder's son, married into the extremely prosperous industrial Koop family, yet he became a well-known liberal. He had taken a degree in philology at Moscow University, an institution with a long tradition of liberalism and clashes with tsarist officials. Returning after his graduation, he became one of the Khortitsa Settlement's most illustrious teachers. When the huge migration to Canada began in 1923, Heinrich decided to stay in Russia, believing that he could best use his talents there. While he was certainly not a revolutionary, his liberal philosophical views, as he propounded them in several post-1923 manuscripts,[7] were decidedly radical by Mennonite standards. Heinrich assumed that his talent, views, and past student activism in Moscow would assure his safety under the new government. For a time it did, and he amassed an estimable record for which the Ukrainian SSR government designated him professor and distinguished pedagogue. But in the early 1930s, following Stalin's final triumph over his opponents and his enforcement of collectivization, the authorities rounded up Epp and sent him to the slave labour camps in the Gulag. He perished there without a trace.

In contrast, his brother Dietrich studied at the St Petersburg Teachers' Institute and found its liberal environment so repugnant that he decided not to continue his education at the university. He then became one of the settlement's most conservative teachers, and when the opportunity to emigrate arose, he was among the first to leave.

There were others besides Dietrich opposing those with radical or liberal leanings, including a small number of reactionary Mennonites. One even became the chairman of a branch of the Union of the Russian People, which was sometimes called the Union of Truly Russian People.[8] The ostensible objective of this arch-conservative, ultra-nationalistic organization was to defend the motherland against subversion from the empire's minorities: Poles, Baltic Germans, and especially Jews. While many of its members may have been sincere in their fear of internal subversion, the group's anti-Semitic position was obvious in its support of murderous pogroms carried out by the hoodlum members of the Black Hundreds.[9] It is a sad fact that nascent anti-Semitism was present among the Mennonites long before the revolution of 1917 and the triumph of Bolshevism.

The overwhelming majority of Mennonites, however, retained their conservative, insular, and apolitical views. Most were obtuse enough to believe that their prosperous condition and privileged situation would escape the coming storm, and only when their own concerns were involved did they show interest in matters of the Russian world surrounding them. In those instances they would protest vigorously at every level of government. Otherwise most held to the slogan, 'We are the silent ones in the land' (*Wir sind die Stillen im Lande*).

Many of the secular and religious leaders were even blinder to the meaning of the 1905 Revolution than their followers, perhaps because most were industrialists and/or landed gentry. They had the most to lose from political and economic reforms. Because the less powerful majority had traditionally either been disenfranchised or had ceded decisions to these leaders, this small elite managed to control the election of a local deputy to the Third Duma in 1907.[10] This conservative body replaced the First and Second Dumas, whose liberal majorities of Kadet and *Trudoviki* (Labourite) deputies had recommended far-reaching agrarian and economic reforms. The *Kadet* program of land reform envisioned the alienation of some private lands with compensation to the former owners. It would have had little effect on the average Mennonite village farmer, but a significant one on *Khutor* or estate owners with substantial holdings. This included the landed gentry and several industrialists, such as the Wallmann family of the Khortitsa Settlement and the Schröder family of the Molochna Settlement.

Fearing the spread of revolutionary agitation, and hoping that Petr Stolypin, the iron-fisted premier, could save the country from what the rightist deputies called 'the folly of the Constitutional Democratic Land Program,' the wealthy group allied itself with the conservative Octobrist Party to elect a representative to the Third Duma. Their deputy was Hermann Bergmann, the Mennonite with the greatest land holdings in Ekaterinoslav province.[11] Thus, one delegate represented a Mennonite population of perhaps 20,000 men, women, and children. The area's second delegate represented 1,600,000 indigenous peasants. The disparity in representation might have been greater had Mr Bergmann actually exercised any power. But in this body he is noted for making only one utterance – 'My god!' (*Bozhe moi!*) – when a portion of the chamber's ceiling collapsed on the delegates assembled in the Tavrida Palace.

The conservative alliance held together in 1912, allowing the Mennonites to re-elect Bergmann, and to elect a second deputy, Peter Schröder, in the Tavrida guberniia.[12] It produced further fruit by supporting the Russian landowner, Mikhail Rodzianko, for president of the State Duma. For this support (and perhaps a bribe), Rodzianko interceded on the Mennonite's behalf in 1917 to exempt them from the Land Liquidation Decrees (see chapter 18).

Russian liberals were no doubt resentful over the accord between the conservative Russians and the Mennonites. The Kadet party vainly sought their support and that of other colonists in the elections of 1907 and 1912. Again, in the summer of 1917 they courted the Mennonites to join them in electing delegates to the convention to draw up a constitution for a supposedly liberal and democratic Russia. The Mennonites, supporting their candidate, Benjamin Unruh, flatly refused.

Perhaps P.M. Friesen's massive work on the Mennonites added fuel to the Russian liberals' distress. Published in 1911, the work states that 75 per cent of Russian Mennonites were not only very conservative monarchists, but that 99 per cent considered the words 'democrat' and 'democratic' with deep suspicion on the ground that nothing good, but only evil, could be expected from that form of government. Furthermore, Friesen claims that the Russian Mennonites of the years before the First World War might have supported political parties even farther right than the Octobrists, were it not for the fact that these groups usually were identified with the interests of the Orthodox church and hatred of ethnic and religious minorities.[13]

Friesen, a religious liberal but an extreme monarchist, may have exaggerated his co-religionists' conservatism, especially among the landless cottagers, the skilled workmen, and the growing number of intellectuals. It is true, however, that many men who served in the Russian zemstvo (the all-class elected local and guberniia administrative institutions), and members of the intelligentsia, were perplexed and no doubt resentful at the attitude of the Mennonites, a group historically linked to the radical wing of the Reformation. Why, they must have wondered, did a group which championed the separation of church and state, freedom of conscience, and so many other personal freedoms, refuse to support the most elementary rights for the native citizenry, even the cry by Russian sectarians for freedom of worship and their right to conscientious objection? Unfortunately, with hindsight we can see that the Mennonites' blindness to the plight of their neighbours also made them blind to the tragedy that would ultimately befall them.

CHAPTER FIFTEEN

Class Conflicts within the Khortitsa Settlement

At the time of the founding of Khortitsa, its settlers represented a fairly homogeneous socioeconomic group. In their home region around Danzig the heads of most families were small farmers, craftsmen, and skilled labourers. Records indicate that none of them were particularly affluent or powerful, nor any abjectly poor. Furthermore, since most families were granted the rights to an equivalent amount of land (sixty-five dessiatins, about 175 acres) in the new settlements, they virtually all started out on a relatively equal footing.[1] From the outset there were a few landless villagers, who occupied small cottage lots in the village. Over the next few decades that segment of the population grew, until in most Mennonite villages, and certainly in Nieder Khortitsa, there were almost as many landless villagers as farmers. A significant class structure developed around this difference, which to a large extent was a division between those who had wealth and power and those who lacked both.

The land crisis arose from at least three factors: the Mennonites' accelerating birth rate, the paucity of extra land on which the burgeoning population could establish new farms, and the Russian Land Law of 19 October 1764, which governed Mennonite ownership of land. This stipulated that allotments could not be sold, mortgaged, or divided, and could be inherited by only one child. The family trees in this book attest to the exploding population. The four ancestral families of which I have some knowledge (the Rempel, Pauls, Kovenhoven, and Höppner families) had one, two, three, and eight children, respectively. Since no more than four of the last family's children reached maturity, the effective average family included two adults and 2.5 children. Their size parallels that of the entire migratory group; the 228 families of the first group arrived with an average of roughly 2.7 children. Had the Mennonites maintained this modest birth rate, the settlement would not have required a substantial increase in land for many decades. Instead, the population grew exponentially. This, too, is reflected in the family tree diagrams. Over the next three generations, each of these four family groups produced seven to thirteen children. Even if no more than half reached maturity (and I suspect that more did), the population could easily double every twenty years or even sooner.

With so many offspring, and the inability to divide the land among them, many of the descendants of the original settlers found themselves landless. They joined the equivalently expanding number of descendants of the original cottagers. The landless class swelled further when some new immigrants, slated to settle on new sixty-five-dessiatin parcels in the Molochna Settlement, refused to move there after learning that they would not receive the same generous terms as the original settlers (including a 500-ruble loan, certain subventions, and a period of tax exemption). Despite governmental directives to the district mayor (*Oberschulz*) and Nieder Khortitsa's mayor (*Schulz*), they remained intransigent, until finally the government relented and these new, and landless, citizens stayed in our village.

The burgeoning population would have had less impact on the settlement if new lands had been readily available. Although the founders of Nieder Khortitsa set aside a limited reserve of land for a few additional family farms, most of the surplus acreage lay in lowlands (*limans*) along the banks of the Dnieper River, areas that often flooded during the spring thaw, and in the bottoms of ravines (*balki*) criss-crossing much of the region.[2] Few new families acquired parcels there, however, because the established farmers, when they discovered the ground's fertility, appropriated much of it for their own use. As a result, the landless population soared. Ultimately, 40 per cent of the Khortitsa Settlement's population and two-thirds of Molochna's citizens were landless. Although their situation was not as dire as that of their neighbouring Russian peasants, it was desperate enough to create substantial social friction within the settlements.

The landed and landless classes were not strictly monolithic entities. Over time both evolved distinct subgroups, each with its own status and concerns. At the top of the heap were the prosperous estate owners (*khutoriane*), who had amassed large holdings, mostly by buying up land from destitute Russian nobles. They represented the Mennonite social elite. Next came those owning full farms (*Vollwirte*) of sixty-five dessiatins. When the Russian government finally permitted farmers to divide their lands, two other groups formed: those holding half-farms (*Halbwirte*) and small or quarter-farms (*Kleinwirte*). The proprietors in each group typically had status commensurate with their holdings. Taxes, pasturage, and other rights and obligations were apportioned accordingly. Each landholder's right to vote, however, was equivalent – one man, one vote.

The second, less fortunate non-farming group was likewise subdivided into the *Anwohner* (or *Aunwohna*), who owned their cottages, and the *Einwohner* (or *Enwohna*), who rented. The residents of these homes were primarily skilled or unskilled tradesmen. In Nieder Khortitsa, which lacked the diversified trades found in the villages supporting industries or commercial ventures, the teamsters and river boatmen were primarily renters, whereas craftsmen such as blacksmiths, tinsmiths, wheelwrights, carpenters, roofers, cabinetmakers, tailors, or millers typically owned their dwelling as did the few professional people, such as teachers and widows of retired farmers, who lived among them. In most villages the cottages were located at one end of the village or on a narrow street behind the farmers' homesteads. In Nieder Khortitsa these homes lay primarily close to the Dnieper (see Map 6, page 268), and so the inhabitants were called, somewhat derogatorily, Dnieper-end (*Nippaenja*) dwellers.

The plight of these two groups touched my family in various ways. Mother, who was very service oriented, often fed them and was much concerned with their welfare. A few of Father's relatives (including his cousins – Wilhelm, Peter, Johann, and Jacob Rempel) were cottagers, as were some of his first wife's cousins. Father had minimal contact with them, in part because many drowned their sorrows in alcohol, which he hated. But also, I suppose, as a self-made man, he expected them to raise themselves by their own bootstraps, much as he had done.

Father could not avoid their plight entirely, however, because the fortunes of the *Nippaenja* boatmen were entwined with his two businesses. The boatmen made most of their income by transporting grain and watermelons during the summer and fall, and thus their fate, like Father's, depended very much on the uncertainties of harvest deficits and surpluses, trade embargoes, and cholera quarantines. Furthermore, these men had little capital beyond their investment in their homes (if they owned them) and boats.[3] So, in years when their income proved

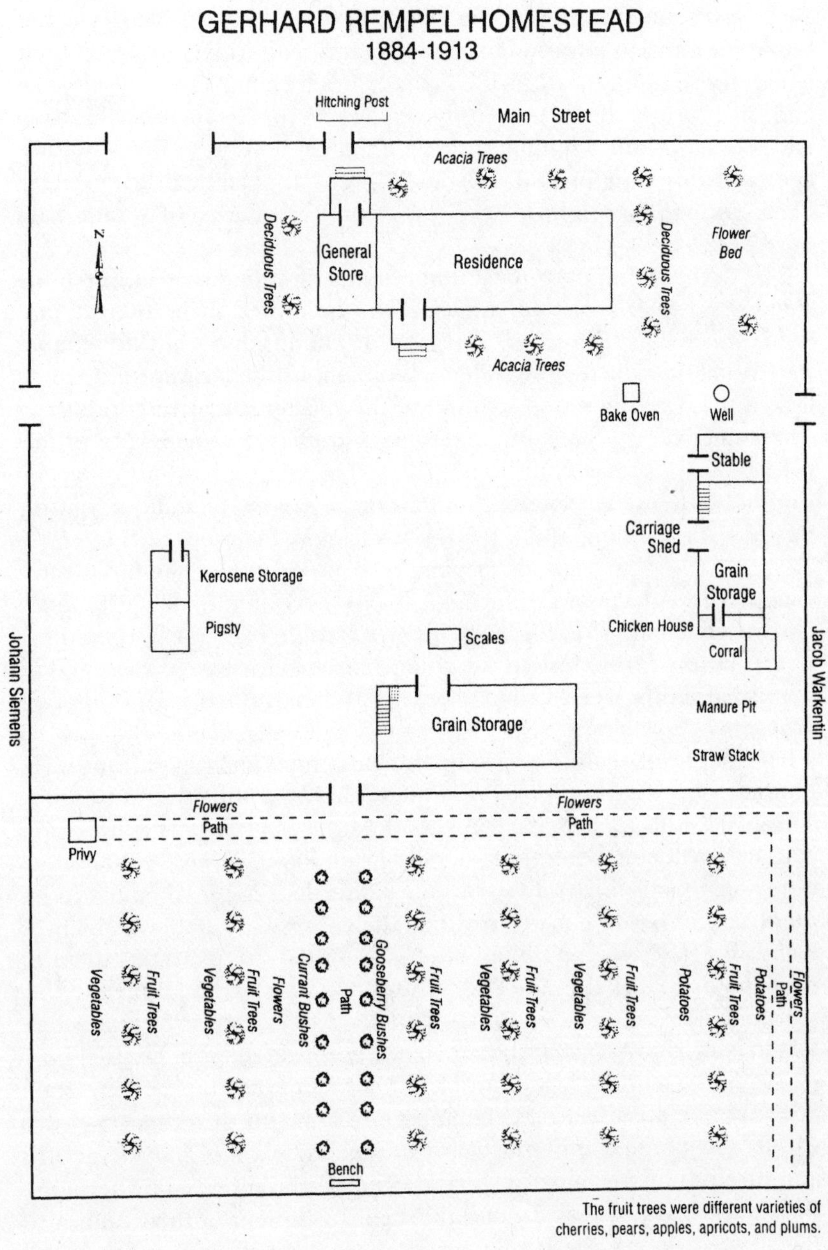
GERHARD REMPEL HOMESTEAD
1884-1913
Hitching Post
Main Street
Acacia Trees
Deciduous Trees
General Store
Residence
Deciduous Trees
Flower Bed
Acacia Trees
Bake Oven
Well
Stable
Carriage Shed
Grain Storage
Kerosene Storage
Pigsty
Chicken House
Scales
Corral
Johann Siemens
Jacob Warkentin
Manure Pit
Grain Storage
Straw Stack
Flowers
Path
Flowers
Path
Privy
Vegetables
Fruit Trees
Vegetables
Fruit Trees
Flowers
Currant Bushes
Path
Gooseberry Bushes
Fruit Trees
Vegetables
Fruit Trees
Vegetables
Fruit Trees
Potatoes
Fruit Trees
Potatoes
Path
Flowers
Bench
The fruit trees were different varieties of cherries, pears, apples, apricots, and plums.

Map 5

too meagre to last through the winter and spring, Father's general store carried them on credit for supplies of kerosene, flour, sunflower oil, and household sundries.

The Land Law of 1764 had ramifications beyond dividing the population into landholding and landless classes. It also consolidated power in the hands of the landholders, because it stipulated that only landholders had the right to vote or hold office in the village assemblies. This allowed the elite to dictate policy on the use of communal and reserve lands. All too often this group appropriated these lands for their own exclusive use. Until the 1860s, the Russian government supported this concentration of power, on the assumption that it encouraged the model farming practices for which the Mennonites were noted.[4] The landless class finally received some relief through the reforms of Alexander II. These abolished the colonists' special status along with many of their privileges, and placed the Mennonites under the administration of the general government. The directives further stipulated that Mennonites must provide land for their landless out of a special fund. This stimulated the 'daughter' colonization programs, through which a substantial number of landless families were resettled on lands the 'mother' settlement had purchased, mainly from financially strapped noble Russian families. Apart from a few lay and clerical leaders, most of the farmers bitterly resisted this program. Had they known that its most progressive provisions were the work of Alexander Klaus, a student of the famous socialist, Nikolai Chernyshevskii, the farmers would no doubt have resisted with even greater vigour.

Unfortunately, the much-praised daughter colony policy benefited the sons of established farmers much more than it did the landless cottagers. This was mainly the result of rising land prices in the more desirable regions of European Russia. While the Mennonite estate owners and industrialists could still afford to buy nearby large estates from the Russian gentry, the villages had to purchase cheaper land for daughter settlements in more distant areas in central Russia, east of the Volga, and in the northern Caucasus. Even land in these remoter districts cost more than the average cottager could afford. For example, in 1910 Khortitsa purchased an estate of 9,414 dessiatins from Count Viazemskii in the Saratov guberniia to found Arkadak. It paid 172 rubles per dessiatin. As the minimal size required for a profitable farm was fifty dessiatins, a prospective farmer's land could cost 8,600 rubles. Although the down payment might be no more than 1,000 to 1,500 rubles, the added cost of farm equipment, buildings, and moving expenses drove the start-up costs beyond the reach of all but the offspring of landed families. Furthermore, since only 179 families established farms there, the program hardly reduced Khortitsa's landless population.

To compound the matter, the Land Commission turned a blind eye to many abuses of the system. Thus, many estate owners' sons, some of whom had no intention of farming nor even of settling on the land, received grants. I know personally of two examples in Nieder Khortitsa: Heinrich Pankratz, one of the village's best farmers, acquired three grants for his sons, and Peter Vogt sold his half-farm to another neighbour so that he could acquire a larger grant in Arkadak. In similar fashion, the sons of two prominent bankers in Khortitsa and Rosental (Krahn and Funk) received land, although neither intended to farm. The abuses in Arkadak were so serious that a special commission sent to investigate cancelled some of the grants. Despite this the landless families remained resentful, with obvious reason. In an attempt to redress these mistakes, Khortitsa purchased a similar-sized estate from Count Volkonskii in Tambov guberniia in 1913. While the per dessiatin price (340 rubles) was almost twice that of the Arkadak land, the Land Commission hoped that a longer amortization period, and some financial subventions for the neediest farmers, would offer hope to villagers of more modest means. Unfortunately, the outbreak of the First World War halted the settlement.

Even with the daughter colony program and Stolypin's reforms, Nieder Khortitsa's *Nippaenja* population remained at about 30 per cent. Although most of these families were close relatives of the well-situated farmers and businessmen, they were still generally regarded as the low-lifes (*podonki*) of Mennonitism. Most owned their homes on plots large enough to raise their own fruit and vegetables, yet the sandy soil required more effort to achieve good yields than was true of the farmers' lands. A significant number of the men became alcoholics, and most lived a haphazard, perhaps carefree, life. Support for their widows and orphans was niggardly and a shame on the community. What saved those in most dire need was their relationship to the more affluent villagers, whom they could count on for a load of straw to patch their roof, or chaff to feed their cow, and so forth. Many rarely attended church, using the excuse that their clothing was not suitable. To a large extent their Mennonitism related perhaps less to faith than to their pro forma baptism at age twenty, which they needed if they were going to claim such community privileges as marriage, eligibility for Alternate Service, and voting.

Grandmother Pauls and daughters

The classier Rempel family (Father's first wife's siblings)

David Rempel (Father's brother) and his wife

The Pauls family, ca. 1888

Grandmother Pauls

The 'America' House, ca. 1910

Father, Gerhard Rempel

Mother, Maria (née Pauls) Rempel

Brother Johann

Sister Maria

Brother Heinrich

Sister Neta and her husband, Jacob Pankratz

Brother Gerhard Rempel and his wife, Tina

Khortitsa High School graduating class, 1917 (author, far right, back row)

Medical Corps of VZS Hospital Train 194 (ca. 1916)

School class photograph (with Jacob Rempel [arrow])

Aunt Susanna

Aunt Catharina and her husband, Jacob Janzen

Aunt Helena and her husband, Kornelius Braun

The Pauls homestead

The Village of Khortitsa, 1910 by Henry Pauls

As it became obvious that few of the cottagers could qualify for land allotments in the daughter colonies, these luckless souls lowered their sights and demanded more achievable concessions at home. This often resulted in shouting contests at the village assembly meetings (*Schultebotts*). They focused on four main issues: (1) more equitable access to communally owned pasture lands, meadows, and woodlands; (2) fairer distribution of taxes, with greater emphasis on property tax and a reduction of poll taxes; (3) grants of home sites on wasteland (*Unland*) for newly married couples; and (4) greater democracy in the village assembly meetings. This latter meant allowing them to vote on issues concerning the whole citizenry, prior notice of village meetings, and the equitable apportionment of communal services.

The first issue – access to communal pasturage – became a problem in virtually every settlement in New Russia almost from the time it was established, and acutely so with the burgeoning population and number of herd of cattle. By the 1840s, when the Mennonites shifted from rearing sheep to growing grain, the existing landowners falsely claimed that the pasture lands had been awarded to their forebears as private property. In fact, the Russian government's Guardianship Committee overseeing the settlements of 'foreigners' was clear on the issue – the lands were to be communal. However, the landowners remained intransigent in refusing to share the lands.

Between 1864 and 1871, the issue became even murkier. During that time the government abolished the category of colonists as a separate entity, designating them instead as 'settler-proprietors' who owned land outright. Unfortunately, the statutes did not delineate who owned the communal lands nor what rights the landless might retain. For twenty years, various ministries and courts debated questions such as how many head of cattle each group – landholder and landless – could graze on communal lands, what fees to charge members of each group, how many small livestock were equivalent to a horse or ox, and so forth. Although the government ultimately worked out grazing formulas, the landless were forced to accept whatever decisions the village assembly made.[5] Fuelling their discomfort was that much of the land they were allowed to use was subject to spring flooding. During that time the assembly awarded a fisherman, Heinrich Rempel, the tract's exclusive and lucrative fishing rights. How, the landless argued, could the assembly award such a monopoly, and should not he at least pay fees as well? The issue remained a subject of bitter controversy in many villages until the revolution, twenty-five years later.[6]

The second major issue between the haves and have-nots arose over taxation. For fifty years prior to the revolution the landless class complained about the burden of poll taxes. They were so onerous that even a Russian agricultural authority, V.G. Postnikov, wrote that he had seen few cases in which so many agencies and services were supported in this regressive fashion as in the Mennonite settlements.[7] Only in the late 1890s, when the cost of maintaining the Alternative Service was shifted to property taxes, did the landless gain a little relief from the staggering poll tax.

The third issue was that the landless be allowed to purchase home sites at reasonable cost for their recently married children. This matter was of little import in the smaller villages, such as Blumengart, Burwalde, Rosengart, Insel Khortitsa, and Neuenburg, where virtually all the citizens were landowning farmers. They not only controlled the assemblies, and were thus able to assign lands to their offspring, but they also had the finances to purchase lands for them in the new settlements. It mattered less also in Khortitsa and Einlage where the factories and mills were obliged to provide housing for their workmen's families. In Nieder Khortitsa, however, the problem was acute, and I vividly recall the heated arguments that filled my father's store after a spokesman for the cottagers somehow found out that each village had been required, at the time of its founding, to set aside acreage for building sites that equaled one-sixth of the homestead lands. Surviving records do not provide a foundation for his claims that this land was to be provided at no cost. Perhaps it was only based on some oral tradition. In actual practice, some villages had provided a restricted number of such lots on an as-needed basis, but only upon payment of a specified fee.

Certainly, Nieder Khortitsa's elite could have satisfied the landless group's demands by granting them parcels on the Huggels, a sandy wasteland, either gratis or at a nominal fee. Only a small portion of this was ever used for pasturing and the remainder could have accommodated fifty to sixty building sites, each about fifty by a hundred feet in size. A second wasteland site, lying on the village's southern border, could have likewise been assigned to housing. Those in power refused to make any such concessions. But after November 1917, the landless took matters into their own hands, and they began carving building sites out of these sections without the farmers' approval.

The fourth issue the landless wanted addressed was the creation of a more democratic system of government. Initially, only those males holding land could vote or hold office, as stipulated in the Colonist Code (*ustav kolonistov*) during the rule of Catherine the Great. Legislation adopted between 1864 and 1870 abolished these restrictions. Under the new law, every adult Mennonite male had the right to cast one vote on all matters affecting the entire population (but not those affecting a specific property). In Nieder Khortitsa, where every male could thus in theory vote in the village assembly (*Schultebott*), usually no more than twenty farmers attended the meetings. The absentees may have been uninterested in the topic at hand, but many non-farmers also felt unwelcome. Perhaps their claims were justified. Or, because many dissidents lived at the end of the village, they may not have received notice of the meeting, conveyed either by a *Zaddel* (note), handed from house to house, or, if called on short notice, by a teenager riding on horseback, shouting, 'Go to the assembly meeting at the Mayor's house immediately' (*Stracks biem Schulten toom Schultebott toopkohme*). Others refused to attend for particular, and sometimes numerous, reasons. For example, the Reverend Jacob Sawatzky refused to attend because of an offensive anti-Semitic remark one leader had made to a Jewish resident, and his own treatment by the farmer-elite. Many Sundays he preached in neighbouring villages, but rather than ride with his team of horses, already worked during the six-day farming week, Reverend Sawatzky walked the distance, when any of the farmer elite could easily have driven him there, using their teams of horses reserved for pleasure drives. Compounding the grief, I imagine, was the fact that often the host village did not even offer him Sunday dinner.

Father Intervenes

For a few years a third class of citizens coexisted with the old landed and landless classes. These were the recipients of small allotments (*nadelshchiki*), awarded under the Stolypin land reform program after the revolution of 1905–6. Although the plan was designed for Russian peasants, the Nieder Khortitsa teamsters petitioned the Ekaterinoslav bureau of the agency administering the Stolypin land reforms (*Udel'noe vedomstvo*) to become eligible for this program, as well. Father's signature appeared at the top of the petition. In further support of the teamsters, he was instrumental in hiring Bernhard Fast, a Mennonite legal expert from Zagradovka, to draft the document.[8]

The teamsters' petition for land aroused immediate and bitter opposition from the farmers. If the petition was successful they stood to lose in two ways. First, many of the farmers rented their own surplus lands to the teamsters. They would no longer realize their rather exorbitant rents. Second, the farmers themselves had often rented the *Udel'noe vedomstvo* lands, and these would then be unavailable to them. Village meetings on the subject in 1907–8 were heated. I personally recall the bitter wrangling in our store between the teamsters and the farmers. Responding to their petition, the Land Commission in Ekaterinoslav dispatched a delegation to inquire about the general grievances and the specifics of the petition. Later, they directed representatives of both groups to appear at a hearing in Ekaterinoslav, which was followed by further investigations in Nieder Khortitsa. These mainly evaluated the likely success of the prospective recipients, judging them much as they would Ukrainian peasants, on the basis of the buildings they owned, their credit, family size, equipment, and livestock.[9]

The commission ruled in favour of the teamsters, and those who qualified received twelve- to twenty-four-dessiatin allotments, depending on family size. Each parcel was allotted as a single plot, rather than in several strips. Since the land was close to the village, the teamsters were allowed to keep their homes rather than having to move them to the newly acquired land. In general, the remaining terms, for instance, the cost per dessiatin and the repayment period, resembled those granted the Ukrainian peasants. The allotments, called *nadel*, gave the new farmers a designation of *nadelshchiki* (allotment-holders). Those living along a narrow cul-de-sac at the end of the village were also referred to as *kutok* people. Since their land was not in the Khortitsa administrative district (*volost*), but rather in the Belenkoe volost, they formed their own village assembly, elected a mayor (*Schulz*), and paid their land and other special taxes to the Belenkoe volost. However, they remained members of Nieder Khortitsa's civil community and church congregation. As such, they enjoyed the rights of villagers, which included access to pasturage, meadow, and woodlands. They paid poll taxes to support community institutions, teachers' salaries, and school maintenance. All of this left ample opportunity for quarrels in civic and church matters between the age-old order and the new class of teamster-farmer.

The Farmers' Retribution

By 1909, the farmers were so enraged at Father's assistance to the new *nadelshchiki* that they boycotted his store and refused to sell him their grain. For a brief time their actions all but wiped out the family income.

Fortunately, Father soon found alternate sources, and the family resumed its comfortable, although modest, life. First, he shifted his grain business to dealings with farmers in seven other Mennonite villages with whom he had always enjoyed close personal and business relations. In doing so he expanded his operations. This, combined with the industrial and commercial expansion that followed the Russo-Japanese War and the Stolypin land reforms, made Father's business more profitable than it had been when he had traded with the intransigent farmers of our home village.

The store's business, however, never recovered. While it remained open for several more years, it retained little of its former trade beyond that with the landless cottagers, teamsters, and *nadelshchiki.* These customers generated little profit, because the store carried most of them on credit. Some could pay up during the following season, others simply defaulted. Parenthetically, I should note that Father's account books included many families carried from year to year with but tiny repayments. Then, after the economic chaos of war, revolution, and civil war, the debts became uncollectable. My brothers and I resolved the question after the death of our parents. Early in 1921 a boatman appeared at the house offering to pay off his substantial prewar debt of fifty or sixty rubles with a several-hundred-thousand ruble note, then worth the price of a tiny packet of matches. With a bit of gallows humour, we resolved to buy the matches and burn the account books to warm up our evening's simple but treasured porridge, itself worth several million rubles at that time.

To make up lost revenue, Father took on a new and hazardous business – raising watermelons. In some years he reaped a substantial profit, selling the melons either to local markets in Alexandrovsk, to Jewish merchants who shipped them to distant cities, or to Ukrainian teamsters (*chumaky*). The latter bought directly from Father, arriving at his fields with their ox-drawn *arbas* (high, ladder-sided carts). After loading hundreds of straw-cushioned melons in each wagon, they resold the fruit in their peasant villages. In other years, my father faced catastrophe, either because the government embargoed the melons during cholera epidemics or because competition from other farmers depressed prices to the point that it was not economical to harvest the crop. Since Father had to lease the land, hire labourers to weed the patch and harvest the melons, and employ teamsters to cart them to market, his losses could be considerable.

The family realized one further source of capital when Father sold an Orenburg farm that he had owned for years. Although he had leased it to local farmers, the rents had never met the expenses of ownership. Thus, the sale not only staunched an outflow of money, it brought in enough for Father to buy the barren lot of a burned-down farmstead that stood a few hundred feet from our home on which, as mentioned, he built a new home, barn, stable, and large *Spitja*.

The Rapacity of the Elite

Unfortunately, the elite farmers not only monopolized village governance, but over the first decades of the twentieth century they regularly plundered the environment. Criticism of their policies seemed only to increase their steamroller tactics. At least four egregious acts that I witnessed leap to mind.

I must have been five or six years old when this group decided to cut down a huge grove of tall poplar and elm trees for their personal use and/or to sell for firewood. The clump, which probably predated the Mennonite settlement, stood along the Nizhniaia Khortitsa Stream where it emptied into the Dnieper. It was a beautiful spot for picnics and afforded shade for boatmen waiting for prospective passengers to Alexandrovsk and for us youngsters during our day-long frolics on the sandy beaches of the river. The stand was, if anything, public or communal property, and not theirs to cut. Public outcry did not deter them. Nor did the tragic death of a peasant labourer, killed by the branches of a falling tree. The group felled virtually every tree and none ever grew there again. Only the tall elms along the border with two Niebuhr flour mills were left standing. This act of grace was likely the result of district or regional prohibitions on the destruction of trees of a certain size or species. The reprieve was short, however. They, too, were cut during the wartime coal shortage.

Their next act occurred nearby, along the bank of the Dnieper. At this spot the bank rose sharply to a massive rock formation about fifteen to twenty feet high and half a mile wide. The spot was idyllic, for you could see the sandy bottom of the then-unpolluted river. It was also useful. On Saturdays the women did their washing there, using the numerous rocks as washboards. During the late spring and summer the *duby* and *berliny* docked about fifteen feet offshore to load grain from the area's farms. We youngsters used the boats as diving boards, often to the annoyance of the Jewish grain merchants' representatives (*priiomshchiki*), who released a stream of indelicate expressions in Yiddish, Plautdietsch, Ukrainian, or Russian. The naked Mennonite urchins usually responded in kind, although with a less rich and colourful vocabulary. About 1906 to 1908, the government wanted to acquire and move the rocks from there to form a barrier on the Dnieper's west bank, which would create a shipping channel deep enough for passenger ships and freighters. With alacrity, the power brokers sold the rights to the picturesque rock formation. After nearly a year of dynamiting, the desecration was complete. The once lovely beach was desolate, and a nearby lumberyard was put out of business. Soon the area was nothing but a stretch of unsightly weeds with the wretched hut of the poorest boatman in its midst.

The next victim of the insatiable appetite of these farmers was the large mulberry plantation created in the 1840s to support the incipient Russian silk industry. Although that enterprise never took hold, the plantation remained a large oasis of perhaps fifteen to twenty acres, densely planted in mulberry and interspersed with elm. The predatory farmers argued that maintaining the plantation was a useless luxury, whereas cutting it would generate revenue and create pasturage. Most of the trees were cut, but the extensive underbrush refused to die, and the land could not be used for grazing. Its tree stumps and scrub remained as silent accusers of purblind stupidity.

Their final regrettable act involved a large pond (*Tränke*). Located in a long, broad valley towards Blumengart, it was used by the community's cattle and horses. Every village had at least one pond some distance out, where herds could reach water without being driven home. They were built around the mid-nineteenth century under the edict of the Guardianship Committee. Surrounding poplars and willow offered shade and cover for the animals, and many of the ponds were stocked with carp and catfish. And what did our village fathers do with our pond? Under the assumption that the village would gain a few dessiatins of grazing land, they allowed the dike, which impounded the water of the pond, to break. To replace it they dug a well and flanked it with two long watering troughs. But instead of gaining pasturage, the low-lying land that had once been the pond's bottom, became a muddy swamp during the wet months and an expanse of barren hardpan during the dry season. This same shortsighted group was also inexplicably opposed to the government's planting grass and willows to halt erosion and drifting sands. I even recall several farmers' sons boasting at school how they had 'planted' some of the trees with their roots in the air and their tips in the ground.

Throughout my childhood these twelve to fifteen, powerful farmer families held the mayor's office and otherwise controlled the local administration.[10] Typically, they would rotate the assistants' (*Beisitzer*) positions among themselves as well, or parcel the positions out to the friends and relatives among the half-farmers. Some of the most ambitious half-farmers also coveted the position of the mayor's flunky (the 'tenthman,' or *desiatskii*), in hopes the job might some day propel them into the mayor's position itself. One of his jobs entailed transferring the sign belonging to the village mayor (*selskii starosta*) every third year from the old mayor's home to the new mayor's gate, an event celebrated with huge buffet (*zakuski*) and enough vodka to leave many in a tipsy state.

No matter how hard outsiders strove to break that monopoly, they never breached its entrenched barriers. One poignant example I recall was of a farmer named Janzen who everyone knew wanted a post in the village administration. He was so desperate to be elected that he did not care what office it might be. He was a successful man, but owned only a half-farm. For this reason, and perhaps because he was a bit odd,[11] Janzen was told each year 'Just wait. Next year' (*Wacht mau blooss. Oppjoah*). Invariably, he would respond, 'You always say next year, and still give nothing' (*Jie saje ema oppjoah, an doch jeft daut nuscht*). This went on for so many years that his nickname became Next Year Janzen (*Oppjoah Janzen*).

The farmer elite's exploitation might have continued unabated except for the emergence of two protest groups. The first was made up primarily of the sons of a few of the farmers and of those engaged in the milling industry. In many ways these resembled the division of interests described in Turgenev's *Fathers and Sons.* As in the novel, many Mennonite sons preferred careers in milling, commerce, teaching, or other professions to taking over the family farm.[12] Most were slightly alienated from the faith of their forebears. Some associated with rebellious students and occasionally joined in their public protests. One group persuaded David H. Epp, the editor of *Der Botschafter,* to publish an anonymous letter (evidently written by my brother Johann's friends Dietrich Warkentin, Kornelius Kethler, and Johann Siemens) exposing the shenanigans of Nieder Khortitsa's powerful elite.

That the opinion of these young people carried any weight was in part because of the role played by a second group, the female members of three families – the elderly widow Wiebe and her daughters, Maria and Tina; Mrs Johann Siemens and her four daughters; and my mother and sisters Neta and Mariechen.[13] As a group, they gave moral and financial support to the village teachers in creating a public library and furthering other educational programs. Individually, they were very outspoken in their disdain for the local officials' depredations of communal assets, lack of interest in educational and cultural matters, and even the lifestyle of some of these local champions of law and order (*bliustiteli poriadka*). Although women had no official voice in the Mennonite church prior to the revolution (their role was to decorate the meeting place and prepare the elaborate meals for the *Brüderschaft* conferences), and could not vote on either civic or church matters, many had a strong hold on their husbands' purses, and they were equally strong in demanding that the men support their view at the next village assembly (*Schultebott*).

A few of the more enlightened village men provided at least silent endorsement for the women's views. Three I recall well were Heinrich Rempel (called *Füla Rampel* for his supposed love of flowers and aversion to work), who had an encyclopedic knowledge of local folklore; Franz Dyck, a small farmer and teamster and great raconteur of his Siberian adventures as a medical orderly during the Russo-Japanese War; and Jacob Janzen, who was quite open in his opposition to the officials' actions.

I cannot say how pervasive the rapacious practices were throughout the settlements, but I suspect that Nieder Khortitsa was not an isolated case. Certainly, the desperation of much of the landless class characterized most of the settlements. The perplexing aspect of these situations is that as a group, Russian Mennonites were not only prosperous, but recorded enviable achievements in education, welfare, and culture. As examples, I can mention their mutual aid practices, support of general and specialized hospitals and schools, afforestation stations, generous contributions to alleviate suffering among their Ukrainian and Russian neighbours, and support of missionary activities in the Far East. And, in fairness to the powerful farmers, their aims were sometimes for communal good. One example was their enforcement of fire regulations. The traditional Nieder Khortitsa wooden home resembled those of the ancestors in the Low Countries and the Vistula region, with living space, stables, and storage attached under one straw-thatched roof. One spark could within minutes become a conflagration. To reduce this hazard the group granted lower insurance rates to those who used fire-resistant building materials, and they insisted on firewalls between home and stable sections, wide streets, and adequate set-backs between neighbouring farm buildings. I suppose that Nieder Khortitsa's citizenry, despite its callous materialism, contributed in a respectable degree to these social goals. One wonders, though, how much more our people could have accomplished if we had given more thought to the needs of our immensely less fortunate neighbours, the Ukrainian peasants.

CHAPTER SIXTEEN

Growing Interest in Education

Until nearly the end of the nineteenth century the education that the average Russian Mennonite student received was rudimentary. To be sure, it was superior to the offerings in the adjacent Ukrainian peasant villages and adequate to serve the needs of a future farmer or homemaker. Nevertheless, as the twentieth century neared, alternative careers to farming became important, and these required a broader grasp of languages, mathematics, history, literature, and/or technical skills. Over the next few decades Mennonites made large improvements in their educational system and created many new schools. This came about despite numerous obstacles presented by the government, especially to the establishment of schools devoted to the liberal arts, women's secondary education, or religion. To circumvent the government, Mennonites sometimes resorted to ruse. For example, the Molochna Settlement gained the Odessa Education District's approval to establish a boys' school with an advanced liberal arts curriculum only by camouflaging it as a school of commerce.

However, the government did not impede the creation of new central boys' high schools (*Zentralschulen*), which were essentially teacher-training institutions. These were originally founded by orders of the Ministry of State Domains in the mid-nineteenth century for the dual purpose of raising the level of education in the settlements and of training instructors who could teach the Russian language. With this encouragement the Khortitsa Settlement and its daughter colonies founded schools at Nikolaipol, New York, and Orenburg, as well as in the Khortitsa Settlement itself. The settlement further improved the quality of teacher-training by creating a teachers' seminary with a two-year pedagogical program, which by 1914 was extended to a three-year course of study. This gave the teaching profession an honoured, if poorly paid, role in many of the settlement villages.

This was not entirely true in Nieder Khortitsa. Although it, like the rest of the villages, moved towards better education, it still lived up to its reputation as a near-frontier outpost, and relatively few families were concerned with educational opportunities or facilities for their offspring. Few of the most prosperous farmers encouraged their sons to acquire higher education, and those who did favoured technical training in milling or business, not teaching. Hence, most of the impetus for higher education in our village came from its non-farmer families.

No family was more interested in education than ours. The matter obsessed Father, primarily because he regretted his own poor education, but I suspect also because Mother's family had been prosperous farmers and he, in turn, wished us to excel in some other arena. After the 1905 Revolution my father acquired another, even more compelling reason to educate his children – his certainty that further revolution was in store for the country. How often he drilled me with: 'I cannot buy land. I could not do that for your older siblings and I cannot do that for you or Jacob either. But what I can give you is an education which no one can take away from you if a revolution comes' (*Laund kaun etj nich tjeepen. Daut kunn etj nich fe diene ellere Jeschwista, en daut woa etj uk nich fe die enn Jasch tjenne. Oba etj kaun die eene Bildung jäwe. Dann hast dü eene Bildung, dee tjeena die wajchnehme kaun wann de Revolution tjemmt*). Whatever his motives may have been, all of us reaped the benefits of Father's preoccupation with education.

The Oldest Children

Neta, the eldest child, had only a primary education. I am not sure why she did not attend the Khortitsa high school for girls in 1898, but I assume that either our parents had not yet clarified their thinking on a girl's need for a secondary education or that in the early years following its 1895 establishment the school had not acquired the high reputation it enjoyed a few years later, when German Lutheran and Catholic colonist families from the surrounding guberniias were as eager to send their daughters to the school as were the Mennonite founders. Furthermore, at the time – especially with a view of their growing family's needs – my parents may not have been able to afford the tuition, which was a proviso the Odessa educational system had demanded for the school's establishment.

Gerhard was the family's problem child. Father insisted that he attend high school in Khortitsa after he finished the primary grades, in 1900. Although very bright, Gerhard was an indifferent student, and the school dropped him from the roster in the third quarter of his first year. He stayed at home for several years after that, helping Father in the store. But when Gerhard showed Grandfather's weakness for alcohol, Father decided to send him to a school with a good accounting curriculum in Simferopol in the Crimea. Although Gerhard protested vigorously, Father insisted, and in the end, Gerhard did well there. Although he succeeded in his accounting jobs in various milling companies between 1906 and 1917, his life was beset with misfortune. His vision in one eye was weak, and his marriage seemed unhappy. His wife had grown up on the estate of prosperous relatives, and she disliked housekeeping and the task of rearing the couple's five children. She also resented having to live on an accountant's salary.

Johann's situation was the reverse of Gerhard's. He eagerly enrolled in the Khortitsa high school in 1903. Graduating four years later, his record indicated what his parents had long believed – that he was keenly observant, analytical, artistic, and had a prodigious memory, as well as an observant eye for nature. Our parents hoped that this precocious son would become a high school teacher, a position then regarded as distinguished. With that objective, Father planned to send Johann to the *gimnaziia* in Alexandrovsk, assuming that would expedite his admission to the St Petersburg Teachers' Institute. Completion of that program was sine qua non for an appointment in a Mennonite high school. But just after Father arranged Johann's room and board in Alexandrovsk, someone reminded him that the Khortitsa Settlement stipend, which had supported Johann through high school, obliged him to teach in a Mennonite village school for several years. Thus, instead of going to Alexandrovsk, Johann returned to Khortitsa to take the two-year training course in the teachers' seminary there. After completing the course in 1909, he took a position in the Neuendorf elementary school, where he taught for four years, before taking a similar position in Kronsweide. Johann returned to this school for another year after Alexander Kerensky demobilized all former teachers who had served in the Alternative Service medical corps.

Then in 1918 Johann and a friend, Kornelius Grunau, established a high school in Nieder Khortitsa. Although the tsarist government had impeded Mennonite efforts to create new schools, the new provisional government favoured the idea of setting up experimental private high schools (*Zentralschulen*) in local villages, at least in part as a way to employ the more educated of the young Mennonites without job prospects when they returned from wartime alternative service posts. Nieder Khortitsa, which lacked a high school, seemed ripe for such an experiment, and my brother Johann and his friend were the logical choices to found it. This time, the village's prosperous farmers refrained from sneering at education, for the chaos of the early phase of the civil war showed even the most hard-headed, tight-fisted 'pound' (*Pundmennist*) Mennonite that land and other material assets were of little lasting value, while the advantages of schooling and the professions might endure.

Kornelius Grunau had studied in Rosental and Alexandrovsk, then graduated from Moscow's best-known school of commerce. While in school he had spent his summers working in the business office of Alexandrabad, a fancy Mennonite-owned health resort located in a picturesque spot on the Dnieper just north of Alexandrovsk. It was converted to a military hospital shortly after war broke out, and for the duration, Kornelius worked full-time in the office. His business experience made him the obvious candidate to be the principal of the new school. And since the teaching staff of the Khortitsa high school held Johann in such high regard, they assured him and Grunau that they would accredit the students as long as they took their year-end examinations in Khortitsa. With that assurance the two men launched the project.

Their school began well, supported in part by the Khortitsa high school, which furnished textbooks and other educational materials. Despite the disruptions of the civil war, all twenty of the first-year class passed their exams with high marks. The teachers, pupils, and parents looked forward eagerly to the next year's school opening.

Johann's return to Nieder Khortitsa was particularly important for Mother and Father, because it represented the culmination of their dreams to see their children educated, and his presence at home was a huge support in the turbulent times of the civil war. Beyond that, the new village high school allowed them to keep my brother Jacob at home while attending school and thus saved the expense of his board.

During the next few years Johann held several important jobs. First, he was elected chairman of the village soviet, or council, and then he was minister of the village's congregation. For a year and a half (1920–1) he resumed teaching, but a new Soviet decree forcing all minister-teachers to give up their school positions aborted his career. Shortly thereafter, during the famine, Johann worked for almost a year with the local branch of the American Mennonite Relief Administration. After his emigration to Canada with his family, he began a long and productive career with Mennonite organizations in his adopted home.

The 'Second' Family's Schooling

With Johann successfully trained, Father then turned his attention to his 'second' family's education. Mariechen finished the six-year elementary curriculum in five years and entered the Khortitsa high school for girls (*Mädchenschule*) in 1906. She lived in Rosental with Grandmother Pauls, who by that time was boarding female students (Lutheran and Catholic, as well as Mennonite) who came from all over southern Russia. This arrangement exposed Mariechen to a broader world as well as saved our parents the extra cost of board.

In 1910, when Mariechen graduated, few Mennonite girls studied beyond high school. Although our parents discussed the possibility of educating her to become a teacher, there were virtually no positions open to women, and so it was hard to justify the expense to send her to the Alexandrovsk *gimnaziia.* This was regrettable, for she would have made a superb teacher. I suspect, too, that our parents based their decision on the fact that my brother Heinrich was then in high school, and they could not afford the expense of room, board, and tuition for two children. Finally, Father needed help in his expanding grain business and, by age sixteen, Mariechen was his primary assistant, and working with more aplomb and perspicacity than any of his sons would ever muster.

Illness aborted Heinrich's educational career. He was a bright boy, and the only one of my siblings who showed interest in taking over Father's store. So it was natural for him to enroll in the Khortitsa boys high school as soon as he completed the elementary grades, in 1911. Unfortunately, his chest pains intensified, and he was often too weak to attend classes or missed them while visiting the doctor. The following summer our parents sent him to Orenburg for a health cure. There his diet of *kumys* – fermented mare's milk – and the dry desert air seemed to assuage his chest pains, but shortly thereafter he returned home and his health declined. Unable to maintain his studies, Heinrich dropped out of school part way through his second year. Although he optimistically intended to manage our general store, in subsequent years his health vacillated, and despite numerous cures (among them drinking copious amounts of ginseng tea) he ran it only sporadically until political conditions of 1917 doomed the enterprise entirely.

With my older siblings now schooled, it was my turn. I suppose I was somewhat inclined to rebel in school. It was not that I did not like school, for I enjoyed it immensely, and did well in my studies. History was my favourite subject, although I also liked literature and folklore, and never tired of Grandmother Pauls's stories of past experiences on Khortitsa Island. I have to admit that in high school I occasionally procrastinated in doing assignments, although not often, because the teachers did not tolerate such behaviour. My procrastination was probably a form of rebellion, for I was tired of hearing that I should emulate Johann and Mariechen's excellent attainments.

The day I started high school is still vivid in my mind. It was not an auspicious start. I knew that Father had made arrangements for me to room and board with *Hottentot Panna*, where Johann and Heinrich boarded for portions of their high school days. I have no idea why the students had nicknamed Mr Penner thus, although it had something to do with their dissatisfaction with the food. The Sunday noon meal was the main problem, for no matter what season of the year it might be, it was always the same – *Rollkuchen.* There was never any other dish, and we were *so* dissatisfied when returning from church the smell of frying *Rollkuchen* greeted us before we even reached the steep incline leading to the Penner home. Added to this was my trepidation about the home's location in the slightly tough Tomakovka district of Rosental, where factory and mill workers lived.

An argument I had earlier with a peasant boy named Petrushka sharpened my queasy feelings that first day. The boy was my age, a relative of Marika, the Ukrainian peasant woman who had worked for us for years, and Father had just engaged him to care for his horses and drive him around on his grain-buying trips, the jobs I used to do during the summer. The reason for our fisticuffs has long escaped me, but its reality is still with me. Father, on entering the stable and instructing us to harness the team and be ready for imminent departure, demanded to know the basis of the quarrel. I responded evasively; not so Petrushka, who replied that he was angry at my good fortune, that having finished six years of school I now had the opportunity for even more, while he had only had two years of school in Razumovka. I must point out that the Orthodox church prohibited Petrushka from attending Nieder Khortitsa's schools for fear of contamination with Protestant ideas. Even so, en route Father lectured me endlessly on my fortunes as compared with those of the local peasant boys. How often I had heard that, and how much more often I would hear it in the next few years!

Thus, I entered high school in 1913 and finished four years later. While there I boarded with *Hottentot Panna* for two and a half years, then roomed at two other boarding houses in Rosental. I received a small stipend (about twenty-five rubles) from the volost scholarship fund until the demands to support the alternative services in 1914 obliterated the fund. Many of the most prosperous farmers in Nieder Khortitsa resented my having been a community-supported *Kolonies-Jung*, and one, Peter Siemens, who could have easily supported a dozen students, stopped me on the street and inquired if I was not ashamed of having accepted a student grant. I said no. After all, my grades were good and my stipend small. Moreover, since 1903, our parents had had at least one, at times two, of their children in high school. Although it did not occur to me at the time, but only years later in Canada and the United States when I was grateful for further scholarships, I often thought about how much more help our prosperous farmers could have given to educate the less fortunate children in our village.

In the early summer of 1917, when it was uncertain whether the Khortitsa Teachers' Training Seminary (which had been transformed into a hospital) would get back its building, Father packed me off to Barvenkovo to take preparatory lessons before entering its school of commerce. The city was an important railroad junction next to a large peasant village in the Kharkov guberniia, and several large Mennonite flour mills were located there. My brother Gerhard worked as an accountant in one of them.

I had no desire to study commerce, nor to enter a business career, but Father realized that Heinrich's health would never improve enough for him to take over the family business. A test of wills ensued between Father and me. Of course, I did not contest openly, for in those days children did not fight head-on with their parents, but some conflict was inevitable. After all, he had lectured me so often to hold fast to my principles, to maintain my individuality, and to stick to my guns unless the fair interests of others demanded compromise. This situation, I felt, warranted just that. Father and I were so much alike that a clash was certain. Both of us were the shortest of several brothers; both of us were tireless; and both of us persevered with unusual tenacity in pursuing our goals. In fact, close relatives asserted that the only difference between us was that Father had complete control of himself, whereas I would explode on occasion. In the end, Father's will prevailed. However, my business education lasted a brief seven weeks, cut short by a tragic incident in Barvenkovo (described later). Then, much to my relief, Father fetched me home.

Fortunately, the Khortitsa teachers' seminary opened shortly after my return, and so I was able to realize my dream in education. Virtually all our prewar instructors were back, teaching either in the teachers' seminary or the adjacent high school. Some taught in both. I most enjoyed the courses that the head teacher, Heinrich Heinrichovich Epp (better known as *Chichikov*) taught. His manner put students at ease. Slouching in his chair behind the desk, his hair tousled, utterly at ease with himself and the world, usually with a preoccupied, occasionally anticipatory expression of humour on his face, he would look up from some scribbled notes, and his soft musical voice would bring student hubbub to an instant stop. His Russian literature class was superb, especially covering the nineteenth-century golden age of Russian prose and poetry. His occasional detours into Russian history lent further interest to his discussions of Tolstoy, Turgenev, Dostoevskii, or Gogol. Epp also excelled in his class on teaching methods, where his critiques of our initial teaching efforts were very constructive.

My own initial foray into teaching was a fiasco, and must have appeared even worse because it followed the performances of Jacob Penner, the brightest of my classmates, and of Jacob Pauls, who was a born teacher. While Chichikov's comments on my performance were severe, they were so constructive that I still remember them with gratitude seven decades later.

In stark contrast, I feared Chichikov's brother, Dietrich Heinrichovich Epp (known as *Eppski*), as did many of my fellow students. He had a no-nonsense attitude that the students met with deference. When he asked questions he expected a straightforward response, whether right or wrong. And you could expect a chewing out if you tried to bluff. His presence on the playground was equally intimidating. There was something of the instantly obeyed platoon commander about him, straight as a ramrod, ready to bark an order. My most memorable experience with him occurred after I had cut classes one Monday, after attending the Sunday funeral for the minister in our home village. When I showed up on Tuesday morning, Epp glared at me and wanted to know why I had not been in class the preceding day. To my response that I had stayed home after the funeral, he exploded: 'The funeral was on Sunday, not Monday. What a lackadaisical attitude towards study!' Perhaps I had it coming, but even decades later, when I occasionally encountered him in his newspaper office in Rosthern, Canada, I felt uneasy in his presence.

I graduated from the teachers' seminary in the spring of 1920 and began teaching in my home village. There were four of us teachers that first year, including Kornelius Grunau and my brother Johann. These two were promised the munificent annual payment of ten bushels of wheat, or their equivalent. I was to be paid eight bushels.

The last of my parents' children, Jacob, finished elementary school in 1917. He, like Johann, had a vast interest in nature, and I remember the two often studying my elder brother's herbaria. There was, of course, no question that Jacob would follow tradition and enter the Khortitsa high school. But the family's fortunes had declined steadily throughout the war, and by 1917 were indeed precarious. How could our parents support two boys away from home? The resolution to this dilemma appears in a subsequent chapter. Jacob's educational achievements stand above all of the siblings, not just for his world-wide recognition in entomology, but also for the increased challenges he faced. Although orphaned in 1920, Jacob finished school in Khortitsa, then continued as an émigré in Canada, and then at Cornell University, where he obtained his doctorate.

From 1903 to 1920 our family always had one, and often two, children attending school in Khortitsa, a record no other Nieder Khortitsa family equalled. It was, therefore, natural that Father and Mother often looked back with satisfaction upon our achievements. How unfortunate that they did not have the opportunity to see three of their sons in the teaching profession. Had times been different they might have even seen Mariechen in a teaching career, as well.

The Education of Life

Much of the education that my siblings and I received was of the practical sort that we learned at home. Father had few illusions about life. His philosophy was that little came your way except through your own efforts. Furthermore, he preached, if you sometimes made mistakes, and lost out, you should not blame others, nor gloat when someone who had mistreated you later came to you asking for help. He practised what he preached.

For example, in 1909 two Russian surveyors came to Nieder Khortitsa to survey a series of narrow valleys branching off the broad one through which the Nizhniaia Khortitsa stream meandered towards the Dnieper. Several of these off-shoots on the north side were badly eroded, steep ravines. The surveyors, who I imagine were from the Forestry Department, made preliminary surveys of the areas most urgently needing conservation – ditching, draining, and tree planting. The Mennonite bigwigs could not endure the thought of a Russian official presuming to teach them how to plant trees. So they asked Father to drive the officials to areas they intended to survey. As Father had a team of horses, but no spring wagon (*Federwagen*), he borrowed one from a farmer, and needing help with the measuring tape, asked me to come along. I do not recall whether my Father ever mentioned the fee he was paid, but I remember his satisfaction in telling Mother that, while so many of the local farmers and the *Schulz* would not sell him their grain, they were only too glad to hire him so that they would not have to deal with these Russian surveyors.

This experience reinforced a lesson that Father had always endeavoured to teach his family – if work is honourable and must be done, it can be done, and should never be regarded as beneath your dignity. We were to observe this on countless occasions after 1917–18, in both the Old World and the New. Mother reinforced this. How often I recall her reciting from Schiller's '*Das Lied von der Glocke*' to me (or to Mariechen who, like me, was prone to rebel at times):

Man must go out
Into the hostile world,
Must work and strive,
Must plant and create,
Contrive, amass,
Must wager and risk
To gain fortune.

(Der Mann muss hinaus
Ins feindliche Leben
Muss wirken und streben,
Muss pflanzen und schaffen

Erlisten, erraffen,
Muss wetten und wagen
Das Glück zu erjagen).

The Higher Education of Other Village Youths

Few Nieder Khortitsa parents shared my father's prescient sense that education in general, and a teaching career in particular, might provide their children with a safety net in a world soon to collapse. Some farmers sneered openly at Father's compulsion, but most were simply indifferent. Two small factions, however, acknowledged the value of an extended education. The first was a set of financially secure families. Several of their children, swept along with the mill fever epidemic, studied flour milling in Germany.[1] None of them finished the prescribed course, and they returned home with little more than fancy student uniforms and other paraphernalia common to German youth organizations. Aside from drinking songs, they seemed to have learned little else.

A few other young men were schooled within the Russian higher education system, the foremost being Kornelius Grunau, mentioned earlier. At least two young men went beyond the Mennonite schooling system: Abram Epp (Grunau's cousin) took a commercial course in Kharkov and Kornelius Kethler, son of a local windmill owner, attended school in Moscow. After Abram Epp returned to Nieder Khortitsa in 1917, his brother Peter and a cousin, Heinrich Sawatzky, also a son of a local farmer and longtime Mennonite minister (Jacob Sawatzky), joined in a series of speculative business ventures. With the constant changes of political regimes during the next three years the fortunes of these ventures fluctuated violently. At times they made enormous paper profits, but in the end they lost everything when the new 'government' expropriated them.

A second, smaller group of youths became teachers. It is a measure of how poorly valued the teaching profession was in my village that each of them was marked with physical or social stigmata. Dietrich Warkentin, my brother Johann's good friend, was lame, and Abram Mantler and Franz Unger came from 'the wrong side of the tracks.' Dietrich was the son of a once-prosperous farmer whose venture into the lumber business had failed. His father's disapproval of Dietrich's desire to teach produced a rift between the two, so Dietrich left our village to teach in Arkadak. His two brothers, both well-read but narrow-minded autodidacts, were similarly disinclined towards farming, but for some reason did not pursue a formal education.

The careers of Abram Mantler and Franz Unger illustrate some of the class discrimination in our village. Abram was the son of a poor widow, whose husband may have been a craftsman or one of the numerous river boatmen. I remember her well, because she frequented our home and I often accompanied my mother when she took food to their cottage when family members were ill. Both then, and later when I roomed with Abram during my first year in high school, I recognized that the members of the Mantler family all had an air of quiet dignity about them that seemed to bespeak an easier mode of life in the past. Yet Abram's *Nippaenja* background prevented him from obtaining a teaching position close to home, and it was not until after the revolution that the Young People's Organization (*Jugendverein*)[2] accepted him as a member. I assume that Abram may have received modest financial assistance from some farm family in addition to a volost stipend, because his mother was too poor to pay his room and board. Franz Unger's family was related to several of the village's wealthier families, but they themselves were poor and disaffected – one of his brothers was an alcoholic and two others were executed by the Cheka (Soviet secret police) as one-time bandits. His father was a teamster-boatman who occasionally hauled grain for my father. The income they derived from this labour was insufficient to send Franz to high school, so he obtained a teaching certificate without a degree, which at least enabled him to teach in a *Judenplan*[3] village.

After the civil war, both Franz Unger and Abram Mantler were deeply committed to providing their poor Mennonite compatriots with the same educational opportunities that the children of the formerly wealthy farmers enjoyed. In the early 1920s, they saw promise in the new regime's reforms and so felt it was their mission to stay in the Soviet Union, rather than emigrate to Canada. That was a tragic mistake. I saw Franz for the last time at a teachers' conference in Khortitsa in 1921 or 1922. During the breaks I spoke with him and several fellow teachers from similarly poor backgrounds, all of whom deplored the old Mennonite establishment that had made their education so difficult. However, for the most part they shared an enthusiasm for the post-1917 changes. The German communist who chaired the meeting was one of many expelled from his country who had found a haven in the Soviet Union. Since the Soviet government had to employ these émigrés somewhere, it placed them in the schools for ethnic minorities. This particular man had no qualifications, but he glibly spoke on the 'complex system,'[4] a new educational theory that the official party line believed would lift the Russian illiterate masses to heights surpassing anything the bourgeoisie (*burzhui*, at the time the term had an infinitely worse connotation than the term *kapitalist*) countries of the West had achieved.

In an enigmatic letter I received from Franz Unger in 1983 (my first contact in more than sixty years) I learned something of his life in the Soviet Union. After a stint in the *Judenplan* schools he taught in numerous schools in the Krivoi Rog and Kamenka districts. Although he seems to have escaped the early Stalinist purges, he was sent into exile in central Siberia during the Second World War. Cryptically, he noted that at times he had 'lived in separation' and that he had met some of my relatives 'in camp.' His caution veiled the details, but the meaning of his comments was clear. His letter also described Abram Mantler's fate. He had taught in the Arkadak Settlement, where he was also elected to the Mennonite ministry. This dual role of teacher-minister later caused his dismissal from teaching. This was common treatment during the Soviet days, as were his exile and death in the Gulag.

PART FOUR

Fading Hopes: War and Revolution

CHAPTER SEVENTEEN

The Outbreak of War

In the summer of 1914 our family's future looked bright. Grandmother Rempel had died the previous November, but her passing seemed as much relief as loss – her health had been failing rapidly during the previous year, and she had often expressed her desire for relief from life's burdens. Otherwise, everyone in the extended family was healthy and in good spirits. The future of the eldest children seemed secure. Neta and her husband, Jacob Pankratz, lived in Arkadak and had avoided many of the difficulties that most homesteaders in the daughter colonies faced. Their eldest daughter, who had been frail since birth, was thriving, which relieved Mother and Mariechen from the burden of making periodic trips to Arkadak to tend the couple's children while they built their home. Gerhard, who had often been in financial difficulties, had a secure bookkeeping job.

Father's grain business was flourishing, as it had been for the past several years. This was despite the Balkan Wars (1912–1913) and despite a dispute with a grain trader who falsified the records of his wheat sales. The case went to court and father won, saving his business from catastrophic loss. Mariechen was Father's indispensable assistant, and Heinrich's heart condition was improved greatly – at least his chest caused him less pain and he no longer coughed up blood – so he was helping Father in the less-taxing aspects of the business. I was eager to start my second year at the high school in Khortitsa while Jacob was happily enrolled in the local primary school. Mother was the hub of our universe and the person who stabilized the busy household and business. As always, she was in excellent health, and her high spirits seldom wearied.

Completion of our new homestead capped the family's satisfaction that summer. It was not only new and large, but also more private than our old home (see Map 5, page 122). There the neighbours on both sides could look directly into our courtyard and so observe all the family's activities. This made us feel as if we were always on stage, especially because we were busy unloading and reloading grain in and out of the *Spitja* from spring until autumn. Once this building was full, we would temporarily store the excess in the open, or if the grain became damp, shovel it back and forth to air-dry. When we failed to detect weed seeds in someone's grain before the whole lot was unsacked, we had to winnow it in the yard.

The worst aspect of this was that the head of the household on one side, Peter Siemens, was a wealthy farmer with unlimited leisure and quite assertive views. Although we were close friends with his wife and children, he was another proposition. No matter what the subject or activity, this self-appointed inspector ambled over to comment, ostentatiously puffing at a Havana cigar held in a gold-rimmed holder and invariably wearing a Panama hat, yellow silk jacket, and gold watch chain stretched across his tubby stomach. He looked, we thought, like a jaundiced bulldog, and we called him Bulldog Siemens. Then he bought a Saint Bernard to scare the peasants, after which we called him Saint Bernard Siemens.

On the surface my father seemed immune to the neighbour's taunting comments, but it must have irked him. Siemens left no doubt that he was one of the old established families in Nieder Khortitsa, while Father had come from one of the lower orders. Perhaps Siemens was trying to nettle Father because about a decade earlier he, too, had begun trading grain and had built himself a big *Spitja* on one side of his yard. This enterprise offered Father little competition – it turned out to be more of a weekend hobby for our neighbour than a thriving enterprise.

Whatever the reason, throughout the First World War Siemens maintained his superior air. For much of the war we feared that the government would apply the land liquidation decrees (described in Chapter 18) to us, take our lands and send us to Siberia. If this happened, our neighbour repeated incessantly, he and his family would be evacuated in a train furnished with sleeping compartments, while our family would be moved with the lower-class people – in freight cars.

But if the man's disdainful remarks did not ruffle Father, they certainly irked Mariechen, who was the one who checked and weighed the grain. Worse still, etiquette prevented her from displaying anger towards this elderly man. Representatives of the grain buyers (*priiomshchiki*) also had to show some restraint at Siemen's condescending tone, particularly if they were – and they were more often than not – Jewish. The teamsters, however, were unbeholden to the man and ready to tell him where to go if he did not mind his own business.

The position of our new home put a stop to this nosy neighbour's visits. The house and large *Spitja* were built right along the sidewalk of the village's main street, with the storage building on the corner. This configuration created a semi-enclosed courtyard. All the loads were brought in from the side street, and our yard itself was virtually free of business traffic. The stable and barn were also built close to one of the interior borders, so that side was relatively private as well. Moreover, neither of our new neighbours, one a teamster and the other a landless cottager, showed any interest in either our business or family affairs.

Alternative Service at the Outbreak of War

My brother Johann travelled through European Russia during the summer of 1914. The previous year he had visited Kiev, Moscow, and St Petersburg. This time he went eastward to the Central Volga region. After stopping in Nizhnii Novgorod, he took the train to Arkadak to stay with our sister Neta and her husband. En route, in July 1914, he met one of the top leaders of the Constitutional Democratic party in the State Duma (I do not recall whether it was Miliukov or Rodichev). Johann, who favoured the Kadets, pressed him for his views on political matters, and whether the Sarajevo incident would spark war. Events soon answered that question, although I do not recall the Russian politician's reply.

Wild rumours that bandied between the peasants and tradesmen congesting Arkadak's street engulfed Johann as soon as he stepped off the train. Some speculated that war was breaking out with Great Britain. Others said no, it must be with France and Germany. Some even suspected that Mother Russia would go to war with Japan again. Seized with apprehension about the imminent war, Johann checked his passport and saw the notation: 'Assigned to army reserve status at the time of draft in 1911.' Until then, he had scarcely considered the meaning of this. Now it became clear. Over the next few days, as facts slowly dispelled the rumours, Johann watched the melee of the first groups of reservists departing for the front – youths exhilarated with vodka and visions of the glorious deeds they would do for the Tsar, followed by throngs of anguished mothers, sweethearts, and wives.

Dispirited, Johann returned home and there found his mobilization orders to report to Ekaterinoslav on 3 September. For the next few weeks, preparing Johann for what we assumed would be a brief stint became the focus of family activities, including such details as finding him a water-repellent rucksack and a louse-comb. Early on the morning of 2 September, a string of straw-lined rack-wagons rolled into our silent village to pick up the first group of draftees. One stopped by our gate where we waited with Johann. I recall Father managing a hearty, 'Well son, I hope you'll be back home within three months.' Johann mustered a light-hearted tone that did not fit his prescient words: 'After three years, Father.' Mother whispered, 'God be with you,' and kissed him farewell. Then he was gone. It was more than three years before we saw him again.

In peacetime, Mennonite men traditionally spent their three years of alternative service at forestry stations (*Forsteien*), but it was clear that 'army reserve status' now meant they would serve in some war-related capacity, presumably as medical orderlies. Soon thousands of young Mennonite men signed up for such posts in agencies operated by the All-Russian Zemstvo Union (*Vserossiiskii zemskii soiuz* or *VZS*), the All-Russian Union of Cities (*Vserossiiskii soiuz gorodov* or *VSG*), the Russian Red Cross, the United Council of the Nobility, and several smaller organizations. Thousands more Mennonite men continued to serve in the established forestry stations, in the Department of Road Construction, or on experimental farms.

Johann served his first two years on the All-Russian Zemstvo Union (*VZS)* hospital train number 194 and then was transferred to the hospital train headquarters in Moscow. There he served with about seventy-five other Mennonites (mostly from the Khortitsa Settlement) on the staff of the agency chief, Prince Boris Saltykov. After the February Revolution, in 1917, Johann worked primarily as a mediator, arbitrating disputes between Mennonite and non-Mennonite members of the hospital staffs.

Gerhard's poor vision, his faint heart murmur, and large family (he had five children by then) kept him out of the draft. Heinrich's more serious heart murmur kept him from serving, too. Jacob and I were too young for service, although I surely would have been called up in the summer of 1917 or 1918 had the Old Regime not collapsed when it did. Many of the men in my extended family served until the revolution.[1]

The conscription of Mennonites continued from September 1914 until early 1917. In this period, about 40 per cent of the, perhaps, 200 draftable men (between the ages of nineteen and forty-two), of Nieder Khortitsa served in one fashion or another. From across the Russian Empire, more than 13,000 of the roughly 33,000 eligible Mennonite men served. Unfortunately, inequalities existed regarding where the men served. Some were financial. For example, funds from the *VZS*, *VSG*, Red Cross, United Council of the Nobility, and other, smaller agencies supported the men who served as military orderlies. Those who served with the Red Cross were the luckiest, because at least some received more pay than the regulations required. In contrast, the Mennonite community as a whole had to provide at least 80 per cent of the support – including food, clothing, transportation, and housing – for the 6,500 men who served in other government establishments, such as the forestry camps and road crews. This burden was in addition to the increased local, district, and national taxes that the war effort entailed. And while theoretically the government supplied the remaining 20 per cent of the men's support, paying them 20 kopeks per day for each day they actually worked, payments were often tardy.

Other inequalities had a more personal and direct effect. Men stationed on the Caucasian front, or assigned to guard forests, rightly complained that they could not get leave, even when there was a serious hardship at home.[2] The forestry workers may have been miffed that they served in a dull, remote region while the medical corpsmen's jobs carried an aura of humanitarianism and heroism. Of more dire import, as the war progressed inflation eroded the 20-kopek allowance to a farcical pittance. In late 1916 or early 1917, the government became increasingly delinquent in paying its share of the food and clothing allowances. Then it withdrew all payments to non–ethnic Russian servicemen. This meant that our servicemen's families had to make up the shortfall which, obviously, hit the poorer families hardest.

Allegations of preferential treatment surfaced, and they were not without basis. Teachers, other professionals, and wealthy men received priority placement. For example, in the Khortitsa Settlement, and specifically in the village of Khortitsa, several servicemen charged that all the local teachers mobilized in the autumn of 1914 were assigned to the Mennonite hospital established in the recently completed teachers' seminary building. The men of several local manufacturing families, among them the Hildebrands and Wallmanns, were equally fortunate. Their assignments allowed them to live at home with their families and to continue their professional careers, at least on a limited basis. A similar situation occurred at the headquarters of the Russian Red Cross in Ekaterinoslav, where many of the teachers from the nearby Nikolaipol Settlement and Kronsgarten high schools (as well as from nearby estates) filled key staff positions. In 1916, when most of the headquarters was transferred to Odessa, the remaining staff members were usually men from nearby homes. In many instances these favourable assignments were undoubtedly the result of the recipients' special qualifications. In others, the complaints were justified. Two of my Rosental uncles in the service harboured this suspicion, and I am certain that they were not the only Rosental and Khortitsa servicemen who did.[3]

Yet despite these quibbles, most of the men who served in the alternative services with whom I spoke at the time, or even decades later, expressed a deep sense of satisfaction that they had been privileged to help in a Christian fashion in a time of conflict – to bind wounds rather than inflict them – and they were grateful that the government had honoured its pledge to allow us to exercise freedom of conscience. One of their few regrets was that authorities, at the behest of the Orthodox church, had strictly prohibited their evangelizing among the wounded and sick they tended, and only with the fall of the Old Regime could they establish relations with the Christian Soldiers Union, which represented Russian sectarians such as Baptists, Shtundists, and Evangelical Christians.

The Early Impact of the War

The carefree summer days of 1914 vanished rapidly. Almost immediately the war began to damage grain exports from southern Russia. The closing of the Dardanelles at first depressed prices for cereal grains, flour, and other by-products, but within several months the prices rose again as the government increased purchases to feed its burgeoning armed forces. Such benefits were soon obliterated by a combination of factors that stifled the grain market – inflation and the Russian government's restrictions and virtual monopoly on trade. Father found it increasingly difficult to stay in business, especially as the control of buying, storing, milling, and selling became concentrated in the hands of people with influence in the regulatory agencies. As 1915 progressed, Father's problems were exacerbated by restrictive government policies aimed at hampering the business of traders from German-speaking regions.

Father's business survived through 1915. The Khortitsa Settlement produced a near-normal crop that season, even though many farmers had been mobilized and the government had requisitioned many of our horses. These requisitions hit the poorer farmers harder than the wealthier ones, for they relied exclusively on horses as their draft animals, while the wealthier used oxen as well.

The government's requisition of horses furnished me with one of the many wartime experiences that I still remember. It was either the late spring or late autumn of 1915, a slack time for farming. Obeying government orders, Father travelled to Nikolaipol where our horses were to be inspected by the army. Those deemed worthy would be 'selected' for cavalry remounts and the artillery. However, there was little chance that they would want Father's horses, and indeed the army rejected our nags.

Father took me along, and perhaps because I had never visited the Nikolaipol area (which is north of Khortitsa), he decided to show me the various Mennonite estates (*khutora*) filling the district. We visited Mother's former brother-in-law, Heinrich Heinrichs, in Eichenfeld (Dubovka), where I became fast friends with two cousins, Heinrich and Kornelius. I was awestruck by that family's prosperity, although I secretly felt smug in observing that their horses did not compare well with the beauties that a few of the farmers in our village possessed. We stopped briefly at Reinfeld to visit another cousin and then left for Petersdorf, a small, beautiful hamlet where Mother's good friend Maria (née Siemens) Peters and her husband lived. From there we rode past two of the Wallmann and Heinrichs estates, stopping at neither. My father pointed out the affluence evidenced by their landscaped gardens, impressive structures, and well-tended fields; he also drew my attention to the stark contrast between these estates and the few Ukrainian peasant villages interspersed among them in this veritable Mennonite paradise that stretched roughly twenty-five miles west of the Dnieper and fifty miles to the north of Khortitsa Settlement. Father also voiced his concern that so few of his Mennonite contemporaries seemed to be aware that their good fortune could instantly crumble to nothing if the tsarist government collapsed. That the Mennonite state within a state could survive another revolt like that following the Russo-Japanese War was unlikely. Father felt sure that the next time would be far worse – and that there would be no Stolypin able to quell it.

Indeed, the fate of these beautiful hamlets just four years later was grim. Eichenfeld was totally destroyed in 1919 by the peasant anarchist bandits led by Nestor Makhno and known as Makhnovites. Heinrich Heinrichs was the first of more than eighty Eichenfeld residents to be slaughtered on a single day in October. Reinfeld was similarly attacked, although cousin Johann Rempel, at least, survived. So too, the Makhnovites plundered Petersdorf and murdered several men, including Johann Peters.

1916

As the war that was supposed to have been won within a few months ground into its third year, everyone's life became darker. The loyalty of Mennonites to their homeland remained unshaken, but many began to doubt the superiority of an autocratic monarchy over a democracy. No one could avoid noticing the government's appalling disorganization, its profligate waste of food and material, and the unbridled corruption. Most had heard the rumours of Grigorii Rasputin's immense and vulgar machinations and his evil influence on the Tsarina. They were also aware of the savage criticism that many of the centrist and liberal State Duma deputies heaped on the government. Only a few of us read Russian newspapers, which were rigidly censored anyway, and our German-language newspapers had been proscribed. Nevertheless, most of us received letters from relatives serving as medical orderlies at the front, and these painted a bleak picture of the deteriorating morale of the troops and the generally desperate situation. Then came the catastrophic news that the government would apply the land liquidation provisions to us. This was on the ground that we were 'German by acculturation' if not of German origin. This could mean exile to the eastern territories.

The protracted war essentially destroyed my father's business. The confiscation of horses and conscription of manpower left the farmers no alternative but to cultivate less land. Furthermore, after the government consolidated virtually all aspects of the grain trade and put it in the hands of a few companies, Father had to depend increasingly on favours from the Jewish merchants he had dealt with in the past or from the giant Mennonite concerns like the Niebuhr mills. This often amounted to nothing more than storing their excess wheat in our *Spitja*, which otherwise stood empty most of the time. As income became increasingly meagre, as well as uncertain, Father supplemented our family resources by buying eggs and butter from local farmers and peddling them in Alexandrovsk.

We soon felt the impact. Our team of dappled grey horses, recently rejected by the cavalry, was sold to a farmer in Schöneberg. Our first decent wagon was, too. In place of the team, Father bought a good-looking, but lame, black mare, which he kept only briefly before selling her to a peasant in Razumovka for a few rubles. Father replaced her with another black mare, this one possessing what he looked for in a horse – four sturdy legs and a strong body. She was so undistinguished in appearance that neither the government, nor even the bandits who pillaged our area in 1918 and 1919, requisitioned her. The same was true for Father's 'new' wagon, pieced together from parts cannibalized from sundry others. Both the wagon and horse left Heinrich and me mortified, for only the poorest peddlar would have driven such a nag and contraption.

In spite of the strained economy and many inconveniences, our life maintained its prewar equanimity to a large degree. Our family did not suffer in any way, nor could we say that we were 'on short rations' (*Schmalhans war bei uns Küchenmeister*). We rarely ate beef, but we had chicken and pork several times a week. Mother rationed butter and eggs, but there was no lack of home-grown vegetables, and fruit was free for the picking from June through late autumn and bountiful, as dried or canned, in the off-season. While we could not raid the pantry freely, we always had plenty of home-baked white and dark bread and watermelon syrup to spread on it. In terms of other consumer goods like clothing, if my memory serves, we fared about as well as other common Mennonite folk. When I consider our experiences in the years that were to follow, and long before the famine of 1920 to 1922, it seems to me that we lived in paradise (*Schlaraffenland*) during the early war years.

CHAPTER EIGHTEEN

Harassment and the Confiscation of Property

Our family lived in modest material comfort throughout the war. One issue did cause us great anxiety, however, as indeed it did every Russian Mennonite family: Would the government confiscate our property and/or exile us to the eastern territories? Even before the First World War some officials in both the government and the Orthodox church vocally opposed the colonists and their rich holdings. Then, as war broke out, the Russian ultra-nationalists gained further prominence, and as they did, colonist bashing became ever more virulent. By early autumn 1914, government corruption was obvious, as was its military unpreparedness. Certainly, tragic Russian defeats in the Masurian Lake region in September 1914 revealed the hollowness of early chauvinistic slogans such as, 'We will smother the enemy by our hats,' that is, by numerical superiority (*shapkami vraga zabrosaem*). Urban unrest was palpable. Peasants renewed their vociferous demands for land redistribution. The gentry and the nationalists recognized the government had an easy solution to both problems: seize the properties of the German-speaking colonists, on the ground that they were of 'enemy descent' – defining that term broadly – and thus, create a dragnet to whisk away as many of them as possible.[1]

On 2 February 1915, the government issued two land liquidation decrees. First came Article 350, On Land Ownership and Land Tenure of Certain Categories of Russian Subjects of Austrian, Hungarian, or German Emigration. Second was Article 351, On the Liquidation of Land Ownership and Land Tenure by Russian Subjects of Austrian, Hungarian, or German Emigration in the Boundary Zones.[2] The language of the decrees was deliberately vague. Up to the very eve of the government's collapse in 1917, neither the Council of Ministers, the

Ministry of the Interior, nor the First Department of the Senate (the supreme court) ever defined what certain sections of the decrees meant, nor had they resolved any of the serious controversies that arose in the process of forcing the sale of property. The results were at times so contradictory that the decrees were likened to rubber bands, which could be stretched or relaxed as deemed opportune at different times by different civil servants. In the Duma itself, deputies outraged by this broad miscarriage of justice, referred to these measures as illiterate decrees (*negramotnye ukazy*). Their protests were to no avail. Instead, the government enlarged on them, in December 1915, in the summer of 1916, and again in February, 1917.

The big question for Mennonites was, would the decrees apply to them? Would they be labelled as 'German,' as various chauvinistic newspapers and extreme nationalistic leaders assumed? Or would they be identified as 'Dutch,' as they themselves had long maintained?

Fortunately, and contrary to many Mennonite writings, relatively little Mennonite property was expropriated prior to the collapse of the Old Regime. Several things explain this. First, the initial confiscations took place only within a narrow boundary region, in which few Mennonite properties lay. Unfortunately, one of this small number belonged to Father's first wife's brother Heinrich, who owned a flour mill in the huge peasant village of Malaia Lepetikha.[3] Mennonites as a whole, however, were not subject to the decrees until August 1916, when the government, indeed, declared Mennonites to be of German descent, and even then the war effort and bureaucratic inertia delayed property appraisals and sales. Furthermore, the Mennonites mounted an aggressive campaign to overturn the application of the decrees to themselves. No sooner were they declared to be German than their leaders sent delegates to Petrograd to argue for our Dutch ancestry. The delegates were armed with an extensive collection of Dutch-related materials: Bibles, old letters, genealogies, books, catechisms, and other religious materials. To this effort, our family donated a treasured family register which, sadly, was never returned. These representatives stressed that the government itself had as often as not identified us to be Dutch, not German origin. Several contemporaneous but unofficial records – mostly diaries – indicate that the delegates took along sufficient money to bribe influential officials in several ministries and to hire a lawyer who supposedly knew his way around the centres of power. There are hints that among those so bribed was acting Minister of the Interior A.D. Protopopov, Rasputin's unsavory protégé. Although bribes were a fact of life, revelation of a payoff to this disreputable man would have discredited the Mennonites' overt actions as well.[4]

Perhaps, too, the government was less zealous in applying the decrees to the Mennonites for economic reasons – tax revenues had declined wherever expropriation had actually taken place. Furthermore, public sentiment was not uniform. Many liberal newspapers and deputies in the Duma denounced the stupidity and criminality of the government's anti-colonist policies. With a lack of consensus at the national level, many local and guberniia zemstvos pleaded with the government to abandon or postpone implementing the decrees. Financial institutions joined the cry, and in the summer of 1916 the Minister of Agriculture assured the colonists that if they planted their lands to the fullest extent possible, they would be permitted to harvest both autumn and spring crops. This put a temporary halt to the decrees.

As 1917 unfolded, however, the situation deteriorated, as central and guberniia governments began to lose authority. Many local officials proceeded on their own to arbitrarily appraise properties at ridiculously low prices. Furthermore, the State Peasant Land Bank, which was the privileged buyer, could set its own prices, irrespective of prior appraisal. This amounted to virtual confiscation, because this institution did not have to pay cash for the property. Rather, it could 'purchase' it with bonds bearing 4.5 per cent interest, redeemable only in twenty-five years, non-transferable, and inheritable only in direct line of succession. Worse, yet, the appraisals were often made by unqualified officials, who had no idea of the property's original cost or current value, the difference between purebred and common livestock, or the value of farm equipment, business inventory, home furnishings, or possessions. The national bank was allowed to deduct 5 to 10 per cent of the appraised value if it felt the farmer had not planted his crops to the fullest extent possible. Another 5 per cent could be deducted, if in *the bank's opinion,* the farmstead did not have adequate kitchenware, fuel, fodder, fertilizer, or reserve grain. Adding insult to injury, the decrees then stipulated that, if the expropriated property would produce more if temporarily left in the original owner's hands, the bank could allow the farmer to remain on the land, provided that he planted the crops and kept the farm in 'proper' condition. In return, the government would provide his family with a subsistence payment. Small wonder that most Mennonites lost confidence in the Minister of Agriculture's promise that they could reap the 1917 spring harvest.

The government also planned to confiscate, rather than purchase, most Mennonite communal property, including schools, teacherages, hospitals, churches, civic buildings, and land reserves. The effort snowballed as local leaders began confiscating other properties. The all-Mennonite school for the deaf and mute (*Taubstummenschule*) in the village of Tiege was forced to surrender its capital fund of 70,000 rubles, and the Khortitsa Settlement its most prized possession, the 1800 Charter of Privileges.

It is impossible to estimate how much property the government expropriated prior to the tsarist collapse. This is partly because of the difficulty in distinguishing Mennonite from non-Mennonite names as published in the local newspapers. Also, the papers often stated that the property had been sold, when in fact it had only been appraised. Without doubt, however, the amount of land to which the decrees might have been applied was enormous – probably at least two to three million dessiatins.

Apart from Father's former brother-in-law, Heinrich Rempel, none of our family lost property under the decrees. However, these odious measures were indirectly responsible for the forced sale of Insel Khortitsa to the city of Alexandrovsk. Everyone in the Khortitsa Settlement regretted the action, but few more than Grandmother Pauls and her family. Her forebears, Jacob Höppner and Peter Hildebrand, had been among the founding families of the island village, and her son Bernhard had purchased the Höppner ancestral farm.

The background to this virtual confiscation went back to the settlement's establishment. At that time, the island was part of the Potemkin estate awarded to the Mennonites, but from the earliest times the settlers had to defend portions of their land against claims by the peasants of Voznesenskoe, situated directly across the Dnieper on its east bank. Their claim involved a small, heavily wooded island situated in what we called the Big Dnieper, its eastern channel. Although the regional court had settled the suit in favour of the Mennonites in 1800, the peasants continued to steal timber from the island. In 1800 Alexandrovsk, situated just south of Voznesenskoe, had been little more than a military fort, but by the end of the nineteenth century Alexandrovsk's rail and river junctions had made it one of the most important trading centres in New Russia. Over the years the river had shifted its main channel, eventually building up several sandy beaches along the island's eastern shore. Beginning in 1910, Alexandrovsk made claims to the largest of these beaches, which were by then heavily wooded. The Mennonites refused to concede the claim, and eventually the issue resulted in a protracted suit in the Ekaterinoslav court. Pending resolution, the city's inhabitants and peasants from nearby villages continued to raid the timber groves. After war broke out, and the Mennonites were labelled to be among those of 'enemy descent,' the city's claims became more insistent and the peasant raids bolder.

Uncle Bernhard Pauls headed the team of Mennonites in their fruitless negotiations with the city of Alexandrovsk. By late 1916, the city representatives insisted that the only way to resolve the contest was for the islanders to sell the entire island, including the village homesteads and all other physical possessions, to Alexandrovsk, which would then lease the holdings back to the Mennonites on a long-term basis. It was clear that the Mennonites would likely become subject to the land liquidation decrees, and therefore, a Mennonite lawyer and several prominent businessmen advised the islanders to agree to the sale.

The city met its financial obligations, but it refused to protect the former owners (now leaseholders) against the increasingly aggressive peasant raids. After several islanders were murdered, the remaining residents realized they would have to abandon their island properties. This affected everyone in the Khortitsa Settlement, but our family felt a particularly keen loss, because it meant giving up two of the extended family's favourite homes: those of Mother's brother Bernhard Pauls and of her cousin Bernhard Hildebrand. The latter property was our family's favourite weekend vacation spot and, as the historic Höppner property, held a prominent place in all our psyches. This house had an immensely serene quality. An attractively tiled oven walled part of the large living room. The other main rooms – the dining room, study, large kitchen, and adjacent summer kitchen – were airy and well lit. A variety of fruit trees, berry bushes, grape vines, and mulberry and walnut trees grew close to the kitchen. Just across the street and perhaps twenty feet beyond lay the Dnieper's sandy beach, which invited swimming any hour of the day from late April to late September. Behind the farm lay the heavily wooded Höppner dale (*Höppnerläajcht*), with its narrow lane leading to the private Höppner family cemetery which was on a high plateau almost in the centre of the island. From here the land rose gently to the north and descended towards the southern lowland, the *Bütendick*, where the youth of Nieder Khortitsa held their May festival, as well as other spring and autumn outings. This spot was typical of southern steppe *plavni*, areas densely wooded with oak, elm, beech, linden, poplar, and willow, interspersed with hay fields and shallow stagnant pools. A narrow estuary connected this lowland with the western arm of the Dnieper, directly opposite part of Nieder Khortitsa.

I visited our cherished island for the last time in 1921. My purpose was to round up my brother's stray cow. The neglect and decay I saw just a few years after Mennonite inhabitants had left their beloved homes was indescribable. Inevitably, the typical Mennonite characterization of things 'Russian' occurred to me: 'Well, isn't that just what you would expect from a rundown Russian farm?' (*Ess daut oba eene rajchte rusche Wirtschauft?*).

Although we lost our beloved island, we Mennonites suffered far less from the land liquidation decrees than did the German Lutheran and Catholic colonists. However, all German-speaking colonists – including the Mennonites – suffered substantial harassment and humiliation. These came from two spheres: the incredibly corrupt machinery of government and, within both lay and church spheres, a chauvinistic yellow press. This group of publishers had labelled Baptist teachings as products of perfidious Albion already years before the war, but they now called them German teachings. Some demagogues even suggested that the government declare all Protestant teachings to be pagan.

As demeaning as these charges were, official corruption nettled more, and proved the Russian proverb concerning bribes (in tsarist days called sinless money and under Bolshevik rule, *kontributsiia*): 'The law is like the tongue of a wagon, which can be turned in many directions, and the more you grease its coupling, the easier it turns.' Over the wartime years, Mennonites often were forced to grease those wheels. For example, in early August 1914, the Khortitsa church held a conference, at which delegates discussed how to contribute money and materials to the Russian Red Cross. As was usual, those attending spoke German, and they opened and closed their sessions with a prayer for the safety and welfare of the royal family. A short time later, the chief of the county (uezd) arrested the church elder, Isaak Dyck, for speaking German, even though the language had not yet been outlawed. He also arrested the Khortitsa district (volost) mayor and executive secretary on the grounds that they had permitted the elder to speak German. All were taken to Ekaterinoslav, where the government threatened to send them into Siberian exile. But after the Khortitsa volost paid a large sum of money to the government official in charge, the men were released.

Officials harassed other clergymen, even one Mennonite minister who concluded his sermon with the Lord's Prayer ('*Dein Wille geschehe*

...'). Only after a long interrogation did the minister manage to convince local police that he had not meant 'Kaiser Wilhelm's will be done.' In another case, a well-known Molochna evangelist, Heinrich D. Braun, managed to escape deportation to Siberia by fleeing to Petrograd, where Assistant Minister of the Interior Prince M.D. Volkonskii shielded him.

Russian religious officials were equally zealous in vindictively labelling someone as German. For example, two Heinrichs brothers, who had years earlier given money to a Russian evangelical congregation for the construction of a meeting house, were arrested and exiled to a northern guberniia of Russia. Similarly, the government told a wealthy Mennonite named Siemens, who had purchased a German airplane in 1913, that he could not fly the plane unless he purchased a special licence, which Siemens refused to do. Although he returned the plane, the governor got even in 1915, arresting Siemens and exiling him for the duration of the war.

Another egregious act concerned a family named Zacharias. Childless, they had adopted a number of orphans, including a Ukrainian peasant child. In accordance with state and church law, the couple raised the child in the Orthodox faith and sent her to the priest in the neighbouring village for weekly instruction. When the family cook, a Ukrainian woman, committed suicide, the priest attending her funeral noticed the young girl, and upon making inquiries, was told of her Ukrainian parentage. A month later the police arrested Mr Zacharias and took the child. Zacharias was sentenced to six months in prison. Relatives advised him to make a contribution to the priest and police, but he refused to do so and served out the sentence.

Village farmers and businessmen were increasingly at the mercy of unscrupulous police who felt uninhibited in the way they ruled over the 'dirty – or disreputable – Germans' (*parshivyie nemtsy*). Most of these acts were caused by allegations too ludicrous to believe. For example, the police searched a farmer's premises looking for a German airplane that they were sure landed there at specific hours of the morning and evening. The plane turned out to be the farmer's cream separator. Or, if on occasion a policeman overheard a farmer speak Low German, he interpreted it as an anti-Russian statement and threatened punishment. Such incidents were, of course, mere excuses to extort money, or a piece of salt pork (*salo*). In the cities, Mennonite businessmen were often blackmailed with claims that their official scales were not in order. Father paid many bribes to clear his three scales, usually with ham, tea, sugar, or a sack of oats for the horse of a shining upholder of the law (*bliustitel poriadka*).

Wartime restrictions were often more annoying than punitive, precisely because no one knew if they were to be observed or if they were only a vehicle for extortion. The situation was aggravated by the on-again, off-again style of enforcement. Just as the population began to think the government had dropped some rule – for example, that we could not hold a church service in German, or that no more than three people could gather – the officials unexpectedly resumed its application, sometimes with vicious force.

The governors of several guberniias (especially of Kherson and Tavrida) were notorious for their own arbitrary acts. Most vengeful was the head of the Ekaterinoslav guberniia, Kolobov, who ordered the Khortitsa volost to surrender the brotherhood's most precious document, the Charter of Privileges, which Tsar Paul had issued on 6 September 1800, apparently on the assumption that its surrender would invalidate its contents. Of course, such an act could not nullify an imperial order, and the document was returned to Khortitsa in 1917. Makhnovites stole it again in late 1919, what happened to it after that remains unknown.

Young men in alternative service certainly knew of the harassment suffered at home. Although it cannot be said that their fellow servicemen discriminated against them, our men resented the fact that their loved ones at home were being treated as second-class citizens – while they themselves were serving their homeland at the front.

The anti-colonist sentiment that was sown among the peasants by the government during the war was to bear bitter fruit for everyone. Some saw clearly the peril that would come. In 1915 to 1916, liberal and leftist members of the Duma repeatedly discussed the possibility that the land liquidation decrees would trigger pogroms against the colonists, and that there would be a new form of the bloody Pugachev terror (*Pugachevshchina*), with consequences just as frightful as those attending that peasant upheaval in the Volga region during the reign of Catherine II. These predictions proved true. Paul Miliukov, the liberal leader of the Kadet party reportedly quoted a peasant spokesman in Saratov region as saying that if the government failed to expropriate the lands of the colonists and distribute them among the peasants, they themselves would one day cut colonists' throats and seize their properties. The anti-German riots in Moscow during June 1915 were equally prophetic. Angry mobs, intent on destroying German businesses, looted and sacked more than 700 stores and offices, but the crowd got out of hand and many of their targets proved to have English, French, and even Russian owners.

What more might be expected of an illiterate population primed by the government about 'perfidious German-speaking colonists' and the need to secure the purity of Russian Orthodoxy? As early as 1916, we saw Ukrainian peasants ride through Nieder Khortitsa, as they did in other Mennonite villages, point to a particular farmstead and say, 'When the revolution comes, that will be my property. I will drive out its owner and seize everything.' By 1916, the peasants of New Russia were in no mood to share the lands they hoped to seize from the colonists, nor to stop at that. Miliukov pointed this out during debates in the Duma, saying, 'He who starts with the properties of the colonists will inevitably end up with yours.' To this, representatives of the gentry and other chauvinists naively rejoined, 'Our peasants know the difference between the property rights of Germans and those of our Russian people.' An openly cynical deputy, Strukov, baldly urged that the land liquidation decrees be extended to the Mennonite lands to deflect peasant unrest away from the nobility. Events after October 1917 proved the bloody truth that the nobility would not be spared the wrath of the peasants. Ironically, Ukrainian peasants pillaged Strukov's estate long before they touched Mennonite villages in the area.

CHAPTER NINETEEN

Revolution and Reform: Challenges to the Old Guards

Most Russian Mennonites felt cautiously optimistic about their future as 1917 began. Rasputin's murder the previous December had removed his malevolent influence over the royal family and its inner circle. In January the government ruled that we would not be subject to the expropriation decrees, so it seemed that our property rights were more secure. On 15 March the tsarist regime collapsed. The new Provisional Government quickly declared sweeping reforms in a Charter of Freedom. These measures included the abolition of the land liquidation decrees, removal of all limitations to Russian citizenship, and the enfranchisement of all men twenty years or older. To further set Russia on a democratic course, the Provisional Government planned to hold elections later that year for delegates to a new Constituent Assembly.

We felt less dread for our future. Nevertheless, it was clear that the new Government held power only tenuously. It was being constantly threatened by forces to both its political right and left, and by local governments and agencies which often paid little heed to central policy. Thus, some local governments continued to appraise Mennonite lands, threatening to expropriate them.[1] Fortunately, virtually no property was actually confiscated. But other forces began to menace Mennonite servicemen. Disgruntled local soviets of soldiers pressed officials to send the alternative servicemen to the front to fight. The provisional government upheld the alternative servicemen's noncombatant status. Still we felt betrayed when it arrested as spies thirty-eight repatriated Mennonite orderlies from the zemstvo hospital train 189.[2]

To the best of my knowledge, there has never been a formal study of how the Mennonites felt about the downfall of the monarchy, but I would guess that opinion was divided, in part along issues of self-interest. Certainly, the small farmers and businessmen were relieved that the expropriation decrees no longer threatened their property. However, the industrialists and the landed gentry felt uneasy, suspecting that the radicalized Russian masses would produce a republican form of government. Under such a regime, they were likely to lose more than they would with a liberalized monarchy in place. The refusal of the Mennonite elite to ally with the Constitutional Democrats in electing delegates to the Constitutional Convention reflects its unyielding conservatism, and especially its fear of that party's mild land reform program. Assuredly, most of our servicemen were overjoyed with the prospect that the new government would bring the war to a rapid close. I believe that the monarchy's downfall also relieved Khortitsa's lay and church leaders. Abram Dyck's diary mentions that the Khortitsa authorities telegraphed Prince Lvov and Mr Rodzianko on 14 March 1917, congratulating the provisional government's leaders and declaring their eagerness to assist in the reconstruction of the country. Dyck also mentions that Elder Johann P. Klassen of the Schönwiese congregation had declared during a sermon: 'It is spring outdoors and spring in our political situation.'

Generally, however, Mennonites were too sober and dispassionate to be swept up in the enthusiasm that possessed much of the Russian intelligentsia. I remember some naive comments, such as, 'Russia has set an example to Western Europe and the entire world in how to bring about the most sweeping political and social change without a bloody revolution.' I do not recall whether the Khortitsa high school teachers shared the intelligentsia's innocent fervour. However, some of us students were greatly affected, and joined enthusiastically in singing well-known revolutionary songs. Students in the Molochna Settlement were probably equally caught up by the mood of the times. Professor B.H. Unruh mentioned that when news of the overthrow reached the School of Commerce in Halbstadt, the students were preparing to march to a nearby Ukrainian village to join crowds of celebrants, when a Russian teacher pleaded with them to stop.[3] Certainly, some astute Mennonites must have felt wary about how the Russian masses would exercise power. My brother Johann mentioned how apprehensive he felt when Count Saltykov told him and a group of his servicemen colleagues, 'some day we shall wade in blood.' Events a few months later proved Saltykov right.

As conservative as the majority of Mennonites were, there is no denying that in the early days of the 'greatest, bloodless revolution,' some of the alternative servicemen were swept by revolutionary sentiment. In many ways their wartime experiences had primed them for this. Widened horizons had jolted many out of their hidebound parochialism, spurious sense of superiority, and air of self-satisfaction. Men stationed in Odessa, Moscow, or Petrograd had become acquainted with the richness of Russian culture – its architecture, literature, music, and theatre. Those who served in the central and western regions of Russia lived in majestic, albeit remote, settings that contrasted dramatically with the treeless steppes of the south. Irrespective of where the men served, they saw for the first time the enormous gulf between the status of their families and that of the Russian peasantry. At home, they had probably referred to their Ukrainian day or seasonal labourers as 'the stupid Russian' (*de domma Russ*), but now they saw daily the bestial treatment that officers meted out to common soldiers, the harsh conditions in which the masses eked out an existence, and the hopelessness they felt of ever achieving the well-being of even a Mennonite small farmer (*Kleinwirt*). Small wonder that many of our young men blamed the old tsarist regime for the urban unrest and soldiers' desertions, and felt relief at the demise of the Romanov dynasty.

The servicemen's criticism did not stop at Mennonite boundaries. They demanded change within the community as well, voicing their dissatisfaction at two informal meetings in Molochna and Moscow, and at three major conferences held between May and August 1917 in Halbstadt and Orloff. Even before the war, many young men were unhappy with the structure of church leadership. They believed that it held a monopoly of delegate positions to the annual sessions of the All-Mennonite General Conference. Furthermore, they felt this body expected the laity to simply rubber stamp its decisions. At that time few of the young men felt free to express their discontent. Now, as revolutionary sentiment filtered down to the servicemen, they voiced their concerns.

In late March or early April 1917, Mennonite servicemen in Moscow dispatched a delegate to the Molochna Settlement to lodge a complaint against Mennonite community leaders over the way they ran the brotherhood's affairs. For obvious reasons, the clergymen who recorded this meeting left sketchy details. Shortly after, however, the servicemen invited three prominent members of the clergy, Professor Benjamin Unruh and H.B. Janz of Molochna, and David H. Epp of Khortitsa, to a follow-up meeting in Moscow. From then on, my brother Johann, who was at this meeting, often referred to the conflicts between the entrenched Mennonite status quo and the young servicemen and intellectuals who desired change in terms of Turgenev's *Fathers and Sons.*

One of the 'fathers' to attend the subsequent Moscow meeting, Professor Unruh, later recorded his reactions to this gathering:

> On the occasion of our visit in Moscow in April we [the Elders] had convinced ourselves that in this field, our society, in the capacity of its responsible institutions, must seize the initiative and hold the reins tightly in its hands. Among the Mennonite corpsmen things fermented strongly, and at the Moscow conference, to which we were invited, we were presented with a project for the reorganization of the General Conference in such a way as to make it concern itself directly with national, cultural, and sociopolitical issues. This we found unhealthy. We took the stand that the church as such address itself solely to the consideration and solution of church matters. However, a Congress, to be sure in close contact with the General Conference and its executive committee, the Committee for Church Affairs, ought to be responsible for the rest of the problems of our national-cultural existence.[4]

According to my brother Johann, Unruh himself presented a talk he had entitled, 'What Is Important Is Not How We Appear, But What We Are' (*Wir wollen nicht Schein, sondern sein*). The servicemen's reaction to Unruh's speech was chilly. Many felt Unruh was too voluble, pompous, assertive, and transparently obvious in his ambition to retain his position of elder or leader (*starshii*). They likewise viewed his suggestion that a Mennonite Congress review matters outside the religious domain as a tactical move to deflect their demands for reduced clerical influence and for more radical changes in the All-Russian Mennonite agencies. Actually, the servicemen wished to change the spirit of the Mennonite 'state' within Russia, and infuse it with a younger, lay generation, as much as they wished to change its form.

In contrast to Unruh's high-handed delivery, Elder David H. Epp electrified the group by speaking in Low German (*Plautdietsch*). H.B. Janz later wrote, 'For a long time the mood remained at the freezing point, until Elder David Epp commenced to talk to them in Low German and about the traditional Mennonite *Plumemooss.* Then the ice was broken, and once more they were happy and light of heart, and they persevered.' Janz mentioned further: 'If dissatisfaction among the servicemen did not make itself felt in prewar times, the situation now was different. It was not that protests or refusal to serve or to pay [the so-called barracks tax] were now being registered. There was, however, intense fermentation.'[5]

The servicemen's dissatisfaction sprang from many sources, but certainly the undemocratic control of the General Conference topped their list. P. Heese, a member of a prominent Ekaterinoslav family, wrote candidly:

> The long sojourn [of our fathers] in undemocratic Prussia and Russia resulted in a development which diverted from the fundamental principle [of democracy]: the General Conference, which dealt not only with spiritual matters, but also with secular affairs, was not a democratically elected organ, but rather a privilege of the ministry. There probably always were people to whom this privilege was a thorn in the eye. However, they lived separated from others and therefore did not oppose it. But now there were hundreds [of Mennonite servicemen stationed in Ekaterinoslav during the war] assembled who influenced each other and decided at last to come to grips publicly with this issue.[6]

The outcome of the Moscow meeting clearly did not satisfy the servicemen, and so further discussions were set to take place in Halbstadt in May and June. The first session, from 3 to 5 May, was a Conference of the Delegates on Alternative Service. Here the young men hoped to vent their dissatisfaction concerning the office of the head, or plenipotentiary, of the Alternative Service System. Theoretically, the conference elected this man each year, but in practice his term was renewable indefinitely. Delegates were either clergymen or men largely chosen by the local clergy, and this meant that the plenipotentiary was their creature. Although the conference determined budgeting and other policies, the plenipotentiary had enormous latitude in their execution. The then-incumbent, David Klassen had held the office for so long that he seemed to have a lifetime sinecure and thus the powers of a little tsar. It is not surprising, therefore, that the servicemen were eager to wrest control from the clergy in the selection of the man who held so much power over their lives.

No official documents of this meeting exist, and the attendees' recollections also furnish few details. We do not even know if the servicemen who arrived at the conference the first morning were invited to attend or simply appeared and confronted the conference with a fait accompli.[7] First, the servicemen proposed that the conference replace the office of plenipotentiary with an executive committee of six delegates from church congregations and six servicemen. The proposal was accepted. But apart from this coup, the servicemen evidently accomplished little and went away somewhat bitter.

A month later, in June 1917, the General Conference met in Halbstadt.[8] The servicemen again sent delegates, this time including my brother Johann. Evidently, they accomplished little at this meeting also, except to acknowledge the need to convene a general conference in Orloff in August.[9] Here, too, while even the stalwart defenders of the status quo must have recognized the inevitability of change, the conflict was obvious between the young men, who had caught the spirit of change, and their reactionary elders. In discussing how to help the struggling forestry workers who increasingly depended on support from their own families, the servicemen requested that the congregations pay for at least the men's essential needs. The Mennonite 'fathers' said this was impossible: the treasury that funded them was already 120,000 rubles in arrears, and many Mennonites, despite their prosperity, were refusing to pay their fair share into the fund. The 'sons' then requested that a new levy be imposed, which the leaders rejected on the basis that a levy would simply produce a greater resistance to paying. Next, the servicemen suggested that a property assessment could pay for the forestry workers' clothing. The elders rejected this, on the ground that the property lists had already been drawn up and distributed. They likewise rejected the idea of an income tax, after a lawyer advised the General Conference that it did not have the authority to levy one, because this was the privilege of the Alternative Service Committee. Since the latter committee had already held its annual meeting, the young men asked that it meet again to discuss this issue. The elders responded, 'Perhaps, but why call it when the provisional government may ante up its share of funds in September?' The servicemen then suggested that the community might send food directly to the forestry workers. The nay-sayers turned down this suggestion because the Minister of Agriculture and the local food committee refused such assistance. Finally, the young men wondered if some groups might follow the example of the Odessa teachers who were donating 1 per cent of their salary to the families of their mobilized compatriots. No one supported them on this.

Ultimately, the congress offered many resolutions expressing the gratitude of Mennonites to the men for their valour and self-sacrificing performance. Yet the Brotherhood owed them much more. When the men were mobilized, an elder had told them that they should not worry about their wives and families, because the congregations would support them. Now, one of the Orloff delegates, another elder, pointed out that this amounted to a promissory note that they had to pay off. Other leaders, however, questioned whether the families were actually needy. Their solution was to send out a questionnaire to determine need, rather than acknowledging its reality. Surely, the poorest servicemen's families felt betrayed.

Having dispensed with this one, the conference took up more general, and potentially more volatile issues. Much time was spent on agrarian reform. The initial speaker on this topic, Dr Peter Dück, provided a recitation of obvious needs: to abolish the strip system, to extend grants to peasants and to resettle them from land-poor to land-rich regions, to organize producers' cooperatives, to increase crop yields, to introduce trades and crafts to the peasants and raise their cultural level, and so forth. These reforms generated little controversy. However, the next speaker, H. Fröse, stirred a lively debate. He raised broader, philosophical concerns: should the laudable objectives be achieved through private enterprise or state action? Should land reform meet just Russian needs or should it meet the needs of peoples elsewhere? Differing views on these humanitarian issues produced heated interchanges. The old guard objected to particular proposals as too socialistic – especially those limiting landholdings, establishing eight-hour work days,[10] and instituting full enfranchisement. One delegate accused Fröse, who was from Moscow, of confusing Christianity with a particular political doctrine. Professor Unruh observed that Christianity had no direct relationship to either capitalism or socialism and that religion sought primarily to further the Kingdom of God. To this Fröse responded that he fully understood that Christianity and socialism were not identical, but that socialism was still more in tune with Christianity than was capitalism.[11]

Despite the obvious conflict between the old guard and the Young Turks, the conference made great progress on several reform issues, especially those dealing with Mennonite education. The provisional government had already demobilized all public school teachers, and those attending the meeting were vocal advocates of reform. They were particularly concerned that few elementary school graduates went on to high school and that it was therefore imperative to encourage continuation classes in the home communities. Furthermore, they suggested that communities should set salary schedules so that teachers would not have to barter and bargain with the village authorities for their wages. Finally, they urged villages to respect the sacrifices that their servicemen-teachers had rendered and reinstate the men in their former jobs.

The intense interest of the delegates in educational reform is obvious from the number of related topics that they took up: teacher-training, job security, retirement pensions, clarification of educational aims, minimum compensation, unification of education from kindergarten through secondary level, the founding of a teachers' training seminary on a higher level than the two existing ones, the formation of a central Mennonite Board of Education, and even whether the schools should be incorporated into the national system and thus be supported by the state.

It is a credit to the delegates that, in addition to these educational reforms, they discussed the need for significant reforms in a variety of other spheres, including freedom of the national press, the establishment of a Mennonite press separate from the Mennonite church, and the creation of a parliamentary form of government set up under a democratic constitution. Furthermore, recognizing that the national government would certainly undergo sweeping change, many delegates recommended that Mennonites send a permanent representative to Petrograd. Some delegates, mostly teachers, also suggested that they establish a four- to six-week orientation program covering the major political and social issues confronting the citizenry, which they would offer to youth and adults alike. Finally, the conference nominated Professor Unruh as the Mennonite-supported candidate for the upcoming national constituent assembly elections.

Regrettably, when the entire Mennonite brotherhood had a chance to vote, their turnout was shamefully small. The Mennonites decided to combine efforts with the Union of Russian Citizens of German Origin (*Verband russischer Bürger deutscher Herkunft*). This group likewise selected Professor Unruh (along with a second candidate, Baron Meyerdorf) to represent the Tavrida guberniia. The same alliance selected, I believe, former Duma deputy Ludwig Lutz, Pastor Georg Baier, and two Mennonites, Johann Esau and Peter Funk, to represent the Ekaterinoslav and Kherson guberniias. In the end, however, the election was moot, for the soon-to-be Bolshevik takeover obliterated the freedoms that we had hoped would democratize our homeland.[12]

At least through this early post-tsarist period, which lasted from spring until autumn 1917, our family's prospects brightened. A major factor boosting our morale was Johann's return home in June. Earlier that month Alexander Kerenskii[13] had demobilized all former teachers, which allowed Johann to attend the second Halbstadt meeting. Shortly thereafter, he returned to Kronsweide to resume the teaching post he had held there prior to the war. While waiting for school to open that fall, he and Heinrich Dyck, a teacher from the Khortitsa high school, registered voters in several villages for the upcoming elections to the constituent assembly.

The younger children's opportunities seemed similarly good. First, the impending end to the war brightened Maria's marriage prospects. She had two suitors, one the son of a prosperous farmer, the other a young teacher and son of a poor widow. An engagement to one or the other seemed imminent. Jacob had just completed elementary school, and there was no doubt that this eager youngster must enter the Khortitsa high school for boys in the coming fall quarter. Best of all, the recent improvement in Heinrich's health seemed permanent, which meant he could assist Father in a hoped-for business upturn. However, my father must have had residual concerns about Heinrich's health, and perhaps for this reason, he sent me off to business school in Barvenkovo.

The superficial stability of the new government began unravelling in July 1917. With the collapse of the provisional government's Brusilov offensive, the troops became more demoralized than ever. Large contingents deserted, taking their arms with them. Other troops, slated for the front, refused to go. In mid-August, the soldiers' wrath erupted in the train station at Barvenkovo. My brother Gerhard's home, where I roomed, faced the station, and I had a ringside seat to the unfolding drama. Just after a train pulled onto its siding, going either to or from the Galician area, we heard shots, then shouting. We soon discovered that mutinous soldiers on the train had murdered three of their officers. For several days, the train remained at the siding, with the soldiers refusing to let anyone remove and bury the bodies of the slain officers, while taunting curious citizens to look at how ordinary soldiers meted out military justice.

The meaning of this action was not lost on the Mennonite owner of the mill. Apprehensive that unrest would erupt among the civilian population as well as the military, and that he would have to curtail operations, he informed his employees that he would terminate their jobs in a few weeks. Perhaps the expropriation decrees had already primed him to look for buyers (principally within the Jewish community) before the government had a chance to take over his mill.[14] Gerhard and several other employees sued the company to retain their jobs, but their action was fruitless, and soon after Gerhard wrote to Father for instructions about me. Should I be boarded elsewhere or sent home? Initially, Father answered that I should stay there and board with a

Ukrainian widow. But our parents must have understood the ominous portent, because not long after that, my father came to bring me home and to deal with Gerhard's joblessness. Anticipating that the Khortitsa teachers' seminary would be reconverted from a military hospital back to a school, Father planned to enroll me there. Gerhard's situation was more problematic. Although married and the father of five children, Gerhard had never managed fully on his own, nor was he able to curtail his wife's spendthrift ways. The home they had had in Nieder Khortitsa was occupied by a brother-in-law of Father's first wife, and it would not become vacant until they moved in the fall of 1917. From then on, Gerhard's family finances were precarious, and much dependent on our parents.

Gerhard's semi-dependence and the cost of Jacob's and my schooling presented a formidable burden for our parents, but there was no question of our attendance. Yet where could Father find the funds for our room and board? After much deliberation, my parents decided that Mother would temporarily move with Jacob and me to Rosental, where we could stay with her sister-in-law Mrs Kornelius Pauls, whose husband was still in war service. Since Mother could cook and care for us, it would save the cost of room and board. Her decision to take on this task was proof of the seriousness and importance that both my parents placed on education.

Although everyone thought the plan was a temporary expedient, neither Father nor Mother believed that the country's situation would stabilize any time soon. My mother was probably more aware of the unstable political situation than were most Mennonite women, since Father talked frequently of strikes and labour unrest in Alexandrovsk. He was keenly aware of the terrible injustices that the common people suffered, and of how the highly privileged position of the Mennonites contrasted with the abject poverty of much of the peasantry and urban working class. Likewise, my father recognized that the discrimination that many of our people practised against the non-Mennonite residents in our midst could not continue.[15] My brother Johann's political ideals were strongly influenced by the Constitutional Democrats and by his voluminous reading and travels through European Russia. Father, however, was a pragmatist. He had long ago concluded that no Russian government, particularly a democratically elected one, would permit a continuation of the islands of people of different tongues, religious beliefs, and particularly of a vastly higher standard of living to exist within the state. For my father, the question was whether the walls that had shielded us for so long would give way of their own accord or be breached only by violence.

When I returned home from Barvenkovo, however, I found life proceeding in its normal August hubbub of preparing the winter larder. Mother kept us boys busy picking and peeling the summer's bounty of fruit that she and Mariechen then canned and dried, or in the case of watermelons, squeezed for the endless gallons of juice that they boiled down into syrup. As August came to an end, Jacob and I began preparing for the school year in Rosental, and Mariechen became noticeably irascible, often giving me gruff digs in the ribs. Perhaps I had it coming for teasing her about her two suitors. It took almost sixty years for me to learn the real cause of her anger that summer. Mariechen had hoped desperately to be able to go to the women's *gimnaziia* in Alexandrovsk to prepare for a teaching career. This field was just opening to women, and even Nieder Khortitsa had engaged a female teacher – Frieda Priess from Schönwiese. As the revolutionary changes of the past few months had stimulated a new attitude within the settlement, Mariechen had come to believe that she would have a solid place within the teaching profession. Instead, she was kept at home with the added burden of taking on further household tasks during Mother's absence while tending our needs at school. It must have added insult to injury, especially since she believed the country would soon erupt, and she would have no chance of schooling after this year.

As things turned out, Mariechen's apprehensions were justified. The Bolshevik seizure of power in late October 1917 was a death knell for Father's business, extinguishing hopes that our parents could pay our room and board. Thus, the idea that Mother's stay with us in her brother's house in Rosental would be brief was illusory. I suppose at times I resented this arrangement. Our limited quarters made studying difficult and our comrades' visits unpleasant, especially since Mother's presence curbed our rowdier inclinations. Certainly, I failed to appreciate at that time the sacrifices Father and Mother made for us financially and the grief their on-and-off separation entailed.

Jacob enrolled in the boys high school, and I in the Teachers' Training Seminary. About half of my high school class enrolled along with me. It was the first year the school operated in its new building which, although completed in 1914, had been occupied as a Red Cross hospital during the war. More striking than the building's newness was the relief from the repressive hold the tsarist government had previously exerted over both teachers and students. Classes were now co-educational; we did not have to wear student uniforms, and teachers had more latitude in what they could teach.

The political turmoil in Petrograd, Moscow, and other cities seemed remote. Khortitsa's two bookstores had sufficient books and school supplies for the students, although the selections were limited. The teachers, however, must have felt more inconvenienced by the community's delay in providing adequate funding because of the burden of supporting roughly 7,000 servicemen. Still, the community was able to stretch finances enough to reopen the model school (*Musterschule*), where students observed classroom instruction and did practice teaching under the superb guidance of Gerhard Peters.

Into the autumn of 1917 the political situation seemed tolerably normal. Vandalism and thefts, especially of horses and livestock from neighbouring estates, became more frequent. However, such episodes were not novel in themselves. Householders seldom left doors or windows unlocked, and certainly no farmer ever left tools or equipment in the fields. As Christmas neared, our time was filled with the usual festivities of the season and heightened expectations that in the new year we would move into more spacious quarters in the home of another uncle in Rosental. There we could occupy an ample basement apartment, complete with kitchen. This was not to be. From the beginning of January 1918, the situation deteriorated apace. The civil war arrived, and it was to last for nearly four years.

PART FIVE

From Dream to Nightmare: Civil War and Makhnovite Terror (*Makhnovshchina*)

CHAPTER TWENTY

The First Phase of the Civil War, January to March 1918

Three periods delineated Russia's fratricidal civil war, at least as it affected the Mennonites in our area.[1] During the first phase, from January to March 1918, Bolsheviks made their first thrusts into our region. Ukrainian peasants, emboldened by the chaos and favourable decrees of the Bolsheviks, began seizing land. Thievery and banditry were commonplace. Although rapes and murders were rare, they did occur. Later even these crimes were common (as we see in subsequent chapters). Throughout the second period, German troops occupied the territory, giving Mennonites a false sense of security and hope for our future. Upon withdrawal of German troops in November 1918, the final and most catastrophic stage erupted, as Bolsheviks, autonomous Ukrainian forces, and counter-revolutionary White Armies battled for control over our strategically important area. Intertwined with that chaos was the worst terror – the occupation of our area by the Makhnovite bandits. That period ended in the autumn of 1920 when the Bolsheviks finally defeated their opponents. This chapter deals with the first phase.

In the first weeks of 1918 the Dnieper River represented a fluid boundary between the many groups battling for the control of southern Russia. Over the next three months control of this amorphous front shifted seven times among the various combatants. Initially, along the river's west bank, troops of the Ukrainian Rada (called *Haidamaky* or *vilny kozaky*) struggled to maintain their tenuous hold. Led by the socialist Simon Petliura, this group had several months earlier declared Ukraine an autonomous republic. Among its adversaries were Bolsheviks, who moved southward from central Russia towards the Dnieper's east bank, the Crimea, and the Don Cossack region. As they progressed they steadily gained control of railroads and important ports. Ukrainian troops in our region were too weak to effectively oppose the Bolsheviks. However, bloody skirmishes erupted between the Reds and a third amorphous group of counter-revolutionary forces, particularly in Alexandrovsk, which was the nodal point of two railroads, as well as a major port. This counter-revolutionary group included detachments of Cossacks and former army officers (whom the Bolsheviks dubbed *Kadety*) retreating from the Austro-Hungarian front or fleeing from central and northern guberniias. Each tried to reach either their Don or Kuban home districts, or gathering points for the White (or volunteer) armies commanded by General Denikin. Most of these men passed through our area successfully. Others were caught and disarmed by members of the Red Army, especially by elite troops consisting of former Black Sea Fleet sailors, or members of international brigades, of whom the Latvian and Chinese units were notoriously ferocious.

While these heavily armed, loosely organized, and undisciplined armies were threatening us, two other completely lawless groups ravaged the countryside. The first was of Ukrainian peasants who seized our lands. Initially, they focused on the estates neighbouring their villages, and some of the outermost lands belonging to individual Mennonite villages and to the Khortitsa Settlement's communal leaseland (*Pachtartikel*).[2] The other group consisted of anarchists, people from the working class, army deserters, and peasants. Armed to the teeth, these marauders adopted the Bolshevik slogan, 'Plunder the Plunderers.' They seized anything they could lay their hands on and exacted tribute (*kontributsiia*) from individual households, or even entire villages. Often they took hostages and exacted ransom for them.

Both types of jacqueries ravaged Ukraine throughout 1918–20, adding immeasurable grief to the suffering inflicted by the main forces of the civil war – the Bolsheviks and the White counter-revolutionaries. Calling themselves partisans, their actions were more often motivated by lust for plunder or revenge against specific people than by any desire to rectify general social conditions.

In the early months of the Russian Civil War, the worst gang of cutthroats in our area were those who followed Marusiia Nikiforova, a notorious gangster who called herself a terrorist-anarchist. Later, when the conflict became even bloodier, the two main groups of partisans (*povstantsy*) in the Ekaterinoslav, Tavrida, and Kherson guberniias were the Makhnovites and the Grigorievites – the huge followings of Nestor Makhno and Nikifor Grigoriev, respectively. Scores of other minor would-be partisans or revolutionaries added to the chaos.[3] Actually, aside from

Bessarabia, which was nominally under Rumanian control, and much of the Tavrida guberniia, which the White Army held during most of the civil war, every Ukrainian guberniia had its share of these *atamans* (or *batkos*) with peasant followings. These peasant revolts shared many features, although they varied somewhat in character and objectives, partly because of local conditions (whether land was controlled by the gentry, colonists, or peasants) and partly because of the bandits' ethnic hatred of the German colonists and/or Jews.

In southern Russia, the *Makhnovshchina* (literally, Makhno terror) outlasted all other jacqueries. The duration and ferocity of this terror may be explained by a number of characteristics unique to the Makhnovites. First, the Makhnovites were geographically concentrated in an area of great strategic and tactical value to the Bolsheviks, who used them from time to time as a buffer between themselves and the White armies. Second, the heartland from which Makhno himself and at least 90 per cent of his following came was surrounded by large, wealthy settlements, which were mainly composed of Mennonites, but also included Lutheran, Catholic, and other German settlers. These provided the rebel army with a supply base, richly stocked with horses, wagons, livestock, foodstuffs, clothing, and money. Moreover, Makhnovites had an intense hatred for these settlements, fuelled by vicious anti-colonist propaganda campaigns promulgated off and on from the time of Alexander III right up through the First World War.

Most of the bandit leaders referred to themselves as *batko,* the Ukrainian for 'little father,' although a few used the old Cossack designation for leader, *ataman.* Grigoriev, who had distinguished himself in the imperial army during the Great War, preferred the title *ataman,* while Makhno used *batko.* The terms were not reserved exclusively for chiefs, however, and leaders of subgroups of brigands within the larger bands often assumed the title of *batko,* as well. Among the most vicious of these subchieftains was Batko Pravda (Little Father Truth).

Only one of these groups (that of Nestor Makhno) is 'credited' with the true anarchist goals of establishing a stateless collection of communes. Such claims for Makhno's movement, commonly called the *Makhnovshchina,* come primarily from non-Russian apologists, some of whom make profoundly misjudged and untenable claims.[4] Everyone who survived the ravages of this band knows that these claims are patently false. There may very well have been a few philosophical and syndicalist anarchists in Guliai Polie, Makhno's huge home village of peasants. But contrary to apologists' claims, the *Makhnovshchina* was not motivated by philosophy, nor did the Makhnovite band of outlaws ever exert any influence among the urban working classes. Certainly, if any Makhnovites were philosophical anarchists, their ideology did not curb the plunderous rampaging and horrible slaughter of hapless victims, which the bandits termed 'entering as expense.'[5]

All the combatants, whether Red Army, local bandits, former peasants, or deserters from the tsarist army, forcibly requisitioned anything they wanted. Only the White Army officers occasionally offered to pay, and then only in depreciated tsarist paper money, or *karenki* (small pieces of paper money issued by the provisional government), or equally worthless paper currency issued by a Ukrainian government during the brief months of autonomy given it by the Kerenskii regime in the summer and autumn of 1917. Demands by combatants followed a common pattern. Several heavily armed men would burst into a house and with blood-curdling, blasphemous curses, demand money, clothing, food, animals, fodder, bedding, wagons, or whatever else they wanted or thought was available. In the worst cases, and this was especially true during the raids in 1919, they killed the head of the household, or raped its young women after first forcing them to cook them a meal. These invasions took place at any hour of the day or night. People bold enough to ask an intruder for identification were treated to an assault or at least an explosive string of two-story-high (*dvukh-etazhnye*) or three-story-high (*triokh-etazhnye*) expletives. When the intruders found the doors locked, or if the homeowners did not open them fast enough or demanded a search warrant, they would fire shots through the door or windows and shout, 'And here is a permit for you' (*a vot tebe nash mandat*). Should someone have ventured to ask what they were looking for, the answer could have been almost anything: weapons, counter-revolutionaries, food, or simply the opportunity to rummage through the house so that they might find something, anything, that they might consider valuable (*posharit'*).

None of the villages of the Khortitsa Settlement escaped the ravages of the bandits. Nevertheless, Khortitsa, Rosental, Einlage, and Nieder Khortitsa, being of greatest geographical and administrative importance, were hardest hit. Everywhere, demands for material fell most heavily on those who possessed the most – farmers, mill owners, and businessmen. Yet the suffering of the teamster-farmers, who had finally acquired small land parcels during the Stolypin land reforms, was perhaps the most tragic. Their little holdings, lying beyond the settlement's land complex, and close to several Ukrainian peasant villages, were easy targets for land 'requisition.' With the breakdown of district and higher governmental authority, peasants simply seized land, with the justification that both the Bolshevik and Ukrainian Rada governments had abolished land ownership for all but those who worked their tracts without hired help. The decrees, of course, were vague and as yet scarcely enforceable anywhere in the southern Ukrainian guberniias.

In February 1918, the Bolsheviks established a tenuous hold over our area. Local workers saw their chance to wrest control of village government from the entrenched leadership of prosperous farmers. Led by a former factory worker by the name of Balkov, these workers replaced the old district (volost) administration, centred in the village of Khortitsa, with a new district soviet consisting of workers and peasants as deputies. The new Bolshevik authorities in Khortitsa and Ekaterinoslav then instructed each of the district's other villages to set up similar soviets. Nieder Khortitsa's deputy representative was a shiftless man named Wall, who had already Ukrainianized his name to Vallenko.[6] When Vallenko returned from Ekaterinoslav, where he had been instructed on the powers of a local soviet, its administrative methods, voting qualifications, and electoral procedures, the landless Mennonites (*Nippaenja*) held elections for the village soviet. Elated at the reversal of roles, the landless shut the former propertied elite out of the process and, of course, tossed Peter Unger, the last mayor (*Schulz*) elected by that class, out of office. The property owners protested vehemently. Balkov retorted that if they caused the local soviet trouble, he would dispatch them to areas from which they would never return.

One of the first actions that the new and proletarian soviet took was to demand that all cottagers be given sufficient acreage to grow crops, and a home site, if they did not own the dwelling they occupied. The obvious source of land to satisfy these demands belonged to the formerly wealthy farmers – acreage left untilled during the last year of war and wasteland (*Unland*) that the farmers had expropriated long ago. There had been conflict over these lands since the 1850s. Not surprisingly, the farmers continued to resist demands to share the land with the landless teamster-farmers. Funk recalls that at some of these village meetings the two sides came to blows over this issue. Ultimately, however, a modest number of building sites and some farming strips were set aside for the newly empowered group.

The antagonism between the propertied and non-propertied classes sometimes erupted over issues not related to land. At one point, the Nieder Khortitsa soviet demanded the redistribution of all clothing according to new principles of liberty and fraternity. Small wonder that enmity developed among the people, or that many threatened reprisal should the roles once again be reversed.

Although members of the propertied class in Nieder Khortitsa were able to limit or delay the seizure of their possessions by fellow Mennonites, they were helpless to prevent 'requisitions' by partisan bandits and the Bolshevik authorities in Khortitsa and Alexandrovsk. Bolsheviks made near-daily raids on the villages, seeking booty – anything in our wardrobes, larders, or granaries to which they could 'give feet.' These raids were certainly illegal, and theoretically, of course, we could refuse the partisans' armed 'requests.' When we reported thefts to the local Bolshevik authorities, however, they did little to protect us. Often, it transpired that the Bolshevik authorities had actually authorized the bandit raids. The Bolsheviks did the bandits one better, demanding *kontributsiia* from the *burzhui,* as well as seizing goods from 'enemies of the masses.' To thwart the raids, most householders spent part of their nights trying to hide anything of value, in haystacks or by burying things in their gardens or fields.

Between January and March 1918, the Bolsheviks demanded payment of three large bribes. Initially, they required the Khortitsa villages, in combination, to pay them two million rubles within three days. When the district failed to raise this sum, the Bolsheviks seized six hostages, and released them only after they had received payment of somewhat less than one million rubles. The next month, Bolshevik authorities demanded that Alexandrovsk pay a tribute of three million rubles and levy a property tax on its inhabitants for another one million rubles. Both sums were to be paid in three weeks. Again, the Bolsheviks took hostages, for again the sum could not be met. Undeterred, the Bolsheviks levied more tributes – 800,000 on the Khortitsa volost, 500,000 on the Nikolaipol volost, and 40,000 rubles on the village of Einlage. Seeing additional sources of funds, Bolsheviks levied *kontributsiia* fines on several of the wealthiest Mennonite industrialists. The men were not able to raise the entire payment rapidly enough, and so they borrowed the balance from local farmers, promising to repay the debt as soon as times returned to 'normal.' Conditions did, in fact, improve, but the industrialists reneged on their promise, claiming that Bolsheviks had extorted the money from them and that therefore they were under no moral obligation to repay. This abrogation of debt fuelled the rising divisions between Mennonites of various social classes.

No one knows how much money Bolsheviks actually garnered from Mennonites during the early part of 1918. To some extent this is because just as several large payments were due, Alexandrovsk and many of the neighbouring Mennonite villages were over-run by the notorious anarchist Marusiia Nikiforova and her gang. Although Nikiforova and her recruits were every bit as vicious as the Makhnovite bandits who had devastated our home area a year later, her reign of terror was brief.

In early February 1918, our situation improved sharply when the Ukrainian Rada signed its separate peace with the Central powers, thereby allowing German and Austrian troops to occupy our region. On the night of 30 March, word arrived of the rapid advance of the German Army on Alexandrovsk. In response, hundreds of Nikiforova's thugs swarmed across the Dnieper to Nieder Khortitsa and Einlage, set on a plunderous massacre of the villages nearest the river. Fortunately, an advance force of German troops had reached Nikolaipol (about fifteen miles north of Khortitsa) the day before. In response to our desperate appeal for help, the Germans quickly dispatched about 200 men to our villages. The terrorists beat a hasty retreat back across the Dnieper, but not before gunning down several German soldiers and blowing up a section of the bridge at Einlage. The villagers buried the soldiers in the Khortitsa Mennonite cemetery in a ceremony that many of us attended. The relief and gratitude we felt for their sacrifice was indescribable, for it seemed that they were our saviors and had brought our trials to an end.

During this early upheaval, most families lost their material possessions, but virtually no villagers had been killed – although peasant bandits had murdered a few of the wealthiest estate owners outside the villages. Our home in Nieder Khortitsa was searched several times, and always some food or clothing was confiscated. But otherwise our family was left relatively alone, perhaps because we had no land or herds of animals to expropriate, and no wagon or other movable property deemed worth taking. The family may also have been spared threats to life or demands for tribute because the *Nippaenja* who briefly controlled the village soviet were grateful to Father, whose general store had carried their debts over many winters. Those of us who stayed in Uncle Bernhard Pauls's home in Rosental – Mother, Jacob, and I – were even luckier. As this house was deemed to be that of a 'worker' (Uncle had been a mechanic in the Lepp-Wallmann factory during the last year of the war), no one molested us.

In my view, many Mennonites found their property losses less important than the loss of status they had endured. Those who had held wealth and power had been themselves subjected to insults and indignities from their former 'inferiors' – the stupid Russian (*de domma Russ*), the unwashed and unkempt *muzhik* – who forced them to surrender property, to perform menial tasks for them, and even to suffer their physical assaults. Thus, it is not surprising that when the Germans occupied the region – and the tables were once again turned – threats of revenge were heard everywhere. Unfortunately, those who followed through on these threats later paid dearly, when power again shifted to the Ukrainian peasants.

CHAPTER TWENTY-ONE

Nominal Security under Foreign Occupation, April to November 1918

In late March and early April 1918, a few days after the advance guard of Germans routed Marusiia Nikoforova's bandits, the main German occupation force, joined by a troop of Austro-Hungarians, seized Alexandrovsk. The entire Old Colony settlement experienced immense relief, and we were eager to feed and house these troops. That they spoke German no doubt added to the warmth of the reception, not least because the Russian government had proscribed that language during the war. Many villagers were thrilled at the idea that they might again buy farm implements and other goods unavailable during the war. The teachers were particularly keen to obtain new books.

I first encountered the German troops in Khortitsa on 2 or 3 April. A large contingent of wagons had been sent from Nieder Khortitsa to transport troops and their equipment back to that village to rout the Nikiforovites and Red Army units that still controlled the Dnieper River boat crossing between Nieder Khortitsa and Alexandrovsk. Jacob Epp, my boyhood friend, was among the throng. Swept up by the moment's excitement, I cut classes, hopped aboard his wagon, and joined the column of several hundred infantrymen and a few mounted officers. As our procession trundled south, Jacob and I marvelled at our experiences during the past two months – of Bolshevik coercion, Ukrainian peasant thefts, bandit raids, and now our apparent rescue.

When we got to Nieder Khortitsa, a German soldier signalled us into the yard of Peter Unger, who with the Bolsheviks gone resumed his office as mayor. As Jacob and I hopped off the wagon to watch the proceedings, we noticed the German soldiers' fatigue. Mounted on an ancient Oldenburger horse an officer rode by while two disgruntled soldiers were unloading our wagon. With a nod to the officer, one soldier grumbled under his breath to the other, 'Comes the day, then he is one of the first whom we beat to death' (*Kommt der Tag, dann ist er einer der Ersten, den wir totschlagen*). Clearly, revolutionary sentiment had infected the German troops, just as it had earlier swept through the Russian Imperial Army.

I recall a more pleasant experience some weeks later at the teachers' seminary. Many of the students and staff were out on the school's verandah, meeting with several German officers, most wearing uniforms, although one or two were in mufti. Earlier, these Germans had visited Halbstadt and several other villages in the Molochna Settlement. The attractive, prosperous appearance impressed the soldiers tremendously, although the men indicated some dismay at the monotonous uniformity of the villages, with their broad main streets flanked by homes and farm buildings of nearly identical architecture and almost military placement. The Germans preferred Khortitsa and Rosental, with their irregular streets, and more diverse architecture of new brick facades, together with aged thatched structures, and the surrounding rolling, wooded countryside.

Our school's barren courtyard did not impress the Germans. The Russian government had requisitioned the buildings for a hospital when war broke out, just months after construction was complete, and in the intervening years the villages had had little money to landscape the grounds. Commenting on the bleakness, one German waxed ecstatically on what the same courtyard would look like at home, with every corner planted with salable flowers and vegetables. What a boon that would be to his hard-pressed family at home. His reverie did not impress us Mennonites, who had not yet faced such hard times.

The German presence raised an imperative issue over which virtually every Russian Mennonite struggled – since life in Russia had become so difficult, should we remain there or should we emigrate en masse? Even before the war many Mennonites had considered the possibility of moving to South America, perhaps to Argentina. Now, another set of alternatives seemed to present itself. The first choice was to emigrate to Germany. If that were not possible, perhaps we could resettle in parts of the Baltic countries that Germany might annex as spoils of war. A third possibility was that Germany might annex those portions of Ukraine that it now occupied, in which case we could remain in our homes. Lastly, even if Germany did not annex our area, we ardently hoped it could secure special privileges for us in whatever formal treaties it made with Ukraine.

I am not aware of any study indicating what action Mennonites did indeed prefer. Certainly, most desired some sort of allegiance with Germany, but I suspect that only the wealthiest class and a few intellectuals who had married into the industrial and milling families, or had studied in Germany, wanted full German citizenship. In Nieder Khortitsa, I can recall only Gerhard Warkentin and his two sons, Jacob and Isaak, being deeply imbued with pro-German sentiment. This modest response probably reflected the entire population of the Khortitsa Settlement, for we held no Ludendorff festivals,[1] like those celebrated in the Lutheran Prischib or the Mennonite Molochna settlements in the summer and autumn of 1918.

Yet understanding the gravity of the situation, groups of German-speaking colonists held a conference in Prischib, the centre of the German Lutheran and Catholic Molochna settlement, shortly after the arrival of the German troops. The Abram Dyck Diaries note:[2]

> H. Epp and Jul. v. Kampen have returned from the Prischib Conference where by virtually unanimous vote it was decided that all Germans in the Tavrida, Ekaterinoslav, and Kherson guberniias will accept German citizenship, place themselves completely under German laws, and joyfully declare themselves to be ready to bear each and every duty connected with German citizenship. Furthermore, they permit themselves to express the supplication that Germany would make use of the century-old cultural work (*Kulturarbeit*) done by them and their forebears, that it (Germany) would create out of the Tavrida guberniia, including the Crimea, a state subordinate to Germany, and leave them, that is, the German colonists, in the new state entity as precursors and pioneers of Germany. But should this not be possible, then they petition Germany to undertake a re-emigration of these people to the mother country under its protection.

Unfortunately, the diaries do not state whether the two Mennonite representatives voted with the 'almost unanimous,' nor whether other Mennonites attended the conference.

German authorities, however, did not favour our emigration. Nor did they want to grant us German citizenship. During the last week in April, the German consul, meeting with Mennonite representatives in Khortitsa, recommended that we remain in Ukraine, retain its citizenship, and continue to grow grain. The Germans, claimed the consul, would protect us if needed. Not content with this response, several private delegations of Mennonites went to Germany to explore other possibilities.

Heinrich Epp of Khortitsa went to Berlin at least once, ostensibly to obtain school supplies, but more likely to request citizenship for the Mennonites. Evidently, Epp received the same response – that we should remain where we were.[3]

Although neither of my parents wished to become German citizens, or to emigrate to an area that their forebears had left more than a century before, the German occupation pleased Father in that it restored order. However, he remained sceptical of the supposed long-range German objectives for our area. He may have read the Germans' desire that we 'remain in Ukraine and grow grain' as serving their war aims more than our future security. Certainly, the German overthrow of the Ukrainian Rada, with whom it had concluded a treaty of peace and recognition in February 1918, gave Father serious concern. The Rada, composed of Ukrainian Socialists and Nationalists from the former Austro-Hungarian Galicia, enjoyed wide support among the Ukrainian Nationalists in the guberniias of historic Ukraine (Kiev, Kharkov, Poltava, Chernigov, Podolia, and Volhynia). But few of that region's peasants, or the peasants in the former New Russia, who had already appropriated much of the lands of the gentry and wealthier peasants, shared this support. With such weak backing, the Rada was unable to raise a significant army. The Germans replaced the Rada in late April 1918 with an unabashedly reactionary regime headed by Pavlo Skoropadskii. The leader's Ukrainianized first name and assumption of the ancient designation of leader (*Hetman*) hardly disguised the fact that he was a puppet of the Germans or that his regime was established to further Germany's annexationist aims for Ukraine, Crimea, and parts of the Caucasus. Skoropadskii was a landowner possessing 30,000 to 40,000 dessiatins, and a former tsarist general. He soon filled his government with aristocrats from the old order, including Count Kanist, Prince Golitsyn, Count Lansdorf, Count Sabanskii, and General Dragomirov. To give their agrarian policy (which was to restore the lands to the former owners) a Ukrainian patina, they formed the new bread – or grain growers – party (*khliboroby*). My father, who more than most Mennonites felt the pulse of the indigenous masses, could hardly avoid sensing their hatred towards Skoropadskii and his cronies.

Beyond the question of acquiring German citizenship, another issue, with even more wrenching and divisive potential, arose at the Prischib Conference.[4] This involved the organization of self-defence (*Selbstschutz*) units in Mennonite settlements. The German soldiers were to organize these and furnish both weapons and training.[5] Opinion on the *Selbstschutz* remained divided throughout the entire German occupation. Nonetheless, by the end of the 1918 school year, many of the villages in the Khortitsa Settlement organized self-defence units, and the German soldiers handed out weapons to any male deemed trustworthy. According to the Funk diary, in Nieder Khortitsa the Germans dispensed two wagonloads of rifles, ammunition, hand grenades, and even one machine gun. I was certainly aware of the first three items, but cannot recall the machine gun. My sense is that about half the village men accepted weapons.

Heinrich and I took rifles and ammunition, but as in many families, our parents differed on whether we should have done so. Mother strongly opposed armed resistance, while Father was ambivalent. On the one hand, he was a pragmatist and a firm believer in the sanctity of property. But he also was aware that the Ukrainian peasant – and landless Mennonite as well – had ample reason to rebel against the existing order. Nevertheless, he felt Heinrich and I were old enough to decide our own course.

The Nieder Khortitsa *Selbstschutz* was never cohesive, nor organized enough to march and shoot targets, much less consider how to behave in a real conflict. The Funk diary claims that some of us once went to Rosental-Khortitsa for a joint exercise with their unit, though I cannot recall this event. Perhaps it took place after I had returned to school. However, I well remember watching the Rosental-Khortitsa unit with its twenty or thirty members, marching back from one of the Rosental valleys lustily singing, 'I once had a comrade, a better one you wouldn't find' (*Ich hatt' einen Kameraden, Einen bessern findst du nicht*). Overall, however, the self-defence movement never gained much strength in the Khortitsa Settlement, and I cannot remember a single instance in which more than a handful of men shot at bandits. In contrast, a strong self-defence movement arose in the more pro-German Molochna Settlement, where later hundreds of youths fought the peasants and partisans.

Why did some Mennonites abandon non-resistance? There are several reasons for this. Certainly, the Germans encouraged the young men's protective instincts and 'manliness.' Then, too, as the Germans argued, since no stable government was likely to emerge soon out of the chaos in Ukraine, we would have to protect ourselves from future outbursts of long-simmering Ukrainian peasant hostility. Given the terror suffered in previous months, and the uncertain future, many youths listened to the siren voices to defend our lives and property with arms. As one who succumbed, I think revenge motivated many Mennonite youths (sometimes encouraged by our elders), hoping to punish the 'stupid peasant,' who with impunity had robbed us of our hard-won belongings.

Many Mennonites in both the Molochna and the Khortitsa settlements vehemently opposed armed resistance. Fighting violated one of the fundamentals of our faith: pacifism. Some found the desertion of pacifism and an allegiance to Germany to be hypocritical, when only months earlier we had disclaimed any German heritage. Several Mennonite ministers and intellectuals voiced the pragmatic concern that armed 'defence' might simply invite retaliation. Soon after the Germans arrived, Mennonites who had lost property in the preceding months denounced the offending Ukrainian peasants (and the occasional poor Mennonite) as collaborators with the Bolsheviks or bandits. Landowners vehemently demanded restitution of their lands. To contain the furor, the German command ordered that expropriated movable property be returned, but that no one penalize culprits beyond restitution. General Eichhorn similarly decreed that the 1919 crop belonged to whoever had planted it. Nonetheless, in the Khortitsa Settlement, the Germans flogged some of those accused of collaboration, while in Molochna, they even executed one such man. A civil war of an unexpected sort had come to many a Mennonite village.

Alarmed over the conflicts and the *Selbstschutz*, church and lay leaders held a conference in Lichtenau, Molochna, to discuss every aspect of historic Mennonite non-resistance, including its biblical basis, our 400-year adherence to its basic principles, its fate during the First World War, and the potential wisdom or folly of abandoning the principles of pacifism now.[6] Held between 30 June and 2 July, 1918, the composition of the conference participants reflected the import of the matter. Of its 283 attendees, nineteen were elders and 139 were ministers.[7] David H. Epp's opening comments foretold the agonizing discussions that followed. Although Epp entreated members to deliberate 'guided by the spirit of love and brotherliness,' he reminded them that the Berdiansk District Commander of the German Army was pressuring Mennonites to form self-defence units. He expected the conference to sanction the self-defence units by 4 July, and required a list of congregations that clung to non-resistance. Epp's peremptory demand must have had a strong impact on everyone present.

Minutes of the meeting reveal that many felt that non-resistance was not a viable option and should either be abandoned or become a matter of individual conscience. Others argued that each congregation could decide the issue for itself, provided it tolerated the contrary views of individual members. Opinion also differed on whether we should base non-resistance on biblical sources or historical precedent, with some speakers noting that our sixteenth-century Anabaptist forebears in the Low Countries had not been unanimous on the subject.

Those opposing armed resistance pressed their view passionately, noting that defending material possessions was the primary motivation of many who agreed to bear arms. The minutes do not clearly show whether anyone suggested that taking up arms might thrust us into deeper trouble than if we held to pacifism, but decades later, several who had attended claimed other participants had expressed that view and that they had left the conference deeply depressed. Compounding this situation was the common knowledge that several Molochna villages had offered boot-money (*Stiefelgeld*) and other assistance to prospective volunteers to join the *Selbstschutz* and that some *Selbstschützler* were increasingly intolerant of those who refused to join.

Faced with a deadlock, the conference appointed a special commission to draft a resolution which a majority could approve to guide all Mennonite congregations. Drawn mainly from the Molochna clergy, a group accustomed to handling the contentiousness of Mennonite gatherings (better known as the 'Mennonite sickness'), the commission crafted a diplomatic masterpiece, which read: 'The General conference holds fast to our present confession in respect to non-resistance. It finds this grounded in Jesus Christ's behaviour during his sojourn here on earth and in his word; the conference, however, recommends each separate congregation not coerce the conscience of any of its members who think differently on this question.' Stripped of its pious language, the majority in effect ratified a fait accompli – that reality had obliterated our privileged non-resistance – while acknowledging the necessity to tolerate differing points of view.

My impression is that many delegates believed, without saying so, that we were taking a wrong turn. Perhaps they felt, as I do now, that for years our churches and schools had failed to teach our students the basic Mennonite beliefs and history, that we had enjoyed privileges without having to fight for them, and that we simply paid lip service to Goethe's injunction: 'Whatever you inherit from your forebears, strive to attain it in order to call it your own' (*Was du ererbt von deinen Vätern, erwirb es um es zu besitzen*). Might not a deeper foundation in our historic beliefs have lessened the aberrant acts of many and saved us all from some of the retributive horrors later inflicted by the Makhnovites?

Despite this wrenching moral struggle, life in the summer of 1918 under German occupation, seemed almost normal. The Ukrainian economy began to revive. Jewish businessmen, who had begun buying Mennonite businesses in 1917, continued to do so through the summer of 1918, even offering the seller a choice of payment in tsarist currency or Reichsmarks, with deposit made in Ukraine or Berlin. Many stores in Alexandrovsk reopened, although with a limited selection of merchandise and grossly inflated prices. Trade in the city's produce market was lively, as was the bartering in the stalls of the bazaar. There we often found our own clothes or household items, requisitioned months earlier by Bolsheviks or bandits. Attempts to reclaim stolen items were always futile, since the peddlars combined forces and threatened violence. My family was affected minimally, because the numerous raiding parties had requisitioned little from us – we had little they deemed valuable, and Father's previous benevolence to the *Nippaenja* who had briefly controlled the village soviet spared us further, I believe.

This apparent return to normalcy buoyed Father's hopes of reviving his grain trade. His expectations may have been based on rumours that the Crimea and its ports, having never been part of Ukraine, might be retained by Germany to protect its interests in the Caucasus and Middle East. Father reopened the general store, perhaps to keep Heinrich's business interests alive until normal times resumed. He transferred the shelving and counters from our old home to the grain warehouse (*Spitja*) of our new home, but with virtually no stock available, the venture was doomed.

Some industrial and commercial entrepreneurs began modernizing their businesses as means and materials became available, despite the precariousness of the Skoropadskii regime under German occupation, and the confused state of currency in circulation (the old ruble, the *kerenki*, *grivenik*, *chervontsy*, and many kinds of regional money). For example, the new Jewish owner of the two former Niebuhr mills in Nieder Khortitsa outfitted the buildings with electricity and offered to provide electric power to any nearby Mennonite household. He was reportedly ready to bring a telephone to our village as soon as the materials became available. Thus, on the surface, conditions for some people appeared tolerable, if not altogether promising. Most of all, our family was overjoyed during that brief summer respite by two events, Mariechen's wedding and the silver wedding anniversary of my aunt and uncle (described in the next chapter).

As autumn approached, however, apprehensiveness about the future returned. The disciplined German troops, whom no one dared disobey, were replaced with squads of poorly disciplined Austro-Hungarians. Peasants and workers, seeing their chance to retaste the 'freedoms' of anarchy, refused to collect grain and cattle for the German occupiers and sometimes even sabotaged their transport. Punitive army expeditions to offending villages only inflamed their Ukrainian inhabitants. Guliai Polie, soon to be the Makhnovite capital, was just such a village. Rumours of German reversals on the western front circulated, fanned perhaps by the unease felt among the various anti-Bolshevik factions that had collected in Ukraine during its occupation.[8] Familiar with the unreassuring reports from the Mennonite representatives who had travelled to Germany to discuss our ultimate status under German protection, former industrialists and estate owners were the first to worry.[9] And, of course, anyone with open eyes could see that the Skoropadskii regime rested on German bayonets, not popular sentiment. By late September, German military officials advised strengthening our self-defence units and offered us more arms. Virtually every farming family or propertied citizen possessed a gun. Abram Löwen, the unprincipled *Selbstschutz* leader who had built a reputation as avenger of the wrongs visited upon the formerly prosperous citizenry, was in his element, strutting about Nieder Khortitsa with a sawed-off army rifle, short enough to hide under his overcoat, if need arose. Bandit raids resumed, especially on isolated Mennonite estates near Schönfeld and the Molochna villages near Guliai Polie, which was Makhno's main base of recruitment. Increasingly, the brigands simply murdered the owners. This was but a foretaste of the tragedy that unfolded over the following years.

CHAPTER TWENTY-TWO

A Short Respite: Two Celebrations

In the tumult during the German occupation, our family managed to enjoy two joyous events. First, in June 1918 Mariechen married Heinrich Klassen, the son of a once-prosperous farmer, and few weeks later my Aunt Justina and Uncle Jacob Janzen celebrated their twenty-fifth wedding anniversary on the Wilhelmstal estate. Both events were striking portraits of life as it once had been.

Mariechen's impending marriage delighted everyone in the extended family, but especially Grandmother Pauls, Tante Sus, and the two bachelor uncles with whom Mariechen had boarded while attending high school in Rosental. She was almost twenty-four, an age tantamount to spinsterhood by Mennonite standards of the time. She had had her share of suitors, but, as she told me decades later, she had always wanted to take an advanced degree that would allow her to teach before she married. Nevertheless, when the revolution dashed her hopes of a career, she accepted the inevitability of marriage.

Times were unsettled and resources scarce, yet Father and Mother attempted to host a wedding comparable to those of prewar times, perhaps because Mariechen was their only unmarried daughter, or simply their favourite child. More likely they wished to reward her for helping Father in his grain business and assuming Mother's role while Mother took care of Jacob and me in Rosental. I suspect they felt she had refused an earlier proposal from a young teacher because of these duties. In any event, the flurry of normal wedding preparations ensued.[1]

As distinct from my parents' rushed wedding, most young couples courted for several months.[2] If the couple's parents approved of the match, their engagement was announced in church on two successive Sundays. This gave anyone an opportunity to object or 'forever hold his peace.' The announcement surprised few, since the marriage had undoubtedly been the subject of conjecture and gossip throughout the village. The speculation was more fun in the rare case that the groom came from a distant village. Then everyone was eager to know what the groom looked like, his family's worth, and how he happened to have found so and so's Trintje, Lentje, Süestje, Sauntje, or Listje.

If an 'outside' suitor actually netted a local maiden it meant that he had already passed a test from her male friends and even perhaps the man's rivals. In Nieder Khortitsa the future bride's close male relatives and/or friends traditionally hid behind farm buildings or in adjacent orchards waiting until the invader's carriage drove through the farmyard gate. Then they greeted the startled suitor with rifle shots. The practice had two meanings. It could warn the suitor that he was trespassing on forbidden terrain, and test the suitor's (or his coachman's) ability to handle his frightened horses – in normal times a spirited, matched pair decked in fancy coloured flynets and Russian-style harness collar (*khomut*). (If the suitor was particularly pretentious, his coachman might even dress in full Russian livery.) The gunshots could also have been fired at the behest of the maiden, apprising the suitor that she favoured his quest, in such case, obviously a good omen.

Sometimes a maiden inflicted another custom on a suitor from another village, whom she wished to reject, when she was either too timid or disingenuous to tell him so directly. If she let her brothers or young male friends know, they hid outside. After the suitor entered the house, they tied a basket to the rear axle of his carriage. The basket, called a *Tjiep*, was oblong – about two feet wide by four feet long – shallow, round-bottomed, and used to haul chaff from the barn's fodder bin to the horses' troughs. The coarse village expression for this practice at that time was, 'That man has received a basket' (*De Maun haft 'ne Tjiep jetjräajen*), meaning the woman rejected his proposal. The only time I witnessed this practice was when, as a child, our neighbour's daughter rejected a man from Burwalde.

Once the couple had announced the engagement, they made endless prearranged visits to relatives and close friends, usually entailing a meal, or at least coffee and *Tweebaktjes*. The wedding itself, which usually occurred three or four weeks later, rarely was held on a Sunday or when crops were being planted, harvested, or threshed. But that left plenty of days during the slack time of May and July, and after late August or early September when the threshing was finished, and the weather was certain to be good.

Only those outside the village received wedding invitations, and since the settlement's postal service was somewhat haphazard, they were hand-delivered by members of the bride's family. The inscription on the inner left side of the card usually read something like, 'God willing, the nuptials of our daughter [name] to [groom's name], son of [name of parents] will take place on [day, date, and hour], to which you are respectfully invited.' The bride's parents signed the card. Invitations sent within the village itself circulated like a chain letter, with a list of names written on the envelope or the inner right side of the card, the first person delivering it to the next on the list, and on down. Most families had extensive relationships of one degree or another to most people in the village, so the question of who to invite or not without causing unhappiness, resentment, or a family rift could be agonizing. Usually, the local teachers were invited if either partner had a sibling in school or their parents were consequential in village affairs.

Weddings were traditionally held in the bride's family home. Thus, our household's activities took on a feverish pace, particularly during the last few days before the ceremony, when it seemed like a beehive. If the bride's father was a farmer, the family usually held the ceremony in its huge barn (*Scheune*), which could accommodate several hundred people when the machinery had been removed. The storage bins for grain and chaff were curtained off, and the rest of the barn was cleaned and festooned with greenery. Wooden benches, six to eight feet long, which flanked every Mennonite's dining table, were collected from friends and neighbours and set up around the interior. A large table was placed near the entrance where the wedding party would sit.

Father was not a farmer, so we used our large grain storage building. Virtually empty at the time, its brick walls and cement floor were easy to clean, and its exposed roof beams were perfect for hanging garlands of flowers. Friends and relatives of both the bride and groom helped out. Neighbours and friends brought ingredients over to use in the traditional wedding fare – especially butter, eggs, and flour for *Tweebaktjes*, *Bultje* (the large loaves of white bread to be served with *Borscht*), and various pastries. Although Mother prepared the dough, the future groom carried batches of it to neighbouring women who baked the delicacies in their ovens. She herself roasted huge batches of beef to serve cold and cooked kettles of *Borscht*, *Zwiebelsuppe* (onion and potato soup), and *Plumemooss*.

The high point of the betrothal period fell on the night before the wedding. Early that evening a huge assemblage of guests – couples and singles, young and old – arrived at the home of the bride's parents for the wedding shower (*Poltaowend* or *Polterabend*). Once everyone arrived, the couple unwrapped their gifts, to the accompaniment of loud 'oohs' and 'ahhs' of admiration and approval. By the time Mariechen married, the war and revolution had made most household articles extremely scarce, so many of the gifts were homemade items and preserves. With the gifts opened, the older guests left, because the *Poltaowend* was really an event for the young to sing, play games, or stage a play, usually a light farce in *Plautdietsch*.

Mariechen's wedding festivities opened with the groom's arrival, and the air filled with *Flintenschüsse* from his former service comrades who had hidden in nearby yards. Shortly after, Mother served *Borscht* and *Zwiebelsuppe* to relatives and out-of-town guests, and then the ceremony began sometime between one and two. Once the guests sat down, the ministers and the parents of the bride and groom took seats at the head table. Then the bride and groom walked in, arm in arm, and sat on garlanded chairs facing the minister, the Reverend Sawatzky. After his brief prayer the esteemed Elder Isaak Dyck delivered a sermon entitled: 'Commend Thy Ways to the Lord' (*Befiehl dem Herrn deine Wege*), then questioned the groom and bride, blessed them, and led the guests in song. Coffee and *Tweebaktjes* were served at the brief reception that followed.[3]

The younger guests stayed for a while after the ceremony, engaged in light banter, and then left to tend to their farm and domestic chores. The elders lingered on for another hour or two, neighbouring with relatives and acquaintances before departing. Several hours later Mother served cold meats and *Plumemooss* to a small number of relatives and out-of-town guests. The latter often stayed overnight and through breakfast the next day. Close relatives might stay on for several days.

The wedding party began after supper, and was decidedly a young people's affair. Maria belonged to Nieder Khortitsa's *Jugendverein*, as did Johann. This was a youth club, and members got together frequently to sing and play games. Before the war, few children outside the most prosperous families were members, but with the war over, and the return of our servicemen, membership had expanded more democratically and interest turned increasingly to plays. Maria was one of the group's most popular members, so virtually everyone else in the club came to her wedding, making the evening a lively affair. Games and singing dominated, no alcohol was served at these events, nor was there any dancing. Athough not really taboo in Nieder Khortitsa, it was still a few years before the younger generation began dancing the waltz, polka, and chardash. The most popular game was a variant of musical chairs (*Schlüsselbund*). Three rituals ended the celebration around ten or eleven o'clock. First, the crowd hoisted the bride and groom, seated in garlanded chairs, into the air, while the men sang, 'High (in the sense of happy) shall they live, happy shall they live, three times high' (*Hoch sollen sie leben, hoch sollen sie leben, dreimal hoch*). Then thrice they shouted, 'bitter' (*gor'koe*), a signal for the groom to kiss the bride, and 'sweet' (*sladkoe*).

Next the bride gave away her wreath or veil, much as modern brides toss their bouquet. For this traditional presentation (*ausspielen,* literally 'playing out') the unmarried women blindfolded the bride, encircled her, and sang a folksong (well-known from Carl Maria von Weber's *Der Freischütz*):

We twine a maiden's wreath for you
From silk of violet-blue,
Escorting you to games and dance,
May joy your life enhance.
refrain:
Beautiful green, beautiful green maiden's wreath.

Wir winden dir den Jungfernkranz
Aus veilchenblauer Seide;
Wir führen dich zu Spiel und Tanz,
Zu Glück und Liebesfreude.
refrain:
Schöner grüner, schöner grüner Jungfernkranz.

When the song finished, the girls turned the bride around three times, and, by obvious prearrangement, positioned her so that she could give the wreath (or veil) to the girl she hoped would next become engaged. The groom gave away his corsage similarly, after which the bride's wreath was replaced with a cap (*haube*). Again the women circled her, and this time they sang:

Give up the wreath and leave it be,
Life's duty, another, will decree.
May for your lot, the holy vow,
God grant you strength and joy of now;

A bonnet frame your lovely sight,
Your lot in life, may it be light.

Gib her den Kranz, du brauchst ihn nicht.
Dich ruft nun eine andere Pflicht.
Da du den Ehestand dich geweiht,
Gott schenk dir Kraft und Freudigkeit.
Die Haube sei hinfort dein Schmuck,
Und geb' es Gott kein schwerer Druck.

The event, which began with Mariechen's engagement and the ensuing prenuptial activities (*Veatjast*), then the wedding ceremony (*Tjast*), was completed the next day with a post-wedding clean-up (*Nohtjast*) – returning benches, pots and pans, tables, and bits and pieces borrowed from neighbours, friends, and relatives. Following lunch, most of the out-of-town guests who had stayed the night departed. Our lives then resumed their normal routine. As customary, the bride and groom moved immediately into his parents' home, where they remained for about a year, before moving into the small *kutok* section house that Grandfather Rempel had built in 1890 for his daughter Elisabeth.

A Wedding Anniversary

My Aunt Katharina and Uncle Jacob Janzen's silver wedding anniversary furnished the second high point of that summer, in part because they celebrated it at their Wilhelmstal estate, in the district of even more impressive Mennonite estates, and an area I had visited only once before. Most of the family was too busy to make the four-day journey, so Mother (who was Katharina's older sister) and I went with Mariechen, her new husband, and Mother's youngest brother, Uncle Johann. My new brother-in-law's parents still owned a spring wagon (*Federwagen*) and several excellent horses, so the trip was comfortable.

We left Nieder Khortitsa late in the afternoon and stayed overnight at Grandmother Pauls in Rosental, so we could leave the next morning before dawn. The lilting calls of nightingales accompanied our first miles. Then as the sun rose, a glorious August morning unfolded. Within an hour, we turned off the main road and headed towards Neuendorf and Wilhelmstal. Here, the deeply bifurcated terrain of our home area gave way to limitless steppe, a horizon broken only by prehistoric earthen burial mounds (*kurgans*) dotting the landscape.

This land, with its spaciousness, strength, beauty, fertility, and the lore of ancient warriors, remains deep in my psyche even today. While Mother and Mariechen chatted and Uncle Johann and Mariechen's husband Heinrich discussed their military experience, my gaze wandered over the expanse of steppe. I imagined endless hordes of Scythians, Sarmatians, Huns, Goths, Pechenegs, Khazars, and Avars sweeping across it in peaceful or plunderous pursuits. Lofty songs my high school companions and I had sung about the exploits of Kievan Prince Igor or Glorious Prince Oleg against the ravaging nomads ran through my head.

> As valiant Oleg now prepares
> To take revenge against the senseless Khazars,
> Their villages and fields, for their brazen attacks,
> He consigns to the sword and fire.
>
> *Kak nyne sbiraetsia veshchii Oleg*
> *Otmstit nerazumnym Khozaram.*
> *Ikh sila i nivy za buinyi nabeg,*
> *Obriok on mecham i pozharam.*

When we reached Wilhelmstal, everything seemed normal, yet an air of apprehension about local civil unrest, and the future in general, was obvious. The older adults felt it keenly, but even we youths were not immune. Perhaps that explains why my brother-in-law Heinrich and I brought an army rifle along, just in case we encountered hostility from passing peasants en route. The weapon distressed my Uncle Johann, however. Bringing a rifle was stupid, he said, and brandishing it openly invited violence.

Johann said no more until I exercised my folly the next afternoon during the anniversary luncheon. It was a huge outdoor affair, with tables laden with traditional Mennonite foods. The weather was hot and swarms of flies hovered over the table, undeterred by peasant servants waving branches. With the heavy meal and the heat the guests began to nod off, and I, bored with the whole affair, took the rifle down to the pond. I fired at some ducks, missed every one, but rudely jarred the guests out of their torpor. Uncle Johann, knowing who must have created the fright, stormed down to the pond and gave me such a dressing down that the words smarted for months. It was, of course, an act of utter stupidity, and not just because, as Uncle Johann reminded me, I could not hit a crow at short range with a shotgun he had earlier tried to teach me to fire.

Woven into my memory of Wilhelmstal are two other estates – one a much grander Mennonite property and the other a Russian's land. The former, Zachariastal, had so far not been touched by bandit hordes or local pilfering peasants and so the house remained magnificent. Outside, too, everything looked thoughtfully planned, from the orchards and tree plantation, to the fields and ponds. The innumerable farmyard structures were well maintained, including the capacious barns, a flour mill, oil press, and even a brickyard. Servant quarters and a school building completed the outlying buildings. How this prosperous estate contrasted with the nearby Russian estate (*khutor*) belonging to the Savitskii family, which I visited with my cousins to deliver an invitation to the anniversary party! The Savitskii estate, like others I could barely see from the road, evoked scenes from Gogol's writings – a picturesque, but unkempt Georgian house with its cherry orchard nearby, a woven willow fence with posts topped with pots, haphazardly arranged mud huts for the servants, and everywhere a sense of inefficiency and neglect. Mennonites of the time summed this up as 'a typical Russian state of affairs' (*daut es 'ne ajchte rusche Wirtschauft*)!

How grand, joyous, and enlightening the trip had been and how poignant it seems now. Although none of us suspected it then, this was the last time the extended family would assemble together in the Old World.

CHAPTER TWENTY-THREE

The Civil War Deepens, November 1918 to September 1919

Defeat of the Central Powers on the Western Front led to the withdrawal of German troops from our area, as well. Their departure doomed the puppet Skoropadskii regime they had installed, and with its collapse, a power vacuum resulted. This, in turn, sucked each of the major factions of the civil war back into our settlement. During November and early December 1918 the fighting was mostly between the Whites (the counter-revolutionary forces led mostly by former tsarist officers and Cossacks) and the Yellows (led by the Ukrainian Socialist Petliura and so-called because of their yellow flag). Jumping into the melee shortly thereafter were the Reds (the Bolsheviks) and Blacks (the partisan bandit groups named for the colour symbolizing revolutionary anarchism).

Petliura and his followers might have been the logical heirs to rule the region, but their chances of winning broad support for a Ukrainian Nationalist-Socialist state were slim. Ukrainian peasants had already expropriated much of the land and so saw little benefit to themselves. Settlers of different ethnic backgrounds (Great Russian, Greek, Armenian, Jewish, and Balkan as well as Germanic) had no desire to live under Ukrainian rule. Lacking the support of these groups, Petliura's forces were no match for the loose collection of Cossacks, Kadet (former officers of the Imperial Army's VIII Corps), and civilian counter-revolutionaries making up the White forces in the region.

In late 1918, there was skirmishing between the Yellows and Whites in Neuenburg, Khortitsa, and Einlage, but these did not affect our security per se, although both groups constantly requisitioned clothing, food, horses, and fodder, in the case of the Petliurovites, under threat of force. To the best of my recollection, our local self-defence unit (*Selbstschutz*) was involved in only three skirmishes during this time. In the first instance it prevented a detachment of Petliurovites from crossing the Einlage bridge. In the second, it stopped a group of Free Cossacks (*vilni kozaki*), allied with some peasant riff-raff from the village of Voznesenskoe, from crossing the same bridge without their escort, thus assuring that they harmed no one along the way. In the third, it repelled a group of Cossacks who demanded that they forfeit their guns. My only defiant act was refusing a Petliurovite order to report to Ekaterinoslav for mobilization in their army.

In December 1918, the Bolsheviks swept back in and re-established control. With them came the soviet system, this time with Comrade Starko in command. In an attempt to starve out their adversaries across the Dnieper River in Alexandrovsk, they installed a special garrison in Nieder Khortitsa, whose function was to interdict black market sales of flour, oil, butter, eggs, and meat. This merely stimulated smuggling, which, once a simple trade plied by peasant women and peddlars, now became a more dangerous game played mostly by Jewish and Mennonite men. Rather than end our misery, the Bolshevik presence meant there was one more party requisitioning household goods, money, horses, or whatever they needed or wanted. Often their justification was that the victim had earlier collaborated with 'the enemy': the Germans. Or they might claim the village had failed to resist 'the enemy,' as if we had had the power to do so.

Next came the bandits, who reappeared in force within weeks. On either 8 or 9 January 1919, a large number of brigands rode into nearby Burwalde and terrorized the population for hours, seizing whatever clothing, food, and money they could find and demanding additional *kontributsiia* of 15,000 to 17,000 rubles from local farmers.

The *Selbstschutz* was by this time unarmed and helpless, but the attack did not go unavenged. Several citizens rushed from Burwalde to Khortitsa to beg protection from Bolshevik Comrade Starko. Responding with about a dozen of his guards, Starko chased the bandits across the Dnieper, which at the time was frozen, caught them in Voznesenskoe, and brought them to Khortitsa where he sentenced them to death.

I witnessed the execution. The three brigands (some acquaintances recall more) were lined against a brick wall outside my classroom. With villagers as witnesses in the street, and my fellow students at the window, the firing squad summarily shot the bandits. Although the Burwalde victims requested that their stolen goods be returned, Starko refused, claiming that the culprits were Petliurovites, and thus the goods were military booty, not civilian losses.

An equally bloody incident took place virtually the same day in Nieder Khortitsa. This time it involved Abram Löwen, who had championed the *Selbstschutz* and its activities during the German occupation. He was to be the source of much of our grief throughout the next six months. This incident began with the sudden arrival at the office of the village soviet of four men from Alexandrovsk who demanded that they be driven to Tomakovka. The group's identity was a mystery, although some claimed they were peasants from that city who had joined the Petliura forces and who were now trying to flee home from the pursuing Makhnovite bandits. The peasants had not actually threatened anyone, but Löwen and his cohorts, Abram Günter Jr, David Neufeld, and Jacob Töws, trapped the four and insisted that the men be shot on the spot. When a crowd of citizens interceded, Löwen grudgingly allowed a village youngster to drive them towards Burwalde. As soon as the crowd dispersed, Löwen and his three friends hitched a team of horses to a spring wagon standing nearby and set off in pursuit of the group. Catching up with them near Schöneberg, the four men from Alexandrovsk dismounted and fled into the valley in vain hopes of escape. Löwen reputedly killed them all, although some rumours claimed that Neufeld shot one. They left the bodies in the field.

When the citizens of Burwalde heard of the shooting, they sent a party out to bury the bodies. Deeply agitated and angry, they also sent a representative to report the incident to the Khortitsa district soviet, fearing that Burwalde would be associated with Löwen's dastardly act, and made to pay for it. Reaction in Nieder Khortitsa was divided. One group of villagers insisted on the immediate need to reorganize the self-defence unit with Löwen in command. The more level-headed demanded that Löwen be held under house arrest for at least a week, to show nearby peasant villages that we did not condone such acts. According to Funk's diary, the village assembly met, and resolved the issue by sentencing Löwen to a week in jail. His incarceration was actually shorter than that, for his friends released him the next day.

Löwen's vicious act had terrible repercussions for our village, for it made Nieder Khortitsa a general target for every passing bandit and partisan, each demanding that we surrender him. When we could – or would – not, they used this as a pretext for punitive demands and violent acts. That did not deter Löwen, however. In February 1919, as the marauders' raids increased, Löwen cornered two bandits just after they had raided Heinrich Pankratz's home. Löwen shot at both, killing one outright and wounding the other, who managed to escape. The crowd gathering at the scene wholeheartedly endorsed Löwen's action.[1] But after the heat of the moment had cooled, the division of feelings towards Löwen became even more acute. Those who feared repercussions, or repudiated the immorality of Löwen's deeds, were even more resentful of him, while others – particularly the formerly prosperous farmers or the mill owners – championed him.

Shortly after, Löwen furthered his reputation as an avenger by capturing two armed men who came to town demanding that the local soviet help find him. Instead, the authorities arrested these men and turned them over to Löwen, who later boasted that the men 'vanished of their own accord.' There seemed little doubt in his meaning.

In late March, our village was again 'saved' from reprisals for Löwen's actions by a quirk. At that time the bandits and Bolsheviks had formed a tenuous alliance against their common enemy, the White Army, which threatened the Reds along the entire Ukrainian front. With this alliance the Bolsheviks forced the partisan bandits to be more restrained, and for a time the raids, made under the pretense of finding Löwen, became less frequent.

Up to this point no one in the village had been killed. That changed on 21 March. Reverend Johann Rempel was plowing his field several versts from the village, with the help of his eldest son and a Ukrainian peasant boy from Razumovka, when unknown marauders stole the preacher's horses and shot the three people. The senior Rempel and the peasant boy died. As evidence of their restraint, the Bolsheviks pursued the culprits, apprehending them in Ekaterinoslav, and returned the horses and wagon to the widow. I have no idea what they did with the killers. Miraculously the son, who had been left for dead, survived with a bullet lodged in his head. Of course, no surgery was possible. Fortunately, a dramatic sneeze at my brother Johann's wedding eighteen months later dislodged the bullet.

The Razumovka peasants were so embittered by the child's death that a week later, when the Red Army arrived to requisition goods, they gave chase to the soldiers, killed one, captured several others, and shoved them under the ice on the Dnieper. The peasants boasted to us in Nieder Khortitsa that they knew better than the Mennonites how to handle would-be expropriators. However, their glory was short-lived. Within days the authorities sent a force to Razumovka, ransacked the village, and arrested about twenty men that they believed were guilty. Some of the men were released, and others fled. The village was fined 100,000 rubles. In this case, the soviet authorities made no distinction between Ukrainian peasants and Mennonite 'counter-revolutionaries,' which elicited a measure of satisfaction among some of our citizenry.

A little while later the actual battle front between the White and Red armies approached our area. The Bolsheviks stepped up their pace of requisitioning Mennonite goods, whether the victims lived in the villages, on estates, or in the region's hamlets. It was small consolation that these expropriations were done by at least a nominally legal system of government, and much less haphazardly than the never-ending seizures by the partisans or bandits. During this time, local administrative agencies underwent endless reorganization – the regular soviets were replaced or augmented by the creation of special committees: first it was the committees of the poor (*komitety nezamozhnykh*), which a few weeks later were replaced by the food-provisioning committees (*prodovol'stvennye komitety*), then by new local soviets.

In April 1919, my brother Johann was elected chairman of this new village soviet (council), replacing Johann Funk who was drafted into another position. Their friend Kornelius Warkentin was re-elected secretary of the soviet. My brother 'qualified' for his position, which had to be filled by someone from the proletariat, because his occupation as a teacher placed him among the toiling masses. The job was not only thankless and exhausting, but very unpleasant. As chairman, Johann was supposed to oversee the requisitioning of goods. Then there was the almost daily invasion of soldiers and party officials demanding to be fed. Johann rotated this chore among the village families, and inevitably some turned bitterly on Johann with the complaint that their turn came too often.

Another of his distasteful tasks lay in quelling vendettas arising between many former prosperous farmers and the *Nippaenja* or *kutok* proletarians. This was especially true when the worker, who might even be a distant relative of the farmer, had made common cause with the Bolsheviks or even the local bandits. Two of the troublemakers, Kornelius and Heinrich Wall, had, as noted, changed their name to the Ukrainianized Vallenko. The worst was a young man named Götz (or Jaetz). One of the wealthier local farmers, who had raised Götz as a foster child, had evidently punished him, so one day Götz appeared in Johann's office, accompanied by several Red Army soldiers. Götz demanded that Johann produce the farmer because 'he beat me once and now I want to beat him, and get an indemnity of 500 rubles.' Johann reminded Götz that when the latter had been Johann's student, he too had punished the boy. Was Johann also to receive a beating? 'Oh no, you were my teacher and had the right to punish me,' was his response. The farmer escaped the beating but evidently paid some indemnity.[2]

The most onerous aspect of Johann's job as chairman of the soviet was the requirement that he keep a gun at home, and, if need be, use it to keep the peace. This civic duty, of course, conflicted with his religious commitment to pacifism. The dilemma became obvious in a dramatic incident in May. Looking up from his desk in the headquarters of the soviet, which was located in Father's old general store, Johann spotted a troop of nineteen heavily armed youths marching down the main street. Red Army troops came out of their garrison, which was across the street from Johann's office in one of the old Niebuhr-Wiebe flour mills, and demanded their identity. Rebuffing the Reds, the band continued down the road towards the Ukrainian peasant village of Belenkoe. The Red Army soldiers then sought help from the Khortitsa district soviet, which sent two soldiers to Belenkoe. They reported back that the youths were Ukrainian soldiers (led by a man named Chaikovskii), who had fortified themselves on a hill called Lysaia Gora. Hearing this, Abram Löwen rushed to Lysaia Gora to join the anti-Bolshevik Ukrainian ruffians. Two weeks later he led a raiding party on the Nieder Khortitsa Red Army garrison, capturing the soldiers, taking them back to their hilltop bastion, and in typical Petliurovite fashion, executing the one Jewish soldier along the way.[3] One Red soldier escaped, reported the melee to Johann, then hurried off to Khortitsa to report the incident. Father, hearing of the skirmish, realized that Johann was now in peril. If the Bolsheviks in Khortitsa suspected that Johann had failed to challenge the Ukrainian peasant raiders, who knew what they would do? Acting quickly, Father rushed to the garrison, still occupied by a few members of the peasant band, and persuaded one of them to 'disarm' Johann. The ploy worked, for when the Red soldiers arrived from Khortitsa, they believed Johann's story that the peasants had surprised and disarmed him just as they had the garrison soldiers.

There is a postscript. The Bolsheviks sent a new detachment of soldiers to wipe out the Chaikovtsy group still entrenched on Lysaia Gora. Löwen later bragged that the group had repelled the Red soldiers by the clever ruse of displaying a 'three-inch artillery piece,' fashioned from a tree trunk and two carriage wheels. Whether this was true or not, Löwen returned unharmed to the village, and Chaikovskii's Ukrainian band eventually left their hilltop and melded into the peasant population.

From March through June of 1919, the peasant bandits and Red Army soldiers alike stepped up their demands for goods. The army also ordered us to either produce Abram Löwen or pay a fine of tens of thousands of rubles. Löwen was continually evading capture, and the fines were always due. To ensure that they were paid, the officials often took innocent hostages. This made Löwen's exploits pale even to his one-time admirers.

Nieder Khortitsa had no telephones. Most of the farmers had lost much of their land, leaving them with lots of free time on their hands. The men of the village used to hang around the soviet headquarters, endlessly rehashing Löwen's heroics, as well as each new rumour about a soon-to-be change of government. Some of the men were sure that the counter-revolutionaries would win, with the help of French or British troops. Others decried the timidity of the village leaders and boasted of the strong-arm tactics that they themselves would use on the Reds and bandits should they become the elected leaders. Yet as soon as expropriators of any sort rode into town, announcing their arrival with a rifle shot, these 'militant' Mennonites would scatter like frightened birds, hoping to get home without running into the uninvited visitors. And as soon as the coast seemed clear, they would reassemble, again bewailing their leaders' 'spineless' accession to the marauders' demands.

I lived in Khortitsa at this time, enrolled in my second year at the teachers' seminary. That autumn classes began in the seminary building as usual, but as fuel became more scarce, we moved first into the high school, and then into the beautiful home that had belonged to the Wallmanns, but was now the headquarters of the district soviet. The new occupants, of course, had no trouble getting fuel. Our move must have been facilitated by the soviet's professed interest in 'liquidating illiteracy,' a task that required new teachers. Among my most poignant memories of that time, when I studied in one of the Wallmanns' lovely panelled, high-ceilinged rooms, were the wonderful, rich aromas that wafted into the hall from the soviet's dining room. I never suffered from malnutrition while rooming with my Aunt Lena and Uncle Kornelius Braun, but the household's food was meagre, like everyone else's. Not so for the soviets.

In June 1919, the front shifted and battles between the Reds and the Whites were before us. The White Army took Alexandrovsk and quickly seized control of the east bank of the Dnieper, both north and south of the city. In reaction, the Makhnovites withdrew from their recruitment base in Guliai Polie and sought safety with their Bolshevik 'allies' in our area, on the west bank of the Dnieper. This meant that many in the Red Army units stationed in our villages were really bandits, controlled only nominally by the Bolsheviks. It made Johann's job as chairman of the village soviet all the more dangerous.

Towards the end of the month, Johann was working at his desk in the village soviet office when he heard a loud thumping noise. Looking up he saw a heavily armed man whose legs became wooden stumps below his knees. Without a glance or greeting the man sat down, unfastened his stumps, and laid them out on the floor. Removing two revolvers from his pockets, the man put them on the desk, eyed Johann for a time, and then asked, 'Who among you is Löwen?'

Johann belittled Löwen, stressing that no one in Nieder Khortitsa liked him, and that outsiders demanded him only when they wanted something else. This comment piqued the visitor's interest. After consulting companions, who addressed him as Batko Pravda, he casually asked whether the village had an apothecary. Replying, 'No,' Johann asked what he needed. Pravda's easy response of, 'morphine,' and a closer look at the *batko*, told Johann he faced an addict, and a particularly violent one if in need of a fix. Sensing danger, Johann suggested they find the village midwife (*Hebamme*). The two set off in the *batko*'s wagon, Johann seated next to the driver, Batko Pravda in the rear with his bodyguard. Locating the midwife at a funeral, Johann whispered that she give him five or six tablets, but no more. Satisfied that this was her entire supply, Batko Pravda swallowed one or two tablets, and departed with a much improved demeanour – and no more demands for Löwen.

A few days later Johann reaped his reward. Bolshevik headquarters in Khortitsa had ordered the settlement to outfit a hospital train with beds, blankets, cookware, medicine, and so forth, threatening to arrest or execute the local soviet chairmen of any villages failing to meet their huge quota. Johann rode to Khortitsa to argue that Nieder Khortitsa could not meet the demand, leaving his wagon and driver in nearby Rosental. Entering the village of Khortitsa, several bandits grabbed Johann and hauled him off to the district headquarters nearby. Responding to Johann's attempts to explain his errand, the peasant guard shrugged as if to say, 'My hut is at the end of the village. I don't know a thing.' (*Moia khata z kraiu. Ia nichogo ne znaiu*). Hearing a familiar thump-thump, Johann realized his fate rested with Batko Pravda. The dreaded man gave Johann a puzzled look, then recognizing him, asked why he was being detained. Learning Johann's business, he escorted him into the office of Comrade Deviatka, the military commander of the region. The pair freed Johann. That was Johann's final encounter with Batko Pravda, although not with Comrade Deviatka.

I had returned home a few weeks earlier, expecting a leisurely summer, as Father's business was almost non-existent. Apart from helping Mother around the house I anticipated leisurely days with my friends, swimming in the Dnieper. I was wrong. As the White Army consolidated its control over the east bank, our side filled up with Red troops. The shelling between forces across the Dnieper increased, with neither side particularly focused on military targets. Fortunately, whether by design or poor marksmanship, the Whites in Alexandrovsk did little damage to our village. The shelling was an added nightmare for the farmers, harvesting what sparse grain remained after troops had trampled through their fields. As far as I know, shells killed only two civilians in our village at the time: Gerhard Vogt, a man in his thirties, and Lieschen Siemens, a ten-year-old girl.

The Reds positioned two artillery pieces in our neighbour's orchard, setting their observation post at a distance, on top of the area's highest ancient burial mound (*kurgan*), and communicated by field telephone. The troops conscripted the youth of Nieder Khortitsa, myself included, to guard the length of wires connecting the two positions. Assigned a post near the top, I often borrowed the troops' field glasses to view targets in Alexandrovsk. Most often they seemed targets of opportunity, rather than of military importance. I recall that one soldier, seeing several White officers exit a building, ordered the artillery crew to fire, shouting, 'Watch out, officer' (*beregis' kadet*).

At home, as we daily lost more clothing with each search of our house, we began hiding our possessions, indoors and out. With the Makhnovites set to retreat as the White Army advanced, they threaded through our village, collecting any last items they could carry. Attempting to save what we could, we made a plan to hide our best clothes in the stable. While Heinrich stood look-out on the main street, I dashed into the backyard, but was barely off the porch when two Makhnovites, riding along the side street edging our corner lot, spotted me. In a flash they were in the yard, eagerly surveying my precious load.

What to do? Father sent Jacob to fetch Johann from the soviet office, assuming that as local soviet leader, he could thwart retribution. Johann arrived, cool-headed and persuasive. I had only been trying to hide the clothes from the White Army, which would surely target our household first, argued Johann. The fabrication saved me from a beating or worse, but not the family's trove of trousers.

I recall only two instances in which Johann lost his composure as chairman of the soviet. The first occurred in late spring 1919 during a house search. The armed men demanded a large sum of money from my father. Unable to produce it, they lashed Father's head and face with their lead-laden whips (*nagaiky*). Someone ran to get Johann. By the time he arrived, Father's face was bloodied, with strips of flesh hanging from his cheeks and chin. Enraged, Johann dashed in front of Father. The bandits then turned their fury on Johann, until they understood his threat to arrest them. I suspect Johann did not bother to report the incident to district headquarters. It would have been fruitless.

The second instance involved the infamous Löwen. Caught at last by the Bolsheviks, he had, as usual, escaped. One of the hapless captors, blaming Johann, sauntered into his office and threatened him with dire measures if he did not produce Löwen. The harangue went on until lunch. Persuading the guard to eat at a neighbour's home, Johann bolted from the office, leaving a note for his assistant saying that he had been summoned to the district office in Khortitsa and would be gone for several days. Panicked, he dashed home and had Jacob hitch up the wagon. Asked where they were going, Johann told Jacob, 'Anywhere but Khortitsa.' In agitation, the two headed towards Blumengart, Johann so frenzied he leaped off the wagon, commanding Jacob to drive as fast as possible while he trotted beside. By a circuitous route, the two finally reached the safety of a cousin's house in Schönhorst. Jacob returned the next day and Johann only several days later when no one seemed to be after him. And so he resumed his duties as though nothing had happened.

The actions of several Mennonite revolutionaries – the most notorious of whom was Peter Thiessen – compounded Johann's problems with the Reds, the Whites, the bandits, and Löwen. Thiessen made several forays into Nieder Khortitsa early in the summer of 1919, but Johann's ordeal with him began on 16 July. As the White Army advanced towards our village, the Red Army prepared to retreat, threatening to beat any farmer who refused to exchange his horses for the soldiers' exhausted beasts.[4] When Johann persuaded a soldier to return a farmer's horse, the farmer invited my brother to stay for lunch. As they sat down to eat, a policeman arrived and hauled Johann to the military headquarters. Commanders Deviatka and Thiessen awaited him there. When Deviatka stepped out of the room, Thiessen – who had earlier served with Johann in the alternative service – tried to warn him that someone had accused him of a serious offence.

A minute later, Deviatka escorted a twelve-year-old boy from Burwalde into the office. The lad accused Johann of burying a machine gun on our property.[5] Seeing that the two Bolsheviks were not joking, Johann questioned the boy. Raising his arm as high as he could, he asked, 'Was the gun this tall?' To the boy's, 'Yes,' Johann laughed that he must have buried a ten-inch artillery piece in his yard, not a machine gun. Deviatka, warning Johann not to make light of the matter, turned to the boy, thrust a gun in his mouth, and demanded that the child answer each question with 'Yes' or 'No.' With a brief interruption for supper, the interrogation resumed. Deviatka was determined to arrest Johann and asked who would replace him as chairman of the soviet while he was jailed. When Johann mentioned a name, Deviatka's henchmen arrested the man. After this, Johann refused to supply more names, but Deviatka's underlings combed the villages near Khortitsa that night and arrested 100 men. No one ever knew for what reason.

The prisoners were held overnight in a filthy jail, then loaded into freight cars with the retreating southbound Red Army. White Army Cossacks shot at the train, but no Mennonites were hit, and Deviatka, soon finding his captives an encumbrance, released most of them when they reached the small town of Marganets. Although he demanded that Johann and seven fellow captives remain with him, they too eluded Deviatka's grip. Initially, they trekked home on foot, then they hitched a ride on the wagon of a Ukrainian teamster from the Nieder Khortitsa area who was also returning home. The peasant had been forced to carry material for the retreating Red Army, but he dropped out of the column after feigning that one of the axles of his wagon had cracked.

The White Army crossed the river two days later and life briefly brightened. Our new occupiers abolished the soviet form of government, restored Peter Unger to his old position as mayor (*Schulz*), and relieved Johann from the onerous chairmanship of the soviet. Over the rest of summer, Johann resumed preparation for the upcoming school session and, of equal importance, began courting Susie Epp, the daughter of a former teacher and sister of my friend Jacob Epp. My brother Heinrich was in equally good spirits, hoping that England and the United States, whose supplies were keeping the White Army alive, might export the goods we needed to rejuvenate Father's store. My father, I suspect, had no illusions that matters would change substantially.

While few Mennonites, even the formerly prosperous ones, openly collaborated with the Whites, I think that most hoped for their ultimate victory. I recall only one Nieder Khortitsa youth (named Bergen), who actually joined the White forces. However, several Mennonites from the Molochna Settlement served in the White Army as officers, and one named Schröder pleaded with the students at the teachers' seminary to join their cause. Our teacher, Dietrich Epp, counselled against this, but suggested instead that we guard the Einlage bridge for the Whites.

That plan seemed safe enough, and not really belligerent, so I signed up for duty, along with several classmates. As fate had it, I never served. A few days later, I contracted malaria, which left me bedridden for five weeks. I was given quinine, but by the time I was up and about most of the group had been assigned to encircle the major portion of Makhno's army at Uman. Two of my classmates remained to guard the bridge. To my parents' relief, I re-enrolled in school in September and thus escaped the terrible fate that befell my friends. The explosive break-out of the Makhnovites at Uman, and their lightning return to Khortitsa in an effort to reach their home base at Guliai Polie altered our situation, closing school for three months and, as we shall see, shattering most of our lives.

CHAPTER TWENTY-FOUR

Makhnovite Terror (*Makhnovshchina*): The Initial Stage, 21 September to 23 October 1919

In early September 1919, we hoped that order had returned permanently. The White Army's rapid advances into the central guberniias of European Russia suggested that they might hold this ground. Father's grain trade looked promising. By late August, the docks in Alexandrovsk were so loaded that he wondered where further shipments could be stored. The family's educational prospects also appeared auspicious. Enrollment at Johann's high school had increased substantially, attesting to its success. Jacob was now old enough to attend, and the location of the school in Nieder Khortitsa meant he could live at home. I went back to Khortitsa to finish my last year of teacher training, boarding again with my Aunt Helena and Uncle Kornelius Braun in the adjacent village of Rosental. I was particularly eager to get back to rekindle my friendship with a Miss S.P. who had caught my eye the previous year. Until her brother told me she was engaged to her village's youngest teacher, I had fostered hopes of a deeper relationship with her. Apart from this disappointment, the opening days of school were happy. The rest of my close friends were back and I loved school, especially my literature class, taught by Heinrich Epp. Being spared from serving in the White Army added to my pleasure.

Our optimism was soon shattered, however. As the White Army advanced towards Moscow, it left its rear, including our region, thinly guarded. The Makhnovites capitalized on this tactical error. Around 20 September, rumours circulated that a large Makhnovite cavalry troop, accompanied by numerous machine-gun detachments, had broken through the White Army's encirclement at Uman and headed for the two main Dnieper crossings at Einlage and Nikopol. The rumours were reinforced by reports that White Army authorities in Alexandrovsk had ordered all boats brought to the east bank and that no further transportation would be allowed from our side. Next day they were confirmed.

Seven decades later I can still remember the events of Saturday, 21 September 1919, when the Makhnovites poured into Khortitsa. On my way to school that morning I passed the old volost administration building (*Gebietsamt*) and was surprised to see my father, who hastily related the calamity of the previous day. After finishing his business in Alexandrovsk, he had headed for the Dnieper ferry as usual, but approaching the river, numerous people, including the White Army officer Bergen from Nieder Khortitsa, told him no one was allowed to cross back to the west bank. To reach home, Father walked all night along the east bank, through Alexandrovsk, Voznesenskoe, and past Alexandrabad to reach the Einlage bridge where he could cross to our side of the river. Throngs of travellers, all with the same intention, filled the road. Traffic across the bridge was prohibited, but the guards, my friends Andres and Kröger, still let people cross that morning.

Late that afternoon the ominous news played out. Lost in thought, I stood in front of the Rosental elementary school, adjacent to the teacherage where I boarded with my aunt and uncle, and at the intersection of the village's main street and a side street that ran towards the Dnieper's historic landing called *Tsarskaia pristan'*, and on to the Einlage bridge. First vaguely, then acutely, I felt the earth vibrate, the air hum, and then the burst of loud sounds – of hoof beats, neighing, grinding wagon wheels, and shouts – and soon the main street from Khortitsa was overrun with mounted soldiers, armed with rifles, sabres, revolvers, and hand grenades dangling from their belts. Clearly, these were all Makhnovites. Several *tachanki,* Mennonite spring wagons, each drawn by four beautiful horses, followed the first cavalry troop. One, drawn by four matched white horses, carried Batko Makhno and a few of his closest minor batkos.

The procession raced past me along the main street, then suddenly halted a few hundred yards east at the small bridge leading over the steppe stream that we called the Little Jordan. Realizing that they had missed the turn-off to the Dnieper bridge, they demanded directions from a passing farmer, veered back towards me, and poured down the side street towards the river. With the main street now empty, farmer Gerhard Schröder slowly approached with the oddest team imaginable, a tiny pony hitched with a camel. The camel, it seems, had been expropriated by the Makhnovites from some Tartar farmer, and later 'traded' for Schröder's good horse.[1]

When they reached the bridge, the Makhnovites found it guarded only by my friends. They seized the two and gave them the choice – to stand and be shot or jump over the side. Both jumped, landing in the Dnieper river, about eighty to ninety feet below. Kröger died. Andres was luckier. A Ukrainian fisherman picked him out of the water and smuggled him home. Somehow during the next terrible months of Makhnovite occupation, Andres eluded capture; ultimately he emigrated to Canada.

Within hours, thousands of 'partisans' overran Rosental and Khortitsa. By the next morning they had captured the White Army garrison in Alexandrovsk and established a secure hold on the east bank of the Dnieper as well. One of the first acts of the Makhnovites was to release the inmates from the city prison and then blow it up. Next the rear columns and camp followers entered the city, looting and terrorizing the civilian population, while the lead troops raced on to their home base area of Guliai Polie and several of its neighbouring villages.

Days later the Makhnovites occupied the entire Khortitsa Settlement, and for the following month they controlled a huge area, roughly thirty miles wide by 100 miles long, from northeast of Khortitsa to Guliai Polie. It included the Nikolaipol, Khortitsa, and Schönfeld Mennonite settlements, and many once-prosperous Mennonite estates of the Ekaterinoslav guberniia. Even in 1919, Mennonite properties in this area were still incomparably richer than those of the neighbouring Ukrainian peasants, and they became the happy hunting ground for brigands and local peasants to plunder and terrorize, day and night. Alexandrovsk and its suburb, Schönwiese – nodal points of rail and river transport, and home to numerous factories and flour mills, most of them owned by Mennonites – were the choicest and most lucrative prizes.

Mennonites throughout the bandit-held corridor all faced the same terror. Like wild beasts the Makhnovites stormed into all but the poorest houses, ransacking and stealing anything in sight – clothing, bedding, pillows, curtains, dishes, food, and of course, horses and wagons. No matter what time of the day or night, the plundering always began with the command, 'Mistress (*khoziaika*), prepare us a meal and be quick about it.' Meanwhile, the bandits ordered the owner (*khoziain*) to stable and feed their horses and sack some grain for their departure. Those who did not move swiftly enough, not to mention anyone who offered resistance, were whipped. Some were tortured or murdered.

At least during this time the Makhno search parties occasionally missed a village, giving its citizens a respite during which they might bury their few remaining valuables in barns, yards, orchards, or distant fields. We students were more fortunate than the general population. No matter how callous the brigands were towards everyone else, they considered teachers members of the working class and left them alone. Of course, the school buildings themselves offered nothing of value to the bandits, so they became a blissful refuge from the turmoil swirling outside.

The situation worsened in mid-October. Bolsheviks advanced from the north, forcing the White Army to retreat south towards a potentially safe area in the Crimea or Don Cossack regions. But to get there, the White Army had to blast its way through the Makhnovite-held corridor that held us, and across its base in Guliai Polie-Pologi. This, in turn, forced the Makhnovites back across the Dnieper to our villages. Thus, on 22 October, when the Whites entered the outskirts of Alexandrovsk, remnants of the Makhnovite bands fled helter-skelter across the Dnieper river into the Khortitsa Settlement. My friend Franz P. Thiessen, who worked for the Niebuhr flour mill in Schönwiese, watched the retreat. He estimated that over a three-day period the parade of cavalry, *tachanki*, cattle, sheep, oxen, camels, women, children, and camp followers included at least 60,000 people. Many bandits swam across the river. Reaching Nieder Khortitsa cold and wet, they demanded dry clothes, without hesitation. From that moment until Christmas, a force of between 80,000 and 100,000 men occupied the entire west bank of the Dnieper from Nikopol almost to Ekaterinoslav, a distance of about eighty miles. Most belonged to Makhno's band, but more than a few may have been members of smaller bands belonging to other batkos (Savelii Nuzhnyi, for example) who had allied themselves with Makhno. About 30,000 of these brigands occupied the Khortitsa and Nikolaipol Mennonite settlements for the next two months, roughly 500 of them entrenched in tiny Nieder Khortitsa, which normally had a population of about 1,000. The marauders visited a nightmare on the Mennonites of this area – hardly matched anywhere during Russia's devastating civil war.

Throughout the settlement, all semblance of normal life ceased. The bandits, now more vicious than ever, set up artillery pieces in a neighbour's orchard in Nieder Khortitsa, making our house a target of retaliatory shelling. After I returned home in October, a shell whistled through my window one night as I slept, embedding itself, unexploded in the wall just over my head. Bandit searches increased dramatically, with Makhnovites invading homes almost hourly, even searching classrooms. Now concerned for our safety, the teachers disbanded the school in Khortitsa.

With the bandits in absolute control, I could now no longer safely wear my favourite leather boots, a superbly crafted pair, custom-made for Johann in Moscow, and given me in anticipation that I would have to guard the Einlage bridge. For a time I had camouflaged the boots by slipping a pair of long, heavy woolen socks over them, then stuffing my feet into oversized clogs. The boots resembled those that the White Army officers wore, and they would label me a collaborator, and warrant a sure death sentence if I were caught with them on.

Uncle Kornelius, with whom I was boarding in Khortitsa, discovered the boots, and announced categorically that I had to get rid of them immediately. But where? Foolishly, I decided to bury them in the hayloft of the teacherage barn. A mere two hours later my infuriated uncle confronted me, having discovered the boots while digging in the same pile of hay to hide some of the family's cherished silver. Since any connection with the prohibited boots, no matter how slim, might damn him – perhaps even the entire family – as well as me, his next edict was unequivocal. I was to get rid of the boots in some distant place.

Snow had fallen that morning, so I took the teacher's son's sleigh, an axe, and a rope, and with the compromising boots camouflaged on my feet, set out towards the Dnieper to hide them among rocks in the heavily wooded valleys nearby. Skirting the schoolyard, I proceeded along the back fences of several farmsteads until I reached the brickyard dale (*Teajelschienläajcht*). There I found a suitable spot, removed the boots, wrapped them in a sack, wedged them in among some rocks, and covered the rift with dead branches. Tucking my feet back into my clogs, I loaded dry branches on the sleigh, tied the axe conspicuously on top, and prayed fervently that no one would stop me as I ventured back. Providence was on my side and I reached the school grounds safely. I retrieved the precious boots several months later, in February 1920. Aside from a few holes chewed by field mice, they were in excellent condition, and served me well for the next three years.

Uncle Kornelius, however, was not mollified. Initially, I attributed this to his temerity in tight situations, but later – after Tante Lena and the children were in bed, and the bandits' raiding seemingly over for the night – learned what fuelled his rage. The previous night three bandits had burst into a neighbour's home, demanding money. When the neighbour could produce none, the bandits tied him to a chair and forced him to watch as they repeatedly raped his wife. Then, with the vilest curses they had beat him, as well.

After recounting the story, Uncle Kornelius and I sat in his study smoking, the inside shutters closed so that no one could see the light. In an effort to relax, Uncle picked up a copy of the humorous Low-German writings of Fritz Reuter and read aloud passages from *Ut mine Strom Tied* (*My Stormy Days*). One especially timely passage concerned Russian troops, who had robbed locals of everything in northwest Germany:

> Those times were really bad,
> And wars raged round us far and sad,
> And then the Russians cozied up
> To us, then filled their every cup
> They ate and ravaged at their will,
> And left us lice, to pay the bill.
>
> *Daut wea doamals de schlemme Tiet,*
> *aus Krieg wea om ons sid und wiet,*
> *on uns aus Frind de Russen kemen*
> *an aules waut wi hauden, neemen*
> *on rautzenkoal on orm ons freten,*
> *on stoats Betoalung Lies ons leten.*

A consummate actor, Uncle Kornelius read the passage with a superb mimicry of the dialect. With this bit of gallows humour we were finally able to sleep.

School was closed indefinitely on 24 October, 1919 and I walked the ten miles through rain and knee-deep mud to Nieder Khortitsa, stopping along the way at Grandmother Pauls's home. It was evening and the house was dark, everyone fearing that a lighted lamp would attract a new group of cursing, rampaging Makhnovites. Grandmother, Uncle Heinrich, and I sat in the second-story glassed-in verandah, looking out over the moonlit lowlands before us. Grandmother gazed pensively eastward, towards the faint outlines of the high, rocky shores of the Dnieper, near the ferry landing to Khortitsa Island. How she longed to walk those sandy shores, she sighed, to cross the river, and again roam across the island's familiar landmarks – the ancestral farm, the cemetery where most of the Hildebrands were buried, the small private Höppner cemetery and monument, and the other places that she and her brother Kornelius had so often frequented for so many decades.

We felt insecure, although we could scarcely imagine the horrors about to engulf us. Yet Grandmother did not despair of life. She expressed a strong desire to survive the clash of monstrous forces that a world war, two revolutions, and a civil war had unleashed on our hapless land. It was not to be. This was the last time I saw Grandmother Pauls in good health.

CHAPTER TWENTY-FIVE

The Height of the Makhnovite Terror: 23 October to 23 December 1919

Once the Makhnovites consolidated their forces on our side of the Dnieper river, their barbarity became boundless. Everyone in the region suffered, but the bandits unleashed their worst rampages on the Mennonites. On 26 October they killed more than 100 Mennonites in four villages and hamlets. My Uncle Heinrich Heinrichs (whose deceased wife had been my Aunt Anganetha Pauls) was among the first killed. The bandits stabbed or hacked most victims to death with sabres rather than fire shots that would warn other intended victims. The death toll in the Nikolaipol Settlement village of Eichenfeld was eighty-three or eighty-four. Eight people were slaughtered in Petersdorf, three in Paulsheim, and ten to fifteen in several other small hamlets and khutors, virtually obliterating their adult male population. In most cases the savages retreated only after burning the villages to the ground.

Some estate owners fared better, losing virtually all their property, while keeping their lives. This was true for my Aunt Katharina and Uncle Jacob Janzen, whose wedding anniversary celebration I described in an earlier chapter. They belonged to the *Gutsbesitzer*, the estate-owning class which the surrounding Ukrainian peasant population envied, even despised. From the overthrow of the provisional government until the Bolsheviks seized power, many of these families, apprehensive for their safety, had fled their estates for the security of a relative's home in the villages. With the estate owners gone, the peasants had looted the properties, and, in cases of extreme hatred, torched the buildings. These acts ceased during the German occupation, but resumed almost immediately thereafter. Up to then, the Janzens, who seemingly had a good relationship with their peasant neighbours had not been molested, nor had they lost significant property. But by late 1918 they too abandoned their Wilhelmstal home fleeing to Grandmother Pauls's home in Rosental. Leaving everything behind but their best clothing, some tableware, a few cherished objects, and what food they could cram into two wagons, they journeyed to Grandmother's, where they lived for a few months, squeezed into the already crowded quarters. Then they moved to another relative's more capacious home, where bandits stole the family's remaining possessions.

Janzen was fortunate to lose only property and not his life. During one raid, the bandit Petia Thiessen discovered an old picture of the Tsar among the household articles. Deciding it belonged to Janzen, Thiessen pronounced my uncle a monarchist counter-revolutionary and thus subject to death. Only when the home-owner intervened, pleading that the picture was his, an artefact which he thought had been discarded years before, did Thiessen relent. After this harrowing incident, the Janzens moved to what they believed would be safer quarters – the Enns home in Neuendorf – little knowing that the bandit who had just challenged them was the Mennonite son of Mrs Enns by a previous marriage, or that Petia (formerly Peter) Thiessen had married a Ukrainian woman named Katia before joining the Makhnovites.

The bizarre intertwining of the lives of the former *Gutsbesitzer* Janzen family and Petia and Katia Thiessen continued for four months. Shortly after raiding the Janzen's refuge, the Makhnovite Thiessen couple moved forcibly into the home of my Uncle Bernhard Pauls in Rosental, where their presence was a mixed blessing. Both Thiessens eagerly flaunted the possessions they had stolen from the Janzens, knowing that Katharina Janzen was Bernhard Pauls's sister. Katia paraded around in the dress Mrs Janzen had made for her silver wedding anniversary the previous year, while Petia proudly strutted about in Uncle Jacob Janzen's suits. Yet Petia revealed conflicted emotions and loyalties. Like his bandit comrades, he could be cruel, ambitious, ruthless, distrustful, and avaricious. At other times, he acted charitably, giving the Pauls family expropriated food, toys, paper, and pencils, and prohibiting his fellow bandits from raiding the Pauls home. Once Petia even showed remorse, coming into the kitchen where Mrs Pauls cooked, laying his head on the table, and moaning disconsolately about the life he led. But when she suggested he leave the Makhnovites, he groaned that he was too deeply involved to sever ties.

The Janzens and other estate owners were not the only ones attacked by the Makhnovites. Most of the far less-affluent Mennonite villagers suffered indescribable horrors. In Nieder Khortitsa, the Makhnovites justified their ferocious attacks as part of their relentless search for Abram Löwen, the desperado who had many times slipped through their grip. Although many villagers had supported Löwen's goals (and some prosperous farmers had hidden him from time to time), most disapproved of his tactics. By October virtually everyone was tired of the Makhnovite retaliations for Löwen's real or alleged misdeeds. His only available hideout became the poor *Nippaenja* quarter, among former boatman co-workers.

On 5 November 1919, Löwen's exploits came to an end when someone informed the Makhnovites of his hideout. No one knew the betrayer's identity, but most suspected it to be the daughter of a Ukrainian peasant cowherd, a girl named Dunka, who had earlier denounced several farmers to the Makhnovites. Löwen, sensing their approach, fled to Martin Klassen's neighbouring hayloft. More Makhnovites arrived, drawing a crowd of villagers to watch. The bandits were at first too frightened to climb into the hayloft, but one finally volunteered. Finding Löwen unarmed, cowering in the hay, he shot him several times. More Makhnovites charged up to the loft with pitchforks, speared the already severely wounded Löwen, and threw him down to the floor below. Their further mutilation of Löwen's body defied description. The triumphant avengers would not allow anyone to move the body until the next day, when they gave it to his grandmother.

News of Löwen's fate spread swiftly through the village, and his three cohorts, Abram Günter, Jacob Töws, and David Neufeld, fled to another village. Surprisingly, the Makhnovites did not inflict the usual reprisals on the three men's families. That would come a few years later at the hands of the Soviet Cheka.

When my mother learned of Löwen's slaying, she insisted we take food to his grandmother and try to comfort the family. Father, who believed the Makhnovites were watching our house, was apprehensive about this and urged her not to go. But Mother was adamant, arguing that whatever we thought of Löwen, his family deserved our compassion, and she was sure that bandits lurking about our home would understand and not molest her. I went along. On entering the cottage, we found Löwen's body stretched out on the floor of the main room, with Löwen's wife grieving beside it. Just as Mother handed her the food, the cottage door burst open. In stormed several Makhnovites. They kicked Löwen's body, then raised their short-handled, lead-tipped whips (*nagaiki*) as though to strike us. Amidst their cursing and menacing gestures, Dunka arrived, shouting, 'Don't hit him! This is the wife and son of Yehor Yehorovich' (*Ne trohai! Tse zhinka ta syn Yehor Yehorovicha*). I assume gratitude motivated her intercession, since Father's general store had often carried her father on credit for winter 'purchases' of kerosene, flour, and syrup. I assume that the Makhnovites ransacked the house after we departed, for Johann Funk's diary mentions that when he visited Löwen's grandmother, he found the cottage thoroughly pillaged. Löwen's mutilated body was buried shortly thereafter, without a funeral.

Löwen and his three accomplices were not the Makhnovites' only targets. The same week they arrested four other young men in our village: Peter Penner, Peter Pauls, my closest friend, Jacob Epp, and my younger brother Jacob. Evidently, the lad who had falsely accused Johann of possessing a machine gun, had mistakenly identified sixteen-year-old Jacob as a member of the White Army. Penner and Pauls had both been *Selbstschutz* members, but not Löwen's collaborators. The bandits whipped the two, beating Pauls's feet so badly with a ramrod that he could not walk for weeks afterwards.

Jacob Epp suffered a worse fate. He had been a member of the *Selbstschutz* since its inception. What may have turned him into the object of murderous revenge was the fact that he had shot at several Ukrainian peasants from neighbouring Razumovka who had tried to hide bullets in a hollow tree in the Epp backyard, either for their own use, or to entrap Epp. Whatever the reason, for several days the bandits beat Epp so mercilessly that he was unconscious much of the time. Ultimately, they beat Epp to death as my brother watched helplessly. Epp's body was dragged from the room and it disappeared thereafter. Although my comrades and I searched the fields the next spring, when the snow melted, we could not find Epp's body among the corpses.

Finally, the Makhnovites turned their wrath on my brother Jacob. He was terrified, but simply said, 'I am only sixteen. Why are doing this to me, when I have done nothing?' Miraculously, the blackguards, their bloodlust satiated, or perhaps suffering twinges of guilt, released Jacob unharmed.

Soon after my brother's narrow escape, I returned home from school and found everything had changed. Three Makhnovites had taken over our house, commandeering the large *Grootestow*, or guest room, for themselves. As self-proclaimed members of the counter-intelligence (*kontrrazvedka*) of the local garrison, intent on ferreting out White Army members (*kadety*) and other traitors to Batko Makhno and his revolutionary movement, they were the most obnoxious and ruthless of all the village's unbidden occupants. Aside from eating, they slept all day, then towards evening left for their escapades, to hunt down counter-revoluntionaries, and to search houses, pilfering whatever touched their fancy or simply because they enjoyed tormenting innocent people.

After such missions to neighbouring villages, they would return long after midnight, unsaddle their horses, or more often, wake us for the chore. Invariably, they demanded that Mother cook them a hot meal. If they wanted chicken, they would send one of us to the henhouse, and curse if we did not kill and pluck the bird fast enough to please them. And every night, awash in power, they would gloat to Father, who knew most of the settlement's farmers, 'And do you remember this and that one in Burwalde? We worked him over real good!' (*A ty pomnish tekh v Baburke? My ikh khoroshen'ko pokolotili!*). In the event they had murdered someone, they would boast, 'We entered him as expense' (*My ego v raskhod zapisali*), or, another favourite expression, 'We sent him to Dukhonin's headquarters' (*My ego v shtab Dukhonina poslali*).[1] Despite their comradeship, the three men did not trust one another. Often, one or another would demand that we guard some prized stolen article of theirs, like the beautiful boot one ordered us to keep out of the clutches of his two comrades or other plunderers, until his own infected and swollen foot healed.

In late November, the three murderous brigands were ordered to vacate our house. We never asked nor learned the reason why. After a few days' respite, nine new bandits – one a woman – took their place. They were staff members of a combat unit that had suffered heavy losses somewhere on the front. Although thrice the number of the previous group, these 'guests' behaved more decently. They made fewer demands and even tried to protect us from the roving bands of marauders. Some even took an interest in Johann's collection of Russian literature, seemed rather well educated, and may for all one knew have actually been philosophical anarchists.

The woman was particularly decent and impressed me as an intellectual from a fine home, as did her brother. At times we wondered if they were hostages. During the last week of their stay, the woman cried so hysterically that we felt she had gone mad. Her brother and another man asked my mother to pray over her, hoping it would soothe the demented woman's nerves. Mother knew no Russian prayers, so she prayed in German and recited chorale verses, one of which went:

Have oft in the circle of loved ones
rested in the fragrant grass,
and sang me a songlet
and worries would quickly pass.

Hab' oft im Kreise der Lieben,
Im duftigen Grase geruht,
Und mir ein Liedlein gesungen,
Und alles, alles war wieder gut.

These sessions not only quieted the woman, but also revived Mother's spirituality and quiet confidence.

CHAPTER TWENTY-SIX

Hostages

No family in the Khortitsa Settlement, whether rich or poor, was immune to the horrors of the civil war. The most prosperous, however, were targets of one assault that the less-affluent among us were spared: kidnap for ransom. While the bandits readily saw they could squeeze nothing from our modest family, one abduction did threaten us when they demanded that Johann collect the ransom. Doing so imperiled his life.

Johann's saga began in September, when Makhno's forces captured Alexandrovsk and its Mennonite suburb Schönwiese. Many of the wealthiest Mennonites in the settlement, particularly the owners of industrial and milling concerns, lived in these communities on the east side of the river. Frightened that bandits would kidnap or murder them, several affluent families fled west across the Dnieper to the then relative safety of our villages.[1] Most found havens in relatives' homes in Osterwick. The family of Jacob Dyck, a wealthy executive of the Niebuhr Milling Company, hid in our home in Nieder Khortitsa. This remained a sanctuary until the White Army recaptured Alexandrovsk, forcing the city's Makhnovites to flee across the river into our villages. With bandits about to claim our house, my father relocated the Dycks to the Johann Thiessens' home next door.

The shift in control of the two banks of the Dnieper posed a problem for these refugees. Their safety in our now bandit-occupied homes became increasingly tenuous. Meanwhile, their own homes in the Schönwiese-Alexandrovsk area, now occupied by the White Army, appeared to be safe. The dilemma was how to cross the heavily guarded Dnieper. Those caught risked being shot. In spite of the peril, one refugee, gambling on the safety of an alternate route, sneaked south to

Belenkoe, the largest peasant village between Ekaterinoslav and Nikopol. He assumed it was beyond Makhnovite-held territory and planned to hire a boatman to row him to Alexandrovsk. Unfortunately, another bandit gang led by Batko Savelii Nuzhnyi controlled Belenkoe, and one of Nuzhnyi's patrols caught the man. Taken to Nuzhnyi's headquarters, the bandits tortured him until he divulged the other Mennonite refugees' names and hiding places. On his list was Jehor Jehorovich Rempel, my father.

It was one of the many curious twists of this violent period that Father had known Batko Nuzhnyi for years. A local man from Belenkoe, Nuzhnyi had owned a small steamboat which he used to ferry passengers between Nieder Khortitsa and Alexandrovsk, and as a tugboat to pull barges of grain or watermelons between Belenkoe and our village. For years Father used to hire Nuzhnyi to transport his grain and watermelons. The war and revolution had strained Nuzhnyi's business, and the civil war had finished it off. Now desperate, and aware of Makhno's success, Nuzhnyi set up his own band of cutthroats, recruiting followers from the peasants of his native village.

In early October 1919, Nuzhnyi and his marauders had raided Blumengart and Schöneberg several times, but they rarely attacked Nieder Khortitsa. My guess is that Nuzhnyi favoured the former two targets because they were on the fringes of the settlement, while Nieder Khortitsa was more central, and thus a preferred target of competitive peasant raiders from Voznesenskoe directly across the Dnieper. Or perhaps Nuzhnyi initially feared recognition, because everyone in Nieder Khortitsa knew him. But after the Makhnovites took over our village, he rode into town fearlessly, called a meeting at the local school, and announced that Makhno had appointed him commander of the region. That may or may not have been true, since a number of bloody skirmishes – some even murderous – between followers of the two men took place over the following weeks.

I was oblivious to these preliminary events, as I had been away at school in Khortitsa for two months. When I returned home on 24 October, I was perplexed to see shadowy figures – a man carrying a small child – darting from our house into the Thiessens' neighbouring yard. Then, as I walked into our house, Mother handed my brother Jacob a basket filled with food which, she explained, was for the Dyck family hiding next door. The Thiessen cottage remained a haven for only a few more days. With the ranks of bandits swollen into the tens of thousands, the horde began raiding even modest abodes like the

Thiessens'. Father then concealed the Dycks in Abram Vogt's nearby shack.

While Makhno's band might not discover this particular hideout, Batko Nuzhnyi knew Dyck had to be close to our home. Two weeks later Nyzhnyi came for his prey. That dreary morning of 10 November 1919 began with a series of dreadful and inexplicable events. Our three bandit 'guests,' claiming to be Makhno's counter-intelligence agents, left early to 'ferret out enemies of their leader.' Their timing was odd – they usually forayed at night. About an hour later, fifteen bandits barged into our house, demanding that we produce two fur coats that allegedly were hidden there. Although my father had once owned a fur coat, bandits had stolen it months earlier. The bandits rejected our protestations and split into four groups to search the property. One grabbed my brother Heinrich and demanded that he escort them to the attic. I was to lead another group into the granary. Johann had to lead a foursome through the house, while Father was to show the remainder around the yard and out-buildings.

My mother remained in the kitchen, watching the proceedings through the window. As Father emerged from the barn, several of the men suddenly began to hit him. Mother shouted for Johann, who dashed out and threw himself between the bandits and Father. 'Don't you dare beat my father' (*Ne smeite bit' moego ottsa*), Johann cried. At that, two men turned on Johann, and only when the other bandits emerged empty-handed did the merciless quartet stop pounding my brother and father. Shreds of skin hung from Father's bloodied face.

A few hours later, just as Jacob Dyck entered our home with his crippled daughter to inquire about the earlier commotion, another bandit rode up and demanded to know whether the Dyck family was hiding with us. When Dyck admitted his identity, the bandit ordered Dyck and Johann into the wagon awaiting them in the side alley. As my mother carried the child to the Vogt home, the rest of us watched the men depart towards Razumovka. For the next three days we waited, hoping our darkest apprehensions would not prove true.

Yet these events seemed so strange that we were almost as puzzled as fearful. Why, Father wondered, had our three bandit 'guests' departed early in the morning, when they normally went out at night? Why had they not demanded to know Johann's whereabouts upon their return? Did these 'counter-intelligence officers' perhaps already know? Nor could we explain why an abnormally large contingent had searched that morning for two non-existent fur coats, and then severely beaten Father.

Were they actually searching for Jacob Dyck and beating Father because they thought he was Dyck? Or were they frustrated when they realized he was not their man? Could the bandits have been keeping us under surveillance waiting for Jacob Dyck to appear? That would explain the near-immediate arrival of the bandit who abducted Johann and Jacob Dyck right after Dyck entered our house. We also could not understand why the group rode off towards Razumovka rather than Khortitsa, where the Makhnovites usually interrogated their victims.

Our anxiety naturally focused on why they had taken my brother, and the next day the question became dire. Some Makhnovites arrived, demanding we produce Johann. When Father said he had no idea where his son was, the men searched the house and yard, clearly seeking Johann rather than booty since they requisitioned nothing. Instead, they left the impression that Johann's name was at the top of six others on the Makhnovites' hit list for our village.

Three nights later, Johann returned safely. But he stayed only long enough to outline his harrowing experience. Batko Nuzhnyi, he said, had discovered the hideouts of the wealthy refugee families and had assumed that he could kidnap them individually, ransom them, and in return, help them get across the river to their homes in Alexandrovsk and Schönwiese. Knowing that my father was hiding Jacob Dyck, and remembering his trustworthy nature, Nuzhnyi decided to nab his first wealthy hostage and use Johann as the courier to fetch the money.

Months later, Johann recounted the saga in some detail. Nuzhnyi's henchman had taken Johann and Dyck to the batko's headquarters in a stately home in Belenkoe and locked them in a tiny room in the former servants' quarters. Well past midnight their guard shoved them into Nuzhyni's room, where the black-bearded *batko* began his abusive interrogation, threatening torture if Dyck could not produce two million rubles within the next few days. When Dyck insisted that there was no way that he could raise this sum, Nuzhnyi ordered the guard to bring him a light and knitting needles. Prompted by the bandit leader's reputation for torture, Johann pleaded with the brigand, 'I beg you not to torture us in the name of the friendship you once had with my father.' Feigning ignorance, Nuzhnyi asked the father's identity. When Johann offered Father's name, the *batko* said, 'He is a good man,' and sent them back to their 'cell.'

Nuzhnyi rejoined his captives and asked how much they could raise, if two million rubles was beyond reach? Dyck replied 200,000 rubles. That satisfied Nuzhnyi. He then revealed Johann's intended role. Dyck would write a note to his Schönwiese relatives and colleagues, confirming Johann's identity and requesting an unspecified amount of money to ransom a likewise unspecified number of hostages. If Johann succeeded, Nuzhnyi would help the Dyck family get across the river to territory held by the White Army. Without hesitation, Johann agreed to the mission.

He set off into the dank November air at sunrise, with the ultimate fate of more than a dozen people in balance. The threat to him was immediately apparent, as well. A guard on the west side of the Dnieper, spotting Johann nearly across the river, shot at him and his boatman. Johann dove for cover in brush along the shore, where he waited – terrified – counting the minutes in silence. Then, assuming that the guard had either left or lost interest, Johann cautiously threaded his way upstream, wading through a befuddling jumble of rain pools, wagon tracks, and cow paths that criss-crossed the lowland's luxuriant stands of poplars, willows, and wild pear trees.

His captors had not fed him, and Johann was immensely hungry. When he saw a tiny cottage in the woods, he stopped to ask for food. The peasant owner answered his knock with a suspicious glare, and demanded his name. But when he discovered Johann was the son of Jehor Jehorovich Rempel from Nizhniaia Khortitsa and, thus, grandson of a man for whom the peasant had once worked – and whom he had respected – the old peasant invited Johann to come in and eat.

After a simple meal of milk and bread, Johann resumed his trek through the muck, with Schönwiese still another fifteen miles away. He planned to reach it by dark, but miles from his goal, as weariness overcame him, he decided to rest at a deserted estate, hoping the nap would revive him. Avoiding the pillaged house, Johann headed for the barn, which appeared intact. As he swung the massive barn door open, rats scurried out of their nests in the walls, and he saw owls perched high among the rafters. In spite of his exhaustion, he trudged on northward. Then, as darkness came, he heard hoof beats and the sound of wagon wheels behind him, and as the clop and rattle grew close, a peasant's greeting. 'Whoa,' the man called. 'I see that you will not walk much farther' (*Prrrr ... bo ja bachu, tyvzhe daleko ne pidesh*). The peasant invited Johann to hop onto the wagon, loaded high with shrubbery for firewood, and hitch a ride as far as he was going.

Just after dark, the peasant drove up to his Balabino cottage, shared, as was common, with his aged parents. Having graciously asked Johann to eat with his family, the peasant introduced his traveller to his old father. Did Johann know anyone in Ostrov Khortitsa (Insel Khortitsa), the old man wanted to know? For thirty years he had worked there as the smith for Ivan Gildebranda (Johann Hildebrand). When Johann said Hildebrand was his great uncle, he was invited to spend the night. Furthermore, the peasant offered to take Johann the last four miles to Alexandrovsk the next morning. In payment the peasant asked only for a pud (about 36 pounds) of flour when they arrived at the Niebuhr mill in Alexandrovsk.

As soon as they reached the city, Johann met representatives of the families hiding on our side of the river. Initially, some mistrusted Johann. Then someone from the Wiebe family arrived, a man who had known Johann for years. After reassuring the others of Johann's trustworthiness, they quickly collected the 200,000-ruble ransom. In a prescient move, Johann wadded 80,000 rubles worth of bills in small denominations into four bulky wads and the remaining 120,000 rubles consisting of larger bills into two thin packets.[2] Now eager for the success of Johann's mission, they gave him a wagon and driver to carry him back to his pick-up point downstream.

It should have been a simple trip. However, the driver repeatedly lost his way. Then night fell and the only available shelter was a haystack, so they bedded down there. Terrified that someone would waylay them, Johann hid the packets of money in the straw. He slept fitfully through the frigid night, and left with his driver at dawn, his mind distracted by fear of ambush. Only after they had journeyed for about a mile downstream did he realize that he had left one packet of money in the hay. They circled round, fortunately finding the right haystack and the money.

Back at Nuzhnyi's headquarters hours later, Johann sought Dyck before he reported to the *batko.* Dyck, who may have discussed the matter with Nuzhnyi during Johann's absence, now thought that half the money would satisfy his captors, so Johann concealed the two smaller packets in his overcoat pocket. When Nuzhnyi's henchman came for the ransom, Johann tossed the four larger packets onto the bed. A stand-off ensued between Johann, who claimed he could collect only 80,000 rubles, and the bandit, who fiercely demanded the full 200,000. Maintaining his bluff, Johann told the *batko*'s lackey that all of the wealthy families had left Alexandrovsk and that he had been fortunate, indeed, to get as much as he had. The bandit fumed, then suggested 100,000 rubles might suffice. Johann seized the opportunity. If his captors would take him home immediately, he said, his father would give them the other 20,000. This settled the matter and a driver brought Johann home.

Throughout Johann's absence, we maintained our usual nightly precautions, alert to any footsteps, hoof beats, or the creak of wagon wheels – sounds often preceding a knock at the door and a flood of curses. On the night of Johann's return, Heinrich spotted a wagon in the Thiessen yard next door. This was an alarming sign, since by this time virtually no one but the Makhnovites possessed a wagon. But when no commotion ensued, we gradually relaxed, and, with our 'own' three bandits out for the night, we prepared for bed. Father and Mother retired to the corner room (*Atjstow*), Heinrich and I to the little one (*Tjleenestow*). The lamps in the kitchen were to be cleaned and refilled with kerosene the following morning, and the house lay in total darkness.

A sudden tap on the window woke my parents. Father cautiously lifted the curtain, recognized Johann, and rushed to unlock the kitchen door. Fearing our family's bandit 'guests' might return and overhear their conversation, Father and Johann conferred in whispered tones for the next few hours. First, Johann sketched an outline of his mission, then Father related his grave news – that Johann was on the Makhnovites' hit list. It was clear that Johann must accompany the Dycks across the river and take sanctuary with them in White Army territory.

Exhausted, Johann went to bed, shoving it next to the window nearest the Thiessen cottage, leaving the pane closed to the cold November night, but unlatched for easy escape should the Makhnovites appear. He slept dressed, rose at five the next morning, and ate hastily. Then he removed 20,000 rubles from his cache, entrusting the remaining 100,000 to Father, and left the house. Outside, he found the Dyck family ready to leave, bedded on straw on the wagon floor. Father led the horses and driver through the thick morning mist to the Razumovka turn-off. There Father and son said good-bye, little knowing that this was their final farewell.

Over the next several weeks Father ransomed at least seven other hostages with the residual money, each man making his way to Batko Nuzhnyi without his followers' knowledge. For reasons we never understood, Nuzhnyi returned 10,000 rubles to us. Of course, my father had never asked for, or wanted, any rewards, and he found the *batko*'s gratitude perplexing. In fact, it had a dreadful consequence.

To the present day Nuzhnyi's motives in staging the kidnapping and in 'rewarding' Father still puzzle me. Were the kidnappings simple extortion or were they an 'insurance' policy as well? By 'rescuing' prominent Mennonites did Nuzhnyi expect them to help him should the White Army establish a permanent government in southern Russia? On occasion, such forethought moderated the behaviour of other bandits. For example, Makhnovites arrested Jacob Dyck's brother, Abram J. Dyck, in early 1919, holding him prisoner in Alexandrovsk and threatening terrible consequences if he did not raise a large ransom. Yet nothing untoward happened when he failed to produce the money. They allowed his wife and daughter to visit him in jail, and even to hold a birthday party for him there. In this case, the captor hoped that Abram Dyck would protect his Jewish girlfriend from the pogrom that was certain to occur if the White Army – with its Cossack contingent – retook the city.

Such 'benevolence' in no way excuses the bestial acts of the bandit hordes. Yet in recalling the particulars of this horrific period, one should note the diversity of partisan motives and backgrounds and the varied forms that their terrorizing took. One should not subsume the whole bleak drama under the monolithic curse of Nestor Makhno. It is equally important to remember that while much of the bandit force derived from the peasantry, individual Ukrainian peasants showed Christian charity – as they had to my brother Johann – equal to that of the Mennonites.

CHAPTER TWENTY-SEVEN

Typhus: The Nightmare Legacy of the Makhnovite Terror, December 1919 to March 1920

Artillery fire, audible on 20 December 1919, presaged the Red Army's assault on the White Army position in Alexandrovsk. Although we villagers were not eager for another Bolshevik occupation, we desperately hoped that advancing Red troops would at least force the Makhnovites out of the Khortitsa Settlement, because the bandits were infected with typhus. Transmitted solely by body lice from one person to another, epidemic typhus is an opportunistic disease which rages through populations living in the squalid conditions we endured under bandit control. Symptoms begin with chills, progress to fever, generalized pain and malaise, and in worst cases to delirium, renal failure, gangrene, and/or death.[1]

Several of the nine bandits who then lived in our home had contracted the disease the previous week. As the epidemic widened, the Makhnovites' improvised hospitals overflowed with their sick and dying, and their unburied dead. Desperate to save themselves, the bandits commandeered all the settlement's modest medical resources, demanding that Drs Hamm and Hottman, our two nurses, and three auxiliary caregivers treat them preferentially.[2] Care for the infected bandits rapidly overwhelmed these seven, and as the disease spread into the Mennonite population that housed the brigands, the doctors could not serve the settlement's own needs, leaving stricken villagers with no aid but each other's ministrations.

Dr Hamm's daily ordeal began at sunrise when he would find thirty or more stolen *tachanki* (Mennonite spring wagons) awaiting him at the hospital in Khortitsa. Many were heaped high with typhus patients, while one remained empty save the bandit driver waiting to drive Hamm to sick comrades housed in village homes or makeshift infirmaries in the Rosental and Khortitsa schools. On one occasion, the brigands took him to the Khortitsa railway station. There infected bandits lay packed tight on straw mats filling three railroad cars, while their still-healthy leaders lived in adjacent luxurious cars filled with booty. Recognizing the importance of keeping the doctor himself healthy, the officers provided him with a quiet room in the station where he could rest, and with food from the leader's buffet. After treating the patients, Dr Hamm discovered the *zakuski* table, laden with food, even including fresh oranges, apples, and grapes. When he asked why they had not fed their sick comrades the food, the leaders cynically replied, that with limited supplies, they might as well be the ones to enjoy what they had. Despite the bandits' concern for Dr Hamm's health, after days of treating verminous patients, he soon came down with the dreaded typhus.[3]

When the settlement's small cadre of medical personnel could not cope with the needs of the suffering Makhnovites, the bandits forced young Mennonite men, usually students, to attend their sick and wounded. For three days I myself cared for patients in the former Khortitsa girls high school. As sick men arrived in the schoolyard, they stripped off their outer clothes, which I first brushed to dislodge lice, then shook them over a fire until the 'pop' of incinerated bugs ceased. Even with this precaution, lice still swarmed over the patients' bodies and remaining clothes as they entered my classroom ward.

There, in the hot room, we conscripted attendants laid the patients, stripped to the waist, on beds of mounded straw. Each of us cared for thirty or more soldiers, and we had little time to care for individual needs beyond delousing the men's upper bodies. During my three-day service, not a single doctor, nurse, or paramedic visited my ward. We had no medicines. The only relief we could offer these feverish and delirious men was a drink of water. Twice a day we fed a cup of soup to those still able to eat – all sharing the same vessel, since we had only one cup. A bucket in the corner served as toilet. Some patients managed to walk or crawl to it. Others I dragged there. Many simply wallowed in their excrement until they recovered or died.

One bandit patient must have been a Mennonite. In his feverish state he gasped a few words in Plautdietsch (Low German) about his parents. I repeatedly asked him his name, but to no avail. Minutes later he died. I don't think that this bandit was unique. As already mentioned, Petia Thiessen was a Makhnovite, and many residents of both the Khortitsa and Molochna settlements recall other Mennonites participating in bandit raids.

On 18 December, I ended my stint as a hospital orderly and returned home with Jacob Pätkau, a friend sent to pick up supplies for the Nieder Khortitsa bandit garrison. Two bandit guards hitched a ride with us. Throughout the two-hour trip one guard, sitting behind me with a revolver trained at my head, continuously grumbled, 'You are a former White Guardist.' Neither my denials nor pledges that I had tended his sick comrades placated the man, and my fear of him abated only when I sighted the high kurgan (*Groote Schauntz*) marking the approach to our village. Yet I felt little joy. Work and sleeplessness had left me exhausted and I was now infested with lice and feverish myself.

As I entered the back door, I found all the lamps lit. Mother, who had just finished feeding one of our Makhnovite 'guests,' was preparing bowls of soup for Father, Heinrich, and Jacob. My father, who had already shown signs of typhus the day I left for Khortitsa, was extremely feverish. Now Jacob and Heinrich were infected as well. Heinrich, whose chronic angina compounded the pain from the typhus, suffered most. Despite Mother's coaxing, no one wanted to eat.

My temperature rapidly mounted while I anxiously waited for Mother to finish her chores so that she could help me delouse myself. Then I stripped. While I tried to kill all the lice that I could reach on my body, Mother worked over my head with a louse-comb, then bashed the vermin crawling over my underwear and shirt with a hammer, taking special care with the seams. Just before I collapsed and she dragged me to bed, I vaguely heard her say there had been more than 120 lice on my body and clothes.

When I think back, I cannot comprehend how my mother got through the next days, caring for her sick husband and sons, all the while meeting the demands of the nine Makhnovites, especially in our grievously depleted household. After months of Bolshevik and bandit raids, our family had no fresh clothing or linens, nor any of Mother's preserved vegetables and fruits. Except for milk from our two cows, and occasional morsels of requisitioned food that our bandit 'guests' shared, we were on close to starvation rations, with little more than a handful of potatoes and a few small bags of flour left in the cupboard. At least we had fuel. Father had bought and stacked an abundance of straw that autumn, and as long as one of us was able to fetch straw and stoke the oven and stove, we would keep warm.

In memory, the following weeks – particularly the next five or six days – were a feverish blur. But I vividly recall an incident that was in many ways the most bestial that I observed during the entire revolution and civil war. On the morning of 22 December, our bandit 'guests' left as part of the general retreat from the advancing Bolshevik Army. No sooner were they gone than two new bandits barged into the house. In the vilest language, the two demanded Father give them 6,000 rubles, presumably a portion of the 10,000 rubles Batko Nuzhnyi had 'returned' to us. Close to death, Father whispered he had no money, that other bandits had long since stolen Nuzhnyi's 'reward.' Despite his denial and Mother's plea for mercy, the Makhnovites whipped my father with their nagaikas. Hearing the commotion, we three brothers staggered to Father's room and fruitlessly begged the bandits to spare him. Finally, in a moment of clarity, I recalled having hidden a few tarnished prewar copper and silver coins in a matchbox in the attic. Fearful and angry, I creeped to the attic and retrieved my small treasure, with the foolish hope it would soften the wrath of the assailants downstairs. But when I showed one bandit the box, he took a cursory look, and shouted, 'Away with that trash' (*Von s etoi drianiu*), and lashed at me instead of Father. Finally, with blood-curdling screams and vulgarity the two left, empty-handed.

I recall only fragments of the next two or three days, among them that a poor neighbour widow, Mrs Mantler, came to clean the *Grootestow* vacated by our nine bandit 'guests.' She and my mother dragged a double bed and two sleeping benches with pull-out extensions (*Schlopbeintje*) into the backyard. They removed the filthy bedding, drenched the frames with boiling water to kill the lice, and then stuffed the beds with straw, covering them with a few salvageable pieces of linen. After they had tugged the beds back to the *Grootestow,* Heinrich, Jacob, and I moved into that room so that sister Mariechen, her husband, and baby, all now suffering from typhus, could occupy ours. My mother tended us all.

I slipped in and out of consciousness, but was alert on the morning of 23 December, when Mother told us that Father had just died, and that she was herself on the verge of collapse. My memory then skips forward a few hours, when she told us she had found someone to build my father's coffin. Finally, and more clearly, I recall Johann arriving home. He had just learned of our plight, and although he was recuperating from pneumonia, he quickly crossed the river, tragically arriving too late to see Father alive. He found Mother exhausted, but surprisingly composed, and went directly to frail Heinrich, who was in extreme pain and coughing up blood. Heinrich died after lingering for three more days, and only then did we discover that under his ragged outer garments he wore a new summer suit, presumably to save it from bandit confiscation.

Shortly after Johann's return, typhus struck the one remaining healthy family member, my older brother Gerhard. For days he had stoked our oven, but now he too needed Mother's care. Then, miraculously, Jacob Sawatzky, one of Johann's former students who had been away in Central Asia, beyond the typhus scourge, offered his help. Jacob Sawatzky was a godsend. Throughout the village virtually every family was in the same disastrous state, lucky if they had even one healthy member to care for the rest.

After Father succumbed, the death march of typhus continued on through the family and neighbourhood. Our neighbour, Johann Siemens died the next day, his eldest son on the following, and my brother Heinrich one day later. By that point, it took two days to find someone with sufficient strength to nail a coffin or dig a grave. Many families had no wood for a casket. We at least had ceiling planks in our grain storage barn, from which Father's former teamsters fashioned a rough box for his body. The Siemens family still had a horse and wagon, and it carried the coffins to the cemetery. Father's rode next to the equally crude crate holding the body of 'Bulldog' Siemens, the man so certain three years earlier that his wealth assured him a ride into exile in a plush sleeping car – while we would go packed in cattle cars. My father was buried on Christmas Day, 1919, without a regular funeral service. Most of the villagers were sick, and those few well enough to attend listened to the scriptures but were unable to sing the chorales. Nevertheless, our family was luckier than those who arrived at the allotted gravesite with their corpse only to find a stranger's box already filling the pit. I must emphasize that our family's misery in no way exceeded that of most Mennonites in the Khortitsa district.

Johann had no time to lament his failure to see Father before he died. He now tended seven family members who were more grievously ill than he was. At the same time he had to arrange Father's and Heinrich's burials, and bolster Mother's sagging morale. For weeks she had cared for everyone else, including the Makhnovites, drawing on her seemingly inexhaustible physical and spiritual resources. Now, her characteristic spunk withered perceptibly. A few hours after Heinrich died, she got into bed and never left it. Perhaps Mother surrendered life knowing that her frail son no longer needed her care. On the day of Heinrich's funeral she asked Johann to inscribe his coffin with, 'My youth hast Thou demanded, Oh Lord.'

As my mother's life ebbed, each day she seemed more serene. Perhaps she sensed that her remaining children could manage without her. Neta, Gerhard, and Mariechen were married, and Johann would be a strength for Jacob and me, who were at least well advanced in our education. My sister Mariechen, however, felt that Father's death had sapped Mother's will to live. Although the two had been very different in background and temperament, they had complemented each other marvellously – Father with his pragmatism and obsessive drive for improvement and education, Mother with her idealism, joy for life, and calm spirituality.

After 28th December, Mother lay unconscious for hours. But during brief lucid moments she spoke lovingly with Mariechen and us three brothers, always urging her sons to remember Father's concern for their education. Mother's compassion extended beyond our little family group, however, and often during those days she murmured her sorrow for the suffering experienced throughout the settlement, even by those who had been contemptuous of my father. Only a week before Father's death, my mother had noticed only a handful of mourners joining Peter Siemens's passing funeral procession. Siemens, a prosperous farmer, had railed against Father's aspirations for his children's education. Nevertheless, my mother told Father she was going to the cemetery to pay her last respects.

On 4 January 1920, Mother's condition turned critical. In her feverish condition she tried to hum snatches of favourite songs, sometimes the opening lines of 'There above the sea of stars, there is a lovely land' (*Dort über jenem Sternenmeer, da ist ein schönes Land*). Other times she managed a few lines of a well-known hymn:

> Take, Jesus, my hands and lead me on
> to my blessed end.
> I cannot walk alone,
> not one step ...
>
> *Nimm Jesu meine Hände*
> *Und führe mich,*
> *Bis an mein selig Ende,*
> *Und ewiglich.*
> *ich kann allein nicht gehen*
> *Nicht einen Schritt.*

Then her voice slurred into silence.

My mother died on the afternoon of 8 January 1920. During her last hours she was conscious and rational, and with all her children gathered around her bedside, she advised her three youngest. I was drawn from her bedside momentarily to inform a distant relative, Peter Heinrichs, who had come concerned about Mother's condition. As I told him that she was dying, Jacob called out that Mother wished to see me. I got to her bed only to hear her last words: 'Boys, if you can emigrate, then go, even if you have to leave everything behind' (*Junges, wann jie ütwaundere tjenne, dann foat mau wajch, uck wann jie aules velohte motte*).

Neither Mariechen, Jacob, nor I were well enough to attend Mother's funeral on 10 January. Dimly I remember my mother's face in the coffin, brought to my bedside before it was nailed shut. Mother's coffin rode to the cemetery on the Siemens's wagon. Few people attended her burial, not even her mother or siblings. Even if any of them knew of Mother's death – and there was virtually no communication between Nieder Khortitsa and Rosental at the time – all were too ill to travel. The small gathering, consisting of a few remaining healthy friends, neighbours, and *Nippaenja* boatmen and teamsters from the *kutok* part of the village, bravely attempted to sing a few songs from the hymnal. Johann read a few verses from the New Testament. Then they buried my mother.

The Makhnovites Withdraw

The helter-skelter movement of the departing Makhnovites abated during the last days of 1919. Those healthy enough to travel retreated towards their home base in Guliai Polie, but ragtag stragglers, many still ill with typhus, remained. A few belligerent rebels threatened reprisals if we refused them food or did not provide it quickly enough. Most, however, seemed more apprehensive than brazen, knowing that any Bolshevik soldiers they encountered would disarm them, taking their booty, too. Often, as the brigands withdrew, Mennonite men cursed them, some even threatening them with pitchforks. Perhaps it was unchristian of Mennonites to forget the biblical injunction, 'Vengeance is mine, sayeth the Lord.' Yet their rage is understandable.

Now that the Makhnovites had lost power, and could no longer 'plunder the plunderers,' the Ukrainian peasants likewise viewed them as intolerable bandits. The Mennonite brigand Petia Thiessen and his wife Katia were especially vulnerable. It was dangerous for him to flee to a Ukrainian peasant village, where non-Slav, non-Orthodox comrades were now conveniently viewed as 'damn Germans.' Nor could Thiessen stay behind, taking refuge in a Mennonite village where one-time co-religionists would seek him out to settle scores. Bolsheviks would dispossess him not only of his booty. They might even kill him and his wife as enemies of the proletariat. Both Thiessens were too ill with typhus to keep up with the rapidly withdrawing Makhnovites, most of whom were either healthy or rode in bandit-driven wagons. Opting for the least dangerous alternative, the Thiessens drove their wagon to the nearby Ukrainian peasant village of Tomakovka. There, however, local peasants denounced the pair to the Bolsheviks, who confiscated everything except their wagon and horses.

The Thiessens saw the Makhnovite village of Guliai Polie as their only possible refuge. They set out for it by a circuitous route around several Mennonite villages. Along the way they stopped at the home of Petia's mother (Mrs Enns) in Neuendorf. They recuperated there for two weeks, and once again the Makhnovite Thiessens and the ex-*Gutsbesitzer* Janzens, who still lived with the Enns family, crossed paths. Two Janzen cousins, Justina and Mariechen, recalled the strange scene. Petia, who had stolen so much from the Janzens, conceded that he had met the family once before. But neither he nor his mother ever acknowledged the relationship. The Thiessens themselves quarrelled bitterly with each other. Katia endlessly berated the Bolsheviks for having stolen 'their' possessions. Petia retorted that his wife had lost nothing but material goods, while he had lost his honour, his integrity, his home, and the acceptance of his family. I have been told that the Thiessens reached Guliai Polie and eventually landed in the Molochna Settlement, where a remorseful Petia reputedly begged his Khortitsa victims for forgiveness.

Other real or imagined Mennonite bandits fared less well. On 27 January 1922, the Cheka (Bolshevik secret police) executed six men from Nieder Khortitsa, all branded as bandits. Among these were Löwen's three main *Selbstschützer* – Günter, Neufeld, and Töws – who were not bandits in the usual sense. However, the Bolsheviks applied that classification to anyone who had opposed them. The other three – the son of one of the poorest *Nippaenja* families and two Unger brothers – had presumably collaborated with a bandit gang. Their death sentence suggests they had plundered among the Ukrainian peasants, because other bandits, who plundered the Mennonites, Lutherans, or German Catholics, were never punished so harshly. The Cheka refused to release the bodies, and we assumed that they had tortured the men before murdering them.

Once back in control, the Bolsheviks quickly established a semblance of order in our area. An early edict proclaimed that no one was subject to Makhnovite demands any longer. What a relief to be free of the obscenities and threats that had dominated our lives the past two months and to no longer hear the endless sing-song refrain, 'Speculator, speculator speculates, But our Little Father Makhno requisitions it.'

Bolshevik control did nothing to quell the typhus epidemic, however. By the time it had run its course, its toll was staggering. According to Dr Hamm, the population of Nieder Khortitsa in 1919 was approximately 1,000, of whom roughly 900 were Mennonites. Over 70 per cent contracted typhus and 15 per cent of the stricken died. In total, typhus killed 14 per cent of the village's Mennonite men and 7 per cent of its Mennonite women. Infection and death rates may have been slightly lower for the non-Mennonite residents because the Makhnovites found their more impoverished homes less inviting. International health organizations estimate that thirty million Russians suffered typhus between 1918 and 1922. Of these, a similar percentage (or three million) died.

As the typhus epidemic raged through Mennonite villages from December 1919 to March 1920, all of the settlement's medical professionals fell ill. The Red Army, which had driven the Makhnovites out, was either unable or unwilling to provide aid, and so care devolved to those who were healthy and willing to render elementary assistance. Johann became the primary caregiver in Nieder Khortitsa. His training as a medical orderly and service on the hospital trains made him pre-eminently suited for this Samaritan job. For six months of the war he had tended a railcar filled exclusively with soldiers suffering from typhus, cholera, or extreme cases of diarrhoea, and so he knew the importance of hygiene and how best to minister to the needs of his patients.

Johann organized his 'house calls' by dividing the village into two sections, going from house to house in a given section, reserving one side of the street for the morning, the other for the afternoon. Usually, he covered the village in two days, although the work often kept him out until midnight. He maintained this regimen from late December 1919 until March 1920. During this period there was no other man in Nieder Khortitsa well enough to consistently perform these services. Of course, as each of us regained our health we did what we could for each other.

With no real medical training, equipment, or drugs, Johann acted primarily in supportive ways, performing simple household tasks such as fetching fresh water or going to a neighbour's home to collect embers to kindle the straw and manure bricks to heat the house. He did, however, manage to relieve some patients' pain by suctioning blood from their lungs and provided others with camphor which the local pharmacist, Mr Tavonius, had saved from the Makhnovite requisitions. The need to improve hygiene was especially acute. All our homes had outdoor privies rather than indoor plumbing, and by this time few people even had bedpans. This presented an obvious problem for those too sick to get out of bed, particularly when there was no one in the home well enough to help them to get outside. Since few people had been able to save extra linens from the thieves, most families could not even change soiled sheets. The filth and foul air were indescribable. Having experienced similar conditions on the hospital train, Johann was able to help clean up the patients and he did whatever he could about their bedding.

One fortunate side effect of Johann's work was his coincidental service as a conduit of village information. Without telephones, everyone relied on word of mouth for news of the fate of friends and relatives. Often family members living just a short distance away were too sick to visit each other and so had no idea of one another's condition. Johann's near-daily visits kept everyone abreast. And if he could not treat their bodies, his presence alone carried many villagers' spirits through the crisis. He was always willing to tarry with someone wishing to pursue the cherished Mennonite custom of *Nohfaedme,* threading family connections, or to pray with those needing spiritual comfort.

Often Johann felt that the greatest suffering he encountered was not physical. Rather, many people struggled with their faith. How, they wondered, could God have permitted the murder of so many innocent people, the rape of defenceless women, and the commission of so many other acts of unconscionable brutality? At such times Johann wished that the local minister, Jacob Sawatzky, could accompany him to offer solace to the afflicted. That so many of us suffered a crisis of faith is hardly surprising. Later, when some Canadian- and U.S.-born Mennonites wondered how we could have lost faith, resorted to self-defence, or despaired during the revolution, civil war, and blackest anarchy, my reaction was straightforward, 'What do you know of such traumatic experience? And what assurance do you have that your faith would have been firmer, or that you would have offered the other cheek?'

Johann believed that the broader Mennonite community would eventually come to our aid, and perhaps one of his greatest services was to reassure his patients of this conviction. His faith was confirmed in mid-March 1920, when a number of young people from the Molochna Settlement, which had escaped the ravages of the Makhnovite terror, arrived with food, clothing, medicine, and arrangements for the care of our settlement's numerous orphaned children. Their assistance was incalculable. In the long run, however, another initiative of the Molochna Settlement was even more significant – it had sent delegates to the United States and Canada to apprise our co-religionists of our needs and to explore the possibility of a mass emigration to the New World. Although the idea of a mass migration had arisen in the past – for example, a Khortitsa high school teacher, Dr Dietrich Neufeld, had championed immigration to New Zealand – few had considered it seriously. Now, the timeliness of the idea was clear.

By about the 18 or 19 January, I was strong enough to walk the twelve miles to Rosental to visit my Pauls relatives. There I learned that Uncle Jacob's wife had died on 21 December 1919. Grandmother's brother Kornelius Hildebrand and his wife had also died. Twenty-one other members of the Pauls family had been infected with typhus. All had survived except Grandmother herself, who died shortly after my visit.[4]

When I arrived I found my gravely ill Grandmother in Uncle Heinrich's room, the only one they were able to heat. 'I know that your mother and father and brother Heinrich have died,' Grandmother said. 'But how are the rest of you? And did your brother Johann return from the other side of the river?' I told her what I could – of Johann's sad arrival after Father's death, that the rest of the family had survived the crisis, and of Johann's humanitarian efforts. Grandmother said little, except to wonder how long she would hold back death. As I bid her good-bye, it seemed to me that there was still strength in her eyes and voice. I thought she might pull through. In the preceding two months I had seen so many people ill with the disease, Mennonites and Makhnovites alike, that I knew you could not always guess who would live and who would die.

I did not stay long with Grandmother, but spoke a little with Tante Sus before departing. I told her that I hoped to see Grandmother well soon. It was not to be. Grandmother died on 20 January 1920. Perhaps it was fortunate, because it spared her the tragedies that befell our family, and the Russian Mennonites as a whole, over the next three and a half years.

CHAPTER TWENTY-EIGHT

More Desperate Years: A Sketch

Our village, indeed the entire region, had barely recovered from the ravages of war, civil war, and epidemics when mass death again marched across southern Ukraine. This time it was famine and to an even greater extent than the carnage of the civil war, this scourge was indifferent to ethnicity, politics, language, or religion. It affected nearly everyone, high-born or low. Only a handful with political power could be certain of their next meal. My brother Johann described the horror:[1]

> All rhetoric pales before the grim realities of the famine that ravaged the Ukraine in 1921–1922. I might torture the reader for a long time with staggering facts, facts which seem indeed stranger than fiction. A few examples, however, will be sufficient to show the picture of human suffering as we experienced it in those two years. The causes of the famine were many. First, the area of cultivation had been constantly reduced during the years of the war and civil war, due to the lack of manpower and loss of draft-animals; second to the depreciation and destruction of agricultural equipment and the inability of the peasant to obtain new ones; third the drought of 1920 and 1921; last, the voluntary reduction of the sowing area on the part of the peasants themselves, as a protest against the senseless wholesale requisitioning policy of the government. These were briefly the causes of the famine.
>
> The catastrophe was made still more horrible by such diseases as cholera and typhus which raged everywhere. [We lacked] hospital facilities, medicines, trained staff [to combat those and deal with] the indescribable unsanitary conditions in the affected regions. As a result of all this, people died like flies in their homes, on the street, and on the road. Thousands of others left their homes and trekked hundreds of miles into regions where

there still was something to eat. Thus in 1920 thousands of fugitives from the Volga came to the Ukraine, their wagons loaded with household goods, children, women, and the aged, drawn by horses with bones showing through their skins. For months they had been on the road, in rags and filth, living on offal, chaff, bark, and clay, and dying at an appalling rate. And scarcely had they reached the Ukraine when there came the great drought of 1920, but more particularly in 1921. In despair many of them returned to the Volga to die at least in their own homes; for there was no other hope. Others stayed passively awaiting death.

It is now in the winter of 1921. The famine has reached such a scale that words fail to describe it. The crop was a total failure, the grain mostly being so sparse that it could not be cut with a machine and had to be harvested painstakingly by hand. The people go about emaciated and weak, living as they do mostly on all kinds of refuse. Cases of cannibalism are not wanting, parents and children murdering one another. In a window at the headquarters of the Cheka in a neighboring city almost daily were posted pictures of people who had been condemned to death for cannibalism, in order to deter others from doing the same thing. But hunger knows no fear of punishment.

People are digging their own graves for fear that soon they will be too weak to do so and they will remain unburied. But frequently it happens that others bury their dead in graves which someone else had dug for himself or his relations. The dead as a rule are buried naked to save the clothing for the living. And by no means all can afford a wooden box as coffin. One day I saw a place where the father, with four children in the same bed, had been dead for two days, the children too weak to leave the bed and call for help. In the same house, but in another room lay two dead Makhnovites, already in a serious state of decomposition. Still in another room of the same building an old laborer, whom I had known very well, probably in a state of delirium, had tried to jump out of the window, but had been too weak and so had died right there, hanging partly out of the window. But why multiply examples. If help does not come soon ... I shudder to think of the consequences.

Over the worst two years of this crisis approximately seven million people perished. Roughly 3 per cent of Nieder Khortitsa's villagers – thirty-three men and children – died of starvation. This, combined with the typhus epidemic of preceding years and the elevated death rate from various other infectious diseases, left a larger percentage of Mennonite families with single parents. A burst of remarriages occurred, not without a degree of friction. With a touch of humour in those days, villagers often told a story of a wife yelling to her husband, 'Papa, come quickly. My kids and your kids are beating up on our kids.' (*Vurratje, komm schwind. Miene Tjinja en diene Tjinja vepriejle onse Tjinja).*

The death toll would have soared far higher had the Bolshevik government not finally allowed U.S. and Dutch Mennonite Relief organizations to distribute food in 1922. Although none of my family died of starvation, we were certainly malnourished.

During this time I was a teacher, and my government salary (like my brother Johann's) included a monthly food allotment, along with an annual stipend of twenty-three million rubles. With hyper-inflation the rubles were almost worthless and depreciating daily, so that when we were paid we rushed out to buy food if possible, or if not, then at least something of material value such as a pair of socks. Often we did not receive the food ration, and when we did, officials took a portion of it as a bribe. Thus, Johann and I sold everything possible – books, bedding, even the boards from the barn ceiling – to buy a few pounds of potatoes or a small sack of flour.

Our teaching careers were also jeopardized. The Bolsheviks controlled every aspect of education, and they continually harassed us to provide statistics and budgets for supplies, which of course we did not receive. For example, Johann's school, with sixty-seven pupils, had only ten primers, and perhaps only three or four pencils. Then the antireligious campaign intensified and Johann, who was also a preacher, was fired. As a preacher's brother, I was transferred to a school in another village. Here the government required, as it did everywhere else, that teachers carry out its vigorous antireligious propaganda and inculcate its anti-bourgeois philosophy. Such repugnant duties made teaching untenable, but what alternative did, or would, we have?

As it became ever clearer that life would never return to the normality of a decade earlier, in either material or religious terms, Mother's final words – to emigrate at all costs – became our watchwords. In June 1923 the day finally arrived. Following several years of negotiation, the Canadian government agreed to accept Mennonite immigrants if the Soviet government would release us as it had promised. To our great relief (the previous struggles had pauperized virtually all of us) the Canadian Pacific Railroad agreed to lend us the money needed for our passage.

Families split on the fateful issue of whether to emigrate or to stay in Russia in the hope that they could recover their prosperity in the land they loved so dearly. Those who left, survived, and for the most part, flourished. Those who stayed were at best exiled; at worst they starved in the famine of 1932 to 1933 or perished in the Gulag. Many of my distant relatives, school friends, and neighbours simply disappeared in the Soviet system, and I do not know what finally happened to them. I do have knowledge, however, of the fates of some family members. I suspect that these reflect the general outcome for the Mennonites who remained in the Soviet Union.

My sister Neta and her husband, Jacob Pankratz, were sent to the slave labour camps in 1937 on the ground that they had been successful farmers in the distant past. Jacob Pankratz, already badly crippled with arthritis, died two years later. Neta was released a year or two after that and sent to Kazakhstan, having no idea where her children were. For ten years she remained ignorant of their fate, until by chance she met her niece (my brother Gerhard's daughter, Marusiia), who in her own wanderings in search of her husband had heard news of Neta's children.

My brother Gerhard somehow escaped the near-universal round-up of Mennonite men during the 1930s. But with the Nazi invasion, his family (excepting one son and his daughters' husbands) was rounded up and resettled in Poland in 1943.[2] After the war, most of the family made its way to Belgrade, where the Red Army picked them up and sent them into Soviet exile, each family member to a different location. Then in 1951 Stalinist forces sent Gerhard to the Gulag, where he remained incarcerated until some time after his wife's death in 1954.

Among my father's relatives, I know nothing of his brother and sister David and Elizabeth or of their families, but I suspect that they spent time in the slave labour camps. What little I know of the fates of four cousins – the orphaned children of Father's oldest brother Johann – is grim. Of the four, Gerhard died of typhus in 1920 as did Elizabeth's husband, Bernhard Hildebrand. She herself died in the second Ukrainian famine of 1932 to 1933. Johann and his wife Maria (née Regier) survived the famine, but I have no idea of their subsequent fate, nor of that of Katharina, except that her husband, Peter Hildebrand, ultimately made it to Canada.

A similar sad outcome befell most of the relations of Father's first wife. Her brothers Gerhard, Heinrich, and Peter died of typhus, as did Peter's wife, Agatha (née Heinrichs). Sonia Funk (née Rempel), the daughter of father's former brother-in-law, was exiled to Siberia with her husband, Heinrich Funk (a church leader in the Ignatievo Settlement). She evidently died there, while he spent 1930 to 1938 at Solovki, one of the more notorious slave labour camps near Arkhangelsk, on the White Sea. Apparently, after release from that prison term he was sent to other Siberian camps, and then died in Karaganda, Kazakhstan.

On my mother's side, my Aunt Katharina and her husband, Jacob Janzen, were exiled. When those of us who had emigrated to Canada learned their location and privation, we arranged to have food parcels sent to them. By the time they arrived, Jacob had already starved to death, as had three of the couple's children. Aunt Katharina died of starvation a few days after the parcels arrived. A fourth child died somewhat later. Only their daughter Justina eventually emigrated to Canada, but this some years after her husband, Johann Sawatzky, was exiled to a slave labour camp in Siberia. No one knows his fate. The Germans swept Justina and her four children west in 1943, and from there they finally emigrated to Canada in the late 1940s. My Uncle Jacob's wife, Anna (née Hamm), died of typhus; he himself died in internal exile in 1932. Uncle Kornelius died in internal exile in 1938. Uncle Johann died in internal exile in 1937. Aunt Anganetha's husband, Heinrich Heinrichs, had of course been killed by Makhnovite bandits in 1919.

For a time, my uncle by marriage, Kornelius Braun, managed well under the Soviet system. Shortly after we left for Canada, he and my Aunt Helena, moved to Rosengart, where Kornelius became the only teacher. My brother Johann and he corresponded frequently until 1926 or 1927, when Kornelius ceased writing, fearing, evidently that letters from abroad would brand him a *burzhui.* He even forced his wife to walk to other villages to read letters from Canadian relatives, and he never allowed her to bring them home. Ultimately, Kornelius made the mistake of going to church in Khortitsa when his two daughters, Maria and Anna, were baptized in 1929. In response, the Bolsheviks, intolerant of any religious connection to education, ousted Kornelius. However, the Rosengart farmers viewed him so highly that they asked him to become their collective farm secretary and allowed his family to continue living in the teacherage. Although his son was rounded up during the Stalinist purges of 1934 to 1938, Kornelius himself was among the handful of Mennonite men who escaped this fate. In 1943, Kornelius and his wife, two daughters, a daughter-in-law, and four grandchildren were rounded up by the Nazis. He died in an East German displaced persons' camp in 1946, just before the Red Army rounded up the rest of the family and sent them into exile in Siberia. My Aunt Helena died in internal exile in 1953.

My Aunt Susanna and Uncles Bernhard and Heinrich emigrated to Canada. They and my own siblings – Johann and Mariechen and their families, and Jacob and I were among the first of the roughly 21,000 Mennonites to leave Russia between 1923 and 1928. We never looked back, nor did we ever stop blessing the wisdom of our decision.

Some decades after I was already in the New World, I received news that my boyhood friend, Makar Golubkov, son of the Old Believer who bought my grandfather's store, starved to death in the famine of 1932 to 1933. This reminded me that the tragedies befalling Mennonites were not limited to our singular group. Rather, they mirrored the horror suffered by an entire nation's people.

Epilogue

Few dates are so indelibly imprinted on my memory as 22 July 1923. It was the first day of my new settled life in Canada and the United States. That day marked the end of five years of social turmoil and family tragedy. That was the day my brother Jacob and I arrived in Rosthern, Saskatchewan. We were among the first group of Mennonites leaving Russia after the First World War, and virtually all of us were from the Khortitsa area, which during the civil war had suffered more than the other settlements.

When the Canadian Pacific train that had picked us up in Quebec pulled into the small town station in the middle of the prairie, we immigrants discovered a huge enthusiastic crowd of Mennonites from the nearby farms awaiting us. Most of those greeting us were first- or second-generation Mennonites who had migrated from New Russia to Manitoba during the 1870s to 1890s. In the decades that followed they had added new settlements in the newly formed province of Saskatchewan. Most of the expectant crowd hoped to find relatives of their parents and grandparents who had stayed behind in Russia.

Bishop David Töws led the welcome. Almost single-handedly he had reversed the Canadian government's refusal to allow more Mennonites into Canada, as well as to quell opposition to such a migration by a small segment of Canadian Mennonites themselves. The government feared the Mennonites' traditional pacifism, while the Canadian Mennonite minority feared that the Russian Mennonite immigrants might pollute their faith. As a number of preachers and lay leaders added their tearful and joyous reception, Canadian Mennonite families milled through the crowded clumps of new arrivals. Was anyone named such and such? Did anyone come from this or that village? Slowly, the newcomers thinned out as they were matched with a near or distant relative, sometimes just an acquaintance of relatives, sometimes with total strangers who befriended them. Together with their meagre belongings they climbed into cars or trucks and took off for a new home. After several hours most of the more than 300 newcomers had departed. Only small groups of immigrants were still left waiting for some kind person to take them under his wing. Most of these were single men, or groups of related unmarried men, as priority had been given to the aged and families with children. Jacob and I remained among these sad, forlorn souls that no one had chosen.

As the crowd shrank further, Jacob and I became restive, almost frantic. Who would select us? Finally, two men approached our leader, Mr Zacharias, who was himself uneasy that some of us remained. Much to our relief, and astonishment, the pair asked Zacharias if there were any Rempels or Epps from Nieder Khortitsa among the group. Zacharias pointed to us.

The two tall Canadians were Jacob Epp and his brother from Laird, and when they approached us, I recalled that my Grandfather Rempel's sister had married Peter Epp, and the couple had emigrated to Canada in the 1890s. With this information, and our distant relationship established, we piled into Jacob's car and headed out for 'Epp' Road, so named because farms of many Epp descendants were all along its length.

We stayed at Jacob's farm that night, sleeping in a small cottage some distance from the main house. It was late when we went to bed, but shortly after we had fallen asleep we were jolted awake. Brilliant light surrounded the farm. Certain that the whole farm was ablaze we dashed from the cottage, only to behold a spectacle we had never seen. It was a fabulous display of Northern Lights, which both Jacob and I interpreted as a good omen for our future. We were safe at last in Canada. We had found a new home. And, indeed, the ensuing years have been good.

The ancestral home in Nieder Khortitsa is no longer. When my nephew Jacob Pankratz visited the village in 1972, he found nothing but a few barren walls where the sturdy house had stood. The once acacia-shaded family cemetery plot that my mother had so lovingly tended was a similar picture of desolation, with only a few fading reminders that this land had been the hallowed ground of a once-prosperous Mennonite settlement. My nephew was able to identify our burial plot by a lonely grave marker with a barely legible name: Gerhard Rempel. Below it was etched what he made out to be 1831–1881. He wished to know what relationship that man might have had to him.

'That was your maternal grandfather,' I wrote in response. 'But the years were actually 1830–1880.'

My nephew's accounts of our ancestral village rekindled memories of three verses from Adalbert von Chamisso's '*Das Schloss Boncourt*,' a poem I had memorized six decades earlier in Nieder Khortitsa. The poet describes his feelings upon visiting the site of his ancestral château years after the French Revolution. He found not a single building standing. Everything was levelled to the ground and the fields were now being tilled by peasants. Still, he did not curse the fate that had wrought this destruction, but blessed the man who now drew a furrow across what had once been.

My dreams to my childhood, they wing me
I shake my head, old and gray,
To the memories of youth's visitation,
Which long I'd forgotten away.

And there you now stand, fine embankment,
So true in my heart you hold sway,
You are gone without demarcation,
And sand holds your fate and its way.

Oh earth, be faithful and fertile,
I bless you gently and pray
And bless you again, when whoever
Will guide the plow on its way.

Ich träum' als Kind mich zurücke,
Und schüttele mein greises Haupt;
Wie sucht ihr mich heim, ihr Bilder,
Die längst ich vergessen geglaubt?

So stehst du, o Schloss meiner Väter,
Mir treu und fest in dem Sinn,
Und bist von der Erde verschwunden,
Der Sand weht über dich hin.

Ich segne dich mild und gerührt,
Und segn' ihn zweifach, wer immer
Den Pflug nun über dich führt
Sei fruchtbar, o treuer Boden.

Similarly, I now recall every detail of my childhood home, yard, garden, barn and *Spitja,* my father, my mother, and the happy prewar days, and then the horrors of war, banditry, epidemics, drought, and famine that brought that all to an end. But I cannot find it in me to curse the people who caused the change. Rather, I continue to have the deepest feelings of gratitude for the fate that brought me, and so many who are dear to me, to various countries in the democratic West.

APPENDIX I

Terms of Catherine the Great's Recruiting Manifesto of 1785*

1 Free transportation and board from the Russian border to the settlement area.
2 The right to settle anywhere and pursue any occupation.
3 Loans to build houses and factories, or purchase farm equipment.
4 Perpetual exemption from military and civil service.
5 Tax exemption for periods that varied with occupation and place of settlement.
6 Freedom of religion, except to establish monasteries.
7 The right to proselytize among the Muslims, but not among Christian subjects.
8 The right of self-government in agricultural communities.
9 The right to import family belongings duty-free.
10 The right to buy serfs and peasants for those who established factories with their own money.
11 The right to negotiate other terms with the Russian authorities.

* Excerpted from D.G. Rempel, 'The Mennonite Commonwealth in Russia: A Sketch of Its Founding and Endurance, 1789–1919,' *Mennonite Quarterly Review* 47 (1973), 259–308 and 48 (1974), 5–54.

APPENDIX II

Mennonite Articles of Settlement in New Russia*

Articles 1, 7, and *8* guaranteed freedom of religion, the rendering of allegiance by a simple affirmation, and permanent exemption for the emigrants and their descendants from military service.

Article 2 granted the Berislav land tract along with the Tavan and several other islands opposite the tract, and exclusive fishing rights within the tract.

Article 3 granted a ten-year tax exemption.

Article 4 set the tax rate unalterably, after this period of exemption, at fifteen kopeks per dessiatin.** It also provided exemptions from quartering troops, except as they passed through the area, and for doing government road work outside the settlement, although the settlement's own roads had to be maintained by the Mennonites.

Article 5 granted the Mennonites the right to conduct business, establish factories, become members of guilds and trade associations, and to freely sell their products.

Article 6 set up a schedule of loans for those who required assistance. These would be made in five payments of 100 rubles, the first when

* Excerpted from D.G. Rempel, 'The Mennonite Commonwealth in Russia: A Sketch of Its Founding and Endurance, 1789–1919,' *Mennonite Quarterly Review* 47 (1973), 259–308 and 48 (1974), 5–54, and Rempel, 'From Danzig to Russia: The First Mennonite Migration,' *Mennonite Life* 24 (1969), 8–27.

**In 'The Mennonite Commonwealth,' Rempel uses the figure of fifteen kopeks per dessiatin; in 'From Danzig,' he states 'no more than ten kopeks per dessiatin.'

the emigrant arrived in Riga, and the remaining once a month thereafter. Repayment, without interest, had to be made in three years.

Article 9 obligated the government to provide 120 twelve-foot- long oak planks for each family's home and the necessary lumber and millstones for two flour mills.

Articles 10 and *11* granted free transportation for those who had none, and a travel allowance of twenty five kopeks for each adult and twelve kopeks for each child under the age of fifteen.

Article 12 requested that the government not require repayment of the timber and travel allowances.

Article 13 requested temporary housing until the emigrants had constructed their own.

Article 14 provided a subsidy from the time of their arrival until the first harvest of ten kopeks per day per person. This was to be repaid over three years after their ten-year tax exemption had expired.

Article 15 demanded that all pasturage and woodcutting on the Berislav tract be set off-limits so that the emigrants would have adequate fuel and feed for livestock when they arrived.

Article 16 requested that similar privileges be granted for future emigrants, that they be settled in the Crimea or on similar lands near Feodosiia and Bakhchisarai, and that the first emigrants not be obliged to support the second group's settlement.

Articles 17 and *19* requested that Georg Trappe facilitate their efforts in leaving Danzig and that he be appointed the Director and Curator of the new Mennonite colonies.

Article 18 requested that a German-speaking surveyor be on hand when the emigrants arrived, to assist in establishing land allotments.

Article 20 requested that the government issue strict orders to protect the colonists and their belongings against injury, insult, harm, and theft.

APPENDIX III

Special Privileges Granted to Höppner and Bartsch*

1 The flour mills promised in the Articles of Settlement were to be given to Höppner and Bartsch, who would repay the government after fifteen years. They would then become their hereditary property.
2 They would receive twenty dessiatins of land on Tavan Island as their hereditary property, in addition to their standard sixty-five dessiatin allotment.
3 Each deputy had the right to keep a store and bakery, and would received a grant of 800 rubles from the government, also repayable in fifteen years.
4 Each had the right to brew beer and vinegar, and sell the products without restrictions.
5 Neither deputy had to repay the government for their family's travel and subsistence allowances.

* Excerpted from D.G. Rempel, 'The Mennonite Commonwealth in Russia: A Sketch of Its Founding and Endurance, 1789–1919,' *Mennonite Quarterly Review* 47 (1973), 259–308 and 48 (1974), 5–54.

APPENDIX IV

Khortitsa Settlement Villages*

High German	*Low German*	*Russian*
Chortitza	Gortietz	Khortitsa
Rosental	Rosendohl	Kantserovka
Insel Chortitza	Kaump	Ostrov Khortitsa
Einlage	Elloag	Kichkas
Neuendorf	Nieendarp	Shirokoe
Neuenburg	Nieenbaoj	Malashevka
Schönhorst	Scheenhorscht	Vodianaia
Kronsweide	Kroonsweid	Vladimirovka
Schönwiese	Scheenwäs	Shenvize
Kronsgarten	Kronsgoad	Polovitsa
Nieder Chortitza	Nie Gortietz	Nizhniaia Khortitsa
Burwalde	Berwool	Baburka
Kronstal	Kroonsdohl	Dolinsk
Osterwick	Oostawitj	Pavlovka
Schöneberg	Scheenboaj	Smolianaia
Rosengart	Roosegaod	Novoslobodka
Blumengart	Bloomegoad	Kapustianka
Neuhorst	Niehorscht	Ternovataia

* Excerpted from D.G. Rempel, 'The Mennonite Commonwealth in Russia: A Sketch of Its Founding and Endurance, 1789–1919,' *Mennonite Quarterly Review* 47 (1973), 259–308 and 48 (1974), 5–54.

APPENDIX V

Nieder Khortitsa about 1917

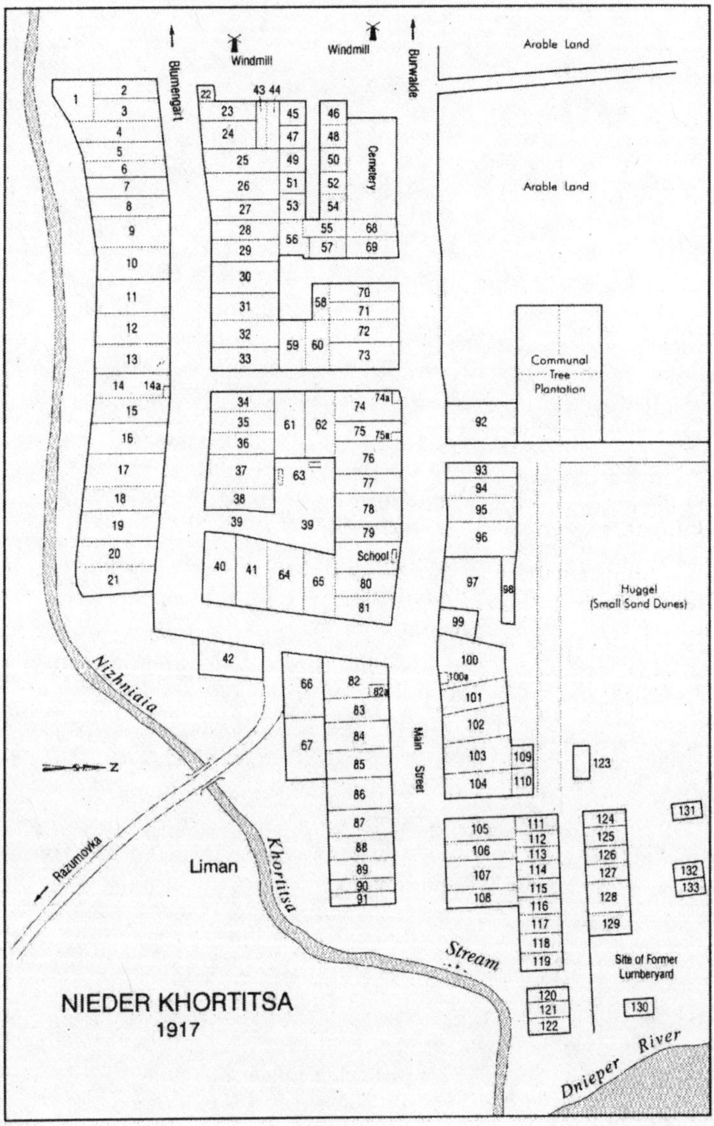

Map 6

1 Cornelius Rempel?
2 Peter and Cornelius Hübert
3 Johann Redekop*
4 Johann Funk
5 P. Dyck
6 J. Krause
7 David Neufeld
8 J. Willms
9 P. Giesbrecht*
10 Cornelius Buhr/Jacob Warkentin*
11 Heinrich Pankratz*
12 Leonid Gerzinuk (blacksmith)
13 J. Janzen*
14 Golobkov (storekeeper)
14a Store
15 Isaak Neufeld
16 Heinrich Klassen*
17 Heinrich Thiessen*
18 Jacob Günter
19 Peter Rempel
20 Cornelius Grunau
21 Widow Sawatzky
22 horse corral
23 Gerhard Klassen
24 Heinrich Rempel
25 Franz Dyck
26 Peter Redekop*
27 Dietrich Neufeld
28 (Peter Günter) Jacob Peters
29 Johann Friesen
30 Isaak Bergen*
31 (Johann Siemens) Jacob Siemens
32 Jacob Buhr*
33 David Epp*
34 Johann Penner
35 Jacob Sawatzky*
36 Harms
37 Heinrich Pankratz
38 Peter (?) Rempel
39 Community Great Orchard
40 David Neufeld
41 Peter Unger*
42 Jacob Epp*
43 Dyck?
44 Kethler?
45 Heinrich Thiessen
46 Peter Wall
47 Johann Günter
48 Peter Thiessen
49 Lettkemann
50 Dyck
51 Pätkau
52 Dyck
53 Johann (?) Rempel
54 Fehr
55 ?
56 David Neufeld
57 Peter Funk
58 Heinrich Penner
59 (?) Pankratz
60 Gerhard Sawatzky
61 Peter Neufeld
62 Heinrich Grunau
63 Community Rental Cottages
64 Gerhard Warkentin
65 Jacob Dyck*
66 David Neufeld*
67 unoccupied
68 J. Peters
69 Cornelius (?) Wall
70 Widow Unger
71 Abram and Peter Vogt
72 Johann (?) Thiessen
73 Gerhard (Lauftje) Rempel (our home from 1913)
74 Johann Siemens*
74a granary

75 Gerhard (Lauftje) Rempel (our home; 1891–1913)
75a store
76 Jacob Warkentin
77 ?
78 Gerhard (Sauntje's) Rempel
79 Peter Friesen
80 Jacob Rempel
81 Peter (Atje) Rempel
82 Jacob Janzen (Storekeeper)
82a store
83 Cornelius Wall
84 Jacob Wall*
85 Abram Günter*
86 Franz Pauls*
87 Abram Schmidt*
88 Abram Thiessen
89 Property of Jacob Pätkau
90 Aaron Mantler
91 Griska Seda
92 Niebuhr and Wiebe flour mills
93 Jacob Martens (blacksmith)
94 unoccupied
95 Wilhelm Pankratz
96 Peter Pätkau
97 Widow Peter Rempel and Peter (Kuita) Rempel
98 school orchard
99 horse corral
100 Johann (Predja) Rempel*
100a Community granary (after 1917 used for church services)
101 Heinrich Penner
101a store
102 Peter Siemens*
103 Peter and David Schellenberger*
104 David Penner*
105 Jacob Bergen*
106 unoccupied
107 Jacob Pätkau*
108 Peter Günter
109 Leppke
110 Widow Thiessen
111 Gerhard ?
112 Jacob Rempel
113 ? Mantler
114 Martin Klassen
115 Martin Klassen
116 Martin Klassen
117 Peter Wall
118 Wilhelm Rempel
119 Abram Unger
120 Peter (?) Rempel
121 ?
122 ('Prussian') Schulz
123 Widow Mantler
124 Jacob Neufeld
125 Jacob Wall
126 Johann Driedger
127 P. ('?') Dyck
128 unoccupied
129 Herdsman's cottage
130 Vogt
131 ? Reimer
132 ?

* descendants of owners of original land grants of 1803, at the founding of Nieder Khortitsa

Nieder Khortitsa Statistics

Until the mid to late 1920s, approximately two-thirds of the village homes were occupied by the same families as in 1917, including the Gerzinuk and Golobkov properties. The remaining one-third were occupied by families with Mennonite names (except the Griska Seda property, later occupied by someone named Bondja?). By that same time, roughly sixty-five more homes had been constructed in the areas designated Huggel, Communal Tree Plantation, and Arable Land. Of these, fifty-five were occupied by Mennonite families, the remainder by families with Ukrainian or Russian names.

Timeline, 1919–1943

1919	village population ~1,000; of these, approximately 894 were Mennonites.
1917–18	4 people died in the revolution.
1919	10 Mennonites murdered by Makhno's bandits.
1920	94 Mennonites died of typhus.
1922	6 men shot by the Cheka.
1921–2	12 men, 5 women, and 7 children starved to death.
1923–8	300 Mennonites emigrated to Canada.
1933–4	11 Mennonites starved to death.
1929–41	78 men exiled or executed.
1941	289 people exiled.
1943	remainder of Mennonites in village evacuated and resettled in Germany.

APPENDIX VI

Genealogy

Figure 1 Six Generations in Russia

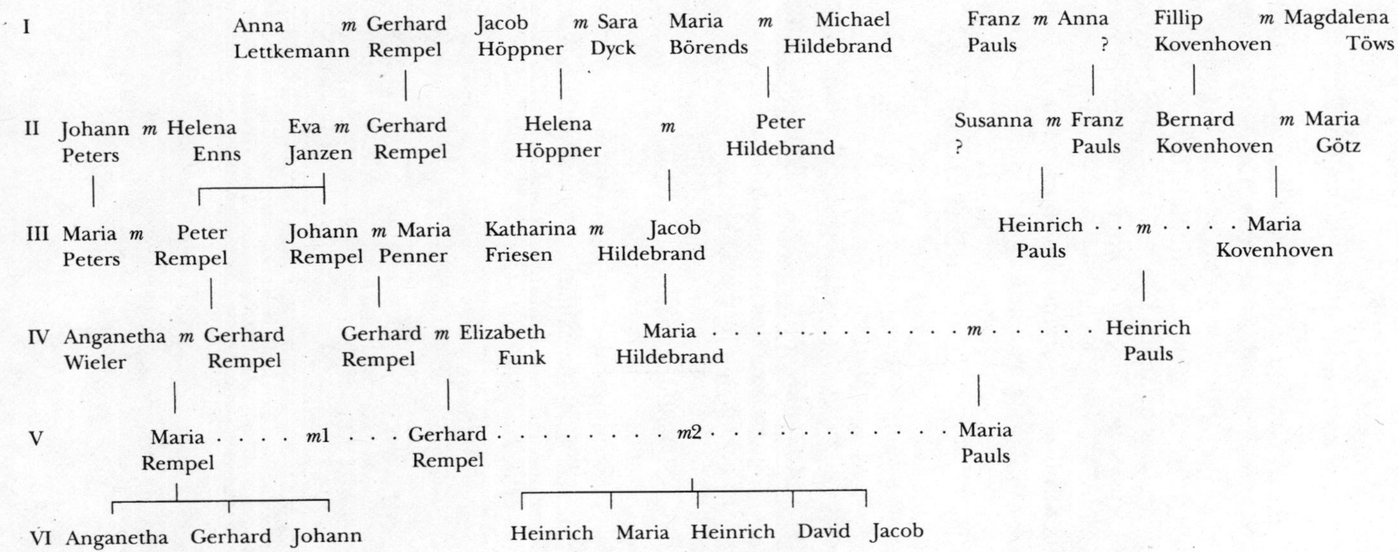

Figure 2 The Original Settlers: The Rempel Family

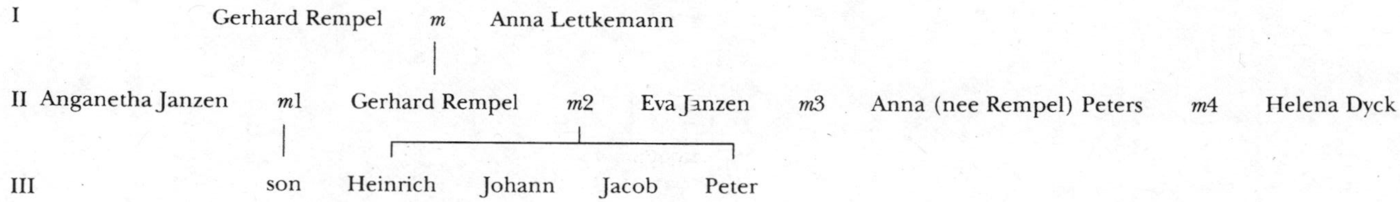

Generation I

Gerhard Rempel b.?; d.?; m. **Anna Lettkemann** b.?; d.? It is unclear where this couple settled. Gerhard's (or Gerd's) name does not appear in the registers of Schönwiese's seventeen founding families, even though church records indicate their residence there in 1797. Perhaps they lived temporarily in Alexandrovsk, then a military fort adjacent to Schönwiese. The family name also does not appear in the register of Kronsgarten's fifteen founding families, or among the remaining eighty-six families temporarily quartered in the previously established eight villages. The only Rempel mentioned is a Johann with a wife and three sons and no indication of residence. Discrepancies between Russian and Mennonite records occur for other Rempel families. Although Johann Rempel is the only name to appear in the early Russian documents, Benjamin H. Unruh's, *Die Niederländisch-niederdeutschen Hintergründe der Mennonitischen Ostwanderungen im 16., 18. und 19., Jahrhundert* (Karlsruhe, 1955), mentions that the families of Wilhelm and Dietrich Rempel arrived and temporarily settled in Rosental in 1795.

Generation II

Gerhard Rempel b. 26 December 1773; d. 28 January 1847; m1. 1799.

Anganetha Janzen, d. 22 March 1801; m2. 1801 **Eva Janzen** d. 3 August 1809; m3. 1810 **Anna (née Rempel) Peters** b. 1766; d. 7 Dec. 1837 (her first marriage to

Peter Peters produced a daughter who married David Penner, and two of this couple's daughters, Katharine and Maria Penner, married Gerhard's sons [see below]); m4. 1838 **Helena Dyck** b. 7 April 1819.

Generation III

Son b. 20 August 1800; d. 5 December 1808.

Heinrich, b. 25 August 1802; d. 24 April 1830; m. 1824 Katharine Penner.

Johann, b. 29 March 1806; d.1885; m. 1826 Maria Penner b. 4 Dec. 1807; d. 16 June 1886.

Jacob, b. 29 January 1807, joined the Frisian church.

Peter b. 28 December 1808; d. 28 July 1855; m. 1829 Maria Peters b. 15 September 1806; d. 19 October 1886.

Figure 3 The Paternal Rempels: My Great Grandparents and Their Children

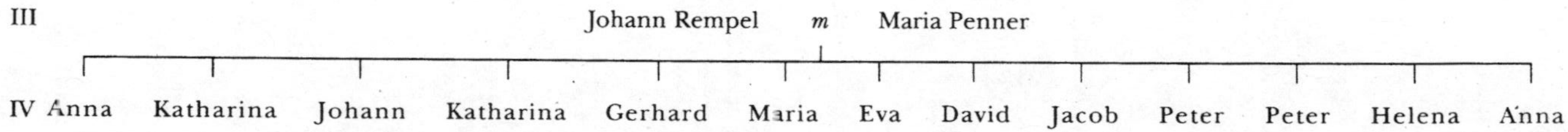

Generation III

Johann Rempel b. 29 March 1806; d. 1885; m. 1826 **Maria Penner**, b. 4 Dec. 1807; d. 16 June 1886.

Generation IV

Anna Rempel b. 1827; d. 1829.
Katharina Rempel b. 1828; d. 1829.
Johann Rempel b. 1830; d. 1847.
Katharina Rempel b. 1832; d. 1895; m. Peter Warkentin, a man of many trades who once built a windmill for my father on the huggels.
Gerhard Rempel b. 27 July 1833; d. 31 October 1901; m. 2 October 1855. **Elizabeth Funk** b. 13 November 1831; d. 30 November 1913.
Maria Rempel b. 1835; m1. Gerhard Penner; m2. Peter Wall.
Eva Rempel b. 1836; m. Jacob Dyck. I believe the couple moved to a daughter settlement.
David Rempel b. 1837; m. Katharina Wiens. They settled in Ignatievo, one of Khortitsa's most prosperous daughter settlements.
Jacob Rempel b. 1840; d. 1841.
Peter Rempel b. 1841; d. 1844.
Peter Rempel b. 1846; d. 1920; m. Maria Penner. One son, also named Peter, allegedly became a revolutionary.
Helena Rempel b. 1848; m. Wilhelm Penner and moved to Orenburg.
Anna Rempel b. 1850; d. 1938; m. Peter Epp b. 1849. The couple had fourteen children. Anna and Peter moved to the Fürstenland Settlement, then emigrated to Canada in the 1890s.

Figure 4 The Maternal Rempels: Father's First Wife's Grandparents

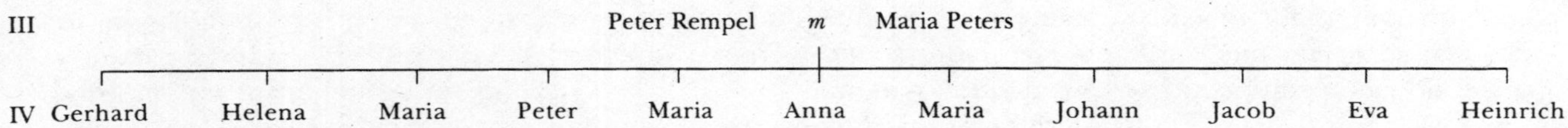

Generation III

Peter Rempel b. 28 December 1808; d. 28 July 1855; m. 1829 **Maria Peters**, b. 15 September 1806; d. 19 October 1886.

Generation IV

Gerhard Rempel b. 10 September 1830; d. 1880; m. 6 November 1855 Anganetha Wieler b. 14 April 1835.
Helena Rempel b. 1831; m1. Johann Hage b. 1820; d. 1860; m2. Wilhelm Schellenberg b. 1836; d. 1900.
Maria Rempel b. 1833; d. 1836.
Peter Rempel b. 1836; d. 1915; m. Justina Reddekop b. 1838; d. 1921.
Maria Rempel b. 1838; d. 1840.
Anna Rempel b. 1839; d. 1898; m. Paul Schellenberg b. 1838; d. 1908.
Maria Rempel b. 1841; d. 1886; m. Abram Giesbrecht b. 1827; d. 1895.
Johann Rempel b. 1843; d 1907; m. Anna Wall b. 1842; d. 1880.
Jacob Rempel b. 1845; d. 1916; m. Katharina Buhr b. 1848; d. 1908.
Eva Rempel b. 1847; m. Isaak Leppky b. 1845.
Heinrich Rempel b. 1848; d. 1920; m. Helena Pätkau b. 1857; d. 1919.

Figure 5 The Maternal Rempels: Father's First Wife's Parents and Siblings

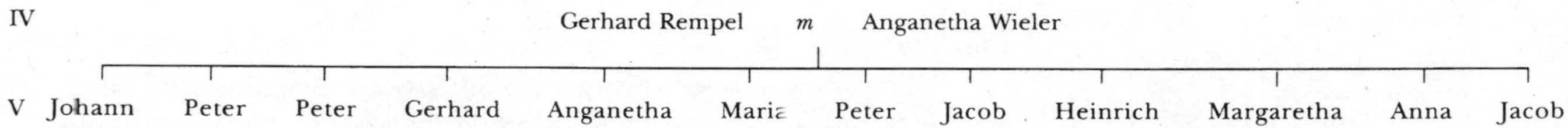

Generation IV

Gerhard Rempel b. 10 September 1830; d. 1880; m. 6 November 1855. **Anganetha Wieler** b. 14 April 1835. She was the daughter of an Einlage schoolteacher, Johann Wieler, and his wife, the former Anganetha Braun.

Generation V

Johann Rempel b. 6 July 1856; m1. Lena Rempel; m2. 20 February 1878. **Helena Unger.** This couple had five sons and two daughters.

Peter Rempel b. 1858; d. 1858.

Peter Rempel b. 1859; d. 1859.

Gerhard Rempel b. 1860; d. 1920; m1. 19 June 1883 Margaretha Dyck b. 1862. m2 to ? Gerhard prospered as a mill-owner until Mennonite Mill Fever bankrupted him as it did many other entrepreneurs during the late nineteenth and early twentieth centuries. Gerhard and Margaretha's children included Sonia and Greta.

Anganetha Rempel b. 1862; m. Isaak Kehler and moved to the village of New York in the Ignatievo Settlement, where her husband taught school, a profession two of their sons followed as well.

Maria Rempel b. 29 February 1864; d. 28 February 1891; m. 22 March 1883. **Gerhard Rempel** b. 2 August 1863; d. 23 December 1919.

Peter Rempel b. 1865; d. 1918; m. 1890 Agatha Heinrichs b. 1867; d. 1920. Peter and Agatha had at least fourteen children (some reports suggest as many as nineteen), most of whom died in infancy or young adulthood. Their daughter, Amalia, eventually immigrated to Canada. Johann Epp's diary states that Peter and Agatha Rempel's oldest son, also named Peter, killed his wife and then committed suicide (See

Kornelius Heinrichs and His Descendants 1782–1979 [Altona, Manitoba, 1980]). However, indirect sources indicate that this man was still living in Siberia in 1978, many decades after the supposed event.

Jacob Rempel b. 1867; d. 1867.

Heinrich Rempel b. 1869; d. 1919; m. 15 October 1889 Agatha Warkentin b. 1870; d. 1913. The couple had three daughters and four sons. Cornelius served in a Moscow facility of the All-Russian Zemstvo Union during the First World War. The Red Army captured and executed him shortly after he was conscripted by Denikin's White Army. His brother, Heinrich Jr., returned to Malaia Lepetikha to marry a Russian girl. Heinrich's sisters, Agatha and Maria, came to Canada. Anganetha's fate is unknown.

Margaretha Rempel b. 1871; d. 1897; m. 26 September 1891 Peter Vogt b. 1870, and lived next door to our farmstead.

Anna Rempel b. 1872; d. 1905; m. Peter Dyck b. 15 January 1872; d. 1920. Their children were Peter and Neta. The son had a warm personality and was particularly handsome and intellectual as well. His mental agility, infectious laughter, breadth of knowledge, and sense of humour were extraordinary, as was his optimistic spirit. He married Lena Siemens, daughter of our neighbor, Johann Siemens, and like his own father, became a teacher. He died of tuberculosis a few years after he reached Canada. Neta married David Epp in Rosental, had six children, and died in Manitoba in 1971. The elder Peter remarried in 1908 and by that wife had another daughter and two sons (J.P., born in 1910 and Victor, born in 1916). My correspondence with J.P. Dyck began after he published two interesting articles on Nieder Khortitsa in *Der Bote* in early 1980. According to his reports, and verified by those of other sources, J.P. was involved in controversial Canadian politics – both right and left leaning – and was committed to an internment camp during the Second World War for pro-Nazi views. Later he became a labour organizer.

Jacob Rempel b. 1878; d. 1879.

Figure 6 The Paternal Rempels: Father's Parents and Siblings

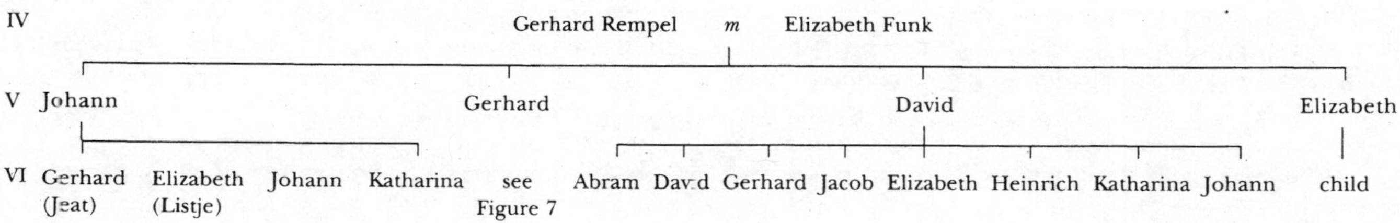

Generation IV

Gerhard Rempel b. 27 July 1833; d. 31 October 1901 m. 2 October 1855. **Elizabeth Funk** b. 13 November 1831; d. 30 November 1913 (she was the daughter of Heinrich Funk and Sara [née Friesen] Funk).

Generation V

Johann Rempel b. 6 July 1860; d. ?; m. 11 February 1879 Katharina Pätkau b. 29 April 1860. The couple's children were Gerhard b. 1879; d. 1920, Elizabeth (called Listje); b. 1881; d. 1932, Johann b. 1883, and Katharina b. 1884.

Gerhard Rempel b. 2 August 1863; d. 23 December 1919.

David Rempel b. 1865; m. 18 May 1891 Elizabeth Wiens, the daughter of Nieder Khortitsa's school teacher. Children: Abram, David, Gerhard, Jacob, Elizabeth, Heinrich, Katharina, and Johann.

Elizabeth Rempel b. 10 May 1869; m. 18 September 1890 Johann Harms. The couple had one child.

Figure 7 My Family

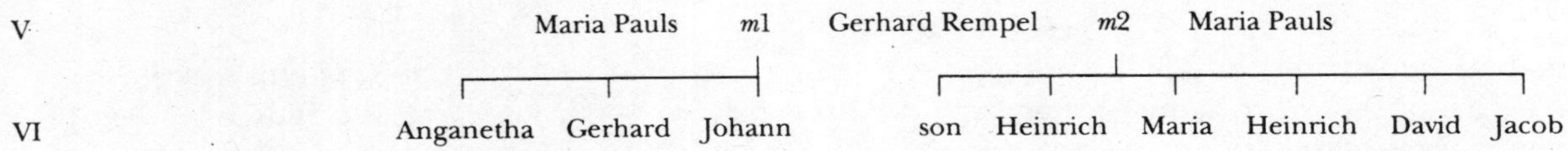

Generation V

Gerhard Rempel b. 2 August 1863; d. 23 December 1919; m1. 22 March 1883. **Maria Rempel** b. 29 February 1864; d. 28 February 1891; m2. 26 November 1891 **Maria Pauls** b. 29 June 1867; d. 8 January 1920.

Generation VI

Anganetha Rempel b. 7 August 1884; d. 1962; m. 11 May 1906 Jacob Pankratz b. 14 September 1884; d.? Children included Heinrich b. 1907, Maria b. 1909, Jacob b. 1910, Anganetha b. 1913, Gerhard b. 1914, Abram b. 1920, Helena.

Gerhard Rempel b. 23 June 1883; d. 1960; m. 28 April 1911 Tina Wiebe b. 8 September 1890; d. 1954. Children: Frieda b. 1912, Marusia b. 1913, Johann b. 1916, Malvina b. 1921, Victor.

Johann Rempel b. 1 February 1890; d. 1 January 1963 m. 23 August 1920 Susanna Epp b. 6 June 1899; d. 1988 Children included Johann b. 1921 d.1982, Gerhard b. 1923, Hilda b. 1925, Alma b. 1926, Agnes b. 1929, Laura b. 1931, Albert b. 1933.

Heinrich Rempel b. 25 June 1892; d. 18 December 1894 (diphtheria).

Maria Rempel b. 10 September 1894; d. 1976 m. 14 June 1918 Heinrich Klassen d. 1953. Children: Henry b. 1919 d. 1920, Henry b. 1921, Mary b. 1923, George b. 1925, John b. 1927, David b. 1929, Jacob b. 1931, Laura b. 1934, Annie b. 1936, Harold b. 1939, Ted b. 1940.

Heinrich Rempel b. 10 September 1897; d. 26 December 1919.

David Rempel b. 17 November 1899; d. 27 June 1992; m. 19 July 1930 Laura Kennel b. 19 January 1901; d. 13 September 1950. Children: Sonia b. 1938, Cornelia b. 1941.

Jacob Rempel b. 26 June 1903; d.1976; m. 1930 Greta Halliday b. 1905 d. 1994. Children: Richard b. 1934, Helen b. 1939, Elizabeth b. 1940.

Figure 8 Original Settlers: The Höppner Family

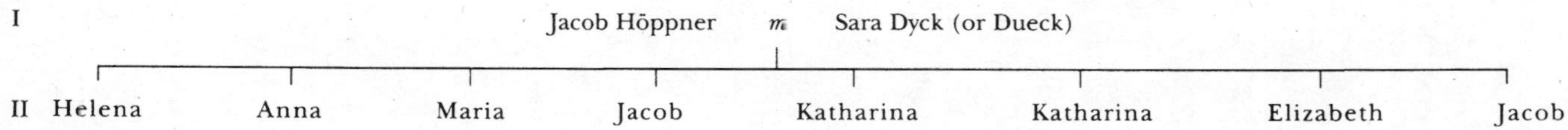

Generation I

Jacob Höppner b. 3 January 1747 or 1748; d. 3 April 1826; m2. 10 December 1773 Sara Dyck. Prior to this marriage, Jacob was married for 42 weeks to a women whose name is unknown.
Sara Dyck b. 17 November 1753; d. 27 February 1826.

Generation II

Helena Höppner b. 11 May 1775; d. 18 June 1833.
Anna Höppner b. 1781.
Maria Höppner b. 1784.
Jacob Höppner b. 1775; d. 1788.
Katharina Höppner d. 1789.
Katharina Höppner b. 1789; d. 1804.
Elizabeth Höppner b. 1792; d. 1804.

Jacob Höppner (2) b. 24 March 1797; d. 19 September 1883; m. 30 June 1821 Anna Brand b. 4 January 1804; d. 24 January 1877. Children: Jacob b. 21 July 1822, Johann b. 1 January 1824, Peter b. 23 August 1825, Anton b. and d. 4 July 1828, Anton b. 14 July 1829, Abraham b. 18 December 1831; d. 22 November 1855, Katharina b. 22 October 1834; d. 28 March 1859, Anna b. 21 January 1837; d. 2 May 1875, Bernhard b. 18 April 1840, Heinrich b. 13 December 1842, Gerhard b. 13 January 1846, Elizabeth b. 9 February 1849. Jacob continued to live on the family farm at Insel Khortitsa until his death in 1883. He was a successful man, and widely known among both Mennonites and local Russian and Ukrainian peasants and fishermen, who referred to him as Iakubenko (the diminutive of Jakub or Jacob). He seems to have had strong ties to several authors who were interested in local folklore as well. Two authors who mention 'Iakubenko' include Alexander Afanasiev-Chuzbinskii, in *Poiezdka v iuzhnuiu Rossiiu. Chast' I. Ocherki Dniepra* (St Petersburg, 1861), and the lawyer / amateur scientist Iakov P. Novitskii, in *S beregov Dniepra. Ocherki Zaporozhia. Putevyie zapiski i issledovaniia* (Ekaterinoslav, 1905). I believe most of this family's descendants emigrated to Canada in the 1870s to 1880s, and by the early 1920s the only families named Höppner lived in Rosengart. Here another Jacob Höppner married Annushka Braun, the daughter of Kornelius and Helena (née Pauls) Braun, and the great, great, great, granddaughter of the first Jacob Höppner.

Figure 9 Original Settlers: The Hildebrand Family

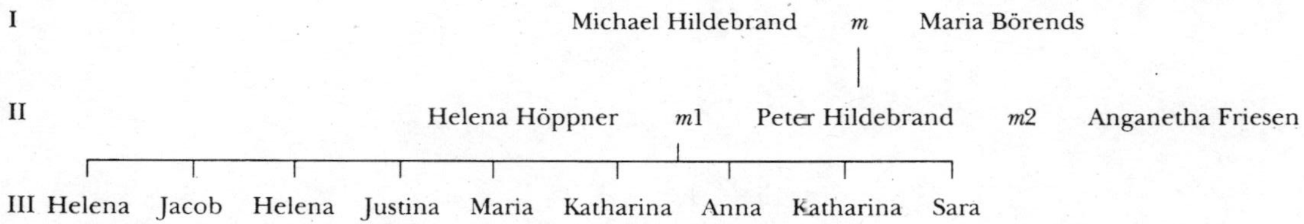

Generation I

Michael Hildebrand b. ?; d.?; m.? **Maria Börends** b.?; d.?

Generation II

Peter Hildebrand b. 3 March 1754; d. 27 March 1849; m1 8 February 1793 **Helena Höppner** b. 11 May 1775; d. 18 June 1833; m2 1835 **Anganetha (née Braun) Friesen**, b. 9 July 1781; d. 17 August 1851 (her first marriage to Jacob Friesen [b. 10 Dec. 1772; d. 6 August 1831] produced a daughter, Katharina Friesen, who married Peter and Helena Hildebrand's son, Jacob. Additionally this first marriage produced twelve more children [Jacob, Kornelius, Anna, Gerhard, Maria, Elizabeth, Sarah, Helena, Kornelius, Johann, Maria, Gerhard, at least four of whom died in 1819, suggesting an epidemic, and two others in infancy]). Peter is indubitably the progenitor of many Hildebrands, but not all who carry this name as is asserted in Neil Heinrichs, et al., eds. *Kornelius Heinrichs and Descendants, 1782 to 1979* (Kornelius Heinrichs History Society, Altona, Manitoba, 1980), 9, and Victor Peters, *Zwei Dokumente Quellen zum Geschichtsstudium der Mennoniten in Russland* (Winnipeg: Echo-Verlag 1965). There were other Mennonite Hildebrands in several colonies from the time of Khortitsa's founding, all named Peter. One lived in Einlage, another in Khortitsa, and a third in Neuendorf. The latter's wife was also named Helena, although in one place her name was listed as Margareta. Substantial movement between villages occurred during the first decade of Khortitsa's development, and these families do not always appear on consecutive lists. A comparison of names and family size, however, shows they are the same as those listed on earlier records. On some Russian lists the name occasionally appears as Gilbert.

Generation III

Helena Hildebrand b. 1 May 1794; d. 3 June 1794.

Jacob Hildebrand b. 3 Sept. 1795; d. 5 October 1867; m. 16 August 1823 Katharina Friesen (daughter of Jacob and Anganetha Friesen) b. 15 May 1806; d. 23 August 1860.

Helena Hildebrand b. 21 November 1798.

Justina Hildebrand b. 6 December 1800.

Maria Hildebrand b. 18 August 1804; d. 1818.

Katharina Hildebrand b. 24 July 1807; d. 5 September 1814.

Anna Hildebrand b. 9 February 1810.

Katharina Hildebrand b. 4 January 1814.

Sara Hildebrand b. 11 March 1817; d. 1867.

Figure 10 The Next Generations of Hildebrands

III Jacob Hildebrand *m* Katharina Friesen

IV Peter | Peter | Jacob | Johann | Kornelius | Katharina | Anganetha | Bernhard | Helena | Maria

Generation III

Jacob Hildebrand b. 3 September 1795; d. 5 October 1867; m. 16 August 1823 **Katharina Friesen** b. 15 May 1806; d. 23 August 1860.

Generation IV

Peter b. 10 June 1824; d. 14 July 1824.

Peter b. 3 May 1825; d. 2 October 1900, who never married, lived in a small cottage on the family farm working at a craft and repairing farm equipment.

Jacob Hildebrand b. 16 March 1827; d. 11 April 1874 (smallpox); m. 1851 Katarina Schellenberg d. 19 November 1888, daughter of one of the few Frisian families living in Nieder Khortitsa. The couple moved to Neu Schönwiese, a village of prosperous farmers.

Johann Hildebrand b. 23 October 1828; d. 17 June 1905; m1. 1857 Sara Peters b. 6 August 1837; d. 4 January 1872, from Insel Khortitsa. When she died fifteen years later, he married his brother Jacob's widow, Katharina (née Friesen – see above). Johann took over the family farm, where he also operated a smithy, and reputedly was one of the best farmers on the island. He was also active in Insel Khortitsa's public affairs and was elected *Oberschulz* (mayor of the volost, or district) twice during the period 1881 to 1887. At some time during his incumbency he helped a group of government employees locate the entrance to a cave along the Dnieper. Oral tradition offers different versions of whether the cave was on Khortitsa Island itself or on the Dnieper's west bank. Mennonites evidently knew of the cave's existence but none had ever entered it. What the officials knew, and the locals did not, was that a cache of coins was hidden there. When the officials found the coins, they gave

Johann, and several other mayors who also helped, a medal. In 1905 Johann developed a kidney infection and moved to my grandmother's house in Rosental, because there were no doctors on the island and no transportation to and from it during that year's high spring floodwaters. He died there after a five-week illness.

Kornelius Hildebrand b. 9 January 1833; d. Jan. 1920; m. 25 July 1854 Anna Epp, daughter of the Flemish church minister, David Epp and sister of Jacob Epp whose diaries appear in translation (*A Mennonite in Russia: The Diaries of Jacob D. Epp, 1851–1880*, ed. and trans. Harvey L. Dyck [Toronto, 1991]). Anna must have joined the Frisian church about the time of the wedding. Perhaps the bride's parents objected strenuously to the marriage, because the ceremony took place at the groom's home, rather than the bride's, with the Reverend Kornelius Unrau, Neu Schönwiese's Frisian minister, administering the vows. Their sixty-five year marriage was one of the longest within both sides of our family. Of their offspring, four daughters married into the prosperous Pries, Görtzen, Martens, and Dyck families. A fifth died of sturgeon poisoning. Their son, Peter, built a home that was regarded as palatial by Khortitsa and Rosental standards. He had one set of twins and a daughter who drowned in the Dnieper, along with two hired maids. A second son, Kornelius Jr., also had a set of twins. Of this younger generation, Kornelius Jr. was the most interested in preserving the family collection of historical materials.

Katharina Hildebrand b. 2 July 1836; d. 24 May 1908; m 22 October 1857 Peter Unrau d. 1904, and moved to the prosperous Frisian stronghold, Neu Schönwiese.

Anganetha Hildebrand b. 23 March 1838; d. 2 August 1907; m. 8 November 1859; Julius Heinrichs, a member of the *Gutsbesitzer* class who lived at Korneevka, a hamlet of several wealthy Heinrichs and their in-laws. He had four children from a prior marriage, the oldest of whom, Helena, married into the even wealthier landed Bergmann family. Helena's husband, Hermann, was elected deputy to the third State Duma (1907–1912) and re-elected to the fourth (the last in Imperial Russia) in 1912. After this marriage the Heinrichs and Bergmann families intermarried to such an extent that a collection of estates owned by one or the other family sprang up between Ekaterinoslav and the Khortitsa Settlement. Anganetha and Julius themselves had ten children, of whom almost half (two sons and two daughters) died at an early age, a characteristic (according to my grandmother) common to the Heinrichs family.

Bernhard Hildebrand b. 11 July 1840; d. 31 December 1910; m1. Anna Peters d. 24 August 1881; from Insel Khortitsa. The couple was married by the Flemish minister, Heinrich Epp, suggesting that the bride may have been of that persuasion. Bernhard became a farmer on the home island and was later elected minister of the Kronsweide (Frisian) church. Following Anna's death, he married Julius Klassen's widow Katharina (née Martens) d. 22 June 1907 from Rosental One of the couple's sons, or grandsons, also named Bernhard, married my cousin Listje (see Figure 6).

Helena Hildebrand b. 28 December 1842; d. 16 February 1898; m. 25 September 1865 Heinrich Plenert, from Kronsgarten, one of the Old Colony's most prosperous villages. The newly married Plenerts moved to Wiesenfeld, which was a sort of daughter colony east of Kronsgarten. It was founded on former gentry estate lands and was reportedly as beautiful and economically successful as the adjacent colony.

Maria Hildebrand b. 2 August 1845; d. 20 January 1920; m. 3 November 1866 Heinrich Pauls.

Figure 11 Original Settlers: The Pauls Family

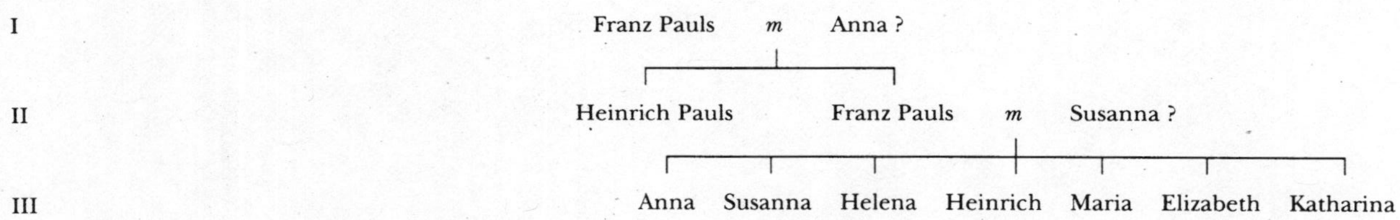

Generation I

Franz Pauls b. 1745; m. **Anna ?** b. 1736. Professor Unruh's list of Kronsweide's 1795 residents (*Hintergründe*, p. 243), contains the names of two Pauls families. The first included Kornelius Pauls (aged 43), his wife Susanna (37), son Johann (11), and daughter Maria (4). The second family included our ancestors, Franz (aged 50), Anna (59), and sons Heinrich (23), and Franz (20). An official Russian source for 14 October 1797, confirms these figures (Report of Efrem Nechaev, secretary of the New Russian guberniia government to the Senate through the *Ekspeditsiia gosudarstvennago khoziaistva, opekunstva i sel'skago domovodstva*, in SHAL: 383/29/159, sheet 7, front and obverse sides.) It states that the Franz Pauls family consisted of three males and one female, while the Kornelius Pauls family consisted of two males and two females. Unruh's report verifies that the Franz Pauls family was our antecedent, noting that on 4 October 1814, Kronsweide had another Pauls family. The father of this one was a Franz, aged 39. This was the age of the elder Franz's son, who was born in 1775. The family's other members included the younger Franz's wife Susanna (aged 35), one son Heinrich (8), and daughters Anna (16), Susanna (14), Helena (12), Maria (6), Elizabeth (4), and Katharina (1). Further confirming this lineage is the fact that son Heinrich was born in 1806. This corresponds to the birth date of my great grandfather, given in family records.

Generation II

Heinrich Pauls b. 1772.
Franz Pauls b. 1775; m. **Susanna** b. 1779.

Generation III

Anna Pauls b. 1798.
Susanna Pauls b. 1800.
Helena Pauls b. 1802.
Heinrich Pauls b. 27 January 1806; d. 26 March 1882; m. 1832 Maria Kovenhoven.
Maria Pauls b. 1808.
Elizabeth Pauls b. 1810.
Katharina Pauls b. 1813.

Figure 12 Original Settlers: The Kovenhoven Family

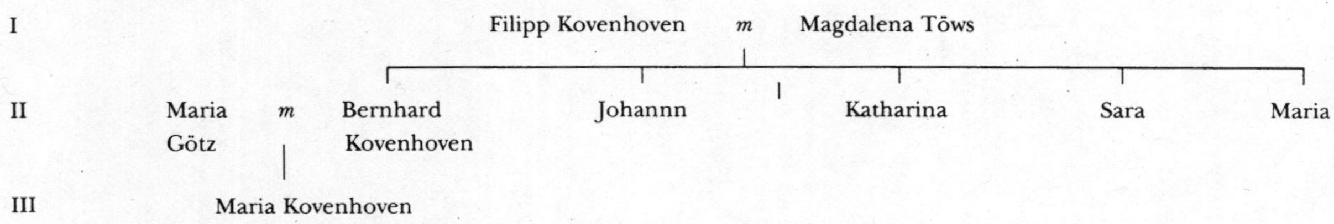

Generation I

Filipp Kovenhoven b. 1748; d. 1806; m. **Magdalena Töws** d. 1806. Evidently only two families named Kovenhoven left Danzig, and the name remained rare within the villages, variously spelled as Kowenhowen, Kauenhoven, or the Russian version of Kovengoven. Unruh's list of Kronsweide's 1795 families includes both. Ours was headed by Filipp (shown as Philp on Unruh's list) Kauenhoven, a tailor, who at some point moved to Khortitsa with his wife, Magdalena and children (Johann, Maria, Sara, Katharina, and Bernhard – born in 1772) and died there in 1806. Family records listed great grandmother Maria Kovenhoven as the daughter of a Bernard Kovenhoven, born in 1772, who married a Maria Götz.

Generation II

Bernhard Kovenhoven b. 12 March 1779; d. 4 October 1852; m. **Maria Götz** b. 22 August 1783; d. 5 April 1875.

Johann Kovenhoven.

Katharina Kovenhoven.

Sara Kovenhoven.

Maria Kovenhoven.

Generation III

Maria Kovenhoven b. 26 October 1813; d. 14 March 1889; m. 1832 Heinrich Pauls b. 27 January 1806; d. 26 March 1882.

Figure 13 Pauls-Kovenhoven Family

III Heinrich Pauls *n* Maria Kovenhoven

IV Bernhard, Heinrich, Maria, Franz, Susanna, Kornelius, Johann

Generation III

Heinrich Pauls b. 27 January 1806; d. 26 March 1880; m. 1832 **Maria Kovenhoven** b. 26 October 1813; d. 14 March 1889.

Generation IV

Bernhard Pauls b. 15 January 1833; m. Maria Peters b. 16 November 1837. She was the daughter of Daniel Peters, who had founded Petersdorf, a hamlet about fifteen miles north of Khortitsa, in the latter 1830s. I am not certain how he acquired the original land, but later, after profiting from the sale of agricultural products during the Crimean War, he bought large tracts of adjacent land. Most of this land came on the market following the emancipation of the serfs, as the local landed gentry were unable to manage substantial land holdings. Maria's dowry included 300 dessiatins (about 800 acres) of choice land. Despite this gift, which should have launched him into a profitable life, success eluded Bernhard and he and his family eventually emigrated to the United States. Here too fortune failed him. At one point he returned to Petersdorf to seek additional assistance. I recall the excitement enveloping Nieder Khortitsa as word spread that an American was about to visit. But his appeals for aid were rebuffed, perhaps because he had joined the Mennonite Brethren Church. Whether his conversion occurred while the family still lived in Russia, or after their move to the United States was a matter of much speculation among my Rosental relatives.

Heinrich Pauls b. 5 October 1835; d. 15 November 1900; m. 11 September 1866 Maria Hildebrand.

Maria Pauls b. 17 July 1838; m. Johann Neustädter, a

man from the wealthy clan which had amassed considerable estates near the Khortitsa Settlement prior to the First World War. Their wealth made them targets for peasant wrath during the uprisings following the Russo-Japanese War.

Franz Pauls b. 21 April 1841; m. Helena Peters, his brother's sister-in-law, who provided a similar dowry. Franz, evidently managing the property more effectively than his brother, founded Reinfeld, a small hamlet west of Petersdorf. The success, however, probably contributed to two later tragedies. In the first case his daughter Mrs Daniel Braun was murdered during a robbery in 1912. Seven years later Makhno's bandits obliterated both the Reinfeld and Petersdorf hamlets and murdered many of their occupants.

Susanna Pauls (Franz's twin) b. 21 April 1841; m. Abram Neustädter, brother of Johann Neustädter. Abram was murdered by peasants in 1905 or 1907, as were several other of the most prosperous Mennonites and non-Mennonite gentry.

Kornelius Pauls b. 1843; d. 1844.

Kornelius Pauls b. 17 June 1845.

Johann Pauls b. 1 May 1848; m. Helena Heinrichs of Einlage, who also belonged to the *Gutsbesitzer.* Using her dowry, which must have been considerable, he set up a flour mill. Some years later he joined the ranks of bankrupt Mennonite entrepreneurs who had suffered 'Mill Fever.' Next he sought his fortunes in the Don Cossack Territory, at the time virgin territory for Mennonite entrepreneurs. I am not sure what venture he undertook or what its fate was, but I suspect it also failed, for the family returned to Khortitsa soon after, where he set up a soap factory.

Figure 14 Pauls-Hildebrand Family

IV Heinrich Pauls *m* Maria Hildebrand

V Maria Heinrich Katharina Katharina Jacob Anganetha Bernhard Johann Kornelius Helena Susanna Johann

Generation IV

Heinrich Pauls b. 5 October 1835; d. 15 November 1900; m. 3 November 1866 **Maria Hildebrand** b. 2 August 1845; d. 20 January 1920.

Generation V

Maria Pauls b. 29 June 1867; d. 8 January 1920; m. 26 November 1891 Gerhard Rempel.

Heinrich Pauls b. 15 May 1869; d. 13 December 1933 in Canada.

Katharina Pauls b. and d. 1871.

Katharina Pauls b. 18 February 1872, d. 20 January 1932; m. 19 October 1893 Jacob Janzen b. 13 April 1870; d. 7 September 1932. Children: Justina b. 14 August 1894; Heinrich b. 5 February 1898 and d. 23 January 1933 in exile; Mariechen b. 23 October 1900; Wilhelm b. 24 August 1902 and d. 31 January 1904; Wilhelm b. 15 June 1905 and d. in exile 19 October 1932; Peter b. 29 June 1907 d. in exile; Johann b. 29 January 1910 d. in exile.

Jacob Pauls b. 9 November 1873; d. 4 October 1932 in Siberia; m1. 8 October 1906 Anna Hamm d. 21 December 1919, who was a member of the Flemish Church; m2. Anganetha Lehn d. 1924. Children: Jacob, b. 27 September 1907; Anna b. 11 October 1910.

Anganetha Pauls b. 21 September 1875; d. 10 September 1914; m. 18 May 1898 Heinrich Heinrichs b. 17 November 1876; d. 26 October 1919. Children included Heinrich, b. 27 February 1899 and d. 20 November 1941; Kornelius b. 28 November 1900; Jacob, b. 13 December 1902 and d. 22 February 1917; Mariechen, b. 6 September 1904 and d. 5 January 1962; Julius b. 15 October 1906 and d. 16 December

1969; Johann b. 15 October 1908; Bernhard b. 11 January 1911 and d. 20 March 20, 1978; Hermann b. 4 February 1912. Anganetha's husband Heinrich was the son of Kornelius Julius Heinrichs and Katharina Peters, two of the most select families of the *Gutsbesitzer* class. He had inherited a portion of his mother's dowry, which must have included 300 dessiatins of land, an amount settled on other Peters daughters who married sons of the previous Pauls generation. This land, combined with that of her Heinrichs husband, would have been an immense estate. Although they had ten children, four died in infancy. When she died in 1893 her dowry was placed in trust for the remaining six children. (Neil Heinrichs et. al., eds. *Kornelius Heinrichs and His Descendants, 1782–1979*, [Altona, Manitoba, 1980, p. 34]). Heinrich himself sold his portion to his brother Julius, then moved to Eichenfeld, where he reputedly became one of the area's most prosperous farmers. This village was part of the Iazykovo Settlement, about thirty-five miles north of Nieder Khortitsa. In her last years Tante Neta Heinrichs suffered poor health. Heinrich married Anna Dyck shortly after Anganetha died. Makhnovites murdered Heinrich in 1919 in the Eichenfeld / Dubovka massacre and Anna died of typhus in 1920.

Bernhard Pauls b. 8 June 1877; d. 29 April 1963; m. 9 June 1902 Helena Epp b. 18 August 1877; d. 1966. Children: Elisabeth, b. 27 March 1903; Heinrich, b. 14 September 1904; d. 1995; Maria, b. 19 July 1906; Helena, b. 26 January 1909 and d. 24 June 1979; Agnes, b. 22 May 1911; d. 1995 Bernard, 23 May 1918. The elder Bernard was the first of the Pauls family to graduate from (or even enroll in) the Khortitsa high school, then studied an additional year in the school's pedagogical program, before becoming the assistant to Jacob Klassen, the executive secretary of the Khortitsa Volost (district) administration office. This was a more responsible position than that of the elected chairman (*Oberschulz*). Its occupant corresponded with the *uezd* (county) and guberniia (provincial) zemstvo agencies and their superior ministries, carried out transactions to purchase or lease land from the nobility, and played a dominant role in all administrative, economic, cultural, and social issues that affected the community.

Johann Pauls b. 1879; d. 1881.

Kornelius Pauls b. b. 26 July 1881; d. 27 March 1938; m. 5 January 1906 Maria Sawatsky b. 18 July 1884; d. 25 December 1950. Children include Kornelius b. and d. 27 April 1907; Kornelius b. 11 November 1908.

Helena Pauls b. 14 June 1883; d. 20 January 1953 in exile; m. 22 May 1907 Kornelius Braun b. 10 August

1883; d. 1946 in displaced persons' camp, Germany. Children: Maria b. 19 July 1909; Anna b. 18 February 1911; Kornelius b. 1914; Johann b. 5 September 1921.

Susanna Pauls b. 3 May 1885; d. 9 April 1980; m1. 16 August 1920 Johann Giesbrecht b. 2 February 1873; d. April, 1922; m2. David Epp b. 12 January 1864; d. 13 September 1942; m3. Peter Neufeld b. 20 December 1875; d. 1966.

Johann Pauls b. 8 May 1887; d. 15 February 1937 in exile; m. Maria Friesen b. 5 May 1898.

Glossary

German (G), Low German (LG), Russian (R), and Ukrainian (U) terms

Anwohner (G), *Aunwohna* (LG), a landless 'cottager' in a Mennonite village, who owned a house, garden, and orchard on a half-dessiatin (1.33 acres) plot

arba (U), ox-drawn Ukrainian cart with high laddered sides

Arbus (LG), *arbuz* (R), watermelon

ataman (R), Cossack designation of leader used by some partisan bandit chiefs during the Civil War.

Atjstow (LG), corner room, usually the parent's bedroom

Auffahrtshof (G), *gostinyi dvor* (R), inn

balka (R), ravine, gully

Baschtaun (LG), *bashtan* (R), watermelon field

Beisitzer (G), assistant village or district mayor

berliny (R), river-plying covered barges

Brüder Gemeinde (G), breakaway, revivalist Mennonite Brethren Church

burlak (R), workman who sacked grain

burzhui (R), bourgeois, used derogatorily by Bolsheviks

Cherkessy (R), one of the most warlike peoples in the Caucasus area

chumak (U), Ukrainian teamster

desiatina (R), dessiatin (English) land measure equal to 1.092 hectares or 2.7 acres *duba* (R), four-oared, flat bottomed barge

ekonomiia (R), landed estate

Einwohner (G), *Enwohna* (LG), a landless villager, often young and recently married, who occupied a rented cottage or rooms in a Mennonite village

Fadawoagon (LG), *Federwagen* (G) German colonist 'Spring Wagon,' used as a Sunday vehicle. The more prosperous farmers in the Khortitsa settlement used a finer, more expensively upholstered version called '*Ungawoagen*' from its manufacture mainly by the Unger Wagonry Company in Einlage.

Forstei (G), Mennonite alternative service, mainly afforestation stations; also designation for such a station.

Gebietsamt (G), volost administration, as well as building housing the administration

Glausschaup (LG), glass-doored china cabinet in Mennonite home

gostinyi dvor (R), see *Auffahrtshof*

Groote Schauntz (LG), high kurgan, or burial mound of pre-historic, non-Slavic steppe warrior/s

Grootestow (LG), living room, or great room in Mennonite home

Grossbauer (G), a farmer who owned more land than a customary village full allotment of 65 dessiatins, but less than a true estate

guberniia (R), province of Tsarist Empire

guter Mann (G), advisor assigned by *Waisenamt* (G) to assist widow (usually with minor children) in financial affairs relating to inheritance

Gutsbesitzer (G), prosperous estate owner

Halbwirt (G), owner of a half farm in a village, usually comprising 32.5 dessiatins

Hüskoagel (LG), a village plot or homestead with house, garden, and orchard

Judenplan (G), Jewish multi-village farming settlements founded during reigns of Alexander I (1801–25) and Nicholas I (1825–55), often with a nucleus of eight or nine Mennonite model farmers in each village

Jugendverein (G), Mennonite youth organization, church or village-related

Kadet (R), popular designation for Russian Constitutional Party of bourgeois-liberal leanings

kadety (R), derisive Bolshevik term for former Tsarist army officers

khutor (R), consolidated farm on private or leased land outside a village, usually larger than a 65 dessiatin village full-farm and smaller than an estate

Kirchliche Gemeinde (G), the established Mennonite church of Frisian or Flemish origin

Kleinwirt (G), owner of a small or quarter village allotment comprising 16.25 dessiatins

Koloniesjung (LG), secondary school (*Zentralschule*) scholarship student

Koloniesgoade (LG), Khortitsa Settlement orchard

kontributsiia (R), extorted payment

kul'turnye liudi (R), cultured, elite society

kurgan (R), see *Groate Schauntz* (LG)

kutok (U), cul-de-sac at the end of the village

Leiterwagen (G), ladder-sided, German-style colonist wagon drawn by four horses

liman (R), system of marshy, reed-choked lakes and streams

Mädchenschule (G), girls' secondary school

Mụmmtje (LG), wife or old woman

muzhik (R), peasant

nadel' (R), small land allotment distributed to landless peasants under Stolypin land reform

Nippaenja (LG), Dnieper-end dwellers, often used derisively

Oberschulz (G), district/*volost* mayor

Oomtje (LG), husband or elderly man

Pachtartikel (G), settlement leaseland, proceeds of which were used to help purchase land for daughter settlements

pẹadhock Sproak (LG), crude, barnyard language

plavni (U), lowland flooded during spring thaw

povstantsy (R), partisans including followers of Nestor Makhno and Nikifor Grigoriev who inflicted great suffering on Khortitsa Settlement

priiomshchik (R), representative of grain merchant

pud (R), measure of weight equal to 16.38 kilograms, or 36 pounds

Scheune (G), barn

Schoawotj (LG), communal work at village or volost levels

Schultebott (LG), village council, also village council meeting

Schulz (G), elected village mayor

Sommastow (LG), or *Sommerstube* (G), room at back of dwelling occupied by newly wedded children or rented to *Einwohner* (G)

Spitja (LG), or *Speicher* (G), granary

sukhari (R), dry bread rations for Tsarist soldier

tachanka (R), German colonist or Mennonite buggy, often used by Makhnovites during the civil war, as an attack vehicle, mounted with a machine gun

Tjoatjemutta (LG), 'Church mother' whose function included preparing young women for baptism

Tränke (G), village watering pond

Udel'noe Vedomstvo (R), agency administering Stolypin land reform

uezd (R), administrative territory similar to a county

Unland (G), waste land

ustav kolonistov (R), special tsarist code of laws applicable to colonists of foreign origin, including Mennonites

Väaschtow (LG), *Vorderstube* (G), vestibule or dining area in Mennonite home

Vaspa (LG), afternoon snack and coffee break

versta (R), verst (English), length equal to 1.065 kilometers or 0.633 miles

Vollwirt (G), owner of a full farm or allotment of 65 dessiatins in a village

volost (R), rural municipality

Waisenamt (G), in tsarist period Mennonite Orphans Administration with court-enforceable executive authority regarding Mennonite inheritance practices

Wirtschaft (G), *khoziaistvo* (R), family full farm of 65 dessiatins with home on small lot in village and with strips of arable land in common fields and access to common pastureland around village

Wolostamt (G), see *Gebietsamt*

Zaddel (LG), *Zettel* (G), a note from house to house announcing important news such as a death or a village assembly meeting

Zentralschule (G), *tsentral'noe uchilishche* (R), boys' secondary school

Notes

Background

1 David G. Rempel, 'From Danzig to Russia: The First Mennonite Migration,' *Mennonite Life* 24 (1969), 8–27. For information on the colony's institutions, see David G. Rempel, 'The Mennonite Commonwealth in Russia: A Sketch of Its Founding and Endurance, 1789–1919,' *Mennonite Quarterly Review* 47 (1973), 259–308, and 48 (1974), 5–54.

Introduction

1 I thank McMaster University historian Richard Rempel, David Rempel's nephew, for this information: e-mail, 24 November 2000.

2 In W.F. Craven and J.L. Cate, eds., *Europe: Argument to V-E Day, January 1944 to May 1945* (Chicago: University of Chicago Press, 1951), vol. 3 of *The Army Air Forces in World War II.* David Rempel authored two chapters 'Check at the Rhine,' 595–635, and 'Battle of the Bulge,' 672–711 and co-authored a third 'From the Rhine to the Elbe,' 756–82.

3 General studies of tsarist and Soviet Mennonite history include: David G. Rempel, 'The Mennonite Commonwealth in Russia: A Sketch of Its Founding and Endurance, 1789–1919,' *Mennonite Quarterly Review* 47 (1973), 259–308, and 48 (1974), 5–54; James Urry, *None But Saints: The Transformation of Mennonite Life in Russia, 1789–1889* (Winnipeg: Hyperion Press, 1989); Harvey L. Dyck, introduction, *A Mennonite in Russia: The Diaries of Jacob D. Epp, 1851–1880,* ed. and trans. Harvey L. Dyck (Toronto: University of Toronto Press, 1991); John B. Toews, *Czars, Soviets and Mennonites* (Newton, KA: Faith and Life Press, 1982); and S.I. Bobyleva, ed., *Ocherki istorii nemtsev i Mennonitov iuga Ukrainy (konets XVIII-pervaia polovina XIX v.)* (Dnepropetrovsk: Art Press, 1999).

4 Rempel, 'The Mennonite Commonwealth in Russia.'

5 This observation is prompted by comments of Orest Subtelny, York University, Toronto.

6 For a dramatic contemporary memoir account see, Dietrich Neufeld, *A Russian Dance of Death: Revolution and Civil War in the Ukraine*, Al Reimer, trans. and ed. (Winnipeg: Hyperion Press, 1977).

7 The post-Soviet era process of reintegrating Mennonites into the history of Russia and Ukraine is advancing rapidly, as seen in following studies: L.V. Iakovliava, et al., eds., *Nimtsi v Ukraini 20-30-ti rr. XX st. Zbirnyk derzhavnykh dokumentiv Ukrainy* (Kiev: Vir 1994); *Voprosy germanskoi istorii. Nemtsy v Ukraine* (Dnepropetrovsk: State University Press, 1996); N.V. Ostasheva, *Na perelome epokh. Mennonitskoe obshchestvo Ukrainy, 1914–1931 gg.* (Moscow: Gotika, 1998); S.I. Bobyleva, ed., *Ocherki istorii nemtsev i mennonitov iuga Ukrainy (konets XVIII-pervaia polovina XIX v.)* (Dnepropetrovsk: Art Press, 1999); and P.P. Vibe, ed., *Nemtsy v Sibiri. Sbornik dokumentov i materialov po istorii nemtsev v Sibiri, 1895–1917* (Omsk: Omskii gos. istoriko-kraevedcheskii muzei, 1999).

8 John B. Toews, *Lost Fatherland: The Story of the Mennonite Emigration from Soviet Russia, 1921–1927* (Scottdale, PA: Herald Press, 1967) and Harvey L. Dyck, 'Collectivization, Depression, and Immigration, 1929–1930: A Chance Interplay,' in Harvey L. Dyck and Peter Krosby, eds., *Empire and Nations* (Toronto: University of Toronto Press, 1969), 144–59.

9 Peter Letkemann, 'Mennonite Victims of the "Great Terror", 1936–1938,' *Journal of Mennonite Studies* 16 (1998), 33–58; Jacob A. Neufeld, *Tiefenwege. Erfahrungen und Erlebnisse von Russland-Mennoniten in zwei Jahrzehnten bis 1949* (Virgil, ON: Niagara Press n.d.); Sarah Dyck, trans. and ed., *The Silence Echoes: Memoirs of Trauma and Tears* (Kitchener, ON: Pandora Press, 1997); V.V. Chentsov, *Tragicheskie sud'by. Politicheskie repressii protiv nemetskogo naseleniia Ukrainy v 1920-e-1930-e gody* (Moscow: Gotika, 1998); *Poverneni imena. Statti, narysy, korotki biografichni dovidky (pro reabilitovani zhertvy politichnykh represii Zaporiz'koi oblasti)* (Kiev: Vir, 1998); *Povernení imena. Dokumenty, korotki biografichni dovidky (pro reabilitovani zhertvy politichnykh represii Zaporiz'koi oblasti)* (Zaporizhzhe: State Oblast Administration, 1999); and I.L. Shcherbakova, *Repressii protiv rossiiskikh nemtsev. Nakazannyi narod* (Moscow: Zven'ia, 1999).

10 His pioneering colleagues included prominently the Mennonite archivist-historians Gerhard Lohrenz from the Canadian Mennonite Bible College, Winnipeg, Manitoba, and Cornelius Krahn, from Bethel College, North Newton, Kansas.

11 His help to fellow émigrés in research, writing, and editing made him into a virtual co-author of several studies, including: G.P. Schroeder, *Miracles of*

Grace and Judgment (Lodi, CA: Schroeder, 1974); and N.J. Kroeker, *Khortitsa-Rosental: First Mennonite Villages in Russia, 1789–1943* (Vancouver: Kroeker, 1981).

12 Helene S. Friesen, ed., *Der Bote Index*, vol. 3, *1964–1976* (Winnipeg: CMBC Publications, 1999), lists twelve articles by him for this period, many of them substantial.

13 David Rempel's rich and voluminous scholarly correspondence, deposited in the University of Toronto's Thomas Fisher Rare Book Library, awaits study.

14 Microfilm deposited in David Rempel Microfilm Collection, Conrad Grebel College Library and Archives, Waterloo, Ontario.

15 For a history of the collection and detailed inventory of its contents, see Ingrid I. Epp, and Harvey L. Dyck, *The Peter J. Braun Russian Mennonite Archive, 1803–1920: A Research Guide* (Toronto: University of Toronto Press, 1996). Rempel's assessment is borne out in new scholarship rooted in the collection: Leona Wiebe Gislason, *Rückenau: The History of a Village in the Molotschna Mennonite Settlement of South Russia* (Winnipeg: Windflower Publications, 2000); and, in preparation, the multi-volume, Ingrid Epp, ed. and trans., *Letters and Papers of Johann Cornies, 1789–1848.* For the Braun Archive's significance to broader Tsarist studies see ground-breaking study by John R. Staples, 'Adaptation, Assimilation, and Alienation in New Russia: The Molochna River Basin, 1783–1861,' (PhD diss., University of Toronto, 1999).

16 E-mail from Leonard Friesen, 6 Dec. 2000.

17 James Urry, 'In Memoriam: David G. Rempel (Nov. 17 [n.s. 30] 1899–27 June 1992),' *Journal of Mennonite Studies* 11 (1993), 224–35.

18 For Mennonite life on the Island of Khortitsa see Is.P. Klassen, *Die Insel Chortitza. Stimmungsbilder, Gedanken und Erinngerungen* (Barre, MS, 1967) and Dyck, *A Mennonite in Russia*, 26–32, 75–116.

19 Paul Robert Magocsi, *A History of Ukraine* (Toronto: University of Toronto Press, 1996), 170–260.

20 See, e.g., Taras Shevchenko, 'I mertvym i zhyvym i nenarozhdenym zemliakam moim v Ukraini i ne v Ukraini. Moe druzhnee poslanie,' in *Tvory*, vol. 3, 111–17. For Shevchenko's treatment of the Zaporozhian Cossack legacy see also, L.F. Borotnykova et al., eds., *Taras Shevchenko i zaporizkyi krai za dokumentamy derzhavnogo arkhivu Zaporizkoi oblasti* (Zaporozhe: Zaporozhe Regional State Archive, 1992).

21 The village is described also by David Rempel's revered older brother Johann G. Rempel, secondary school teacher and sometime chair of the village soviet during the Civil War, and later a Mennonite church elder, in *Mein Heimatdorf Nieder Chortitza* (Rosthern, SK: self-published, 1956).

23 See in particular documents scattered throughout two Communist Party fondy in the State Archive of the Zaporizhzhe Region: 1) PR 1/Opis 1, Zaporizhzhe Okrug Party Committee; and 2) PR 7/Opis 1, Khortitsa Raion Committee of the Communist Party. Extensive microfilm from these fondy can be found in University of Toronto Collection of Microfilmed Mennonite-Related Documents from the Zaporozhe Archive. See Harvey L. Dyck and John R. Staples, eds., *Mennonites in Southern Ukraine, 1789–1941: A Guide to Holdings and Microfilmed Documents from the State Archive of the Zaporozhe Region* (Toronto: Centre for Russian and East European Studies, University of Toronto, 2001).

Chapter 1 Two Russian Mennonite Families

1 For a more detailed discussion of Khortitsa's founding see D.G. Rempel, 'From Danzig to Russia: The First Mennonite Migration,' *Mennonite Life* 24 (1969), 8–27. For information on the settlements' institutions, see D.G. Rempel, 'The Mennonite Commonwealth in Russia: A Sketch of its Founding and Endurance, 1789–1919,' *Mennonite Quarterly Review* 47 (1973), 259–308 and 48 (1974), 5–54. See J. Urry, *None But Saints: The Transformation of Mennonite Life in Russia 1789–1889* (Winnipeg: Hyperion Press Limited, 1989) for an excellent social history of the Mennonite Molochna Settlement, which largely paralleled that of the Khortitsa Settlement.

2 The precise number of emigrants and family groups is not clear. Johann Bartsch indicated in a letter to Potemkin that 307 families, totaling 1,515 people had arrived in Riga, and gone on to Dubrovna. Of these, 215 families (1,117 people) were Mennonite and 92 families (398 people) were Lutheran. However, all Russian records indicate 228 Mennonite families arrived in Khortitsa, and although they fail to indicate the total population, most authorities estimate it between 1,030 and 1,073. Perhaps births, deaths, and marriages occurring along the way account for some discrepancies.

3 This estate was completely surrounded by huge grants that belonged to Potemkin's relatives, acquaintances, and prominent military and civil officials in New Russia's administration. For example, his niece, Countess Skavronskaia, owned 12,000 dessiatins of land between the Middle and Lower (*Nizhniaia*) Khortitsa streams, and adjacent to his property. Count Razumovskii, one of Empress Catherine's former favourites, owned a huge tract that virtually encircled Potemkin's estate. A vast area just beyond belonged to Miklashevskii, soon to be named Civil Governor of New Russia,

while large grants made to Nechaev, Lukashevskii, Privy Counselor Titov, and others, lay farther north.

4 During the 1930s and 1940s a small number of Mennonites – disillusioned by the triumph of Communism, and espousing Nazi sympathies – claimed the Russian Mennonites were principally of German origin. This is not so. Beyond oral tradition I recall that many families had Dutch catechisms or Bibles, and that some had centuries-old family registers, whose entries predating the late eighteenth century were always written in Dutch. Letters the early settlers sent back to Prussia, requesting Bibles and other religious materials, asked that they send Dutch editions if High German editions were not available, stating, 'We can still read the Dutch language.' Numerous Tsarist Russian histories written prior to the First World War mention the Mennonites' Dutch origin, as did a 1910 to 1911 government memorandum, produced in response to right-wing Duma delegates' demands for restricting German land purchases. In my childhood and adolescence, most Mennonites spoke of themselves as '*Wie sent Dietsche.*' The latter word referred to the Low German-speaking, Mennonite ethnic minority, and it connoted a distinction from the German Lutherans and Catholics in Russia. *Dietsche* also implied the superiority the Mennonites felt over both those other settlers and the Prussian Germans. The Mennonites felt particular disdain for the latter. They tolerated them as lower-class workmen, but did not consider them equals they would invite into their homes, much less allow to court their daughters.

5 In virtually all German writings about the Russian settlements, irrespective of religious affiliation or even ethnic origin, *Ansiedlung* referred to a group of villages founded on a given tract of land. The individual villages were called colonies. However, when the immigrants' burgeoning population forced them to purchase new property, often at distant locations, the new group of villages (or colonies) was referred to as a daughter colony (*Tochter-Kolonie*) of the mother settlement (*Mutter Ansiedlung*). Thus when the Khortitsa Settlement purchased large tracts of land from Duchess Koskul' and Captain Morosov in 1869 and 1872, they founded five new villages in a new settlement referred to as a Khortitsa *Tochter-Kolonie.*

6 Kronsweide's farmers soon found its topography and soil inferior, and most relocated farther from the Dnieper, and slightly to the north. This colony became known as Neu Kronsweide and the few remaining farmers renamed the original village Alt Kronsweide.

7 The claim that all 118 families of this group were Frisians, is erroneous. Actually they were in the minority. See David H. Epp, *Die Chortitzer*

Mennoniten (Odessa: self-published, 1889), 54; Benjamin H. Unruh, *Die Niederländisch-niederdeutschen Hintergründe der Mennonitischen Osterwanderungen im 16, 18, und 19 Jahrhundert* (Karlsruhe: Rupürr, 1955), 243; and the Report of Efrem Nechaev, secretary of the New Russia guberniia administration to the Senate through the *Ekspeditsiia gosudarstvennago khoziaistva, opekunstva inostrannykh i sel'skago domovodstva,* in State Historical Archive, Leningrad, collection 383, inventory list 29, file 159 (hereafter SHAL: 383/29/159), sheet 7, front and obverse side.

8 It was also relocated to higher ground in the 1830s when its lack of arable land and problems with spring flooding became obvious.

Chapter 2 The Rempel Clan

1 Every village had many curious examples of these appellations. In Rosental, e.g., men were named Curiosity Sawatzky (*Nieschieja Sewautztje*), Whistling Friesen (*Swistun Friese*), Mosquito or Freckled-faced Friesen (*Moschtje Friese*), Brick Penner (*Teajel Panna*), Honey Pries (*Honig Pries*), Girl Hiebert (*Mejale Hiebat*), Painter Elias (*Foawa Eelis*), Clockmaker Kröger (*Klockemoaka Tjreaja*), and Curly-haired Penner (*Kruskopja Panna*). The Mennonite colonists likewise nicknamed their villages. The origin, meaning, and reasons for particular nicknames are often hard to explain. In some cases these names suggested the inhabitants real or imagined behaviour. In other cases the nickname (*Etjenohme*) was related to the resident's food or beverage preferences, whether real or the figments of wildest imagination. Thus, the Rosentalers were nicknamed *Kvass*-drinkers (*Kruschtjekwaus Drintja*), that is those who drank the fermented beverage made from the little pears call *grushi* in Ukrainian, or *Kruschtje.* Einlage's dwellers were called catfish-gnawers (*Welsgnoagasch*), after their preference for fish. In other cases the nickname connoted condescension or mockery. Thus, Schöneberg's inhabitants were dubbed crane-milkers (*Krauntjemaltjasch*), for which purpose their pockets were supposedly tin-lined to hold the milk. Then there were nicknames illustrating the crudest barnyard humour.

2 Beyond this form of naming, the younger people who had attended secondary schools, practised the Russian form of address, using their first name with their father's name (patronymic) to which they added -evich or -ovich (if male) or -ovna or -evna (if female). Thus, Peter Epp might be known as Piotr Ivanovich Epp and Katia Klassen known as Katia Iakovlevna Klassen. This practice occurred in all colonies, but was most prevalent in those located near cities, or among those people who were in direct contact with Russian officials or professionals.

3 See SHAL: 383/29/159, sheets 5–14. See also Benjamin H. Unruh, *Die Niederländisch-niederdeutschen Hintergründe der Mennonitischen Ostwanderungen im 16, 18, und 19 Jahrhundert* (Karlsruhe: Rupürr, 1955), 210–15.

4 The *Cherkessy* were a warlike people famous for their horsemanship, marksmanship, and dexterity with a dagger. Victor Peters, 'The *Cherkessy* Mennonites,' *Mennonite Life* 26 (1971), 64, includes a legend of a supposed shining post implanted at the foot of a mound on the outskirts of the village, into which mounted youths, riding at top speed, had to plunge their knives, breaking off the tips, in order to be accepted as a true 'brave' of the colony – which is an exceedingly fanciful embroidery on the origin of this nickname.

5 The best article on Mennonite nicknames is by Professor Gerhard Wiens, 'Village Nicknames Among the Mennonites in Russia,' *Mennonite Life* 25 (1970), 177–180.

Chapter 3 The First Three Generations of Rempels

1 My brother, Johann, searched these shortly before Soviet officials confiscated them in 1920. Benjamin H. Unruh in *Die Niederländisch-niederdeutschen Hintergründe der Mennonitischen Ostwanderungen im 16, 18, und 19 Jahrhundert* (Karlsrahe: Rupürr, 1955), 214, 302, verifies the family's stay in Schönwiese. The family lost the one document that might definitively date the ancestor's arrival and initial residence – a large book, written in Dutch, with heavy pigskin bound wooden covers. Our parents never permitted us children to touch it. I remember only Grandmother Rempel occasionally paging through what I assume was a family register going back to the seventeenth century. Unfortunately our family turned this register over to the Russian government in 1915 or 1916 in an attempt to substantiate the claim that the Mennonites were of Dutch, as opposed to German, ancestry.

2 The early settlers moved not only within the settlement but also to distant cities. For example, in 1796 Johann Hamm and Berend Janzen moved to St Petersburg. Janzen returned to Alexandrovsk but Hamm remained in St Petersburg. Records indicate perhaps four or five other families moved to Ekaterinoslav. Two – the Töws and Thiessen families – remained prominent in that community until the Revolution. Still other families moved to Odessa, Alexandrovsk, and Kharkov.

3 See Johann Rempel, '*Das Familienregister des Ältesten,*' *Der Bote*, 23 Feb. 1938.

4 This quiet, isolated room was usually occupied by the parents until a new home was built for them after their eldest son (who would take over the farm) married.

5 See D.H. Epp, *Johann Cornies, Züge aus seinem Leben und Wirken* (Rosthern, SK: 1946), 91–3. Also available in English translation by Peter Pauls (Winnipeg: CMBC Publications, Manitoba Mennonite Historical Society, 1995). Epp names only R and D as the responsible officials.

6 In the Land Law of 19 March 1764, the government specified that the minorat inheritance principle was to apply in all colonies. This meant that the youngest son, not the oldest, was to inherit the farm. A female, either widow or daughter, could inherit and possess the land only until either she, or the daughter, got married. The first male entering the family was to be declared owner of the farm. In actual practice the Mennonites were free to practise their own system of inheritance. This meant the oldest son usually inherited the farm, after having bought out the shares of movable possession from the other family members.

Chapter 4 The Maternal Lineage

1 According to a diary written by Heinrich's descendent, Johann Epp, 'Peter was a thoroughly dissolute and frivolous man ... He frequently deceived his wife and spent her fortune foolishly. When he died, he left his wife penniless and children in bitter poverty.' In fact, Peter died of typhus in the Territory of the Don Cossacks during the turbulence of 1918.

2 In my teenage years, when the Pätkau family owned it, my friends and I enjoyed the winter coziness of their *Sommastow*, or on summer nights, we vied with Jacob Pätkau's sisters' suitors for spots on those same benches.

3 For discussions of these schisms see P.M. Friesen's massive Mennonite history, *Alt-Evangelische Mennonitische Brüderschaft in Russland (1789–1910) im Rahmen der mennonitischen Gesamtgeschichte* (Halbstadt, Russia: Raduga, 1911; reprinted Duderstadt: Mecke, 1991); in English translation as *The Mennonite Brotherhood in Russia, 1789–1910*, trans. and ed. J.B. Toews, Abraham Friesen, Peter J. Klassen, Harry Loewen (Fresno, CA: Board of Christian Literature, General Conference of Mennonite Brethren Churches, 1978); A.H. Unruh, *Die Geschichte der Mennoniten-Brüdergemeinde* (Winnipeg: Christian Press, 1954); Jacob P. Bekker, *Origin of the Mennonite Brethren Church: Previously Unpublished Manuscript by One of the Eighteen Founders* (Hillsboro, KA: Mennonite Brethren Publishing House, 1973); Waldemar Gutsche, *Westliche Quellen des Russischen Stundismus. Anfänge der Evangelischen Bewegung in Russland* (Kassel: J.G. Oncken, 1957); Aron A. Töws, *Mennonitische Märtyrer der jüngsten Vergangenheit und der Gegenwart*, vol. 1, (Winnipeg: Christian Press, 1949) 29–30 or excerpted in translation by John B. Toews, as *Mennonite Martyrs: The People Who Suffered for Their Faith, 1920–1940* (Winnipeg: Kindred Press, 1990).

4 An explanation and correction are in order. In the Russian Mennonite villages the only church buildings existed in the diocese, termed *Kirchspiel*, of several villages. In other villages, church services were held in the school building. This was true until 1921 when the Communist government prohibited all religious functions in the schools. They also prohibited ministers from acting as teachers. Even relatives of a minister could not teach in his home village. So when Mr Bükert spoke of going to church in the school, he referred to the habits of the past.

Chapter 5 Tribulations: My Paternal Grandparents

1 The former cast-iron marker read: 'And now beside this grave in keeping, I stand beside your earthly stone, / And as I once bereaved and weeping, / Before His peace became my own (*So steh ich nun an diesem Grabe, Steh hier an deinem Leichenstein. Und wie ich einst geweinet habe, So zieht nun Frieden bei mir ein*).' The latter was inscribed with: 'This gravestone is not meant for me, / For you, oh wanderer, shall it be! / One day, like I, you too shall pale, / And earthly matters all will fail! / So learn the art, do not defy, / Since only then, you'll never die' ('*Nicht mir gilt dieser Leichenstein, Für dich, o Wanderer, soll er sein! Du musst einst auch wie ich erblassen, Und alles hinter dir verlassen! Drum lern die Kunst, zu sterben früh, Lerne sie, dann stirbst du nie*').

2 Fourteen villages comprised the original Old Colony daughter settlement of Orenburg, until the Molochna Settlement added eight more villages on land purchased from the Deiev brothers.

3 The colonist's contributions received extensive and laudatory acknowledgment from official government agencies and war correspondents. Perhaps the warmest plaudits came from individual commanders whose units the Mennonites transported from one area to another. Small wonder the Mennonites were acutely conscious of the value of their contributions to the motherland. It was not surprising that pre-First World War Russian Mennonite annals referred to the period as the group's 'finest hour.' That says something about Mennonites' historic pacifism. The Russian government was therefore perplexed when its introduction of obligatory military service in the early 1870s triggered the emigration of one-third of all Mennonites (about 18,000) to Canada and the United States instead of accepting alternative service. See P.M. Friesen's massive Mennonite history, *Alt-Evangelische Mennonitesche Brüderschaft in Russland (1789–1910) im Rahmen der mennonitischen Gesamtgeschichte* (Halbstadt, Russia: Raduga, 1911; reprinted Duderstadt: Mecke, 1991); in English translation as *The Mennonite Brotherhood in Russia, 1789–1910*, translated by J.B. Toews et al. (Fresno, CA: Board of Christian Literature, General Conference of Mennonite

Brethren Churches, 1978), 483–9. More extensive comments are found in P.V. Kamenskii, *Vopros ili nedorazumenie. K voprosu ob inostrannykh poseleniiakh na iuge Rossii* (Moscow: n.p., 1895), and some data in P. Alabin, *Pokhodnye zapiski voinu 1853, 54, 55, i 56 gg.*, vol. 2 (Viatka: n.p., 1861). See also N.I. Pirtigov, *Sevastopol'skie pisma i vospominaniia* (St Petersburg: n.p., 1899); Anton Christian A. Hübbenett, *Die Sanitätsverhältnisse der russischen Verwundeten während des Krimkrieges in den Jahren 1854–56* (Berlin: n.p., 1871); and John Shelton Curtiss, *The Russian Army under Nicholas I, 1825–55* (Durham, NC: Duke University Press, 1965).

Chapter 6 Father and His First Wife

1 No photos exist to verify her appearance, perhaps due to her mother-in-law's strong opposition to having photographs or pictures displayed around the house, or my father's extreme reluctance to have his own portrait taken. The only photo I have of him is a daguerreotype, taken for an internal passport to Orenburg, and obviously shot in the wintertime, for he is bundled in fur coat and cap.

2 Every Mennonite family had a similar china cupboard, built into the living room wall, with a central desk (*Schuflod*) below the shelves for china and above drawers to hold linens.

Chapter 7 Unjust Charges

1 Both monuments remained major landmarks for generations of Mennonites until the 1960s when the Soviet government demanded their removal. They now stand in the Mennonite Museum in Steinbach, Manitoba.

2 See D.H. Epp, *Die Chortitzer Mennoniten* (Odessa: self-publication, 1889) for some of the details of this tragic conflict.

3 A third Mennonite, a man named Rempel from Einlage, was set to be imprisoned at the same time as the Höppners, for having fraudulently obtained two farm allotments from Baron von Brackel. Rempel died before the Russians could jail him, and so the government sold his second farm to Johann Andres to satisfy Mr Rempel's debt of 1,045 rubles.

4 In Höppner's days the island was heavily wooded with huge oak, linden, elm, and other trees. Wanton cutting by all the villages during the 1830s and 1840s denuded it substantially. Reforestation finally began at mid-century when Insel Khortitsa acquired the entire island.

5 The Mennonites usually referred to the island as *de Kaump*, a term they had used in the Vistula region to designate the higher ground where they

constructed their buildings out of the reach of flood waters in the generally lowland area. Slightly below the ferry from Rosental to *de Kaump* was another island which the Mennonites called the Small Camp (*de tjleena Kaump*), which the Russians referred to as Oaken Island (*dubovyi ostrov*). Both islands had once reputedly harboured wolf packs. See K.J. Hildebrand's '*Ein Sonntag auf der Insel Chortitsa*' for a boy's fascinating recollections of a wolf hunt after Sunday church service, reprinted in Victor Peters, ed., *Zwei Dokumente. Quellen zum Geschichtsstudium der Mennoniten in Russland* (Winnipeg: Echo-Verlag, 1965).

Chapter 8 Mennonite Service and Supernatural Tales

1 According to Peter's reminiscences, it was he who first met the recruiting agent, Georg Trappe. Höppner was away from his inn when Trappe appeared there, desiring a meal. Hildebrand entertained the man until Höppner arrived a little later. Unquestionably Peter was privy to many later discussions between Höppner and Trappe. Unfortunately Peter's record, written many years later, approaches the events in a naive and simplistic manner, assuming matters were all in the hands of Providence. His treatment of the colonists' later bitter attack on Höppner and Bartsch regrettably sweeps the dissension under a proverbial rug.

2 Presumably he first joined the Flemish church, to which the Höppners belonged, then converted to the Frisian at about the same time as the former church banned his father-in-law.

3 *The Friend: A Religious and Literary Journal*, vol. 3 (Philadelphia: n.p., 1830), 189. I am indebted to Professor James Urry of Victoria University, Wellington, New Zealand, for this reference.

4 The work was probably edited by David H. Epp. It was serialized in *Der Bote* (Rosthern) issues 15 and 22 Feb., 8 and 15 Mar., 17 and 24 June, and 1, 8, 15, 22, and 29 July, 1933 and in *Mennonitische Rundschau* (Winnipeg) issues 15, 22, and 29 Aug., 5, 12, 19, and 26 Sept., and 3, 10, and 17 Oct., 1951, and republished as a booklet, Victor Peters, *Zwei Dokumente. Quellen zum Geschichtsstudium der Mennoniten in Russland* (Winnipeg: Echo-Verlag, 1965).

5 Kornelius Hildebrand, Helena's great grandson, finally aired the matter publicly in, '*Wie man meine Grossmutter fand. Eine merkwürdige Erscheinung bei dem Verschwinden meiner Grossmutter, des Grossvaters Peter Hildebrand Ehefrau*,' *Der Bote*, 24 Jan. 1934, 5. He presents the sketchy details of her tragic drowning and the ensuing supernatural myths, based on notes written by Helena's son Jacob and grandson, Kornelius.

6 His anecdotes are best reflected in his unpublished, '*Lebenserinnerung, 1891.*'

Chapter 9 Piety and Pain

1 Mennonite forestry workers applied this latter expression to fellow workers who were, or imagined themselves to be, literate people, and is derived from the Russian word '*gramotnyi,*' that is, being literate.

2 The Kovenhoven farm was the first one around the corner of the main street, in a short alley leading up a hill to a succession of heavily wooded valleys and thence to the Dnieper, and was, for generations, the favourite site of elementary school picnics and youth outings. Until the late 1920s, when the *dekulakization* policy began, this farm belonged to the Fröse family, who were intimate friends with several of the Pauls.

3 The death and funeral were announced as usual via a black bordered note expressing bereavement that read: 'It has pleased the Lord of Life and Death to take our dear mother to Him' ('*Es hat dem Herrn über Leben und Tod gefallen, unsere liebe Mutter zu sich zu nehmen*'). The note was tucked in a black-bordered white envelope listing the names of guests requested to attend the at-home funeral service, interment, and later repast of coffee and zwieback.

4 All three faiths were still far more affluent than their Slavic neighbours despite the egalitarian changes of the Alexandrian Reforms during the 1860s and 1870s. Though both lay and clerical leaders in Russia began viewing these affluent 'aliens' with increased hostility, the 'foreign confessions' failed to form a united front. Instead they continued to live in their separate and isolated worlds, with mutual suspicion of each other. The Mennonites were still viewed by the other groups as heretics (*Ketzer*), while the Mennonites reciprocated by viewing the Catholics as idol-worshipers, and the Lutherans as members of the Protestant State Church, which in Danzig had been more hostile to them than the Catholic Church.

5 For recipes for these traditional pastries, see N.J. Voth, *Mennonite Foods and Folkways from Southern Russia,* vols. 1 and 2 (Intercourse, PA: Good Books, 1990 and 1991).

6 Decades later Tante Sus mentioned that 'We all attended the services in the Khortitsa (Flemish) church, but were members of the Kronsweide (Frisian) one. Since all of us attended the Rosental village school we learned the Khortitsa Church catechism, but all of us were sent to Kronsweide for baptismal instruction and baptism.'

Chapter 10 A Burdened Life

1 The familiarity that developed between employer and peasant employee was so widespread in all the Protestant colonies, that the Orthodox Church and Panslavist and other nationalist groups blamed the spread of Baptism

and/or Shtundist teachings on the colonists. Later, during the First World War, these groups and extreme nationalist Duma deputies used these interactions as one basis for demanding the land expropriation decrees against the colonists.

Chapter 11 Equanimity

1 The *Waisenamt* was headed by the *Waisen-Schulz*, a highly trusted man, selected by the Elder and Deacon. He appointed guardians for orphaned children and safeguarded their inheritances. The *Waisenamt* invested the orphans' capital until they came of age, lending it at 6 per cent and paying 5 per cent in return, while the property itself served as security to insure the capital involved. This department also designated a Good Man for widows with small children as needed to protect their interests. The elder or local minister oversaw the 'good man's performance.'

2 Nephew of Khortitsa Church elder, Heinrich Epp, and cousin of Dietrich H. and Heinrich H. Epp.

3 Although the land allotment decree of 19 March 1764, for future colonists in New Russia had prescribed settlement on separate land allotments, most settlers had ignored the provision.

4 The 75,000 acre parcel lay both east and west of the Dnieper in an area the Cossacks had called the Zaporozhian Liberties for over two centuries.

Chapter 12 Life at Home

1 When government officials visited they were lodged and fed in all the local farmers' homes on a pre-arranged schedule. This was typical of most Mennonite villages. Actually you could obtain nothing more than the simplest refreshments in other villages, and then only where Old Believers operated a store.

2 These fields were also called *bashtan* in Russian. Father leased this land from neighbouring farmers or, more usually, from one of the teamsters who had received a land allotment under the Stolypin Land Reform Program. Sometimes the *bashtan* guardsmen oversaw several farmers' fields, in which case all provided the guardsman's board on a prearranged schedule.

3 Russian Mennonite churchman, educator, and writer (1878–1950).

Chapter 13 Father's Occupation

1 The farmers usually hired seasonal labor from 10 May to *Pokrov*, (1 Oct.).

2 One of them probably represented a Dutch firm (Meier and Company).

Another, named Alphand, was, I suspect, the famous Russian Social Democrat, Alexander Israel Halphand (or Elfand), who spent years of his life in European exile. Using the name Parvus, he acted as an Imperial German agent, and was engaged under this government's aegis in various lucrative businesses, including the Constantinople grain trade. See Z.A.B. Zeman and W.B. Scharlau, *The Merchant of Revolution: The Life of Alexander Israel Helphand (Parvus), 1867–1924* (London: Oxford University Press, 1965).

3 The unpublished diaries of Abram Dyck, a partner in the Niebuhr milling concern, covering the period 1897 to 1919, paint a detailed picture of the effects of these phenomena on trade.

4 Horses and cattle were pastured in separate common areas, then driven home at dusk. The herdsmen dropped the cattle off at their respective owners farms, but drove the pastured horses (those the farmer had not used that day) back to a common *peadhock*, usually in the village center. The farmers often gathered there to fetch a horse they needed the next day, or to admire their respective horses, perhaps a stallion rented for the summer from the government stud farm. Rightly or wrongly, the cruder aspects of farm language and off-colour stories were associated with these paddock gatherings.

Chapter 14 Apprehension Following the 1905 Revolution

1 The agency administering Stolypin's land reforms. The land had reverted to the state after once belonging to various of Catherine II's favourites. Notable among these was Count Razumovski. His parcel was near Potemkin's holdings and those of his niece, Countess Skavronskaia, on which sixteen of Khortitsa's eighteen villages were established. When these lands fell into government hands they were placed with the Ministry of State Domains. During much of the nineteenth century the Khortitsa Settlement leased large portions of these, first as pasturage for their communal flocks of sheep, later for grain cultivation. Late in the century the government allowed the Mennonites to establish two tenant villages, Kronsfeld and Neu Rosengart, on the land.

2 See P.M. Friesen, *Alt-Evangelische Mennonitesche Brüderschaft in Russland (1789–1910) im Rahman der mennonitischen Gesamtgeschichte* (Halbstadt, Russia: Raduga, 1911); English translation by J.B. Toews et al., as *The Mennonite Brotherhood in Russia, 1789–1910* (Fresno, CA: Board of Christian Literature, General Conference of Mennonite Brethren Churches, 1978), 628.

3 A few came from Nieder Khortitsa, including some Walls, Ungers, and possibly a Thiessen or two. Other revolutionaries named Hübert, Wiebe, and Meder (perhaps not a Mennonite) came from Osterwick, Einlage, and Schönwiese respectively. For more on Thiessen, see D.G. Rempel, 'Mennonite Revolutionaries in the Khortitsa Settlement Under the Tsarist Regime as Recollected by Johann G. Rempel,' *Journal of Mennonite Studies* 10 (1992), 70–86.

4 A second Peter Rempel, a relative of Father's first wife, was later also labelled a radical.

5 The author was an enthusiastic admirer of the Russian communal system and although acquainted with the Mennonite system, never commented on its claimed advantages or disadvantages. However, three of his pupils or colleagues did. A.A. Klaus, who was the author of a large study, *Nashi kolonii* (Odessa, 1869; Cambridge, UK: Oriental Research Partners, 1972), and who held important posts in the Ministry of State Domains, was an enthusiastic admirer of the Mennonite agricultural, social, and various economic institutions. However, Eliseev and Janson, both champions of the peasant commune system, wrote lengthy and extremely critical commentaries on Klaus' book and were particularly critical of the Mennonite land ownership system.

6 The term Kadet was based on the pronunciation of the first letters of the party's designation *Ka* and *De.*

7 *Das deutsche Lehrer-seminar in Khortitsa. Projekt einer Reorganisation des bestehenden Seminars; Die Internationale und die Kommune von Paris*; and *Die russische Revolution.* He expressed even more radical views in *Die deutschen Kolonien der Ukraine in geschichtlicher Bedeutung*, published as an appendix in *Kurzgefasste Geschichte der Ukraine*, translated by Heinrich H. Epp from the Russian (Kharkov: Zentralverlag, 1928).

8 Friesen, *Alt-Evangelische Mennonitesche Brüderschaft*, trans. Toews et al., *Mennonite Brotherhood*, 526. Friesen does not name either the man or the chapter, but some sources indicated the location to be Ekaterinoslav.

9 The Black Hundreds were activist squads of rightist hoodlums operating during the 1905–6 revolutions, who beat and even killed Jews, liberals, and intellectuals.

10 In Russian political annals, the Third Duma (from 1907–12) was often called the 'Dark Duma.'

11 Hermann A. Bergmann (1850–1919), a prominent Mennonite estate owner, was murdered during the civil war.

12 Stenographic reports of the Fourth Duma indicate that Mr. Schröder voted with the Progressivists, who were slightly more liberal than the Octoberists.

13 Friesen, *Alt-Evangelische Mennonitische Brüderschaft*, trans. Toews et al., *Mennonite Brotherhood*, 627.

Chapter 15 Class Conflicts within the Khortitsa Settlement

1 In the early days, prior to 1797, some settlers may have expanded their farms by buying another farm from a deceased farmer's estate, marrying the widow of a landowner, or inheriting property from an infirm or deceased branch-line relative. A few other early settlers may have bribed Baron von Brackel to exchange farmsteads to enrich their holdings.

2 In the Khortitsa Settlement as a whole these surplus lands were not well defined, nor necessarily assigned in relationship to the original number of farms.

3 Most owned a two-oared vessel which could carry five or six passengers or up to ten sacks of grain (roughly 1,800 pounds). A few had gone into partnership with a relative or friend to purchase a *duba* (a four-oared barge) used to ferry up to four teamed wagons across the river. In either case they were extremely proud of their boats, keeping them spotless and well-painted.

4 In 1841, the Minister of State Domains, Count Kiselev, went so far as to threaten the Odessa region German colonists that if they did not emulate Mennonite farming practices he would replace every village and district official with Mennonites from the Molochna.

5 Parenthetically I should note that after the civil war many of these intractable farmers were placated by the concessions of the New Economic Policy and decided to stay in the Soviet Union instead of emigrating to Canada. Within ten years most perished at Vorkuta and other slave labour camps in the Gulag. Unfortunately, the same fate awaited most of the landless who stayed. Their fortunes improved initially under this policy, but soon they too were classified as kulaks, and were likewise exiled to death in Siberia's taiga forests.

6 In addition to my own recollections, I am indebted for this information to Johann Funk, who was secretary to a succession of Nieder Khortitsa mayors.

7 V.G. Postnikov, *Iuzhno-russkoe Khoziaistvo* (Moscow: n.p., 1891).

8 Gerhard Lohrenz, formerly of Zagradovka, confirmed that Bernhard Fast had once been the volost executive secretary of that settlement, and was reputed to be an expert in preparing legal documents.

9 In the absence of pertinent documents I have relied heavily on my brother Johann and sister Mariechen's reminiscences as well as those of several other Canadian refugees from Nieder Khortitsa. Cornelius Warkentin,

village secretary for several years, has been especially helpful in recalling the names of about twenty teamsters who received land allotments, and which of them later sold them to other teamsters.

10 In my childhood the nucleus of this group included Peter Siemens and two Johann Siemens, a Gerhard Rempel (not my father), Abram Günter, Heinrich Klassen, David Neufeld, Jacob Dyck, and Peter Unger.

11 Perhaps he had delusions of grandeur, for he claimed to have met Tsar Nicholas II, who said, 'Are you truly Janzen,' to which he replied 'By God, I am Janzen (*Ei Bogu, Janson*).'

12 Unfortunately none of the farmers' sons from Nieder Khortitsa, who had studied milling in Germany, succeeded in this enterprise because they entered the field just as the 'mill fever' began bankrupting many Mennonites. Three (Abram Dyck, Wilhelm Pankratz, and Peter Epp) then drifted in and out of various types of employment and finally ended up tilling a few acres in the desperate years of the civil war and famine. A fourth, Peter Siemens, married into the wealthy Peters clan and so ended in clover despite his failure in milling. Those who succeeded, including two sons of Reverend Sawatzky, had no formal training. Abram Sawatzky set up business in a peasant village (Mikhailovka) near the Mennonite village of New York, and his brother David took over his father-in-law, Mr Kethler's mill in Nieder Khortitsa. A third, Peter Rempel, who was commonly called *Kueta Rampel*, founded a successful mill in Arkadak. The civil war put an end to all three businesses.

13 The membership of this loosely knit group changed as some of the younger women married and left the village, while others joined when they entered womanhood. Maria Wiebe moved to Schönwiese, where her husband, Jacob Janzen (the son of Brewer Janzen) was elected minister of the Kronsweide church. My sister Neta moved first to Schönwiese and later to Arkadak, while Maria Siemens moved to Petersdorf with her husband Johann Peters. Tina Wiebe died of tuberculosis. Newer members included Anna Pauls (the daughter of Mother's cousin, Franz Pauls) and Anna and Lena Klassen.

Chapter 16 Growing Interest in Education

1 This included Peter Epp, Franz Pankratz, Abram Dyck, Peter Siemens, and possibly Hermann Wiebe.

2 From about 1909 Nieder Khortitsa had a *Jugendverein* of near-grown daughters and sons of the village's prosperous families. They met several times a month in private homes where they sang, played games, read plays,

and at least once a year performed a play on an improvised stage in a farmer's *Spitja*. They also formed a *Gesangverein* (singing club) which gave occasional public performances. Unfortunately they never sang during church services, for the *Oomtjes* and *Mummtjes* would have found that an unheard of breach of custom. Instead the church singing was often atrocious, led by song-leaders who after several false starts eventually hit on a pitch that the assembled worshipers could follow passably.

3 The *Judenplan* communities of Jewish residents were set up during the reigns of Alexander I and Nicholas I. In some of these villages in Kherson guberniia the government planted Mennonite farming families to act as model farmers for their Jewish neighbours. Some time later they were placed in control of the local administration, including running the schools. Until the last decade or two of the nineteenth century the government insisted that Mennonite teachers be as qualified to teach in these schools as in their home schools. However, the government lost interest in the project toward the turn of the nineteenth century, and the Mennonites drifted away from these villages as they deteriorated. From that time on teachers without certification could teach in the *Judenplan* schools. For the early history of the *Judenplan* and the role of Mennonites in its development, see Harvey L. Dyck, trans. and ed., *A Mennonite in Russia: The Diaries of Jacob D. Epp, 1851–1880* (Toronto: University of Toronto Press, 1991).

4 Complex system, or project system. The Bolsheviks used this method for inculcating anti-religious propaganda in school children, treating a certain object from different aspects and its relationship to different things. My brother Johann cited the following example from his teaching days: 'The Cucumber I. What is it? Where does it grow? How? For what used? Pickling. II. Pushkin, the great Russian lyric poet liked pickles; he really was of Negro descent; Negroes live in Africa; Africa is a hot country; our Caucasus is very hot too; III Lermontov, another Russian poet. Lived in the Caucasus for a long time; he wrote a poem called "The Demon:" demon, the invented spirit of darkness is the opposite from Christ ...'

Chapter 17 The Outbreak of War

1 These included my cousins Gerhard and Johann Rempel, sons of Father's deceased brother Johann, and several of his older brother David's sons. My brother-in-law, Jacob Pankratz, was drafted in early 1916, and Mariechen's future husband, Heinrich Klassen, was mobilized in September, 1914. He served three years also on *VZS* hospital train 194 with my brother Johann. Two of Mother's brothers, Kornelius and Johann Pauls, who had recently

completed their three years of alternative service, were mobilized during the early years of the war. Her brother Bernhard Pauls, however, escaped service when he took work as a mechanic in the Lepp–Wallmann factory in late 1916, a job exempting him from service, due to the company's war contracts. Uncles Heinrich and Jacob were over age, as were three of Grandmother's sons-in-laws. Her fourth son-in-law, Kornelius Braun, had a medical exemption.

2 Johann had likewise been distressed that he could not come home from his Moscow assignment to celebrate our parents' silver wedding anniversary. The poem he wrote for the occasion, however, became a cherished remembrance: 'As the train cars sway and creak, / And the wheels clatter in a steady grind, / My thoughts so often are with you. / You dear ones are all on my mind,' ('*Wenn wiegen die Wagen und wanken, und klappern die Räder den Reim, dann weilen so oft die Gedanken, bei euch, o ihr Lieben, daheim.*')

3 Excellent accounts of Mennonite servicemen's wartime experiences in issues of *Der Bote* (Rosthern) from 1924 on, and in Waldemar Guenther, David Heidebrecht, and Gerhard J. Peters, eds., '*Onsi Tjedels.*' *Ersatzdienst der Mennoniten in Russland unter den Romanovs* (self-publication, 1966). The recollections in it stem almost exclusively from men who served in the *VZS* in Moscow and in the field.

Chapter 18 Harassment and Confiscation of Property

1 The question of German colonist land ownership had been a contentious issue at least since 1882, when V. Postnikov voiced concern over the colonists' (and especially the Mennonites') increasing wealth and power (see *Sel'skoe khoziaistvo i lesovodstvo* 140 [April 1882], 221–40, and *Iuzhnorusskoe krestianskoe khoziaistvo* [Moscow, 1891]). A few years later A.A. Velitsyn helped stimulate the anti-colonist views of Alexander III (see *Nemtsy v Rossii,* [St Petersburg, 1893]). Other factors fueled the debate: heavy foreign investment, Kaiser Wilhem II's accession to the German throne in 1888, the concern of Orthodox officials over proselytizing by sectarian colonists, the Baltic Germans' allegedly increasing power in Russian government, military, and society. Now, with the need for land, and the inability to grab it from their usual target – the Jews (who had precious little of it) – the land-rich, so-called German colonists became the obvious sacrificial lambs. The government then launched a slanderous campaign against them. Two newspapers (*Novoe vremia* and *Vechernee vremia*) viciously propagated the attack, as did numerous books, including Serfei Shelukhin, *Nemetshaia kolonizatsiia na iuge Rossii* (Odessa: n.p., 1915)

and Prince S.P. Mansyrev, *Nemetskoe zemlevladenie i pravila 2 fevralia 1915 g* (Petrograd: n.p., 1915).

2 I have dealt with the decrees at length in, 'The Expropriation of the German Colonists in South Russia During the Great War,' *Journal of Modern History* 4 (March 1932), 49–67. The original texts appear in '*Vysochaishie utverzhdenyia polozheniia Soveta Ministrov,*' in *Sobranie uzakonenii i rasporiazhenii pravitelstva, izdannykh pri pravitelstvuiushchem senate. Otdel pervyi, 3 fevralia* 39 (1915), 564–66.

3 French emigrants had founded the village in 1795.

4 Various Mennonites took bribes to Petrograd. The diary of Peter J. Dyck states: 'Once again ... Dav. Dyck, Jak. Neufeld ... and Heinr. Fast went to Petrograd to work with the requisition of land. It is said that 50,000 rubles have been put at their disposal.' See John P. Dyck, ed., *Troubles and Triumphs: 1914–1924: Excerpts from the Diary of Peter J. Dyck* (Springstein, MB: 1981). It also mentions that two Schönwiese men, Jacob Niebuhr and Kornelius Hübert, lobbied effectively with Rodzianko, the President of the State Duma, who they hoped would influence the Minister of Justice, Dobrovolskii, and that the two telegraphed that 'the operation had been successful.' They requested 100,000 rubles, 10,000 of which was to go to Dobrovolskii immediately. They were to deliver the final portion of what amounted to a bribe once his favourable decision was approved. The source of the money is not clear. The *Niebuhr Chronik* mentions the incident as well.

Chapter 19 Revolution and Reform

1 K. Lindeman, *Prekrashchenie zemlevladeniia,* 1917 ed., appendices 6 and 7, 368–72.

2 For an account of the ordeal, see D. Neufeld in *Christlicher Familienkalendar für das Jahr 1918,* ed., A. Kröker (Halbstadt, Russia: Raduga, 1917), 133–46, and also my comments David Rempel, 'Mennonite Medics in Russia during World War I,' *Journal of Mennonite Studies* 11 (1993), 149–61.

3 The Molochna population was somewhat more prosperous and conservative and less 'Russian' than was the Khortitsa citizenry. Prince Boris Saltykov, chairman of the headquarters of the Hospital Trains of the All-Russian Zemstvo Union (*VZS*) in Moscow mentioned to some of my relatives that the Khortitsa men on his staff were more self-confident, more at ease, had a greater sense of humour, and a less 'German' attitude than did the Molochna men.

4 Benjamin Unruh, '*Unsere Koloniepolitik seit Kriegsausbruch,*' *Der Bote,* 5 July 1939, 2.

5 H.B. Janz, '*Einige kurze Mitteilungen über den Forsteidienst der Mennoniten in Russland,*' *Der Bote,* 20 Dec., 1939, 2.

6 P. Heese, '*Die mennonitische Kolonie der Stadt Ekaterinoslav, 18.–1923,*' unpublished manuscript, 58–60.

7 See H.B. Janz, '*Einige kurze Mitteilungen*', and '*Zu der Geschichte des Ersatzdienstes in Russland,*' *Der Bote,* 30 Oct. 1940, 1–3. Indirect information is available in B.B. Janz '*Die Wehrlosigkeit der Mennoniten in Russland,*' *Der Bote,* 15 June 1940 and 29 June 1949.

8 Minutes appear in John B. Toews, ed., *The Mennonites in Russia from 1917 to 1930: Selected Documents* (Winnipeg: Christian Press, 1975), 396–404. My brother Johann's recollections appear in *Mein Heimatdorf Nieder Chortitza* (Rosthern, SK: self-published, 1956).

9 Minutes of the congress appear in the Feb. to July 1938 issues of the *Mennonitische Warte* under the title '*Protokoll des allgemeinen mennonitischen Kongresses.*'

10 A. Kröker, publisher of the *Friedensstimme,* later referred to the eight hour work day as 'lead(ing) to sin, to impoverishment and to neglect' ('*Politische Parteien,*' in *Christlicher Familienkalender für das Jahr 1918,* 33–4.)

11 According to two renegade Mennonites, A. Reinmarus (pseudonym for Penner) and G. Frizen, 'when half-educated Mennonite intellectuals had sought to equate the ideas of Socialism with those of religion, many delegates had demonstratively left the meeting hall, while others had pretended to sleep.' A. Reinmarus and G. Frizen, in *Mennonity* (Moscow: Central Council of Atheist Warriors of the Soviet Union [1930], 30). Unfortunately, this book is so replete with prevarication and outright lies, that I suspect the truth of this statement.

12 Many immigrant writings – interpreting these events differently from the way they transpired – make much of our patriotism to the Tsarist government and of how shamefully that government treated us during the First World War. These accounts seldom mention our relief at the regime's collapse, especially that of the servicemen who saw the need for democratization of our own institutions.

13 Kerenskii was a prominent minister and sometime prime minister of the Russian Provisional Government in 1917.

14 The Dyck diaries mention that by late 1917 or early 1918 the Niebuhr milling company had already sold four of its eleven mills, including two in Nieder Khortitsa.

15 For example, the Mennonites continued to prevent non-Mennonites, except an occasional Old Believer, from buying property in their villages, even after the reforms of the 1860 to 1870s relaxed the prohibitions on non-Mennonites living in Mennonite villages. Other native Russian and Ukrainian businessmen could operate businesses but could only lease or rent the buildings, not own them outright, which they strongly resented. I recall the Zhukov family, who operated the inn and livery stable (*gostinyi dvor*) in Khortitsa for decades, was particularly bitter over the issue.

Chapter 20 The First Phase of the Civil War

1 I have based this account on my own experience and on that of my family and friends. My knowledge of the broader patterns of this terror stem from graduate work at Stanford, especially studying its collections in the Hoover Library. I am also indebted to Johann Funk for the use of his diary and to Katjuscha Thiessen, who kindly gave me access to the diary of her father (Abram Dyck) covering the period 1899 to 1919.

The personal accounts which flooded the Mennonite book market after the tide of emigrants left our homeland in the 1920s verify that all Mennonite settlements endured similar tragedies. Although the particulars of the terror may have been slightly different from one village or family to another, no one was spared.

2 The Mennonites had used the income generated from leasing this land to fund the purchase of land for daughter colonies.

3 Grigoriev operated primarily in Kherson and Kush while Makhno's territory included the Alexandrovsk and Ekaterinoslav *uezdy* (counties) of the Ekaterinoslav guberniia, the Berdiansk and Melitopol *uezdy* of the Tavrida guberniia, and occasionally Mennonite districts in Kherson. Leaders of the minor bands included Selenchuk, Struck, and Debrenko in Kiev, Serepushka and Burlak in Kharkov, Shubu and Sekira in Poltava, and Gladchenko in Ekaterinoslav.

4 See for example, Paul Avrich, *The Russian Anarchists* (Princeton, NJ: Princeton University Press, 1971), 212.

5 As Arthur Adams pointedly noted, deep 'strains of social anarchism – the desire to steal from the rich, to drink one's fill of vodka, to savor the wildest pleasures of rape and murder – were strong among many partisan bands.' See Arthur Adams, 'The Great Ukrainian Jacquerie,' in *The Ukraine, 1917–1921: A Study in Revolution*, ed., Taras Hunczak (Cambridge, MA: Harvard Ukrainian Research Institute, 1977).

6 The diaries of both Gerhard P. Schröder of Rosental and Abram Dyck of Schönwiese mention this man, and I suspect he had a reputation as a policeman or red guardsman.

Chapter 21 Nominal Security under Foreign Occupation

1 German General Erich von Ludendorff led the eastward invasion.
2 The entries are dated 4 and 5 May 1918, although the conference was held toward the end of April.
3 These meetings and excursions to Germany are discussed in the Funk and Dyck diaries. The Molochna Settlement sent Professor B.H. Unruh, Johann Willms, and A.A. Friesen to petition the German government (one diary says the Kaiser) to grant us German citizenship.
4 At the time I roomed with my Uncle Bernhard Pauls, whose brother-in-law attended the conference. The latter predicted the bitter controversy the *Selbstschultz* would raise.
5 There had actually been a small measure of armed resistance since Feb., when Balkov, the regional soviet leader allowed villagers to take rifles out of the village soviet to defend themselves against the bandits. The scale of this resistance changed dramatically with the German presence.
6 John B. Toews, ed., *The Mennonites in Russia from 1917 to 1930: Selected Documents* (Winnipeg: Christian Press, 1975), 404–27; see also D.H. Epp, '*Zur Geschichte der "Bundeskonferenz" der russländischen Mennonitengemeinden,*' *Der Bote,* 3 and 10 November 1926. 6–7.
7 Although designated a General Conference, it was called too hastily for delegates from congregations in the Caucasus, Central and Eastern Russia, Siberia, and Turkestan to attend. Curiously only two men of stature (Reverend Johann J. Klassen and Dietrich Epp) attended from the Khortitsa Settlement.
8 Some anti-Germans were sprinkled among this collection, including a man named Shelukhin, author of a virulent book entitled *Nemtsy v Rossii,* published in 1915. Rumor had it that the Western Allied and Associated Powers also had their agents positioned in Ukraine, attempting to learn German aims there, and in the Crimea and Caucasus.
9 Professor B.H. Unruh repeatedly extolled the supposed serious German government concerns over the fate of all German colonists in his numerous *Der Bote* articles between 1934 and 1938. However, a study of German documents, and of civilian literature dealing with German war aims in and out of parliament, of business and industrial magnates, and of the major

political parties, and of vast number of publications for the occupation period, paints a different picture. See Fritz Fischer, *Germany's Aims in the First World War* (New York: Norton, 1967), first published as *Griff nach der Weltmacht* (Düsseldorf: Droste, 1964), and O. Fedyshyn, 'German Plans and Policies in the Ukraine and the Crimea, 1917–18,' (PhD dissertation), Columbia University, 1962).

Chapter 22 A Short Respite

1 The information in this chapter comes in part from my recollections of pre-war marriages, and even more from my sister Mary's recollections, written decades later.

2 Although parentally pre-arranged marriages were common among the wealthy Mennonite industrialists, businessmen, and land-owners, they were extremely rare in Nieder Khortitsa.

3 As the couple arrived the choir (*Gesangverein*) sang 'The Lord greet you,' ('*Gott grüsse dich*'), then the guests joined in singing Hymn 587, 'How deeply my heart trembles' ('*Wie tief erzittert mir das Herz*'). Following Dyck's sermon, the congregation sang Hymns 590, 'Rise, happy, joyful children' ('*Erhebt euch, frohe Jubelkinder*'), and 597, 'Oh blessed home where Thou hast been accepted' ('*O selig Haus wo man Dich aufgenommen*'). During the reception we also sang Hymn 552, 'We bring Thee the song of praise' ('*Wir bringen Dir des Dankes-Lieder*').

Chapter 23 The Civil War Deepens

1 According to Funk's diary, Löwen trapped the men across the street in the widow Thiessen's home. But another source (a contemporaneous letter by my friend Jacob Epp, which I rediscovered in the 1950s) suggested it occurred in Isaak Neufeld's home. According to the letter, my brother Johann was not only there but shouted at the bandit, 'You beast, you had it coming to you for the way you beat my father earlier on this day.'

2 My brother, Johann, stated that the farmer was Peter Unger. The Funk diary notes a similar incident, with a farmer named P.D. Perhaps this was the same event. Or there may have been several such occurrences.

3 The Funk diary mentions this incident.

4 See Johann G. Rempel, *Mein Heimatdorf Nieder Khortitsa* (Rosthern, SK: self-published, 1956).

5 Funk's diary identifies the accuser as a madman from Burwalde, not a child.

Chapter 24 Makhnovite Terror

1 Schröder's memoir, *Miracles of Grace and Judgment* (Lodi, CA: G.P. Schroeder, 1974), which I helped prepare, is an invaluable record of the 1919 events, especially since he met a number of the *batkos* (including Batko Pravda) while teaching in Schönfeld.

Chapter 25 Height of Makhnovite Terror

1 General Dukhonin, once in charge of the Northwestern Front, was known for his brutality to his troops. His troops killed him a few months after the February Revolution.

Chapter 26 Hostages

1 I am not certain how many families sought refuge in our villages, but the group included at least a Mr. Hiebert, the Abram Koop, and Petrus Epp families, and three Dyck families (headed by relatives, one named Abram, and two others named Jacob).

2 According to Franz P. Thiessen, then employed in the Niebuhr office, the money came largely from various mill stockholders, though a few other people in Alexandrovsk may have contributed as well. But according to Maria Hildebrand, the daughter of Abram Koop who was hiding in Osterwick, some of the money came from various sources in Voznesenskoe and Belenkoe, including one Greek Orthodox priest. I believe this account is confused with a similar set of arrests made in 1919.

Chapter 27 Typhus

1 See B.D. Davis, R. Dulbecco, H.N. Eisen, H.S. Ginsberg, W.B. Wood, and M. McCarty, *Microbiology*, 2nd ed. (Hagerstown, MD: Harper and Row, 1973).

2 Normally most of the medical care within the Khortitsa Settlement's individual villages was performed by a midwife (*Hebamme*) or in some cases a trained nurse (*akusherka*).

3 Dr Hamm's pregnant wife, simultaneously infected with typhus, gave birth prematurely. The infant son survived. Mrs Hamm did not.

4 Figures published in *Der Bote* (17 Nov. 1926) indicate typhus killed seventy-one men and sixty-two women in Rosental. I am not certain of the exact pre-epidemic population of that village but suspect the death toll represented about fifteen per cent of the people.

Chapter 28 More Desperate Years

1 Editor's note: The author's brother, Johann Rempel, published a series of reminiscences in *Der Bote* during the mid to late 1920s, which David Rempel later translated to English. Unpublished, he titled them 'Just Memories.' The quoted material is drawn from two articles in this series.

2 Editor's note: How willingly Mennonites acceded to German demands that they resettle in Poland in 1943 is a matter of debate. The author uses the term 'rounded-up' in the original manuscript, and often used that term in conversation. In a letter dated 21 December 1977 he stated: 'But the Nazi authorities did not consult the people. The orders were: get ready within so many days, or be shot.' His brother, Gerhard, was reluctant to go in part because he hoped his daughters would be re-united with their lost husbands. Certainly many women whose husbands or sons were exiled, wished to stay, hoping for the same thing. Some Mennonites must have believed the Soviet system was preferable to the Nazi regime. This was probably true of the author's uncle, Kornelius Braun. Furthermore, both Gerhard and Braun, sixty years old in 1943, may not have wanted to attempt the arduous journey. However, many Mennonites certainly departed willingly for German-held lands.

A Painter's Recollection of Khortitsa, 1910

HENRY PAULS*

Let us visit the village as it was when I was ten. We will need a guide, so we ask old Mr Redekop (*Oomtje Radakopp* [in lower left corner of the painting]), who knows the village and townspeople. He lights his pipe and points to the carriage in front of us: 'This family will enroll their son in the high school (*Zentralschule*), where he will learn and mature.' Since they come from another village, we call them outsiders (*Butendarpa*).

The new girls' high school (*Mädchenschule*) is across the street and *Oomtje Radakopp* admires this grand building as if he had built it himself. The model elementary school is to the right, while behind and up the hill from it stands the Teachers Seminary, about which our guide comments, 'Now we have better teachers.' To the right of them, we see the L-shaped boys' high school building (*Zentralschule*) with its tower. Teacher Penner maintains the big clock, establishing time from a sun dial he made, while everyone else sets their clocks and watches by the school clock.

Next we come to the big Mennonite Church, which is almost a hundred years old. Four men stand in the gate, and since all speak several languages, they understand each other as they discuss the Bible and the meaning of God's word. The big man with a hat is the Reverend Isaak Dyck (*Ohm Isaak*) a Mennonite church elder (*Ältester*). The Jewish rabbi stands to his right, wearing a blue cap. Next is Teacher Penner, and on the far right, the local Russian Orthodox priest. At home, the Mennonites speak Low German (*Plautdietsch*), while in church and school we

* Pauls painted the representation of Khortitsa that is reproduced in the illustrations following page 124, a detail of which appears on the jacket of this book.

speak High German. The Russian Priest speaks Ukrainian (*Khokholsch*), but in church he speaks Old Church Slavonic. The Rabbi speaks Yiddish at home and Hebrew in his synagogue, but he knows the other languages, too. He tutors our teacher, Mr Penner, who studies ancient Hebrew from books.

As much as we would like to learn from them, we walk on to the light green building – the district (*volost*) administration building. The post office is up the side street, while farther back to the left we see the hospital with its light blue roof. In the distance we see a typical Ukrainian hill, really a Scythian burial mound, perhaps a thousand years old. And way to the right we see Hildebrand's factory that manufactures wagons and farm machines, and notice smoke pluming from its chimney.

Turning back, we see the fence bordering the Lepp-Wallmann factory, which also manufactures farm implements. In the street itself, we encounter a carriage, with a Russian coachman to drive the horses, while three children sit in the back seat. *Oomtje Radakopp* cannot afford even one horse, and disapproves of such ostentation. He says, 'That is how the rich live. Like the youngsters in a one-horse buggy, they are too proud, and pride is the root of all evil.'

Then we meet customers of Dyck's flour mill where *Oomtje Radakopp* likes to stop. He knows this Ukrainian couple, Paraska and Kusma. They just had an argument, and he backed down. The mill owner offers a choice of cash or flour for your wheat, and while Paraska wanted cash, she prevailed. 'Money disappears and ten bags of flour will feed us through the winter,' she says. She is such a talkative woman, persuasive and full of colourful descriptions. *Oomtje Radakopp* savours both his Low German and Paraska's Ukrainian, because, he says, 'In dialect, you have no problem with grammar.'

We go on and meet Mr and Mrs Klassen, out visiting for late afternoon tea (*spazieren to Faspa*). *Oomtje Radakopp* says, 'Mrs Klassen has 17 children. She is still young and getting younger.' (*Mumtje Kloasche haft 17 Tjinja – es uck noch jung – woat emma jinga.*')

A man runs down the street and *Oomtje Radakopp* says, 'What's wrong with old Peters? He runs this way, he runs that way. He runs so fast, he passes himself. He crashes into his own back door.' ('*Waut's los met Ohmtje Peetasch – he rannt emma han on hea – he rannt so schwind – he rannt sitz selvst vebie – on prallt dan jaejni Daea.*')

I was only ten years old and I did not write down all of what Mr Redekop said. So much of his poetry is lost – lost forever!

Index